Telecollaboration in Translator Education

This volume provides a comprehensive treatment of telecollaboration as a learning mode in translator education, surveying the state-of-the-art, exploring its distinctive challenges and affordances and outlining future directions in both theoretical and practical terms. The book begins with an overview of telecollaboration and its rise in prominence in today's globalised world, one in which developments in technology have significantly impacted practices in professional translation and translator education.

The volume highlights basic design types and assessment modes and their use in achieving competence-based learning outcomes, drawing on examples from seven telecollaboration projects. In incorporating real-life research, Marczak draws readers' attention to not only the practical workings of different types of projects and their attendant challenges but also the opportunities for educators to diversify and optimize their instructional practices and for budding translators to build competence and better secure their future employability in the language service provision industry.

This volume will be a valuable resource for students and researchers in translation studies, particularly those with an interest in translator education and translation technology, as well as stakeholders in the professional translation industry.

Mariusz Marczak is Assistant Professor in Translation Studies at the Jagiellonian University in Kraków, Poland.

Routledge Advances in Translation and Interpreting Studies

For more information about this series, please visit: www.routledge.com/Routledge-Advances-in-Translation-and-Interpreting-Studies/book-series/RTS

Telecollaboration in Translator Education

Implementing Telecollaborative Learning Modes in Translation Courses

Mariusz Marczak

Routledge
Taylor & Francis Group

NEW YORK AND LONDON

First published 2024
by Routledge
605 Third Avenue, New York, NY 10158

and by Routledge
4 Park Square, Milton Park, Abingdon, Oxon, OX14 4RN

Routledge is an imprint of the Taylor & Francis Group, an informa business

Library of Congress Cataloging-in-Publication Data
Names: Marczak, Mariusz, author.
Title: Telecollaboration in translator education : implementing
   telecollaborative learning modes in translation courses / Mariusz
   Marczak.
Description: New York, NY : Routledge, 2023. | Series: Routledge
   advances in translation and interpreting studies | Includes
   bibliographical references and index. |
Identifiers: LCCN 2023023216 | ISBN 9781032539942 (hardback) |
   ISBN9781032544519 (paperback) | ISBN 9781003424932
   (ebook)
Subjects: LCSH: Translating and interpreting—Study and
   teaching—Technological innovations. | Translators—Training of.
   | Educational technology. | Internet in education.
Classification: LCC P306.5 .M36 2023 | DDC 418/.02071—
   dc23/eng/20230721
LC record available at https://lccn.loc.gov/2023023216

ISBN: 978-1-032-53994-2 (hbk)
ISBN: 978-1-032-54451-9 (pbk)
ISBN: 978-1-003-42493-2 (ebk)

DOI: 10.4324/9781003424932

Typeset in Sabon
by Apex CoVantage, LLC

Contents

Acronyms and abbreviations

ALM	Audiolingual Method
ALPAC	Automatic Language Processing Advisory Committee
CAT	computer-assisted translation
CMC	computer-mediated communication
COIL	Collaborative Online International Learning
CLL	Community Language Learning
CLT	Communicative Language Teaching
CMS	Content Management System
CoopLL	Cooperative Language Learning
CSA	Common Sense Advisory
DGT	Directorate-General for Translation
EMT	European Master's in Translation
f2f	face to face
GALA	Globalization and Localization Association
GTM	Grammar-Translation Method
GPE	Global Partners in Education
GU	Global Understanding (project)
ICT	Information and Communication Technology
ISO	International Organization for Standardization
ITI	Institute of Translation and Interpreting
L1	native language
L2	target language
LSP	language service provision
MT	Machine Translation
OIE	Online Intercultural Exchange
PACTE	Procés d'Adquisició de la Competència Traductora i Avaluació (Process in the Acquisition of Translation Competence and Evaluation)
QA	Quality Assurance
QMPs	quality management principles
SaaS	Software-as-a-Service

SNA	Social Network Theory
SPSS	Statistical Package for the Social Sciences
TM	Translation Memory
TMS	Translation Management System
TS	Translation Studies
VLE	Virtual Learning Environment
ZPD	Zone of Proximal Development

Introduction

This book is dedicated to the implementation of telecollaboration as a learning mode in academic translator education. Although conceptually conceived of long before the outbreak of COVID-19, its topic seems to be even more relevant today, given the ensuing shift towards distant learning in all sectors of contemporary education, including translation education, in the wake of the pandemic. After all, telecollaborative work modes are now highly likely to be considered as an option in translation courses not only due to the fact that professional translation tends to increasingly involve teamwork in virtual spaces (Pietrzak, 2020; Pietrzak & Kornacki, 2021) but also in response to the COVID-induced changes to instructional practices.

At this point, it needs to be elucidated that telecollaboration must not be interpreted as synonymous with online learning at large – although it is a form of the latter – but rather as a possible didactic choice in Web-based educational settings, with its distinctive features, affordances, related methodology and potential learning outcomes. Its value lies in its potential to facilitate translation students' learning experience, improve learning gains, help translation teachers diversify their practices, increase the efficacy of teachers' instructional efforts, help translation programme graduates both enter the contemporary translation market with greater confidence – derived from the set of transferrable skills which telecollaboration fosters – and ensure their own employability in the volatile language service provision (LSP) market by augmenting their self- and professional development skills. Hence, recommendations for the implementation of project-based assignments in translator education courses by numerous scholars (Gonzáles-Davies, 2017; Kiraly, 2000, 2005, 2012, 2016; Kiraly & Hofmann, 2016; Kiraly & Massey, 2019; Małgorzewicz, 2016; Massey, 2016) or organisations (EMT, 2022).

That said, the extent to which telecollaboration will be utilised in translator education is at the discretion of individual course instructors. Thus, the book sets out to provide translation teachers with an insight

DOI: 10.4324/9781003424932-1

into selected telecollaborative work modes which seem most applicable to translator education and help them make informed and methodologically sound decisions on whether or not to add telecollaboration to the repertoire of learning modes in which they involve their students. Those potentially interested in doing so will be able to not only explore the theoretical underpinnings of telecollaboration as an educational solution but also the practicalities of telecollaboration project and task design, as well as the actual workings of telecollaboration projects, as they can be implemented in academic translator education courses.

What needs elucidating is that the book is limited to translation and translator education rather than interpreting and interpreter training. The choice is primarily determined by the nature of the researched telecollaboration projects which are discussed here, where translation was performed in written mode. The applicability of telecollaboration to interpreter training is also worth investigating, but it would require research involving – *inter alia* – different participants (student interpreters and their teachers), project setups (e.g. online conference interpreting) and skill sets (online interpreting-specific hard skills and oral telecollaboration skills). All in all, in congruence with a noticeable trend in Translation Studies (TS) to often distinguish between translator and interpreter education, it seems reasonable to deal with the problem of telecollaboration in the latter area in a separate publication, for which dedicated research would first need to be conducted.

Pedagogically, what is telecollaboration? The simplest answer to that question could be that it entails education, not training, which implies that telecollaboration aims to foster whole person growth and the development of competences which reach beyond the technologies that it involves. Rather than mechanical and largely reproductive learning, which is conventionally associated with training, telecollaboration comprises student-centred, joint, explorative learning, hands-on practice and reflection on experience, which are conducive to the transformation of learners and the reiterative emergence of knowledge whose scope escapes complete predetermination and planning.

Telecollaboration is a valid educational choice and a work mode convergent with the principles of 21st-century education in that it responds to the contemporary social and cultural perception of literacies as complex, dynamic and community-based social practices. In congruence with that, it promotes learning which involves what Lim, Hung et al. define as "situated cognition, where knowledge, agency and context are tightly intertwined, . . . [and where] literacy practices and contexts are an inseparable coupling" (Lim, Hung, & Cheah, 2009, p. 120).

Moreover, telecollaboration also answers the need to educate innovative, resourceful and efficient workforce, equipped with 21st-century skills, such as critical thinking, risk-taking and social and collaborative skills, by involving learner communities of geographically dispersed and culturally distinct learners in collaboration which is augmented by the use of online resources and computer-mediated communication tools and which consists in learners discerning information rather than simply collecting it. All in all, it could be viewed as a pedagogical measure with which to counteract illiteracy, as it was envisaged by Alvin Toffler, who famously prophesied that "The illiterate of the 21st century will not be those who cannot read and write, but those who cannot learn, unlearn, and relearn" (Toffler, as cited in Hennessy, 2002, para. 1).

Although it originally gained ground as a methodology used to develop language learners' intercultural competence, digital literacy or social agency, with time, telecollaboration has evolved to help learners and course constructors move far beyond intercultural education to promote professional competence in numerous areas, including components of translator and translation competence, as this book will demonstrate.

The book contains seven chapters, which fall into two major parts: conceptual-theoretical and practical-empirical. The former part comprises the first five chapters, which delineate telecollaboration in societal, professional, general educational and translation education contexts; provide an overview of its pedagogical foundations; and characterise telecollaborative work modes which seem most suitable for translator education. The latter part of the book is constituted by the sixth chapter, which discusses actual implementations of telecollaboration as learning projects that were administered in academic translation courses. It also reports on a series of research studies, each based on one of the projects in question, which aimed to investigate specific aspects of telecollaboration-enhanced learning in translator education at university level.

Chapter 1 begins with an introduction to the concept of telecollaboration at large with regard to the etymology of the term, subject-independent perspectives on it and extended definitions derived from the area of language education, where telecollaboration has long been used to develop language learners' intercultural competence. The chapter also anchors telecollaboration to general societal needs, as reflected in the provisions made for telecollaboration-based instruction in global and local educational documents, such as handbooks, standards, frameworks and recommendations, with a particular emphasis on the European context. The chapter ends with an overview of research reports which provide empirical evidence corroborating the effectiveness of selected implementations of telecollaboration in concrete educational settings.

Chapter 2 sheds light on telecollaboration as a solution which, in an era of globalisation, internationalisation and exponential market growth, has found its place in the professional world across different sectors of economy, where it is being used to facilitate international communication and cooperation, increase work efficiency or enhance continuous professional development, as exemplified by various forms of professional training. Most importantly, the chapter discusses how telecollaboration has also been gradually adopted by the translation profession to help it swiftly respond to the rapid growth of the translation market, the need for increased collaboration, the digitalisation of translation and LSP, as well as the proliferation of translator roles.

Chapter 3 demonstrates the extent to which telecollaboration is relevant to the goals of contemporary translation pedagogy in the light of the models of translator and translation competence which guide translation programme and course design, as well as the ensuing teaching and learning practices involved in translator education. In addition, it relates telecollaboration to professional translation standards in order to establish the extent to which the use of telecollaboration in translator education is justifiable by the current trends and procedures utilised in the LSP industry.

Chapter 4 reviews the pedagogical foundations of telecollaboration, as delineated in the field of language education, where it has had a relatively long history of use and where – very importantly – it has been conceptually and empirically researched for nearly three decades now. By doing so, the chapter responds to Kiraly's (2015) concern that, although various teaching solutions have been used in the translation classroom, they have inspired little reflection on their epistemological underpinnings. The chapter opens with a discussion of the main epistemological perspectives on the nature of goals of education, which is followed by an analysis of the compatibility of the concept of telecollaboration with the three major pedagogical approaches to (translator) education corresponding to the aforementioned epistemologies.

Chapter 5 aims to define telecollaboration specifically from the perspective of translator education in recognition of the fact that telecollaboration is an inclusive term and seems adaptable to numerous educational settings. The chapter demonstrates which of the generic features of telecollaboration seem to lend themselves to translator education and which others appear to lack pertinence. The chapter typifies three major telecollaborative designs which seem most suitable for translator education, discusses areas, modes and purposes of assessment in translator-education-oriented telecollaboration and analyses selected issues in implementing telecollaborative work modes.

Chapter 6 is an account of a total of seven telecollaboration projects administered in various courses offered on two MA programmes in Translation Studies at two institutions: the Jagiellonian University in Kraków, Poland (UJ), and the Pedagogical University of Kraków. The projects represent the three basic design types defined in Chapter 5 and involve varying degrees of telecollaboration. For each project, the details of its implementation are first provided, followed by a report on research into various aspects of telecollaboration which, in nearly all cases, was based on the data collected from the project participants or – in one case – inspired by the project participants' observed performance. The project descriptions and overviews provided in the chapter may serve as an illustration of how the telecollaboration-related theories discussed in the preceding chapters may be put into practice or as guidelines on the implementation of telecollaboration for particular educational purposes in Translation Studies courses. In turn, the research results which follow provide insights into multiple dimensions of telecollaboration in translator education and possibly inspiration for further research into specific aspects of this learning mode.

Chapter 7 rounds up the book with a set of conclusions drawn from the research findings obtained, which are delineated with regard to the three major telecollaboration project designs with varying degrees of online and offline collaboration, which were discussed theoretically in the preceding chapters: Online Intercultural Exchanges, telecollaborative translation projects and miscellaneous projects. The conclusions comprise student expectations and attitudes towards telecollaboration, learning needs identified on the basis of the students' experience, the perceived and measured usefulness of the projects, interaction patterns in student-student in-project communication, learning affordances and gains, challenges and difficulties and the students' stance on teacher presence and the electronic tools used.

References

EMT. (2022). *European master's in translation competence framework 2022.* Retrieved from https://commission.europa.eu/system/files/2022-11/emt_competence_fwk_2022_en.pdf

Gonzáles-Davies, M. (2017). A collaborative pedagogy for translation. In L. Venutti (Ed.), *Teaching translation: Programs, courses, pedagogies* (pp. 71–78). London & New York: Routledge.

Hennessy, J. (2002). Embracing the need to 'Learn and Relearn'. *Stanford Magazine*, January/February. https://stanfordmag.org/contents/embracing-the-need-to-learn-and-relearn

Kiraly, D. C. (2000). *A social constructivist approach to translator education: Empowerment from theory to practice.* Manchester: St. Jerome.

Kiraly, D. C. (2005). Project-based learning: A case for situated translation. *Meta*, 50(4), 1098–1111. https://doi.org/10.7202/012063ar

Kiraly, D. C. (2012). Growing a project-based translation pedagogy: A fractal perspective. *Meta*, 57(1), 82–95.

Kiraly, D. C. (2015). Occasioning translator competence: Moving beyond social constructivism. Toward a postmodern alternative to instructionism. *Translation and Interpreting Studies*, 10(1), 8–32.

Kiraly, D. C. (2016). Authentic project work and pedagogical epistemologies: A question of competing or complementary worldviews? In D. C. Kiraly (Ed.), *V&R academic. Towards authentic experiential learning in translator education* (pp. 53–65). Göttingen: V & R Unipress; Mainz University Press.

Kiraly, D. C., & Hofmann, S. (2016). Towards a postpositivist curriculum development model for translator education. In D. C. Kiraly (Ed.), *V&R academic. Towards authentic experiential learning in translator education* (pp. 67–88). Göttingen: V & R Unipress; Mainz University Press.

Kiraly, D. C., & Massey, G. (Eds.). (2019). *Towards authentic experiential learning in translator education* (2nd ed.). Newcastle upon Tyne: Cambridge Scholars Publishing.

Lim, W.-Y., Hung, D., & Cheah, H.-M. (2009). An interactive and digital media literacy framework for the 21st century. In L. Tan Wee Hin & R. Subramaniam (Eds.), *Handbook of research on new media literacy at the K-12 level* (pp. 119–127). IGI Global. https://doi.org/10.4018/978-1-60566-120-9.ch008

Małgorzewicz, A. (2016). Podejście zadaniowe w antropocentrycznej translodydaktyce akademickiej. *Lingwistyka Stosowana, 19*, 149–165.

Massey, G. (2016). Collaborative feedback flows and how we can learn from them: Investigating a synergetic learning experience in translator education. In D. C. Kiraly (Ed.), *V&R academic. Towards authentic experiential learning in translator education* (pp. 177–199). Göttingen: V & R Unipress; Mainz University Press.

Pietrzak, P. (2020). Inside and outside the translation classroom. *Research in Language, 18*(2), 109–117. https://doi.org/10.18778/1731-7533.18.2.07

Pietrzak, P., & Kornacki, M. (2021). *Using CAT tools in freelance translation: Insights from a case study*. London: Routledge.

1 Telecollaborative learning

1.1 The concept of telecollaboration

At its most basic, a definition of telecollaboration may be derived from the etymology of the very word, which is a combination of the English word *collaboration*, denoting a group of people working together towards a common goal, and the Greek prefix *tele-*, which means far off, over a distance (Merriam-Webster, n.d.), as in *television*, *telepathy* or *telemarketing*. Consequently, telecollaboration consists in the collaboration of people located in distant locations with the use of technologies which permit it.

The nature of the aforementioned technologies is elucidated in Encyclopaedia Britannica (n.d.), which generally defines telecollaboration as "the interactive exchange of audiovisual information or conferencing in real time between two or more participants [by means of] . . . telephone calls, voice conferencing, video conferencing, pictoral information exchange, and data or document conferencing" (Encyclopaedia Britannica, n.d.).

However, a more adequate, subject-independent definition of telecollaboration, as it is used for educational purposes, comes from Harris (1999), who described it as "an educational endeavour that involves people in different locations using Internet tools and resources to work together" (Harris, 1999, p. 55). Short as it may be, this definition encapsulates the critical features of telecollaborative education (i.e. the realisation of an educational purpose with the mediation of online technologies by learners operating from distant settings).

Complementary to this definition is Narayan's (2013) view of the affordances created by online collaboration tools, which in her own words "connect learners to other learners, teachers, educators, scholars and researchers, scientists and artists, industry leaders and politicians – in short, to any individual with access to the internet who can enrich the learning process" (Narayan, 2013, p. 11). This definition emphasises the open nature of telecollaboration, which permits learners to transcend beyond

DOI: 10.4324/9781003424932-2

learner-learner interaction and reach the world outside their immediate education context (e.g. to seek information or advice).

More elaborate definitions of telecollaboration come from the realm of language education, where it has been most intensively used as an instructional mode (Dooly, 2008). From the language education perspective, telecollaboration is usually defined as a work mode used to facilitate communication and intercultural learning. For instance, Belz (2003) explains:

> Telecollaboration involves the application of global computer networks to foreign (and second) language learning and teaching in institutionalized settings. In telecollaborative partnerships, internationally dispersed learners in parallel language classes use Internet communication tools such as e-mail, synchronous chat, threaded discussion, and MOOs (as well as other forms of electronically mediated communication), in order to support social interaction, dialogue, debate, and intercultural exchange.
>
> (Belz, 2003, p. 2)

As it can be observed, in her view, telecollaboration permits learners from geographically distant locations to involve in various forms of synchronous (chat, videoconferencing) and asynchronous communication (email, discussion lists, blogs), as well as online intercultural projects.

O'Dowd's (2011) classification of telecollaborative learning scenarios into three major models – the e-tandem model, the blended intercultural model and the model of third generation telecollaborative exchanges – provides further insight into the nature of telecollaboration. Typically, the *e-tandem model* (see O'Rourke, 2007) involves pairs of learners in a collaborative learning task, whereby they act as tutors to each other. In this way, they become responsible not only for their own learning but also the knowledge, instruction or feedback which they provide to their partner. E-tandems (Jager, Kurek, & O'Rourke, 2016) are most of all an implementation of peer learning, where learners assume responsibility for learning and the mutual provision of feedback, while the teacher's role is reduced to the introduction of the task and the relinquishing of the control over the learning process to the learners themselves. Learning success hinges upon reciprocity and autonomy, as the extent of learning and on-topic communication depends on the learners' decisions. However, O'Rourke (2005) and Marczak (2019) have also reported on e-tandems with a far greater degree of teacher control, where the teacher not only structured the e-tandem work but also integrated it into a series of face-to-face (f2f) classes.

In the blended intercultural model, telecollaborative online interaction is more thoroughly interwoven into the fabric of language programmes, hence, the name. In practice, it means that learners participate in class-to-class telecollaboration projects, where online work blends with in-class activities, with the latter devoted to the preparation, analysis of online exchanges as well as post-experience reflection. In this model, the teacher guides the learners' work and involves them in tasks stimulating the development of language and cultural awareness. Some tasks may be relatively simple and require learners to exchange with partners information about their native culture. Others can involve not only exchanging information but also comparing cultural products with a view to reflecting on the cultures in question. The most challenging tasks require learners to work jointly on a tangible product (e.g. an essay or presentation), whereby they can share their conclusions from the intercultural work performed. In fact, learners' involvement in production, not only negotiation, is often viewed now as an inherent feature of telecollaboration (Lamy & Goodfellow, 2010), and it is no longer the distinguishing feature of the blended, or third generation, model of telecollaboration because contemporary e-tandems are also likely to involve products (see Marczak, 2019).

The *third*-generation *model of telecollaborative exchanges* (O'Dowd, 2011) entails the completion of online telecollaboration projects which can foster the development of the participants' communication and intercultural competence alongside online, or digital, literacies. As a result, telecollaborative exchanges can be adjusted to accommodate the teaching and learning needs of a wide group of learners in range of settings, they may involve project partners other than language learners only and they will engage the participants in multilingual, cross-cultural communication for a variety of purposes, including better preparation for their professional lives. It is due to its "multidimensionality and complexity" (Dooly & O'Dowd, 2010, p. 10) that Guth and Helm (2010a) label it as Telecollaboration 2.0.

As O'Dowd (2011) observes, with time, not only models of telecollaboration have evolved but so have the computer-mediated communication (CMC) tools utilised by learners, which has affected the type of content learners work with, the communication modes they use and the sociocultural dimension of the literacies they develop. While initially telecollaboration was largely text-based due to the nature of the online communication tools, it will now incorporate multimodal communication, involving the use of text, voice, images or video. For instance, contemporary e-tandems will not necessarily rely on email, online forums or discussion boards as means of communication but on videoconferencing tools (Dooly, 2008), while in Telecollaboration 2.0, where interaction is facilitated by "'post-typographic' forms of text" (Lankshear & Knobel, 2011, p. 28), communication will involve text messaging, the use of 3D virtual worlds or webcam images as Guth and Helm (2010b) report. Learners will use the resources at hand extensively and not only exchange but also compare and contrast (Guth & Helm, 2010b), contest and evaluate them. Finally, due to the dynamic nature and modes of interaction, in Lankshear and Knobel's (2011) view, the literacies developed in telecollaboration projects are now much less individualised and much more distributed, collaborative and participatory in nature. It might be added that the literacies are no longer set; instead, they are rather dynamic in nature and need to be negotiated by the project partners, given that Telecollaboration 2.0 is likely to be multi-lateral, multilingual and multicultural.

All the skills relating to the handling of the communication tools, modes and content types, appended with the list of social media literacies proposed by Steele and Cheater (2008), which includes informing and participating, communicating and collaborating, creating social networks and sharing, may be collectively viewed as online literacies to be developed in the course of Telecollaboration 2.0 projects.

While the flexibility of designs may be considered as asset which renders telecollaboration suitable for learning in different areas (e.g. economics [O'Dowd, 2016], social studies [Dooly & O'Dowd, 2018], global business, environment, health education [GPE, 2021], science, technology and engineering [see Smyrnova-Trybulska, 2019]), it also poses – as O'Dowd and Ware (2009) rightly point out – a problem to those who would like to produce a comprehensive typology of telecollaborative tasks and designs, which "are as varied as their counterparts in the traditional language classroom" (O'Dowd & Ware, 2009, p. 175).

1.2 Societal needs and educational policies

The integration of telecollaboration into courses delivered at various levels of education and to students of different age finds justification in the needs of contemporary society, which in turn translate into provisions which – with varying levels of explicitness – are made for it in documents likely to affect the shaping of today's educational landscape.

Societal needs. One of the major phenomena indicating the need to develop learners' communication skills – which are inherently part of telecollaborative learning – is globalisation. The globalised world of today is characterised by voluntary or forced social mobility, both physical and virtual. Individual motives for it are likely to differ from person to person and can – *inter alia* – be educational, economic or political, but irrespective of what they are, as people move, so do "goods, services, ideas and cultures" (Orlando, 2016, p. 18). As a result, it is only natural that the number of international and intercultural exchanges which people engage in has grown exponentially, which – as Orlando (2016) rightly observes – translates into increased communication needs to which populations and governments need to respond.

As Guth and Helm (2010a) observe, telecollaboration constitutes an educational response to those needs, especially with regard to the complex nature of 21st-century communication. Even without engaging in any type of physical mobility, people can now communicate with representatives of other language and culture groups; they learn, work or even participate in various forms of entertainment online. Thus, it is critically important that they know how to do it effectively. Consequently, education needs to foster learners' intercultural communicative competence (ICC) and online literacies. Albeit Guth and Helm (2010a) also list language skills as the goals of modern-day education, there is no need for it. Those skills are an inherent component of ICC, as it has been proposed by Byram (1997). As a matter of fact, Byram's (1997) definition of ICC, which he perceives as "the ability to interact with people from another country and culture in a foreign language" (Byram, 1997, p. 71), renders the development of the competence impossible without the simultaneous development of linguistic competence. After all, he envisioned ICC as a goal of foreign language (FL) education and advocated the integration of interculturality into the FL teaching curriculum.

Interestingly enough, online literacies could also be perceived as an inevitable component of intercultural learning, as nearly two decades ago, it already involved the use of Web-based resources and techniques such as virtual ethnography (see O'Dowd, 2006). Yet it must be underlined that ICC can equally be developed offline, through techniques to be used in face-to-face educational settings, hence, the need to list online literacies explicitly.

Online literacies also merit highlighting on other grounds. It must be noted that they exceed the technical, which could be labelled as Information and Communication Technology (ICT) skills. They actually build on ICT skills and derive from them, but they take learning to realms other than simply the effective use of Web-related technologies and computer software. Online literacies are essential in today's society in that they correspond to how people tend to use the Internet. As Guth and Helm (2010a) explain, the Web permits users to participate in various online communities, which make a mark on their social identities. From the sociocultural point of view, it leads to social and cultural hybridity, which manifests itself in people's identification with an increasing number of communities due to frequent interaction, or even immersion, depending on the intensity of the former. Each of those communities will have different characteristics pertaining to how they communicate, what language they use and how they construe their identity, which can easily act as shibboleths (Sharwood-Smith, 2007) that are used to gatekeep and prevent strangers from infiltrating them.

To successfully navigate between disparate online communities, delineated at local, regional, national and global levels, the aforementioned online literacies are indispensable. But the learning outcomes which telecollaboration fosters may extend to yet another social dimension – the preparation of learners for agency which would perpetuate social transformation. Telecollaboration seems to lend itself perfectly to educating learners for what Guth and Helm (2010a) describe as conflict resolution and the study of international relations, and what Byram (2008) calls education for global citizenship, or intercultural citizenship (Byram, Porto, & Yulita, 2019).

Guth and Helm (2010a) believe that telecollaboration may be a catalyst for the development of citizenship-related skills, as it may be used "to promote reflection, understanding, criticism, equality and transformation rather than to perpetuate inequalities and drive forward market-driven agendas" (Guth & Helm, 2010a, p. 23). It is worth observing that, due to the flexibility of telecollaboration designs, translation – as yet another type of telecollaborative activity – could also be incorporated into them as a vehicle for social activism (e.g. in an attempt to counteract human rights abuse), as Baker (2013) illustrates.

Educational documents. An indicator of whether the use of telecollaboration for pedagogical purposes is a justifiable choice is the extent to which its characteristics correspond to the content of documents shaping educational policies and informing curriculum and course design. At this point, it needs to be underlined, though, that the aforementioned documents are generic in nature and usually tend to outline and prioritise instructional goals, action paths and learning outcomes, while delegating the choice of actual practices (e.g. teaching techniques such a telecollaboration) to particular institutions and course instructors. Hence, the provisions for telecollaborative learning which the documents implicitly make need to be sought in educational goals, teaching content and learning outcomes to which telecollaboration is applicable (e.g. using Web-based communication tools for learner-learner interaction orientated towards a shared goal, creating opportunities, international collaboration, joint learning, mobility or developing the knowledge, skills and awareness which are prerequisites of social agency or intercultural competence). Examples of educational documents where more or less implicit provisions for telecollaborative learning have been made are provided next.

At international level, the United Nations General Assembly announced *the Global Agenda for Dialogue among* Civilizations *A/RES/56/6* (United Nations, 2001), which urged national governments and social institutions to foster intercultural dialogue which would "unfold shared meaning and core values and integrate multiple perspectives through dialogue" (United Nations, 2001, p. 3) by creating opportunities for intercultural exploration and understanding.

The *UNESCO Education Strategy* 2014–2021 (UNESCO, 2014) under-lined the importance of preparing students for the challenges of living in an interconnected world, but first and foremost, it placed the need to support education for global citizenship at its core. It perceived learners as agents of change with regard to the promotion of peace, security and democracy but also environment protection or health.

UNESCO's *Education 2030: Incheon Declaration and Framework for Action for the implementation of Sustainable Development Goal 4* (UNESCO, 2016), which sets out a new vision for education for the years to come, advocates inclusive and equitable quality *education*, as well as the promotion of lifelong learning opportunities for all. It sets the goals of pro-viding all learners with skills sustainable for development, including the promotion of global citizenship and appreciation of cultural diversity by the year 2030. It also recommends that learners are equipped for employ-ment in today's volatile job markets, where change is driven by multi-ple factors, including technological advancements. The document finds it essential to diversify learning opportunities through varied education and training modalities. Clearly, telecollaboration can be viewed as one of those modalities. What is more, in relation to Target 25, which – very interestingly – calls for the provision of education in emergency situations, including natural disasters, conflicts and pandemics, it seems indispen-sable. After all, in the wake of the recent COVID-19 crisis worldwide, Target 25 has already materialised through the – *temporary(?)* – substi-tution of f2f instruction for various forms of online learning, including telecollaboration.

The Future of Education and Skills. Education 2030, published by OECD (2018), also posits that education is to prepare learners for the world of work and active citizenship. The document provides a list of cog-nitive and metacognitive skills (e.g. critical and creative thinking), social and emotional skills (e.g. empathy and collaboration), as well as practical and physical skills, *including* the use of online communication technolo-gies, which are to hone learners' agency in education and life. However, most pertinently to telecollaborative learning, the document addition-ally introduces the concept of coagency, consisting in students working towards set goals through interaction with others – also communities – whereby those others can act as teachers.

At local levels worldwide, educational documents also seem to make room to telecollaboration, as if inspired – and rightly so – by the interna-tional guidelines and recommendations cited earlier.

In the Middle East (e.g. Turkey) (Raw, 1998) and Asia (e.g. Japan) (Parmenter, 2003), provisions have also been made for intercultural educa-tion, albeit with a bias towards the promotion or enrichment of the home culture. Although this kind of learning could be viewed as potentially suitable for telecollaboration, it must be observed that for at least two reasons, actual implementation in this particular geographical and educational context could be a challenge. Firstly, for example, Chinese education has traditionally been hierarchical, teacher-centred and instruction-oriented (Wang & Farmer, 2008). Secondly, in settings where intercultural learning is to result in the promotion or elevation of a particular culture (Parmenter, 2003), it would be an attempt to use a very democratic, equity-based and inclusive teaching mode for a purpose which by definition is undemocratic and inegalitarian. By the same token, it is hard to imagine the applicability of telecollaboration to multicultural education in compliance with the principles of the assimilation perspective, which has often been used in the United States of America for immigrants to give up their identities and assimilate with the mainstream American society by adopting its way of life (Ameny-Dixon, 2004).

It must be underlined that the challenges cited earlier are precautionary in nature only and do not, by any means, preclude the involvement of, for example, Middle Eastern learners in virtual exchanges (VEs). For instance, thanks to the European Commission's Erasmus+ Virtual Exchange project, spanning the years 2018–2020, over 27,000 learners from Europe and the Middle East and Africa, participated in VEs, with over 4,000 people also receiving training in selected aspects of telecollaborative learning. Further support to telecollaboration projects between European, North African, Middle Eastern and Asian institutions has also come from the European Commission's eTwinning programme, to be discussed further next.

In the United States of America, the *Standards for Foreign Language Learning: Preparing for the 21st Century* (NSFLE Project, 1996), endorsed by the US Department of Education and the National Endowment for the Humanities, laid out a model of content- and skill-based standards in American FL education, which recommends that learners develop a range of competences with regard to the five Cs, namely, (i) Communication, (ii) Cultures, (iii) Connections, (iv) Comparisons and (v) Communities.

The five Cs seem to perfectly match telecollaborative work modes, which involve the development of corresponding knowledge and skills, including (i) offline and online communication skills, (ii) cultural understanding and openness to otherness, (iii) knowledge in a range of subject areas, (iv) skills of comparing and contrasting, which can be used to explore cultures or issues at hand, and (v) skills permitting learners to participate in, and interact with, domestic and international communities. The last element brings to the fore the concept of intercultural learning based on the exploration of the multiple subcultures constituting home culture, which corresponds to Byram's (1997) vision of intercultural learning in monolingual settings.

In Europe, it was nearly four decades ago that the *Recommendation R (82) 18* of the Committee of Ministers of the Council of Europe (CoE,

1982), on which the *Common European Framework of Reference for Languages: Learning, Teaching, Assessment* (CUP, 2001) is based, listed – among numerous other educational goals – the need to facilitate pan-European communication and increase mobility while counteracting prejudice and discrimination.

Two years later, the *Recommendation No. R (84) 18 on the training of teachers in education for intercultural understanding* (CoE, 1984), published by the Committee of Ministers of the Council of Europe, stressed the need to develop intercultural understanding and respect for the originality of particular cultures as a pan-European educational goal.

Well over 20 years ago, the *Recommendation No. R (98) 6 concerning Modern Languages* (CoE, 1998) of the Committee of Ministers of the Council of Europe highlighted the need to equip learners for international mobility and effective intercultural communication while promoting intercultural understanding and tolerance at primary, secondary and tertiary levels of education. Most importantly, it called for honing adult learners' skills for international cooperation.

At the onset of the 21st century, the *Recommendation 1539 on the European Year of Languages* (CoE, 2001) of the Parliamentary Assembly of the Council of Europe called for the introduction of measures with which to promote social and ethnic integration, while the *Common European Framework* (CUP, 2001), which is seminal to the uniformity of language education in Europe, set *general competences* and *communicative language competence* as the major educational goals. Interestingly, the latter competence was conceptualised on the basis of Byram's (1997) intercultural communicative competence, which – as it has been demonstrated – by definition is often regarded as the goal of telecollaboration.

Towards the end of the noughties, in 2008, the Council of Europe Ministers of Foreign Affairs issued the *White Paper on Intercultural Dialogue* (CoE, 2008), where it was recommended that the educational policies of the member states of the Council of Europe create opportunities for intercultural dialogue and thus promote intercultural understanding.

More recently, *The Recommendation of the European Parliament and of the Council of 18 December 2006 on key competences for lifelong learning (2006/962/EC)* (European Parliament, 2006) highlighted the importance of equipping learners for work and life as an educational goal by listing eight key competences to be developed to foster individuals' personal fulfilment, active citizenship, social inclusion and employment. The competences comprise the following:

1) Communication in the mother tongue;
2) Communication in foreign languages;

3) Mathematical competence and basic competences in science and technology;
4) Digital competence;
5) Learning to learn;
6) Social and civic competences;
7) Sense of initiative and entrepreneurship; and
8) Cultural awareness and expression.

(European Parliament, 2006, L 394/13)

If one is cognisant of the fact that the use of telecollaboration has already been extended to education in mathematics or engineering, it seems that all of the key competences listed earlier lend themselves to being developed through telecollaboration, with the caveat that they are unlikely to be worked on simultaneously, as the ultimate selection of the target competences will depend on a given setup.

In 2018, a survey commissioned by the European Commission's Directorate-General for Education Youth, Sport and Culture (European Commission, 2018) has investigated EU learners' opinions on learning preferences. What draws attention is the respondents' positive stance on educational mobility and collaboration, as illustrated by very high proportions of the over-8,000-strong sample of young Europeans, who expressed the belief that education would be facilitated by an experience abroad (90%) and involvement in innovative projects to study and work together across disciplines and departments alongside international academics, researchers and company representatives (97%). Albeit the respondents were surveyed on f2f collaboration, the data indicate a general interest in international collaboration.

Noteworthy is the fact that, as Helm (2015) reports, although tertiary-level European and American educational institutions have incorporated physical student mobility into their official internationalisation policies and budgetary plans, participation levels are very low: 5% in Europe and only 1% in the USA. Surprising as it might be, it makes room for telecollaboration to be used as a replacement solution through which to involve students in distant learning, including Online Intercultural Exchanges – which by default are telecollaborative in nature – but also to motivate students to partake in physical mobility projects in the future. In fact, research has already demonstrated a positive impact of OIEs on students' willingness to study abroad (see Marczak, 2019).

The Council of Europe's *Digital Citizenship Education Handbook* (CoE, 2019) is a good example of how an indispensable component of telecollaboration (the use of online communication skills and tools) and one of its goals (the development of learners' social agency) can be used to digitally engage students in their community. The document stresses the importance of participation and communication skills, familiarity with sociopragmatic rules, critical thinking, problem-solving and opportunities for unrestrained expression as educational goals. All in all, it implies the usefulness of telecollaboration as a work mode with which to work on learners' digital citizenship.

The European Commission's *Digital Competence Framework*, also known as *DigComp* (European Commission, 2019), reiterates the importance of developing learners' digital competences. As a resource that can be utilised by institutions (e.g. ministries of education) or individual self-learners to inform programme and course design, it advocates the development of digital competence in five areas: (i) information and data literacy, (ii) communication and collaboration, (iii) digital content creation, (iv) safety and (v) problem-solving.

The very list indicates that telecollaboration has a place in education oriented towards the development of digital competence, and it can be used to help learners develop most of the areas of the latter. Yet on closer inspection of the skills which these areas comprise, the adequacy of telecollaborative learning becomes even more evident. For instance, *information and data literacy* covers the ability to locate, retrieve and manage digital information and content. *Communication and collaboration* comprise the ability to interact, communicate and collaborate through digital technologies and practice participatory citizenship. *Digital content creation* regards the ability to create and edit digital content. *Safety* relates to the ability to protect personal data and privacy in digital environments, while *problem-solving* embraces the ability to identify and resolve problems in digital environments. Selective as these operationalisations of the five areas are – the full *DigComp* list is longer – they describe those skills which telecollaboration project can be envisaged to help to develop, given the nature of telecollaborative tasks and tools.

Finally, two recent documents, both issued by the European Commission, explicitly highlight the importance and role of VEs, and thus telecollaboration, within the EU's educational policies. The *European Commission's Communication on Achieving the European Education Area by 2025* (European Commission, 2020b) sets out to complement student and staff physical mobility with virtual and blended mobility formats in recognition of the need to deliver greener educational services and "support the digital path of internationalisation of education providers, in particular higher education and vocational training institutes" (European Commission, 2018, p. 24). In addition, the *Digital Education Action Plan (21–27)* (European Commission, 2020b) makes several provisions for telecollaborative learning and VEs, stipulating that "Blended mobility will be 'mainstreamed' (i.e. integrated) into the Erasmus programme by introducing a 'virtual learning' component to Erasmus and further strengthening successful initiatives such as e-Twinning for schools" (European Commission, 2020a, p. 17), "greater use will be made of VEs between young people and education institutions in Europe, and around the world, to further engage young people in intercultural dialogue and improve their soft skills" (European Commission, 2020a, p. 17), while "In higher education, the European Universities initiative will develop virtual and face-to-face EU inter-university campuses" (European Commission, 2020a, p. 17).

All in all, it seems that contemporary educational policies give priority to themes and competences which do fall within the scope of telecollaboration. The extent to which telecollaborative learning is indeed being utilised to realise educational goals, though, is likely to differ from context to context and depends on course instructors' awareness of the potential of telecollaboration, as well as the methodology behind it. However, the fact that telecollaborative work modes are entering new areas of education, as it has already been discussed, seems to confirm that they are recognised as an effective pedagogical solution.

It finds further corroboration in the proliferation of organisations which mediate VEs worldwide, as it is demonstrated later. At secondary school level, eTwinning, launched in 2005 and since 2014 co-funded by the Erasmus+ programme, is the European Union's platform facilitating the communication, collaboration and project development among the teaching and administrative staff of its member institutions. It currently involves entities from 44 countries, largely in Europe, but thanks to its eTwinning Plus initiative, also from Africa, the Middle East or Western Asia.

At tertiary level, the Global Partners in Education (GPE), established in 2002 and based at East Carolina University in Greenville, NC, USA, is an association of 47 partner institutions from 29 countries worldwide which promotes the use of modern technologies to enhance pedagogical efforts worldwide, arranges for high quality global VE programmes and creates opportunities for collaboration and interinstitutional and international research. Currently, it continues to run its flagship programme, Global Understanding (GU), but it has also launched the Global Business, Education, Environment, and Health International Virtual Exchange (Global BEEHIVE) initiative to extend VEs to areas of higher education which are listed in its name.

The SUNY COIL Center, originally established in 2004 as the COIL centre, is a hub for promoting and professionalising Collaborative Online International Learning – hence, its original name – as well as VE projects. It seeks to further mutual understanding and digital literacies through work modes fostering the development of international students' leadership skills, problem-solving skills or decision-making skills.

One of the more recent developments is the establishment in 2014 of the Stevens Initiative, which not only promotes but also funds VEs organised between educational institutions in the United States, the Middle East and North Africa, while yet another is UNICollaboration, launched in Dublin in 2016 as an organisation for the support of telecollaboration and VE at university level. Its main goals are the facilitation of research and practice into telecollaboration and promotion of telecollaboration at institutional level.

1.3 The effectiveness of telecollaboration in empirical evidence

Research on the impact of telecollaborative work modes on learner success, viewed as the development of competences targeted within the courses under investigation, has been largely dispersed and fragmentary, with the scope limited to specific, often small-scale telecollaboration projects in terms of institutional and individual participation or the number of targeted competences. Therefore, the results – however useful for investigating the specificity of telecollaboration in particular settings – are either hard or impossible to extrapolate.

However, over the past few years, several reports of large-scale research have been published which shed more light on the facilitative effects of telecollaboration on learning outcomes, as they delve into the impact of telecollaboration in contexts involving larger student cohorts, more international partners and varied instructional goals.

What follows is an attempt to synthesise the findings presented in six such reports, published in the years 2017–2022:

- *Global Understanding (GU) Survey Results: Assessment Report for Spring 2021 and Fall 2021* (GPE, 2022);
- *Erasmus+ Virtual Exchange Impact Report 2019* (Helm & van der Velden, 2020);
- *The impact of virtual exchange on student learning in higher education* (EVOLVE Project Team, 2020);
- *Virtual Exchange Impact and Learning Report* (Stevens Initiative, 2020);
- *Evaluating the impact of virtual exchange on initial teacher education: A European policy experiment* (EVALUATE Group, 2019); and
- *SUNY COIL Stevens Initiative Assessment* (Guth & Helm, 2017).

Global Understanding (GU) Survey Results: Assessment Report for Spring 2021 and Fall 2021 (GPE, 2022) is the latest in a series of annual surveys measuring the impact of intercultural exchanges held as part of the aforementioned GU project. The report pertains to the 15th iteration of the project. It is based on research with a pre-test/post-design where data were collected by means of surveys and measured perspective taking and empathy, the effects of the VEs on the levels of students' course satisfaction, intercultural communication competence, interactional anxiety, motivation to partake in physical mobility programmes and intercultural understanding. 727 from 39 higher education institutions from 25 countries located in North America, South American, Africa, Europe, the Middle East and Asia took part in the pre- and post-testing, but the original sample size amounted to 1,678 participants.

Erasmus+ Virtual Exchange Impact Report 2019 (Helm & van der Velden, 2020) provides findings on the impact of the Erasmus+ Virtual Exchange (EVE) pilot project, which was offered as part of the Erasmus+ programme providing opportunities for online intercultural learning. The objectives of EVE were – *inter alia* – to encourage intercultural dialogue online, provide an online complement to Erasmus+ physical mobility, hone students' critical thinking, media literacy, online and social media skills and promote citizenship. The data were collected through pre-exchange surveys, filled out by over 5,500 students, and post-exchange surveys, filled out by over 2,000 students. The sample contained students from Europe, North Africa, the Middle East and Western Asia, while the survey questions elicited the respondents' self-assessment of the individual levels of their linguistic, intercultural and digital competences.

The impact of virtual exchange on student learning in higher education (EVOLVE Project Team, 2020) reports on a large-scale research study into the impact of VE on student learning in higher education. The main goal of the EVOLVE project, which the report pertains to, was to elevate the status of VEs in higher education programmes to that of the mainstream. Quantitative and qualitative data were collected through varied instruments, including pre- and post-surveys, as well as interviews, portfolios and information-gathering sheets respectively. As a result, 248 students reported on the level of their competences before and after the completion of the VEs they participated in and – in an attempt to triangulate the data – also reflected on the details of the experience. The merit of the report lies in the fact that it presents data elicited from 16 different exchange projects, involving a total of 34 international institutional partners.

The *Virtual Exchange Impact and Learning Report* (Stevens Initiative, 2020) brings findings on the impact of VE projects administered between summer/fall 2019 and spring 2020 by educational institutions which had been awarded Stevens Initiative grants towards that end. The research conducted by the Stevens Initiative involved over 3,500 secondary school learners and higher education students from the United States and 11 other countries across the Middle East, North Africa and the Palestinian territories. The data were collected through pre- and post-experience surveys which measured potential changes in the participants' intercultural competencies throughout the VE projects and student satisfaction with the projects.

Evaluating the impact of virtual exchange on initial teacher education: a European policy experiment (EVALUATE Group, 2019) reports on findings relating to the Evaluating and Upscaling Telecollaborative Teacher Education research project, which examined the impact of virtual-exchange-enhanced learning on the development of digital-pedagogical, intercultural and linguistic competences in teacher trainees. The report provides data based on a substantially large sample of over 1,000 student teachers from 34 international teacher training institutions, who participated in a total of 25 VE projects. Quantitative data were collected through pre- and post-surveys, while qualitative data were elicited through learner diaries, portfolios, essays, interviews, records of in-project online interaction and products.

SUNY COIL Stevens Initiative Assessment (Guth & Helm, 2017) reports on the impact of telecollaborative learning in the context of a VE project administered as part of the Stevens Initiative grant. The project involved secondary school learners and higher education students from the United States, North Africa and the Middle East. The SUNY COIL Stevens Initiative involved telecollaboration, supplemented with study visits between SUNY schools and higher education institutions from the Middle East and North Africa. The data were elicited through pre- and middle-reflection questions, as well as post-project assessment questions answered by 112 participants, and they were analysed both quantitatively and qualitatively. The researchers focused – *inter alia* – on measuring increases in students' intercultural competence, intercultural communicative competence, digital literacy, team skills and language competence.

The findings cited in the aforementioned reports demonstrate that the VEs under examination effected gains in several areas, including intercultural competence, language competence, digital literacy, disciplinary skills and knowledge, transversal competences, citizenship skills and student satisfaction. In what follows is a breakdown of the competences into the corresponding components whose development was observed. The data in brackets refer to project names, not the publications, in order to avoid the need to multiply relevant citations.

Gains in intercultural competence are evidenced by reportedly increased levels of students' confidence in situations involving intercultural communication (Erasmus+ 2019, EVOLVE, Stevens Initiative, GU 2021, SUNY COIL), confidence in interaction with representatives of other cultures (EVOLVE, GU 2021), confidence in collaboration (EVOLVE, SUNY COIL, Stevens Initiative), mediation skills such as translation, interpretation and explanation and the ability to negotiate conflicts (Erasmus+ 2019, EVOLVE), knowledge of other cultures (Erasmus+ 2019, EVOLVE, Stevens Initiative, GU 2021), interest in exploring culture-dependent beliefs, values and traditions (EVOLVE), curiosity (Erasmus+ 2019, GU 2021), sensitivity to different ways of expression displayed by the culturally other (EVOLVE), self-reflection on – and resulting awareness of – the culture-boundedness of their own perceptions (EVOLVE), the ability to detach from own perspectives (Erasmus+ 2019, EVOLVE, Stevens Initiative, GU 2021, SUNY COIL), awareness of cultural diversity (EVOLVE, EVALUATE, SUNY COIL), as well as the hybridity of cultures and individuals (EVOLVE, EVALUATE).

Gains in language competence were discovered such as increases in the level of students' language confidence (Erasmus+ 2019), vocabulary range and control, grammatical range and control, propositional precision and thematic development, spoken fluency, linguistic adaptation, manifested in the used of adjustments, repetitions, rephrasing to facilitate understanding (EVOLVE) and FL skills at large (Erasmus+ 2019, EVOLVE, EVALUATE, GU 2021, SUNY COIL).

The impact on digital literacy was observed as significant progress in students' ability to curate and create online resources, proactive involvement in online exchanges (e.g. using artefacts to promote discussion), the maintenance of a positive tone by using friendly language, humour or emoticons and emojis, attempts to self-establish through expressive graphics and exchanging personal information, reciprocity manifested in efforts to help exchange partners establish themselves by using praise, giving space or showing empathy and respect (EVOLVE) and online communication skills (EVOLVE, SUNY COIL).

The participants of the VEs also reported increases in the level of skills and knowledge relating to the academic disciplines they studied and the objectives of the courses they attended (EVOLVE).

Gains in transversal competences – understood as universally relevant across occupations and viewed as pivotal to personal development – were observed with regard to group work, self-management (EVOLVE), empathy and preparedness to help each other (Erasmus+ 2019, EVOLVE, GU 2021), positive attitudes towards the culturally other (Erasmus+ 2019, Stevens Initiative), collaboration (EVOLVE, SUNY COIL, GU 2021), time management (EVOLVE), problem-solving (Erasmus+ 2019, SUNY COIL), teamwork (Erasmus+ 2019, SUNY COIL) and flexibility (SUNY COIL).

Improvements in the VE participants' citizenship skills were mostly observable through increased knowledge pertaining to topical social issues (e.g. gender roles, health issues and religious beliefs) (Erasmus+ 2019, EVOLVE).

Finally, the exchanges also reportedly resulted in the students' readiness to recommend participation in VE programmes to their friends (Erasmus+ 2019, EVOLVE, EVALUATE, Stevens Initiative, GU 2021) or to maintain the relationships established with individual project partners after the conclusion of the project (Erasmus+ 2019, EVOLVE, Stevens Initiative, EVALUATE) and high levels of overall student satisfaction with the VE-based learning experience (Erasmus+ 2019, EVOLVE, EVALUATE, Stevens Initiative, GU 2021).

Table 1.1 presents an overview of the seven competences on the development of which – in the least – the VEs in question have been reported to exert an impact.

What merits note is the fact that the set of competences reportedly developed – at least partially – are congruent with the standard goals of telecollaborative learning and are likely to equip students for future life by preparing them to function in intercultural settings (intercultural competence and language competence), involve in online communication (digital literacy), function in professional settings (subject competence), affect social change (citizenship skills) and find motivation for lifelong learning (student satisfaction). What is more, it must be stressed that in each of the projects analysed, evidence was collected from multiple VEs, which increases its reliability.

The previous juxtaposition was an attempt to organise and accumulate the findings for better orientation in the *status quo*, with the caveat that the reports were not compiled as a concerted effort of their authors. Each report was prepared independently, focused on the impact of VEs on selected competences and involved different methods of data collection and analysis, which has a number of consequences.

Firstly, by no means should it be presumed that VEs warrant the development of these competences in their entirety and in all circumstances, hence, use of circles in Table 1.1 to graphically indicate partial or conditional development. In the case of specific sub-competences, the findings were based on strong evidence (e.g. quantitative data which depicted statistically significant levels of progress) for which effect sizes could be computed. Yet in other cases, progress could only be inferred from qualitative data (e.g. the participants' reflections or records of students' in-project performance).

Secondly, although the reports communicated cumulative quantitative results indicative of overall positive learning outcomes, it must not be overlooked that certain proportions of the samples in question displayed no, or minimal, learning gains. The same applies to qualitative accounts of individual students' records of performance, which demonstrated no or little learning progress.

Table 1.1 An overview of competences reportedly developed in VE projects in the years 2017–2022

	IC	Language comp.	Digital literacy	Disciplinary comp.	Transversal comp.	Citizenship skills	Student satisfaction
Erasmus+	•	•	•	n.d.	•	•	•
EVOLVE	•	•	•	•	•	•	•
Stevens Initiative	•	n.d.	n.d.	n.d.	n.d.	n.d.	•
GU	•	•	n.d.	n.d.	n.d.	n.d.	•
EVALUATE	•	•	n.d.	n.d.	n.d.	n.d.	•
SUNY COIL	•	•	•	•	•	n.d.	n.d.

Thirdly, the lack of evidence for a tangible impact of VEs on the development of specific competences in some projects cannot be interpreted as instructional failure. In numerous cases, it merely stems from two following: either the initial level of competence development at the beginning of the exchanges – diagnosed through pre-tests – was already so high in individuals that it was difficult to observe substantial progress or the impact of the VE was simply not measured with regard to particular competences.

Fourthly, it would be interesting to see similar impact reports on VEs in areas other than language education, where for well over two decades, VEs have been implemented and researched (cf. O'Dowd, 2021; cf. O'Dowd, 2021). The results of reports relating to VE projects in mathematics, engineering or health education would shed even more light on the effectiveness of this mode of telecollaboration. Yet there is no reason to question the applicability of VE – *mutadis mutandi* – to other educational fields, including translator education, the more that there are numerous other arguments in its favour, which will be discussed in the following chapter.

Most importantly, perhaps, it must be remembered that learning gains in VEs are largely dependent on project and task design. For instance, Helm and van der Velden (2020) observe in the 2018 Erasmus+ report that learning success is most likely to be produced in exchanges conducive to challenge, where learners are required to face and overcome specific obstacles. It was explicated by O'Dowd, who elucidates:

> VE can best enhance students' collaborative and intercultural skills when they are confronted with a range of collaborative hurdles and challenges which require them to find creative ways to collaborate and communicate successfully with their international partners. Simply put, when tasks are carefully designed, VE can help push students out of their comfort zone and this is when skills and attitude development is most likely to take place.
>
> (O'Dowd, 2021, p. 218)

References

Ameny-Dixon, G. M. (2004). Why multicultural education is more important in higher education now than ever: A global perspective. *International Journal of Scholarly Academic Intellectual Diversity*, 6(1), 1–12. Retrieved from www.nationalforum.com/Electronic%20Journal%20Volumes/Ameny-Dixon,%20Gloria%20M.%20Why%20Multicultural%20Education%20is%20More%20Important%20in%20Higher%20Education%20Now%20than%20Ever.pdf

Baker, M. (2013). Translation as an alternative space for political action. *Social Movement Studies*, 12(1), 23–47. https://doi.org/10.1080/14742837.2012.685624

Belz, J. A. (2003). From the special issue editor. *Language Learning & Technology*, 7(2), 2–5.

Byram, M. (1997). *Teaching and assessing intercultural communicative competence*. Clevedon: Multilingual Matters.

Byram, M. (2008). *From foreign language education to education for intercultural citizenship*. Clevedon, Buffalo, & Toronto: Multilingual Matters.

Byram, M., Porto, M., & Yulita, L. (2019). *Education for intercultural citizenship*. In S. Laviosa & M. Gonzalez-Davies (Eds.), *The Routledge handbook of translation and education*. London & New York: Routledge.

CoE. (1982). *Recommendation R (82) 18 of the committee of ministers of the council of Europe*. Retrieved from https://rm.coe.int/16804fa45e

CoE. (1984). *Recommendation No R (84) 18 on the training of teachers in education for intercultural understanding*. Retrieved from www.ohchr.org/EN/Issues/Education/Training/Compilation/Pages/RecommendationNoR(84)18toMember StatesontheTrainingofTeachersinEducationforInterculturalUnderstanding,Nota blyinacontextofMi.aspx

CoE. (1998). *Recommendation No. R (98) 6 concerning modern languages*. Retrieved from https://rm.coe.int/16804fc569

CoE. (2001). *Recommendation 1539 on the European year of languages*. Retrieved from https://assembly.coe.int/nw/xml/XRef/Xref-XML2HTML-en.asp?fileid=16954&lang=en

CoE. (2008). *White Paper on intercultural dialogue: 'Living together as equals in dignity'*. Retrieved from www.coe.int/t/dg4/intercultural/source/white%20paper_final_revised_en.pdf

CoE. (2019). *Digital citizenship education handbook*. Retrieved from https://rm.coe.int/16809382f9

CUP. (2001). *Common European framework of reference for languages: Learning, teaching, assessment*. Cambridge: Cambridge University Press.

Dooly, M. (2008). *Telecollaborative language learning: A guidebook to moderating intercultural collaboration online*. Bern: Peter Lang Publishing Group.

Dooly, M., & O'Dowd, R. (2010). Series editors' preface. In S. Guth & F. Helm (Eds.), *Telecollaboration 2.0: Language, literacies and intercultural learning in the 21st century* (pp. 9–10). Bern, Berlin, Bruxelles, Frankfurt am Main, New York, Oxford, & Wien: Peter Lang.

Dooly, M., & O'Dowd, R. (2018). Telecollaboration in the foreign language classroom: A review of its origins and its application to language teaching practice. In M. A. Dooly Owenby & R. O'Dowd (Eds.), *In this together: teachers' experiences with transnational, telecollaborative language learning projects*. New York: Peter Lang CH.

Encyclopaedia Britannica. (n.d.). *Telecollaboration*. Retrieved from www.britannica.com/science/telemedicine#ref1191233

European Commission. (2018). *The European education area*. Retrieved from www.ecestaticos.com/file/c15945bef2d875b111e9fe94b0e76d4b/1576511759-fl_466_sum_en.pdf

European Commission. (2019). *DigComp: Digital competence framework for citizens*. Retrieved from https://ec.europa.eu/jrc/en/digcomp/digital-competence-framework

European Commission. (2020a). *Digital education action plan (21–27)*. Retrieved from https://ec.europa.eu/education/sites/default/files/document-library-docs/deap-communication-sept2020_en.pdf

European Commission. (2020b). *European commission's communication on achieving the European education area by 2025*. Retrieved from https://ec.europa.eu/education/sites/default/files/document-library-docs/communication-european-education-area.pdf

European Parliament. (2006). *The recommendation of the European parliament and of the council of 18 December 2006 on key competences for lifelong learning (2006/962/EC)*. Retrieved from https://eur-lex.europa.eu/legal-content/EN/TXT/PDF/?uri=CELEX:32006H0962&from=EN

EVALUATE Group. (2019). *Evaluating the impact of virtual exchange on initial teacher education: A European policy experiment*. Research-publishing.net. https://doi.org/10.14705/rpnet.2019.29.9782490057337

EVOLVE Project Team. (2020). *The impact of virtual exchange on student learning in higher education: EVOLVE project report*. Retrieved from http://hdl.handle.net/11370/d69d9923-8a9c-4b37-91c6-326ebbd14f17

GPE. (2021). *Global BEEHIVE*. Retrieved from https://thegpe.org/gpe-programming/global-beehive/

GPE. (2022). *Global Understanding (GU) survey results: Assessment report for Spring 2021 and Fall 2021*. Retrieved from https://thegpe.org/wp-content/uploads/2022/05/GPE-15-assessment-report.pdf

Guth, S., & Helm, F. (2010a). Introduction. In S. Guth & F. Helm (Eds.), *Telecollaboration 2.0: Language, literacies and intercultural learning in the 21st century* (pp. 13–23). Bern, Berlin, Bruxelles, Frankfurt am Main, New York, Oxford, & Wien: Peter Lang.

Guth, S., & Helm, F. (Eds.). (2010b). *Telecollaboration 2.0: Language, literacies and intercultural learning in the 21st century*. Bern, Berlin, Bruxelles, Frankfurt am Main, New York, Oxford, & Wien: Peter Lang.

Guth, S., & Helm, F. (2017). *SUNY COIL stevens initiative assessment: Final report*. Retrieved from www.researchgate.net/publication/324113574_SUNY_COIL_Stevens_Initiative_Assessment_FINAL_REPORT

Harris, J. (1999). First steps in telecollaboration. *International Society for Technology in Education, 27*(3), 54–57. Retrieved from https://virtual-architecture.wm.edu/Foundation/Articles/First-Steps.pdf

Helm, F. (2015). The practices and challenges of telecollaboration in higher education in Europe. *Language Learning & Technology, 19*(2), 197–217. Retrieved from http://llt.msu.edu/issues/june2015/helm.pdf

Helm, F., & van der Velden, B. (2020). *Erasmus + virtual exchange impact report 2019*. Retrieved from https://op.europa.eu/en/publication-detail/-/publication/0ee233d5-cbc6-11ea-adf7-01aa75ed71a1/language-en/format-PDF/source-181006410

Jager, S., Kurek, M., & O'Rourke, B. (Eds.). (2016). *New directions in telecollaborative research and practice: Selected papers from the second conference on telecollaboration in higher education*. Dublin: Research-publishing.net.

Lamy, M. N., & Goodfellow, R. (2010). Telecollaboration and learning 2.0. In S. Guth & F. Helm (Eds.), *Telecollaboration 2.0: Language, literacies and intercultural learning in the 21st century* (pp. 107–138). Bern, Berlin, Bruxelles, Frankfurt am Main, New York, Oxford, & Wien: Peter Lang.

Lankshear, C., & Knobel, M. (2011). *New literacies* (3rd ed.). Maidenhead: McGraw-Hill Open University Press.

Marczak, M. (2019). Successful e-learning: Intercultural development in GPE's global understanding project. In E. Smyrnova-Trybulska (Ed.), *E-learning: Vol. 11. E-leaming and STEM education* (pp. 233–254). Katowice-Cieszyn: Studio Noa for University of Silesia.

Merriam-Webster. (n.d.). *Tele. In Merriam-Webster.com dictionary*. Retrieved from www.merriam-webster.com/dictionary/tele

Narayan, A. (2013). ICT: Change of ICT: Change of paradigm, limitations and possible courses for action for future. In D. D'Souza, U. Singh, D. Sharma, & R. Prabhas (Eds.), *Educational technology in teaching and learning: Prospects and challenges* (pp. 9–14). Patna, Bihar: Patna's Women's College Publications.

NSFLE Project. (1996). *Standards for foreign language learning in the 21st century*. Yonkers, NY: NSFLE Project.

O'Dowd, R. (2006). The use of videoconferencing and e-mail as mediators of intercultural student ethnography. In J. A. Belz & S. L. Thorne (Eds.), *AAUSC issues in language program direction: Vol. 2005. Internet-mediated intercultural foreign language education* (pp. 86–119). Boston, MA: Thomson Heinle.

O'Dowd, R. (2011). Online foreign language interaction: Moving from the periphery to the core of foreign language education? *Language Teaching, 44*, 368–380. https://doi.org/10.1017/S0261444810000194

O'Dowd, R. (2016). Emerging trends and new directions in telecollaborative learning. *CALICO Journal, 3*(33), 291–310.

O'Dowd, R. (2021). Virtual exchange: Moving forward into the next decade. *Computer Assisted Language Learning, 34*(3), 209–224.

O'Dowd, R., & Ware, P. (2009). Critical issues in telecollaborative task design. *Computer Assisted Language Learning, 22*(2), 173–188. https://doi.org/10.1080/09588220902778369

OECD. (2018). *The future of education and skills: Education 2030*. Retrieved from www.oecd.org/education/2030/E2030%20Position%20Paper%20(05.04.2018).pdf

Orlando, M. (2016). *Training 21st-century translators and interpreters: At the crossroads of practice, research and pedagogy. Transkulturalität – Translation – Transfer*. Berlin: Frank & Timme.

O'Rourke, B. (2005). Form-focused interaction in online tandem learning. *CALICO Journal, 22*(3), 433–466.

O'Rourke, B. (2007). Models of telecollaboration (1): Etandem. In R. O'Dowd (Ed.), *Online intercultural exchange* (pp. 41–61). Bristol, Blue Ridge Summit: Multilingual Matters.

Parmenter, L. (2003). Describing and defining intercultural communicative competence – international perspectives. In M. Byram (Ed.), *Intercultural competence. Strasbourg: Council of Europe*. Strasbourg: Council of Europe.

Raw, L. (1998). Intercultural competence: Does it exist? In R. Cherrington & L. Davcheva (Eds.), *Teaching towards intercultural competence. Conference proceedings*. Sofia: Tilia/The British Council.

Sharwood-Smith, M. (2007). British shibboleths. In E. Ronowicz & C. Yallop (Eds.), *English: One language, different cultures/edited by Eddie Ronowicz and Colin Yallop* (2nd ed., pp. 46–82). London: Continuum.

Smyrnova-Trybulska, E. (Ed.). (2019). *E-learning and STEM education. E-learning: Vol. 11.* Katowice-Cieszyn: Studio Noa for University of Silesia.

Steele, K., & Cheater, M. (2008). Connecting with the Facebook generation: Social media strategies. *Presentation to the 2008 AARAO conference, "Diverse perspectives: A new generation of students," June 4–6 2008*, Halifax, NS. Retrieved from www.academica.ca/AARAO-2008

Stevens Initiative. (2020). *Virtual exchange impact and learning report 2020.* Retrieved from www.stevensinitiative.org/resource/virtual-exchange-impact-and-learning-report-2/

UNESCO. (2014). *UNESCO education strategy 2014–2021.* Retrieved from https://unesdoc.unesco.org/ark:/48223/pf0000231288

UNESCO. (2016). *Education 2030: Incheon declaration and framework for action for the implementation of sustainable development goal 4.* Retrieved from http://uis.unesco.org/sites/default/files/documents/education-2030-incheon-framework-for-action-implementation-of-sdg4-2016-en_2.pdf

United Nations. (2001). *Global agenda for dialogue among civilizations: Resolution A/RES/56/6.* Retrieved from http://digitallibrary.un.org/record/452351

Wang, V., & Farmer, L. (2008). Adult teaching methods in China and Bloom's taxonomy. *International Journal for the Scholarship of Teaching and Learning*, 2(2), 1–14. https://doi.org/10.20429/ijsotl.2008.020213

2 Telecollaboration in contemporary translation

Telecollaboration is not only a pedagogical solution. It has also been implemented in the professional world across different sectors, where it is used to facilitate international communication and cooperation, increase overall work efficiency or – interestingly enough – enhance continuous professional development by ameliorating the delivery of various forms of professional training. Against this backdrop, it has also entered the realm of the translation profession to help it cope with the effects of initial internationalisation and ensuing globalisation, including rapid translation market growth, increased collaboration, the digitalisation and technologisation of the translation process and language service provision, as well as the proliferation of translator roles.

2.1 Globalisation and market growth

The factors perpetuating change to, and the rapid growth of, the translation market have been internationalisation (Orlando, 2016) and globalisation (Orlando, 2016; Pietrzak & Kornacki, 2021) – both strongly, but not exclusively, connected with economic activity.

Globalisation. The internationalisation of economic activities began after World War II and over time transformed into globalisation. While internationalisation refers to the increased involvement of international companies in attempts to win a share of the world market (e.g. through investment in foreign countries) (Drahokoupil, 2020), globalisation is its more advanced developmental stage. Its effects from the increased internationalisation of "markets for goods and services, the means of production, financial systems, competition, corporations, technology and industries" (Hayes, 2021) manifest themselves in the "increased mobility of capital, faster propagation of technological innovations and an increasing interdependency and uniformity of national markets" (OECD, 2013).

Globalisation had led to the emergence of what Clunan (2016) refers to as epistemic community, which is a network of internationally dispersed

DOI: 10.4324/9781003424932-3

professionals in a range of disciplines whose recognised expertise and shared norms permit them to provide informed advice to national governments and organisations involved in the establishment and coordination of common policies in response to local and global problems. That in turn makes states increasingly dependent on each other, hence, the notion of interdependency as a marker of globalisation.

However, globalisation exceeds far beyond economics, as it also has social, cultural, political and legal dimensions. As Fernando (2021) posits, it means increased interaction of populations, exchange of ideas, values and cultural products, homogenisation of the world culture, rise of intergovernmental organisations and unification of international law.

Intergovernmental organisations fulfil various roles. For example, the Organisation for Economic Co-operation and Development (OECD) aims to respond to social, economic and environmental issues, the World Trade Organisation (WTO) regulates international trade practices, the United Nations (UN) promotes international peace, security and cooperation, while the European Union (EU) – emblematic of the concept of political, economic, cultural and social unification – attempts to increase the competitiveness of its member states and their people in the globalised world.

Interestingly, in the wake of globalisation, individuals' interaction also increases, as people – driven by social agency – feel the need to resolve problems beyond the jurisdiction of local or national governments. As Tolley (1989) notes, where global issues are at stake, in the absence of political parties and elections which could be used to affect the decision makers, nongovernmental pressure groups are particularly vital. Hence, the exponential growth of nongovernment, non-profit organisations worldwide, which is evident in statistical data. For instance, as Cronin (2013) maintains, between 1909 and 1989, the number of intergovernmental and nongovernmental international organisations operating in the world had grown from 36 to 300 and from 176 to 4,200 respectively. However, the growth rate seems to have substantially increased, as at present, the numbers are unequivocally larger. For example, the Union of International Associations (UIA) processes data on over 68,000 member organisations, while in India, a government-commissioned study had identified 3.3 million organisations functioning in the country alone (Shukla, 2010).

Inevitably, globalisation – in its multiple dimensions – involves increased physical mobility (Orlando, 2016), motivated politically, socially, economically or educationally, as well as online interaction, which is additionally fuelled by the rapid development of Web-based communication tools. As people and organisations involve in travel, participate in international culture and cooperate on global issues (e.g. environment protection, terrorism or international crime), they involve in on-site and online communication and produce vast amounts of printed and digital content which requires translation (Orlando, 2016; Pietrzak & Kornacki, 2021). Consequently, the demand for language services, including translation, is growing exponentially. After all, corporate and private documents, international treaties, legislation, creative content and various forms of offline and online communication, including communication through the social media (Desjardins, 2017) – among numerous others – all need to be translated.

Market growth. The intensity and speed characterising the growth of the translation market are visible in relevant indices, and although the data have been collected with the use of different research methodologies in both local and international contexts, they generally demonstrate upward trends in market size growth.

For instance, according to Statista (2020), the size of the translation market, expressed in its annually computed value in US dollars, has been steadily increasing. In 2009, the market was worth $23 billion. By 2012, it had grown by 10 million to reach slightly over $33 billion. In 2015, it was worth over $38 billion – an increase of 5 billion – while in 2019, its worth amounted to $49.6 billion (i.e. over 11 billion more). Although the dynamics of the growth apparently differed between the three-year-long intervals, the market continued to grow, and over the ten years (2009–2019), its size had more than doubled. Moreover, the growth rate does not seem to be slowing, with its then-projected value of nearly $52 billion for 2021 and roughly $58 billion for 2022.

Nimdzi, a market research and consulting company oriented towards the translation market, provides its own estimates of the size of the language services industry (LSI), also expressed in US dollars, confirming a steady, or even accelerated, market growth. In last year's report (Nimdzi, 2022), it valued the language services market at $64.7 billion in 2022 and estimated its worth to exceed $69 billion in 2023. Given the industry's compound annual growth rate (CAGR) of 7%, for the years 2022–2026, it forecasts growth to $84.9 billion in the year 2026. In the latest report (Nimdzi, 2023), it estimates the CAGR to remain at 7%, predicts growth to $69.3 billion in 2023 and forecasts further growth to nearly $91 billion in 2027. In a similar vein, the International Market Analysis Research and Consulting Group (IMARC Group, 2023) valued the global language services market at $67.2 billion in 2022 and predicted that the market would grow at the CAGR of 6.2% to reach $98.6 billion by 2028.

IBIS World (2023) data illustrate the size of the translation market in the United States alone, but in this context, growth is also evident. Over the past ten years, the size of US translation services has grown from $5.7 billion in 2013 to $9.4 billion in 2023, with the average annual growth rate of $0.37 billion. In this case, a trough could be observed in the years 2014–2015, with the negative growth rates of $–1.4 and $–1.2 billion respectively, but since 2016, a steady growth is observable, disrupted only in 2020, when the rate equalled $-0.3 billion, coinciding with the out-break of the pandemic. For the COVID-stricken year of 2020, though, the growth rate was estimated at $0.5 billion, which additionally indicates another characteristic of the translation market – resilience.

As the *Slator 2021 Language Industry Market Report* (Slator, 2021) reveals, although the COVID-19 pandemic disrupted the market tem-porarily in the first six months of 2020, when the market contracted by 1.6%, swift recuperation followed contradicting the fears voiced by some translators in the face of the COVID-19 crisis, as reported by the French Association of Translators (Société française des traducteurs) (European Commission, 2021). In a survey on translators' beliefs about the impact of the pandemic on their work, nearly 60% of the respondents expressed the belief that negative disruption would be caused by COVID-19. Findings reported by the Common Sense Advisory (CSA, 2021c) research insti-tute also revealed negative expectations among language service provid-ers, 55% of whom had reported a decline in business, with 56% of them believing in the temporary nature of the decline.

In the Common Sense Advisory (CSA, 2021a) examination of the men-tal and professional impact of the pandemic on freelance translators from nearly 100 countries, conducted in the second half of 2020, the respond-ents were even more positive in their outlook, as despite commonly report-ing lower income or reduced workload, the majority (65%) believed the disruption was temporary. The same applies to the CSA (2021d) research conducted among language service providers, where considerably large majorities expected growth in demand (72%) and revenue (65%), while 90% claimed they felt optimistic about the future of the language services sector.

The most interesting finding of this research, though, was the nature of the impact reported. It turned out that while the pandemic reduced demand for translation services in some sectors, it simultaneously increased it in others. Quite naturally, the decline was observed in translation pertaining to the sectors of economy most badly hit by the pandemic, for example, hospitality services (events, travel and leisure), the automobile industry, commercial services and manufacturing. At the same time, increased demand was recorded in sectors of strategic importance for combating the pandemic, for example, healthcare, medical and pharmaceutical industries and the digital market, including social networking, the IT industry and software programming.

In the light of the findings, it may be stated that due to the apparent flexibility of the translation market, where commissions follow peak and troughs in various sectors of economy, even serious crises, while temporar-ily decreasing demand for translation services within certain domains, are – at the same time – likely to offset potential loss of income by increasing demand in other domains. It is this kind of realisation that might have inspired 44% of freelance translators who participated in CSA research in January 2021 (CSA, 2021b) – in the midst of the pandemic – to display a positive outlook on the future of the translation sector, as predicted for the first half of the year and an even greater proportion (51%) of freelancers with the same view, as projected for the second half of the year.

2.2 From collaboration to telecollaborative translation

As it has been demonstrated earlier, globalisation has caused increased demand for translation services, which is evidenced not only by the rapid growth of the translation market but also by its resilience in the face of economic crises. That in turn has stimulated change to the mode in which translation is now being performed.

Simply put, to cope with the volume of content that needs translation, increased collaboration is being observed, irrespective of whether translation is being performed by freelancers or language service providers (i.e. translation bureaux). In corroboration of that, O'Brien (2011) suggests that "Collaboration is evident in all types of translation scenarios" (O'Brien, 2011, p. 17).

In fact, translation has rarely been a solitary activity. As Jansen and Wegener (2013) purport, it is often collaborative in nature, and evidence that it has indeed been so for centuries can be found in the professional literature. For instance, O'Brien (2011) cites the *Septuagint* translation of the Hebrew Bible into Greek, which was reputedly delivered by a group of 72 translators. Hung (2005) provides an account of how Buddhist texts were collaboratively translated into Chinese between the years 150 CE–1150 CE. Monks based in a monastery would first read and attempt to understand the source text. Afterwards, the text would be interpreted into Chinese, collectively revised and consulted with the interpreter. The latter *per se* would frequently be cyclical and potentially involved several rounds of discussion. Finally, the text would be recorded and compared with previous translations, if they were available. Therefore, it was a team effort – a project involving the monks, an interpreter and a scribe where the final version of the translation was negotiated through the intensive interaction of all of the parties involved.

Cordingley and Manning (2017) provide more evidence for the collaborative nature of translation performed between antiquity and the Renaissance, when translation was frequently performed by groups of language specialists who collaborated with one another, contributing their knowledge and skills to the translation at hand. In a similar vein, Bistué (2013) describes how medieval and Renaissance translators also collaborated with one another, as well copyists and printers, while producing multilingual translations, in manuscript or print, where the meaning relations between the different language versions and their physical location on the page required negotiation.

The reason for which translation has been perceived as an individual undertaking stems from more or less deliberate efforts to present the profession as such. It was often in the accounts of the process – the translation metadiscourse of the time, so to speak – that the group effort was overlooked and a solitary translator was brought to the fore, either to give the translation an air of unity and authority or to respond to the politically motivated trend of power consolidation, be it in the hands of state or church (Bistué, 2013; Cordingley & Manning, 2017).

Triggered by advances in computational and corpus linguistics, as well as translation technologies (Bogucki & Lewandowska-Tomaszczyk, 2016), collaboration has now not only significantly increased in volume but it has also transformed into telecollaboration, which is being fuelled by ever-growing demand and facilitated by online communication tools. The collaborative nature of today's translation is nicely expressed by Pietrzak and Kornacki (2021), who observe that "What used to be considered a tedious pen-and-paper job now appears to be a profession which takes numerous forms, oftentimes interactive, multimodal, and collaborative" (Pietrzak & Kornacki, 2021, p. 38). Kang (2019) adds that especially in institutional contexts, "'the translator' is no longer an individual who translates a text solely on the basis of personal training and experience, but also a participant in a situated institutional practice" (Kang, 2019, p. 144), while Mehadzic (2022), as a representative of the localisation market, underlines that translation is a human collaboration.

Members (Hernandez, 2017; Mirza, 2017) of one of the largest and most influential international professional organisations, the Globalization and Localization Association (GALA) (www.gala-global.org), highlight the critical role of collaboration in translation, deeming it necessary for professionals to split tasks, communicate exchange viewpoints and feedback and collaborate with parties involved in translation projects – all in an atmosphere of team spirit.

It must be observed that collaboration is equally likely to be part of translation projects delivered by both in-house translators and freelancers. It is common practice for translators to (tele)collaborate with numerous other stakeholders in the translation process, including companies, agencies (European Commission, 2021), content authors, clients, project managers, revisers, dubbing adapters, editors, publishers and multiple others (Cordingley & Manning, 2017). It holds true even for freelancers, who are often contracted by translation agencies for specific translation jobs. In that case, digitally networked freelancers will deliver translation jointly, which is economically viable in an era of higher workloads, urgent deadlines and increased turnovers. Sakamoto and Foedisch (2017) corroborate this by stating that "Professional translation is now predominantly carried out in virtual-team-style production networks where communication between language service providers (LSPs) and freelance translators' practice is increasingly restricted to computerised methods" (Sakamoto & Foedisch, 2017, p. 333).

Collaboration may also take less obvious forms (e.g. a freelancer working on a text whose translation has been commissioned by a client-author will not only need to communicate with the latter but will also certainly need to consult various resources to cope with the linguistic, cultural or technical challenges which he or she may face in the process). For that purpose, the freelancer may use printed or read-only Web content. Quite often, though, they will find it more useful to reach colleague translators (Mitchell-Schuitevoerder, 2020) via professional virtual communities. As Risku and Dickinson posit, "Freelance workers increasingly look to such communities to fill a need in their working lives for collaboration, mutual learning or knowledge exchange" (Risku & Dickinson, 2009, p. 53). That kind of consultation will not only involve online synchronous or asynchronous communication, but in more problematic cases, it may develop into a longer exchange, with multiple professionals working jointly towards the most adequate solution to the problem at hand. And that, in turn, will ultimately benefit those directly involved and the broader online community. Examples of this kind of asynchronous communication can be found on the virtual translation community site ProZ.com (proz.com) and its forum discussion threads relating to, for example, the resolution of terminological issues or the troubleshooting of computer-assisted translation.

Basing on Social Network Theory (SNA), Risku, Rogl, and Pein-Weber (2016) discuss how a seemingly small-scale project, involving the client-translator dyad, in fact involves a complex network of human actors and tools. While Risku et al. (2016) use the network to tackle the issue of centrality in translation networks, for the purpose of the present discussion, the human actors that they list (e.g. the client, graphic designer, prior contractors, colleagues or online platform members) are particularly interesting, as they exemplify what parties can potentially collaborate with the translator.

The most emblematic example of collaboration in the translation profession is a fully-fledged translation project, completed by in-house translators operating under the supervision of a translation agency. Robinson (2019) provides a simplified account of a possible implementation of a team translation project where translators work on a large text in jigsaw mode, first independently translating different parts of the source text and then exchanging their translations for mutual revision. Subsequently, they introduce the necessary corrections, as suggested by the colleagues, and consult in-house specialists (e.g. terminologists or reviewers), who peruse the final product before it is delivered to the client.

Robinson's (2019) model is quite simple, but the team line-up and workflow structure are likely to be more elaborate and involve various actors. Illustrative of that is the translation production network model, which Foedisch (2017a) proposed to indicate the interdependencies within a dyadically structured translation project. The network starts with the client, who initiates the project and delegates the translation to an LSP entity (e.g. a translation agency). The project manager at the agency begins to collaborate regularly with in-house colleagues (e.g. vendor managers) and, externally, with linguists (e.g. translators, revisers, post-editors), who have been sub-contracted by the translation agency. If the project is large enough in volume, another translation agency may also join in, with its own network of sub-contracted linguists. The model implies that the network of actors collaborating on a translation project may be complex, although the amount of communication between the different nodes of the network will substantially differ.

At this point, it must be reiterated that since "technology has acted as the main enabler for collaborative translation in the modern age" (O'Brien, 2011, p. 19), it has inevitably transformed collaboration into telecollaborative translation. A corroboration of that is inferable from the aforementioned characteristics of present-day translation provided by Pietrzak and Kornacki (2021). In certain contexts, telecollaborative translation is a necessity, as freelancers, in-house translators and other translation agents tend to work from home. In fact, they telecollaborate – even internationally – with actors involved in the translation production network who are physically located in geographically dispersed locations. In the light of that, it may be surprising that the shift towards telecollaboration does not find reflection in terminology used in discourse about contemporary translation, where the term *collaboration* continues to be used, although it is to a large extent synonymous with *telecollaboration*. It is evidenced even by O'Brien's (2011) definition of collaboration cited earlier, which by underlining the pivotal role of technology clearly encompasses telecollaborative work modes while at the same time omitting the prefix (*tele-*) in the very term. The same is observable in the writings of Bogucki and Lewandowska-Tomaszczyk (2016), who discuss professional online collaborative activities while also using the term *collaborative translation*. The previous example might stem from the fact that telecollaboration-enhancing technology has so seamlessly been integrated into professional practices that it hardly needs emphasising. It is simply difficult to envisage present-day collaboration administered in offline mode exclusively, even more so in the post-COVID era of the *new normal*, where telework looks set to occur even more than it did prior to the outbreak of the pandemic.

2.3 The digitalisation of translation

Globalisation, exponentially increasing demand for translation services and the resulting rapid growth of the LSP market have all contributed to promoting collaborative work modes in professional translation. As it has already been stated, the factor which has triggered the shift towards telecollaboration, though, has most of all been the development of ICT, especially the expansion of the Internet and the ensuing proliferation of online communication tools. What can be added as yet another enabler of telecollaborative translation is the appearance of translation technology. The aforementioned developments have been driving the digitalisation (Ehrensberger-Dow & Massey, 2022) of not only the translation process but also – most pertinently to the telecollaborative shift in translation – the translation workflow (Pym & Torres-Simón, 2021).

Mitchell-Schuitevoerder (2020) observes:

> Translations have become projects and translation is only one component in the workflow. The translation project requires management of communications and accounts in addition to the actual translation process. Sheer volume demands a different approach to how we translate and deal with demands.
>
> (Mitchell-Schuitevoerder, 2020, p. 16)

The mediator of the implementation of this new approach is translation technology. It may be posited that the role of translation technology in modifying translation service provision could be compared to that of ICT in perpetuating globalisation processes. Analogically, it could be stated that "The advent of translation technology has totally globalized translation" (Chan, 2015a, p. xxvii). It needs to be underlined at this point, though, that translation technology is a very inclusive term and, as Chan (2015a) explains, comprises all kinds of technology used to facilitate human translation, machine translation (MT) and computer-assisted translation (CAT). However, the greatest share in the digitalisation of the translation workflow belongs to CAT technologies, including CAT tools, translation management systems (TMSs), as well as generic office tools (e.g. email clients or online communicators, which support translation-related communication).

The latter tools were particularly important in the early days, when they aided distant communication and resource sharing between stakeholders involved in the translation process even before CAT tools and TMSs entered the stage. Biau-Gil and Pym (2006) explain:

> electronic formats concern not just our texts, but also our communications with clients and other translators. Thanks to the Internet,

professionals from all over the world can be in regular contact by email or various forms of instant messaging. Work can be sent and received electronically, across national and cultural borders.

(Biau-Gil & Pym, 2006, p. 6)

Historically, work on computer-assisted translation began shortly after the ALPAC report, commissioned by the United States government and issued in 1966 by the Automatic Language Processing Advisory Committee (ALPAC), determined for the years to come that "there is no immediate or predictable prospect of useful machine translation" (ALPAC, 1966, p. 32), having critically assessed the outcomes of research conducted in 1947–1966 on the use of computers to deliver automated translation. Consequently, as funds for MT research were unavailable, in the years to come, researchers focused their efforts on developing not a system which would perform translation for a human being but rather a tool that would assist human translation by optimising and accelerating it – very much in agreement with the recommendations contained in the ALPAC report.

Focusing on the nature of changes, Chan (2015b) divides the history of the development of CAT technology into four major phases, spanning the years 1967 and 2013: germination (1967–1983), steady growth (1984–1992), rapid growth (1993–2003) and global development (2004–2013). Esselink (2020), for a change, distinguishes five such stages, which he delineates by the type of technology prevalent within each of them, namely, desktop tools (early 1990s), server-based tools (late 1990s), project management and collaboration platforms (early 2000s), translation management systems (late 2000s) and cloud translation platforms (2010–now). It is beyond the scope of the present argument to provide a detailed account of the history of the development of translation technology – the more that it has already been done by other scholars, for example, Somers (2003) or Bogucki (2009). Thus, only the distinguishing features of the phases delineated by Chan (2015b) and Esselink (2020) will be discussed to demonstrate major directions in the advancement of translation technology *vis-à-vis* telecollaboration.

In Chan's (2015b) germination phase (1967–1983), two important concepts were born. Firstly, what is now commonly known as translation memory (TM) was conceptualised and materialised at the turn of the 1970s and 1980s, as the concept of CAT was founded on the idea that computer technology could be used to store fragments of past translations which would be automatically retrieved for reuse to aid other translation jobs – all under the supervision of, and subject to verification by, a human translator. Secondly, towards the end of 1980, foundations were laid for an interactive computer translation system which would display the source and target texts in two adjacent windows on the computer screen to let the user introduce necessary edits to the target text using functionalities for text selection and reference text consultation. In other words, the framework was created for the layout of the editor pane, which is featured by all contemporary CAT tools.

As it can be seen, at that time, CAT was largely perceived as human-computer interaction. Efforts concentrated on the technicalities of the process, the identification of possible challenges and adequate technical solutions, which effectively dissuaded the developers from considering other aspects of translation to be incorporated into the tools. Even if functionalities aiding in-project communication had been envisaged at the time, the limited capacity of the computers and the Internet would have inhibited substantial progress in that area. Consequently, the software developed then did not involve features promoting collaborative translation.

Chan's (2015b) steady growth phase (1984–1992), which roughly corresponds to Esselink's (2020) era of server-based translation tools, saw the commercialisation of CAT systems, as corporations such as Trados and Star developed their own software with a view to economising large-scale translation projects. Work continued on the then-equivalent of today's TM, which would identify matches between the source text and the sentence pairs stored in a computerised bilingual dictionary to suggest possible translations, but the matching mechanism had limited capacity permitting the identification of only perfect rather than fuzzy matches. Chan (2015b) also adds that in 1990, the first multilingual terminology management program was released.

This phase marked the beginning of an era in which CAT tools would aid the delivery of corporate translation projects, which at present inevitably involve telecollaboration. Yet due to the then-limited use of the Internet and the concentration of efforts mostly on the improvement of the mechanics of CAT, telecollaboration was not incorporated into the tools of the day.

In Chan's (2015b) phase of rapid growth (1993–2003), which roughly overlaps with that of Esselink's (2020) project management and team collaboration platforms, the commercialisation of computer-assisted systems continued, and their number increased considerably. As the tools developed, they permitted greater customisation and provided increased assistance through automatic and manual text alignment tools, term extractors, the translator's workstation, integration with standard Windows-based software (e.g. word processors), customisable dictionaries, voluminous lexicons, language corpora, compatibility with various file formats, tag management tools, enhanced character coding or MT modules. Most importantly, though, CAT tools shipped with project-oriented and Web-based features, thus opening themselves to the world outside the translator's desk. Corporate translation management software started to support translation project management, even for multi-file and multilingual projects, workflow management, project analysis or shared online TMs. What is more, server-side solutions began to appear, causing the bifurcation of CAT tools into stand-alone desktop applications and cloud-based, multi-user solutions.

The aforementioned innovations apparently gave CAT tool development a new angle, catering for the needs of corporate language service providers or networked individuals who delivered more complex translation projects. And although the integration of project management or cloud resource sharing functionalities did not necessarily provide support for fully-fledged (tele)collaboration, as they mostly permitted a top-bottom, linear administration of specific project stages, an important first step was taken to lay ground for genuinely telecollaborative features of CAT tools.

In Chan's (2015b) global development phase (2004–2013), which dovetails with Esselink's (2020) eras of TMSs and cloud translation platforms, computer-assisted technologies continued to grow algorithmically on an unprecedented scale, perhaps due to global competition. In part, that development entailed the betterment of tools and functionalities already available on the market. As a result, translation technology supported fully automated alignment, automated quality assurance (QA), including checks for terminological inconsistency in target texts, as well as new file formats, including TMX and TBX, which permitted the transfer of translation memories and term bases, and HTML or ASP, which were used in localisation.

As Chan (2015b), Gambier (2019) and Esselink (2020) report, with time, the changes introduced visibly steered towards support for a LAN- and Web-based collaboration communities, including server-based project management, collaborative language translation services with cross-browser compatibility or online integrated CAT and management tools. It is within the current phase that Software-as-a-Service (SaaS) collaborative translation technology began to thrive, which combined functionalities augmenting workflow management, CAT and machine translation.

The main themes of this phase could be summarised as improvement, tool and resource consolidation, networking, resource-sharing, productivity and online LSP. Hence, the emergence of cloud tools permitting the management and delivery of large-scale multinational projects in real time (Gambier, 2019; O'Brien & Rodriquez Vazquez, 2020), with translators, reviewers and project managers being able to access and edit translations, as well as simultaneously use shared and team-editable resources.

Since the publication of Chan's (2015b) paper on the development of translation technology, the globalisation phase has shown no signs of easing, which is evidenced by Esselink (2020) renaming contemporary TMSs as globalisation management systems (GMSs), which are being perfected and now increasingly permit synchronous and asynchronous online communication between project stakeholders, which in combination with other functionalities, such as change tracking, document versioning or segments commenting, facilitate genuine team interaction within "a managed crowd" (Esselink, 2020, p. 110). It is in such translation environments that the epitome of telecollaboration – computer-mediated interaction of team members oriented towards the achievement of a shared goal – materialises. As Gambier (2019) posits, SaaS actually "pushes the translator to become member of an international virtual and collaborative community" (Gambier, 2019, p. 351).

Intriguingly, globalisation seems to have been both the catalyst of change and its product at the same time. As if in a self-perpetuating cycle, it fosters the development of translation technology which would aptly respond to the needs of the contemporary translation market, while fomenting further globalisation of the translation industry. As Chan (2017) himself observes, in congruence with Esselink (2020), continued globalisation of translation is evident in the establishment of online language service companies providing complex, round-the-clock translation services in multiple languages, intensive development and widespread implementation of MT, as well as the utilisation of comprehensive cloud CAT tools and TMSs.

It seems that globalisation is going to promote further development of translation technology, for example, with regard to facilitating the now-rapidly-developing multimedia and multimodal translation, which involves the transfer of meaning between a range of digital content formats, including text, speech, images, videos, animations, diagrams or graphs. This multimodality is likely to increasingly characterise translation, which is particularly visible in the localisation industry, as discussed by Hofmann-Delbor and Bartnicka (2017) or Díaz Cintas and Massidda (2020), the more that contemporary translation comprises the localisation of social media (Desjardins, 2017), including content from file-sharing platforms, social-networking sites, instant messaging systems, be it through professional localisation services or crowdsourcing.

Even in the latter case, which often involves going beyond "an in-house team or group of employees in order to 'assign' a specific task to the masses, in the hope of leveraging the 'crowd's' diverse experience and knowledge" (Desjardins, 2017, p. 22), tools have been developed to support collaborative work modes. For instance, the FTC platform, which has been developed to augment the crowdsourced localisation of Facebook, offers two modules – the input module and the weighting module – which permit contributors to communicate and thus deliver collaborative localisation. As O'Hagan (2016) reports, the input module features community pages and functionalities which permit contributors to share screenshots or video clips, while the voting module enables contributors to benefit from vote-based feedback on the quality of their translations from those who volunteer to provide it.

As an aside, it could be added that despite the somewhat romanticised view of crowdsourcing as an activity performed by lay translators who work for the greater social good, self-development or social recognition (cf. Desjardins, 2017; O'Brien, 2011), paid crowdsourcing is also a fully-fledged professional business model used in today's LSP (cf. Sakamoto, Rodriguez de Céspdes, Berthaud, & Evans, 2017).

In its multiple forms, technology-induced change to translation practices has been enormous. While back in the 1990s, Samuelsson-Brown (1996) already perceived the rapid development of technology at large and the ensuing demands towards translators and highlighted the need for translators to adapt, lest they should lose their competitive edge, today, technology is so interwoven into the fabric of translation that Chan (2017) proposes to define translation as action taken to "transfer one language into another with the aid of technology" (Chan, 2017, p. 269). In the same vein, Massey, Barros, and Katan (2022) state that human translators now perform their tasks in sociotechnical environments, Angelone (2022) reports profound changes driven by technological advancement, including artificial intelligence, as a factor in redefining the roles and responsibilities of the LSP industry stakeholders, while do Carmo and Moorkens (2022) discuss the disruption that so-called intelligent technologies are bringing to translation.

Notwithstanding, it must be noted that the proliferation of translation technology solutions does not automatically entail increased interdependent collaboration, even if specific tools have been developed with teamwork in mind.

Foedisch (2017a) provides an example of how new technology does not always mean increased collaboration. As part of her research into quality assurance in translation projects – *inter alia* – she asked the participants working for a UK-based translation company about the impact of a new Enterprise Resource Planning (ERP) system on collaboration patterns. In return, she (Foedisch, 2017b) found out that, for example, communication with the accounts department, previously augmented by email or instant messaging, had literally ceased, as employees no longer needed to consult humans to obtain the data or information which they needed. They could simply collect it directly from the ERP system.

Although the findings cited earlier do not, as a matter of fact, refer to collaboration but regard mere information exchange within the company in question, they nevertheless signal a problem which is likely to arise in translation projects, for example, due to the introduction of tools for what the Smartcat (2019) company calls connected translation. In an attempt to respond to the exponential proliferation of digital content, which requires

urgent updates and delivery and is fragmented but overwhelmingly voluminous, connected translation platforms can be used to increase productivity –
inter alia – by fully automating the management of source and target
content, distribution of translation jobs and exchange and updates of project
resources, to name a few of their functionalities. In other words, the platforms can help translation agencies build a fully automated delivery pipeline
for automatically managing the translation process and workflow, including
quality assurance, final product delivery or payment. However, what the
platforms eliminate to a large extent is human-human communication and
genuine collaboration. Consequently, although such solutions may increase
productivity, they do not warrant high quality.

More illustration of how new technology may be detrimental to collaboration is provided by translation market representatives themselves.
For example, Hofmann-Delbor and Bartnicka (2017) describe the workflow of localisation projects delivered in *agile* mode, where due to short
turnaround times and constant changes in localised content, localisers
work via online platforms permitting instant access to project resources,
real-time updates and automated file transfer, as well as product delivery, but little, or no, actual collaboration. The *agile* localisation mode and
dedicated platforms often enforce linear progress through the workflow
stages, with limited room or instruments for interaction. Consequently,
this kind of setup not only produces an "isolating and dehumanizing"
(Biau-Gil & Pym, 2006, p. 7) working environment but also, most importantly, as Hofmann-Delbor and Bartnicka (2017) demonstrate, precludes
the exchange of critical information, joint planning and negotiation, which
are necessary to ensure the quality of translation and the final product. In
fact, Hofmann-Delbor and Bartnicka (2017) provide numerous examples
of inadequate or nonsensical English-Polish localisations of desktop software, computer and console games or mobile apps, which stemmed from
mis-, or total lack of, communication.

Apparently, the importance of communication and direct interaction for
the delivery of quality translation services is not overlooked by professionals, who actively seek channels for both. For instance, in a report on
research conducted in association with the Institute of Translation and
Interpreting (ITI) – a UK-based association for in-service translators, interpreters and LSPs – into LSPs' practices in the digital age, Sakamoto et al.
(2017) describe how PMs tend to use various tools for effective in-project
communication, recruitment, marketing and knowledge sharing, including applications which are conducive to genuine collaboration (e.g. Skype,
WhatsApp or even the social media).

Several other downsides of the intense technologisation of translation
have been signalled by Moorkens (2020), who draws attention to the
effects of Digital Taylorism in translation, which is a work system based on

cloud-based tools and micro-tasking that permits translation agencies to have multiple freelancers complete voluminous projects for them through collaborative workflows. Although the system helps employers to cut hiring and infrastructural costs, monitor work and substantially increase turnaround times, it may reportedly be detrimental to translators' motivation and satisfaction levels, which may also be affected by the limited reliability of SaaS tools due to unexpected discontinuation, change of terms or regional unavailability. In the long run, low motivation may additionally decrease sustainable work organisation, worker committal and translators' ability to deal with deep concentration tasks.

References

ALPAC. (1966). *Languages and machines: Computers in translation and linguistics: A report by the automatic language processing advisory committee, division of behavioral sciences, national academy of sciences, national research council.* Washington, DC: National Academy of Sciences, National Research Council.

Angelone, E. (2022). Weaving adaptive expertise into translator training. In G. Massey, E. Huertas-Barros, & D. Katan (Eds.), *The IATIS yearbook. The human translator in the 2020s* (1st ed.). London: Routledge.

Biau-Gil, J. R., & Pym, A. (2006). Technology and translation (a pedagogical overview). In A. Pym, A. Perestrenko, & B. Starink (Eds.), *Translation technology and its teaching* (pp. 5–19). Tarragona, Spain: Intercultural Studies Group, Universitat Rovira i Virgili.

Bistué, B. (2013). *Collaborative translation and multi-version texts in early modern Europe.* London & New York: Routledge.

Bogucki, Ł. (2009). *Tłumaczenie wspomagane komputerowo. Przekład, Mity i Rzeczywistość.* Warszawa: Wydawnictwo Naukowe PWN.

Bogucki, Ł., & Lewandowska-Tomaszczyk, B. (2016). Volunteer translation, collaborative knowledge acquisition and what is likely to follow. In Ł. Bogucki, B. Lewandowska-Tomaszczyk, & M. Thelen (Eds.), *Lodz studies in language: vol. 41. Translation and meaning: New series* (pp. 37–46). Frankfurt am Main: Peter Lang Edition.

Chan, S.-W. (2015a). Preface. In S.-W. Chan (Ed.), *Routledge encyclopedia of translation technology.* London & New York: Routledge Taylor & Francis Group.

Chan, S.-W. (2015b). The development of technology 1967–2013. In S.-W. Chan (Ed.), *Routledge encyclopedia of translation technology.* London & New York: Routledge Taylor & Francis Group.

Chan, S.-W. (2017). *The future of translation technology: Towards a world without Babel. Routledge studies in translation technology: Vol. 1.* London & New York: Routledge.

Clunan, A. L. (2016). *Epistemic community.* Retrieved from www.britannica.com/topic/epistemic-community#ref1181615

Cordingley, A., & Manning, C. F. (2017). What is collaborative translation? In A. Cordingley & C. F. Manning (Eds.), *Collaborative translation: From the renaissance to the digital age* (pp. 1–30). London: Bloomsbury.

Cronin, M. (2013). *Translation in the digital age. New perspectives in translation studies*. Milton Park, Abingdon, Oxon, & New York: Routledge.

CSA. (2021a). *COVID-19 freelancer 2 survey data*. Retrieved from https://csa-research.com/Featured-Content/COVID-19-Industry-Data-Research/Freelancer-2-Survey

CSA. (2021b). *COVID-19 freelancer 3 survey data*. Retrieved from https://csa-research.com/Featured-Content/COVID-19-Industry-Data-Research/Freelancer-3-Survey

CSA. (2021c). *COVID-19 LSP 3 survey data: Overall results*. Retrieved from https://csa-research.com/Featured-Content/COVID-19-Industry-Data-Research/LSP-3-Survey

CSA. (2021d). *COVID-19 LSP 5 survey data: Overall results*. Retrieved from https://csa-research.com/Featured-Content/COVID-19-Industry-Data-Research/LSP-5-Survey

Desjardins, R. (2017). *Translation and social media: In theory, in training and in professional practice. Palgrave pivot*. London: Palgrave Macmillan.

Díaz Cintas, J., & Massidda, S. (2020). Technological advances in audiovisual translation. In M. O'Hagan (Ed.), *Routledge handbooks in translation and interpreting studies. The Routledge handbook of translation and technology* (1st ed., pp. 255–270). London: Routledge.

Do Carmo, F., & Moorkens, J. (2022). Translation's new high-tech clothes. In G. Massey, E. Huertas-Barros, & D. Katan (Eds.), *The IATIS yearbook. The human translator in the 2020s* (1st ed.). London: Routledge.

Drahokoupil, J. (2020). *Foreign direct investment*. Retrieved from www.britannica.com/topic/foreign-direct-investment#ref1181306

Ehrensberger-Dow, M., & Massey, G. (2022). *The changing (inter)face of professional translation: Lecture delivered on 8th December 2021 as part of the centre for translation studies' convergence lecture series*. Retrieved from https://www.youtube.com/watch?v=Hzw6TR-Rah8

Esselink, B. (2020). Multinational language service provider as user. In M. O'Hagan (Ed.), *Routledge handbooks in translation and interpreting studies. The Routledge handbook of translation and technology* (1st ed., pp. 109–126). London: Routledge.

European Commission. (2021). *COVID-19: How has it affected the world of translation?* Retrieved from https://blogs.ec.europa.eu/emt/covid-19-how-has-it-affected-the-world-of-translation/

Fernando, J. (2021). *What is globalization?* Retrieved from www.investopedia.com/terms/g/globalization.asp

Foedisch, M. (2017a). *Managing translation projects: Practices and quality in production networks: A thesis submitted to the University of Manchester for the degree of Doctor of Philosophy in the Faculty of Humanities*. Retrieved from www.research.manchester.ac.uk/portal/files/66048304/FULL_TEXT.PDF

Foedisch, M. (2017b). *Researching technological changes in translation production. An outline of the application of practice theory to translation: A PPT presentation presented at the portsmouth translation conference 2017*. Portsmouth: University of Portsmouth.

Gambier, Y. (2019). Impact of technology on translation and translation studies. *Russian Journal of Linguistics*, 23(2), 344–361. https://doi.org/10.22363/2312-9182-2019-23-2-344-361

Hayes, A. (2021). *Internationalization*. Retrieved from www.investopedia.com/terms/i/internationalization.asp

Hernandez, M. (2017). *10 traits of successful language industry professionals – Rising star winner*. Retrieved from www.gala-global.org/knowledge-center/professional-development/articles/10-traits-successful-language-industry

Hofmann-Delbor, A., & Bartnicka, M. (2017). *Programiści i tłumacze: Wprowadzenie do lokalizacji oprogramowania*. Gliwice: Helion.

Hung, E. (2005). Translation in China: An analytical survey. In E. Hung & J. Wakabayashi (Eds.), *Asian translation traditions* (pp. 67–107). Manchester: St. Jerome.

IBIS World. (2023). *Translation services in the US – market size 2003–2028*. Retrieved from www.ibisworld.com/industry-statistics/market-size/translation-services-united-states/

IMARC Group. (2023). *Language services market: Global industry trends, share, size, growth, opportunity and forecast 2023–2028*. Retrieved from https://www.imarcgroup.com/language-services-market

Jansen, H., & Wegener, A. (2013). Multiple translatorship. In H. Jansen & A. Wegener (Eds.), *Authorial and editorial voices in translation 1: Collaborative relationships between authors, translators and performers* (pp. 1–39). Montréal: Éditions québécoises de l'oeuvre.

Kang, J.-H. (2019). Institutional translation. In M. Baker & G. Saldanha (Eds.), *Routledge encyclopedia of translation studies* (pp. 141–145). London & New York, NY: Routledge.

Massey, G., Barros, E., & Katan, D. (2022). The human translator in the 2020s: An introduction. In G. Massey, E. Huertas-Barros, & D. Katan (Eds.), *The IATIS yearbook. The human translator in the 2020s* (1st ed.). London: Routledge.

Mehadzic, S. (2022). *How software companies can make localization and Agile get along: – Infobip's story*. Retrieved from https://www.smartcat.com/blog/author/semir/

Mirza, C. (2017). *Translators of the future: What skills do you need?* Retrieved from www.gala-global.org/blog/translators-future-what-skills-do-you-need

Mitchell-Schuitevoerder, R. (2020). *A project-based approach to translation technology: Translation practices explained* (1st ed.). London: Routledge.

Moorkens, J. (2020). "A tiny cog in a large machine": Digital Taylorism in the translation industry. *Translation Spaces*, 9(1), 12–34. https://doi.org/10.1075/ts.00019.moo

Nimdzi. (2022). *The 2022 Nimdzi 100: The ranking of the top 100 largest language service providers*. Retrieved from www.nimdzi.com/nimdzi-100-2022/

Nimdzi. (2023). *The 2023 Nimdzi 100: The ranking of the top 100 largest language service providers*. Retrieved from www.nimdzi.com/nimdzi-100-top-lsp/?utm_source=ZohoCampaigns&utm_campaign=Nimdzi+100+Report+-+PDF+of+full+report+now+available+&utm_medium=email#market-size-and-growth-projection

O'Brien, S. (2011). Collaborative translation. In Y. Gambier & L. van Doorslaer (Eds.), *The handbook of translation studies: Volume 2* (pp. 17–20). Amsterdam & Philadelphia: John Benjamins Publishing Company.

O'Brien, S., & Rodriquez Vazquez, S. (2020). Translation and technology. In S. Laviosa & M. González Davies (Eds.), *Routledge handbooks. The Routledge handbook of translation and education* (pp. 264–277). Abingdon, Oxon, & New York, NY: Routledge, Taylor and Francis Group.

OECD. (2013). *Glossary of statistical terms.* Retrieved from https://stats.oecd.org/glossary/detail.asp?ID=1121

O'Hagan, M. (2016). Deconstructing translation crodwsourcing wiht the case of a Facebook initiative: A translator network of engineered autonomy and trust? In D. Kenny (Ed.), *The IATIS yearbook. human issues in translation technology: The IATIS yearbook/edited by Dorothy Kenny* (pp. 25–44). London: Routledge.

Orlando, M. (2016). *Training 21st-century translators and interpreters: At the crossroads of practice, research and pedagogy. Transkulturalität – Translation – Transfer.* Berlin: Frank & Timme.

Pietrzak, P., & Kornacki, M. (2021). *Using CAT tools in freelance translation: Insights from a case study.* London: Routledge.

Pym, A., & Torres-Simón, E. (2021). Is automation changing the translation profession? *International Journal of the Sociology of Language, 2021*(270), 39–57. https://doi.org/10.1515/ijsl-2020-0015

Risku, H., & Dickinson, A. (2009). Translators as networkers: The role of virtual communities. *HERMES – Journal of Language and Communication in Business, 42,* 49–70. https://doi.org/10.7146/hjlcb.v22i42.96846

Risku, H., Rogl, R., & Pein-Weber, C. (2016). Mutual dependencies: Centrality in translation networks. *JoSTrans, 25,* 232–253.

Robinson, D. (2019). *Becoming a translator: An introduction to the theory and practice of translation/Douglas Robinson* (4th ed.). London: Routledge.

Sakamoto, A., & Foedisch, M. (2017). No news is good news? The role of feedback in the virtual-team-style translation production network. *Translation Spaces, 6*(2), 333–352. https://doi.org/10.1075/ts.6.2.08sak

Sakamoto, A., Rodriguez de Céspdes, B., Berthaud, S., & Evans, J. (2017). *When translation meets technologies: Language service providers (LSPs) in the digital age: Focus group report.* Portsmouth: University of Portsmouth.

Samuelsson-Brown, G. (1996). New technology for translators. In R. A. Owens (Ed.), *The translator's handbook* (pp. 279–293). London: Aslib.

Shukla, A. (2010). *First official estimate: An NGO for every 400 people in India.* Retrieved from http://archive.indianexpress.com/news/first-official-estimate-an-ngo-for-every-400-people-in-india/643302/

Slator. (2021). *Translation and localization industry set to grow by up to 10% to USD 26.2bn in 2021.* Retrieved from https://slator.com/translation-and-localization-industry-set-to-grow-by-up-to-10-to-usd-26-2bn-in-2021/

Smartcat. (2019). *Embrace the global content economy with Connected Translation.* Retrieved from www.smartcat.com/connected-translation

Somers, H. L. (2003). *Computers and translation: A translator's guide. Benjamins translation library: v. 35.* Amsterdam: John Benjamins.

Statista (2020). *Market size of the global language services industry from 2009 to 2019 with a projection until 2022.* Retrieved from https://www.statista.com/statistics/257656/size-of-the-global-language-services-market/

Tolley, H. (1989). Popular sovereignty and international law: ICJ strategies for human rights standard setting. *Human Rights Quarterly, 11*(4), 561. https://doi.org/10.2307/762091

3 Telecollaboration in competence models and professional standards

As Piotrowska (2007, 2022) observed, research into the competences characterising translators has been undertaken for roughly the past 40 years. Due to interest in comparative, product-based research in TS before the 1980s, translation theories focused largely on the relationship between the source text and the target text. As a result – as she notes in congruence with Tabakowska (1999) – translation competence was perceived as either the determiner of success or failure in translation. However, since that time, conceptualisations of competence have evolved to serve various purposes, including the psychological modelling of the translator, translation quality assessment and – last but not least – translation pedagogy (Campbell, 1998).

For Piotrowska (2007, 2022), competence models are the keystone of translation pedagogy, as through the target competences which they lay out they inform the teaching and learning processes involved in translator education and help relevant stakeholders, including education policy makers, course designers and teachers, take vital decisions on course content, learning outcomes and assessment modes. In a similar vein, Klimkowski (2015) sees competence models as crucial to curriculum design but also describing the desired effects of TS programmes. Dybiec-Gajer (2013) corroborates that view discussing how – in line with the aforementioned shifts in perspectives on competence – competence models have moved the focus of assessment in translation courses from the quality of the student translations towards the profiling of translation students' target competence.

In a similar vein, guidance for translation pedagogy is provided by professional translation standards, which in an era of the professionalisation of translator education Piotrowska (2022) can be helpful in updating course design and teaching and learning practices in accordance with the current LSP guidelines.

That said, it seems pertinent to analyse how – if at all – telecollaboration correlates with the goals of translation pedagogy, as they are delineated within major competence models and professional standards. With that

DOI: 10.4324/9781003424932-4

in mind, both kinds of documents will first be reviewed to augment recall, and subsequently, they will be examined with a view to identifying elements which legitimise the implementation of telecollaboration in translation courses and also indicate the development of which competences telecollaboration could possibly support.

3.1   Overview of major translation competence models

The starting point for research into competences indispensable for translators was the nature/nurture debate over their origins in the professional literature in the late 1970s through the 1990s. Scholars such as Harris and Sherwood (1978), Toury (1984) and Lörscher (1991) on one side and Hönig (1988) and Kiraly (1995) on the other respectively advocated the view that translation is an innate capacity or an acquired trait – an outcome of effort and perseverance. According to Piotrowska (2007), a solution through which to reconcile the two conflicting standpoints is Kiraly's (1995) distinction between *translator competence* vs. *translation competence*, where the former emphasises "the complex nature of the professional translator's task and the nonlinguistic skills that are required . . . [and] allows us to distinguish between the more general types of native and foreign language communicative competence the professional translator shares with bilinguals (as native translators)" (Kiraly, 1995, p. 16), while the latter denotes "the translation skills that are specific to professional translation and which most bilinguals do not possess" (Kiraly, 1995, pp. 16–17). Although as Whyatt (2012) notes – citing the writings of Tabakowska (2003), Pieńkos (2003) and Piotrowska (2007) – the debate is far from over, Kiraly's (1995) notions of translator and translaton competence demonstrate that certain elements of what it takes to be able to translate may be inborn and natural, while others may require education and training.

The 1990s saw a gradual shift – motivated by the implementation of the Bologna Agreement across Europe (Popiołek, 2020) – towards translator competence, with translation programmes increasingly focusing on the development of the translator as a whole person, with their psychocorporeal dispositions, hence, the increasing popularity of the term *translator education* (Pietrzak, 2020), which indicates that TS programmes aim to "cater for the overall, life-long human growth and functioning [of (student) translators] – as individuals, members of groups, teams, communities and societies" (Klimkowski, 2015, p. 47). Nonetheless, change was slow, as translation competence continued to constitute the essence of translation teaching in the first decade of the 21st century (cf. Piotrowska, 2007).

It is also worth noticing that the notion of competence *per se* is problematic in that, although commonly used in the professional literature, it tends to be confused with other terms such as *ability* and *skill* (Whyatt, 2012). Whyatt (2012), in correspondence with Shreve (1997), proposed that both ability and skill, together with predisposition and competence, be perceived as elements of a developmental continuum through which one can ultimately develop translation expertise. In her view, predisposition is the natural human quality which permits individuals to mediate meaning and which in bilingual children may develop into the natural ability to translate – a potential "coextensive with bilingualism" (Toury, 2012, p. 281). Skill is "an actual demonstration of this potential" (Whyatt, 2012, p. 26) to translate well, which individuals develop to varying degrees. With time, through education or professional training, this skill may evolve into competence (i.e. an up-to-standard ability to perform well) and in the long run into translation expertise encompassing extensive knowledge, skills, training or experience which collectively warrant good performance.

The idea of modelling translation/translator competence has also attracted bitter criticism for a number of reasons. For instance, Pym (2003) posits that multi-componential models of translation competence reflect the view that competence is a linguistically analysable mode of bilingualism. It constitutes a response to historical and social change as well as market demands, involves linguistic, cultural, technological and professional skill sets and – in congruence with the writings of Wills (1996) – entails a *super-competence*, which in its nature is superior to others. Instead, he proposes a minimalist concept of translation competence, which in his opinion is a more fitting response to "rapid technological and professional change" (Pym, 2003, p. 481). He envisages translation competence as the following:

> The ability to generate a series of more than one viable target text (TT$_1$, TT$_2$ . . . TTn) for a pertinent source text (ST)
> The ability to select only one viable TT from this series, quickly and with justified confidence.
>
> (Pym, 2003, p. 498)

This minimalist interpretation of translation competence implies that it is hard to predict what sub-competences exactly a translator needs to be equipped with to make informed choices about the final version of the target text which would be most pertinent to the context in which the translation is being performed.

On the one hand, Pym's (2003) conceptualisation of translation competence may be helpful in dismissing the claim that "the rapid changes [to the translation profession] observed seriously challenge the primacy of universities" (Orlando, 2016, p. 28) in educating translators and that, by default, competence will never catch up with market reality (Pym, 2003), while on the other hand, it avoids the excessive compartmentalisation of translation competence models, criticised by Kiraly and Hofmann (2016). As they state, multi-componential models are often "the product of abductive armchair theorizing" (Kiraly & Hofmann, 2016, p. 72). Even more worryingly, the models imply not only that their components may be multiplied at will but also that those components are "both operationalizable (clearly definable and measurable), and acquirable by learners in a step-by-step, cumulative and essentially linear manner" (Kiraly & Hofmann, 2016, p. 72). The latter is congruent with the concern expressed at the beginning of the present millennium that translation competence may indeed be composed of, for example, "different skills but ones which are interwoven so intimately that, when they are viewed separately, the underlying construct seems to evaporate" (Waddington, 2001, p. 18).

Regardless of all the criticism, programme and course design in contemporary translator education is predominantly competence-based, which dates back to over three decades ago (Dybiec-Gajer, 2013; Hurtado Albir, 2007). After all, from the pragmatic viewpoint, it promotes the modularisation of TS programmes, gives "a particular programme considerable flexibility, and of course allows the overall competence to be acquired to be sub-divided into smaller, more manageable, more easily assessable, gradable units" (Kelly, 2007, p. 137) (e.g. in order to meet the requirements set in educational documents such as the Bologna Agreement in Europe).

Numerous scholars, including Campbell (1998), Kelly (2005), Kiraly (1995), Risku (2002), Schäffner and Adab (2000), Wills (1996) or Grucza (2005), Kielar (1988) and Hejwowski (2012) in the Polish academic context – to name a few – proposed their own components of translation competence, albeit they did so without testing their conceptualisations empirically. Other models, however, are the products of large-scale, methodologically advanced research projects, often undertaken by purpose-created research groups or consortia, for example, the PACTE (2005) model, all versions of the EMT (2009, 2017, 2022a) model and the TransComp model, which was proposed by Göpferich (2009b).

Dybiec-Gajer (2013) names the three competence models which are scientifically established, hierarchically structured, not merely listing their components, and particularly relevant to translation pedagogy as PACTE (2005), EMT (2009, 2017, 2022a) and TransComp (Göpferich, 2009b).

Procés d'Adquisició de la Competència Traductora i Avaluació, commonly known as PACTE (2005), was a research group established at Universitat Autònoma de Barcelona and led by Amparo Hurtado Albir, which in the years 1997–2022 conducted empirical and experimental research into translation competence and the process of its acquisition.

Its model is relevant to professional translation, characterises an expert translator and has been validated through extensive translation process research (Hurtado Albir, 2017). The model comprises mostly procedural, expert knowledge which underpins the translation process and encompasses a total of five sub-competences, complemented with a set of psycho-physiological components elevating the position of the strategic component as vital for the utilisation of procedural knowledge. As PACTE maintains, its model is "a system of competences that interact, are hierarchical and subject to variation" (PACTE, 2002, p. 43).

PACTE (2008) delineates the major model components as follows. The first component is (i) bilingual sub-competence, which relates to the pragmatic, sociolinguistic, textual, grammatical and lexical aspects of mostly – albeit not exclusively – procedural knowledge which is required for bilingual communication. The second is (ii) extra-linguistic sub-competence, entailing largely declarative – often encyclopaedic – world and field-specific knowledge. Next in line is (iii) knowledge about translation sub-competence – mostly declarative, implicit and explicit knowledge about translation and the translation profession. It covers translation functions (e.g. procedures, methods and possible problems), as well as the practice of professional translation, including the market, or target audiences, and other relevant knowledge, (e.g. that of translation associations or tariffs). The following component of the model is (iv) instrumental sub-competence, defined as largely procedural and related to the use of documentation resources and ICT tools in translation (e.g. reference sources, electronic databases or search engines). Finally, (v) strategic sub-competence refers to procedural knowledge necessary to ensure efficiency and problem resolution in translation. PACTE (2008) elucidates that the latter sub-competence is essential, as it links and activates all the other sub-competences to control the translation process at large. More specifically, it is used to administer translation projects, plan and evaluate the relevant translation processes with the purpose of the translation in mind, as well as identify and resolve potential translation problems.

In addition, the model features psycho-physiological components, which PACTE defines:

> different types of cognitive and attitudinal components and psycho-motor mechanisms . . . [which] include: cognitive components such as memory, perception, attention and emotion; attitudinal aspects such as intellectual curiosity, perseverance, rigour, critical spirit, knowledge of and confidence in one's own abilities, the ability to measure one's own abilities, motivation, etc.; abilities such as creativity, logical reasoning, analysis and synthesis, etc.

> (PACTE, 2008, pp. 108–109)

What merits note is that the new PACTE (2005, 2008) model introduced a number of modifications to its original version (PACTE, 2003), which had been developed in 1998 (PACTE, 2000). First and foremost, it removed transfer competence (the ability to transfer meaning from the source text to the target text) from the central position. Although in 1998, transfer sub-competence was believed to *drive* all the others, the new model recognises that in fact all bilinguals can be credited with the natural ability to translate and that expert translation is an outcome of interaction between all the remaining sub-competences. Consequently, on the basis of its research, PACTE (2000) had repositioned strategic sub-competence as the central element of the model to underline its role in coordinating the use of all the other sub-competences in the translation process. Other changes included the replacement of communicative competence in two languages, which had originally been distinguished to illustrate the fact that translation was a form of communication, with bilingual competence, and – more importantly – the renaming of psycho-physiological sub-competence as the psycho-physiological components to emphasise that they cut across all the other sub-competences.

The TransComp (Göpferich, 2009a, 2009b) model of translation competence was developed as part of a project involving longitudinal research into the development of translation competence in translation students which was launched at the University of Graz (UniGraz, n.d.) in 2007.

Proposed by Göpferich and Jääskeläinen (2009) two years later, the model comprises six major competences. The first component is (i) bi- or multilingual communicative competence comprising lexical, grammatical and pragmatic knowledge in the relevant languages, which most of all is necessary for the reception of source texts and the production of target texts. Pragmatic knowledge relates to culture-bound genre and situation-specific conventions. Domain competence (ii) denotes general and domain-specific knowledge necessary to understand and produce source and target texts respectively, or to be able to identify knowledge that needs to be accessed from external information sources to compensate for one's deficiencies in this respect. The third component is (iii) tools and research competence, which entails the ability to use translation-enhancing (electronic) tools and resources (e.g. terminology and translation management systems, MT systems, corpora or term banks). The fourth component, which Göpferich (2009b) distinguishes from PACTE's (2008) knowledge about translation sub-competence, is labelled as (iv) translation routine activation competence and relates to the application of transfer operations, which permit the generation of acceptable target language equivalents. The penultimate component is (v) psychomotor competence, involving abilities to read and write (electronically) with enough efficiency to release some of the individual's cognitive capacity for other cognitively challenging tasks.

Finally, (vi) strategic competence refers to one's capacity to coordinate the use of the remaining competences and hierarchise them.

It needs to be underlined that the last strategy does not only clearly indicate the parallels that can be drawn between the PACTE (2005) model and Göpferich's (2009b) modification of it but also introduces situation-specific motivation as a factor with the capacity to affect the quality of the translator's performance. She views the level of that motivation as directly proportional to the efficiency with which the translator uses their strategic competence and adds that the motivation may derive from both internal (intrinsic motivation) or external (extrinsic motivation) incentives, such as the joy of translation or the remuneration respectively.

Göpferich (2009b) explicitly states that three of the remaining components, strategic competence, translation routine activation competence and tools and research competence, are translation specific in that they demarcate professional translation competence as separate from mere bilingual competence.

What distinguishes the TransComp model is that Göpferich (2009b) anchors the aforementioned components to professional, attitudinal and personal factors which she believes to affect the implementation of the six major competences listed earlier. The professional factor relates to the translation brief which guides a given translation job and the relevant translation norms which need to be complied with. The attitudinal factor involves the translator's self-concept and professional ethos, which are the outcomes of translator education and which additionally highlight the translator's social responsibility and roles, while the personal factor comprises characteristics, such as intelligence, perseverance or self-confidence – to name a few – which constitute the translator's psycho-physical disposition. Göpferich (2009b) finds this last component influential enough for it to potentially affect how fast an individual develops translation competence.

While the PACTE (2005) model is apparently skewed towards professional translation and expertise, all versions of the EMT (2009, 2017, 2022a) model are frameworks for the planning and provision of translator education, developed by the EMT expert group established in 2007 by the Directorate-General for Translation (DGT) of the European Commission. The group's major goal was to implement "a European reference framework for a Master's in translation (European Master's in Translation – EMT) throughout the European Union" (EMT, 2009, p. 1) and to provide a platform for the establishment, comparison and evaluation of translation programmes in Europe in keeping with the Bologna Declaration. Dybiec-Gajer (2013) observes that from the perspective of translator education in Europe, EMT is the most influential model of translation competence, which finds reflection in the fact that as of now, 85 higher education institutions offering translation programmes are accredited members of the

EMT network (EMT, 2022b) – an increase from 54 member institutions reported 10 years ago (Dybiec-Gajer, 2013).

The original version of the model contained six interdependent competences, understood as an amalgamation of aptitudes, knowledge, behaviour and know-how which one needs to perform translation in particular circumstances, including (i) translation service provision competence, with interpersonal and production dimensions; (ii) language competence; (iii) intercultural competence, including sociolinguistic and textual dimensions; (iv) information mining competence; (v) thematic competence; and (vi) technological competence.

Interestingly, the model was originally visualised as a circle, with translation service provision competence in the middle of it and all the remaining sub-competences placed all around it. This kind of arrangement of the sub-competences clearly indicated that in very much the same way in which the PACTE (2005) model promotes strategic sub-competence as its leading component, the original EMT (2009) model centralised translation service provision. Dybiec-Gajer (2013) notes that this in turn denotes the shift in the conceptualisation of the nature of translation competence from linguistic-philological to organisational-professional.

It must also be added that, although each of the competences in the first version of EMT (2009) model was delineated in terms of the relevant components, EMT documentation elucidated that the model constituted the minimum requirements only and was thus open to expansion, depending on the type of translation (e.g. localisation, which the model would be used to educate for (EMT, 2009).

The revised version of the EMT model (EMT Board, 2017) distinguished five major competences: (i) language and culture, including transcultural and sociolinguistic awareness, as well as communicative skills; (ii) translation, comprising strategic, methodological and thematic competence; (iii) technology, relating the use of relevant tools and applications; (iv) personal and interpersonal, which were viewed as a repertoire of generic, transferable skills which enhance graduate adaptability and employability; and (v) service provision, encompassing skills relating to the implementation of translation and to the provision of professional language services.

The 2017 version has been criticised on the grounds that "The visual representation of the different competences . . . 'a series of mechanical cogs' . . . looks quite dynamic at first glance but is actually rather confusing" (Popiołek, 2020, p. 21), the model does not elucidate how its components relate to each other and the sequencing of particular sub-competences is confusing (cf. Popiołek, 2020). However, the three previously cited arguments could be refuted – or at least mitigated – by the argument that due to the rudimentary and open character of the model, a degree of vagueness is inevitable. Perhaps the mechanical cogs are only to be set in motion in the context of a specific translation programme or course, as a result of which the relationship between particular sub-competences will need to be resolved; the cogs will indeed trigger each other in various combinations, depending on a given educational context and the translation (learning) experiences of the students.

At the same time, it must be observed, as Massey did, that the model "reflects an increasing awareness of just how relevant the situated cultural, social and technological contexts of 4E cognition are to the competent (and expert) practice of professional translation" (Massey, 2021, p. 42). On the one hand, it does so by giving more importance to technical knowledge and reflective practice on the use of relevant technologies (e.g. translation tools). On the other hand, it "places distinctly more emphasis on socio-cognitive (inter-) personal competences in contexts of work" (Massey, 2021, p. 42), which Massey demonstrates by citing the constituents of language and culture competence, delineated as linguistic, sociolinguistic, cultural and transcultural knowledge and skills, which underlie professional translation competence.

EMT recently updated the competence framework (EMT, 2022a), leaving the 2017 structure and major components intact. However, in response to increased automation of translation, it has emphasised the importance of "human skills as a differentiator in a technologized employment market, where linguistic, critical, and ethical competences can combine to produce a transversal skill set to equip graduates for the future" (EMT, 2022a, p. 2).

3.2 Telecollaboration in translation competence models

As Massey and Kiraly (2021) opine, the best overview of the competences constituting the common core of translation competence models proposed to date is Kelly's (2007) synthetic model of competence, which is a well-balanced, accurate, comprehensive and ecologically valid representation of the models dominating the contemporary translator education scene. As such, it is representative – *mutadis mutandi* – of the competences which are most likely to guide contemporary translation programmes.

Kelly distinguishes seven sub-competences which, when accumulated, are representative of the apparatus of a competent translator: (i) communicative and textual competence in at least two languages and cultures, which cover active and passive language skills, as well as awareness of textuality and discourse and the relevant conventions; (ii) cultural and/ or intercultural competence, comprising knowledge of native and other cultures on explicit (e.g. encyclopaedic knowledge and observable behaviours) and more implicit (e.g. values, myths or perceptions) levels, as well as awareness of (translation as) intercultural communication and related issues; (iii) subject area or thematic competence, permitting the translator to understand source texts to resolve translation problems by referring to specialised documentation; (iv) professional and/or instrumental competence, pertaining to the use of ICT tools and documentary resources for professional practices; (v) attitudinal or psycho-physiological competence, including self-concept, self-confidence, attention, concentration, memory and initiative; (vi) interpersonal competence, relating to the ability to work with professional (e.g. revisers, project managers, terminologists) and nonprofessional (clients, authors, experts) stakeholders in the translation process, as well as teamwork, negotiation and leadership skills; and (vii) organisational or strategic competence, comprising knowledge and skills which enable the translator to organise, monitor, revise, self-assess and resolve problems. Kelly (2007) deems strategic sub-competence as the overarching super-competence which guides the utilisation of all the other sub-competences.

To establish whether it is advisable to include telecollaboration in contemporary translation programmes, an analysis will be conducted of the extent to which the knowledge, skills or awareness contained within the three major competence models discussed earlier can possibly be developed through telecollaboration. To augment the analysis, Table 3.1 juxtaposes the current versions of the models proposed by PACTE (2005), Göpferich (2009b) and EMT (2017, 2022a), aligns them (wherever possible) to Kelly's (2007) synthesised model and indicates which of their constituents do (●) (at least implicitly) or do not (○) lend themselves to development via telecollaboration.

As the table illustrates, three components of the translation competence models under analysis seem most relatable to – and thus potentially teachable through – telecollaboration. They are what Kelly (2007) synthetically calls cultural and/or intercultural competence, professional and/or instrumental competence and interpersonal competence.

Telecollaboration could be used to develop cultural and/or intercultural competence, as it is defined in the three models on condition that it involves genuine communication with representatives of other languacultural groups (e.g. via OIEs).

In the PACTE (2008) model, telecollaboration-related elements fall into bilingual sub-competence and refer particularly to the pragmatic and sociolinguistic procedural knowledge required for bilingual communication. Telecollaboration, especially in OIEs, seems to be the perfectly fitted for the development of this competence, as it offers translation students opportunities to engage in genuine communication with representatives of other languacultural groups while also sensitising them to issues in bilingual communication.

Table 3.1 Telecollaboration *vis-à-vis* translation competence models

Kelly (2007)	PACTE (2005)	TransComp (Göpferich 2009b)	EMT (2017, 2022a)	Telecollaboration
Communicative and textual competence	Bilingual competence	Bi-/multilingual communicative competence	Language and culture competence	○
Cultural and/or intercultural competence	Bilingual sub-competence	Bi-/multilingual communicative competence	Language and culture competence	●
Subject area or thematic competence	Extra-linguistic sub-competence	Domain competence	Translation competence	○
Professional and/or instrumental competence	Instrumental sub-competence	Tools and research competence	Technology competence	●
Attitudinal or psycho-physiological competence	Psycho-physiological components	Psycho-physical disposition	–	○
Interpersonal competence	–	–	Personal and interpersonal competence	●
Organisational or strategic competence	Strategic sub-competence	Strategic competence	Translation competence	○

By the same token, the TransComp model (Göpferich, 2009b), which advocates the development of bi- or multilingual communicative competence, including pragmatic knowledge in the relevant languages and culture-bound genre and situation-specific conventions, seems to imply the usefulness of telecollaboration. For instance, if OIE tasks involve reflection on experience, they will help students explore the intricacies of various bi- or multilingual communicative situations, while e-tandems, which often involve text-based interaction, may additionally augment the analysis of the selected pragmatic aspects of culture-bound genres.

The EMT (2017, 2022a) model, which contains language and culture competence and promotes the development of transcultural and sociolinguistic awareness, as well as communicative skills, also seems to affirm the validity of telecollaborative learning in translator education. After all, the cognitive, metacognitive and pragmatic/behavioural components of the competence can be effectively developed through reflective interaction with representatives of other cultures, which telecollaboration is most likely to involve.

What also appears amenable to development through telecollaboration is professional and/or instrumental competence. Its near-equivalent component in the PACTE model is named instrumental sub-competence and embraces "Predominantly procedural knowledge related to the use of documentation resources and information and communication technologies applied to translation (dictionaries of all kinds, encyclopaedias, grammars, style books, parallel texts, electronic corpora, search engines, etc.)" (PACTE, 2008, p. 107). The key fragment of the definition of this sub-competence relates to *the use of information and communication technologies applied to translation*. As their name indicates, such technologies comprise not only generic IT tools but also CMC tools. Moreover, as the list of ICTs exemplified by PACTE (2008) is open, it may be assumed – particularly in the light of the professional LSP practices (see Chapter 2) – that it is also inclusive of tools which are used specifically for telecollaboration (e.g. online communicators, project management systems or TMSs). Thus, telecollaboration is most likely to stimulate the development of instrumental competence.

In the TransComp model (Göpferich, 2009b), the corresponding component, which in all likelihood simultaneously relates to telecollaboration, is that of tools and research competence:

> comprises the ability to use translation-specific conventional and electronic tools, from reference works such as dictionaries and encyclopaedias (either printed or electronic), term banks and other databases, parallel texts, the use of search engines and corpora to the use of word processors, terminology and translation management systems as well as machine translation systems.
>
> (Göpferich, 2009b, p. 22)

Firstly, although the competence is seemingly limited to the ability to use translation-specific electronic tools, the examples of tools cited within the model also include generic computer software, such as word processors, and there is no reason why online communicators should be excluded from that category. Secondly, the definition explicitly mentions TMSs, whose functionalities permit telecollaboration through team-text editing (translating), team-reviewing or joint use of translation resources (translation memories or term bases), which can be team updated in real time. Therefore, telecollaboration does seem to be a relevant means of developing the tools and research competence, as it is defined in the TransComp model.

The parallel element of the EMT model is technology competence, which "includes all the knowledge and skills used to implement . . . present and future translation technologies within the translation process" (EMT, 2022a, p. 9). Again, the open nature and future-orientedness of this definition implies that translators need to be able to utilise various tools, including those designed for telecollaboration. However, as many as four of the six operationalising descriptors for this competence are particularly relatable to telecollaboration, as they embrace the knowledge of how to (i) "use the most relevant IT applications, including the full range of office software" (EMT, 2022a, p. 9); (ii) implement CAT tools; (iii) implement language and translation technology, such as workflow management software (EMT, 2017, 2022a); and (iii) handle Web technologies (EMT, 2022a).

The first of the previously cited EMT descriptors could potentially denote a plethora of telecollaboration solutions, including synchronous and asynchronous online communications tools. The second relates to CAT tools, which increasingly provide telecollaborative team translation functionalities, as is the case with the cloud editions of Phrase (phrase. com) – formerly known as Memsource – and Trados (www.rws.com/localization/products/trados-team). The third explicitly cites workflow management software (e.g. of the kind that is used in localisation projects), which are often delivered through cloud platforms permitting collaborative translation and team management, such as Lokalise (https://lokalise.com) or Transifex (www.transifex.com). The fourth, Web technologies, is so inclusive that it inevitably comprises telecollaboration tools – the more that the EMT (2017, 2022a) model stresses teamwork in virtual multicultural and multilingual environments involving communications technologies. All in all, it implies that telecollaborative assignments may facilitate the development of the competence in question.

Last but not least, telecollaboration also seems applicable to the development of interpersonal competence, which is a constituent of the EMT (2017, 2022a) model. In fact, nearly all of the descriptors for this competence relate to a lesser or greater extent to telecollaboration, as they entail the ability to work in virtual, multicultural and multilingual teams via communication technologies and to use social media for professional purposes. Interestingly, while the previously cited descriptors pertain to various elements of telework, another descriptor additionally underlies the importance of collaborative learning *explicité* as a means of fostering self-evaluation and competence development at large. Cogently, the presence of telecollaboration-related elements in this particular competence model further legitimises telecollaboration as a valid instructional choice in translation courses, given the impact of the EMT network on translator education (see chapter 3.1).

3.3 Telecollaboration in professional translation standards

Due to increased professionalisation of translator education, particularly over the past 10–15 years (cf. Dybiec-Gajer, 2014; Pietrzak, 2022), it is pertinent to additionally review professional standards for elements which would, at least implicitly, indicate the relevance of telecollaboration to professional education and training. Professional standards for translation are developed by the International Organization for Standardization (ISO), based in Geneva, Switzerland. This nongovernmental international network of nearly 170 national standards organisations aims to develop and promote international standards for technology, scientific testing processes or working conditions, among others (ISO, 2022a). ISO standards can be credited with an accurate depiction of a particular industry's best practice and requirements, especially "with regard to translator competences and qualifications, translation processes, technologies and some other key professional requirements" (Popiołek, 2020, p. 10), as they are painstakingly developed through a multi-stakeholder process, usually spanning three years and involving contributions from international industry experts, consumer bodies and academia, to name a few (ISO, 2022b). What is more, by default, the standards are also cyclically reviewed and updated in five-year cycles (ISO, 2019), which increases their temporal validity.

There are two ISO standards which are particularly pertinent to the use of telecollaboration in translation and translator education. One of them is the general translation service provision standard (ISO 17100, 2015) – validated as part of the systematic review procedure in 2020 – lays out requirements for translation services and covers all aspects of the translation process, including translators' professional competences. The other is the standard for translation projects (ISO 11669, 2012), which aims to provide general guidance for all phases of a translation project and addresses issues such as the development of structured project specifications, in-project communication, quality assurance and – most importantly – the competences of translators and revisers.

It must be underlined that, as Popiołek (2020) rightly points out, ISO standards define translator rather than translation competence, as they are intended for the documentation and validation of competence and qualifications in practice. A thorough analysis of the aforementioned documents falls outside the focus of this publication; therefore, it will not be carried out. Instead, competences delineated within the standards will be outlined, and the elements of the standards explicitly or implicitly related to the implementation of telecollaboration in the translation process will be briefly reviewed.

At first, the professional competences of the translator which have been delineated in the general translation service provision standard (ISO 17100, 2015) will be discussed. They contain a total of six competences: (i) translation competence, which entails the ability to translate in accordance with the purpose and specifications of a translation project and the relevant linguistic conventions, as well as resolve content comprehension and production problem; (ii) linguistic and textual competence in the source language (SL) and the target language (TL), which comprises receptive competence in SL, fluency in TL, the knowledge of text-type conventions and the ability to use the latter to produce translations; (iii) competence in research, information acquisition and processing, which refers to the ability to efficiently acquire linguistic and specialised knowledge for handling SL comprehension and translation into TL, experience in the use of research tools and the efficient use of relevant information sources; (iv) cultural competence, which covers (the ability to use) information about SL and TL cultures on explicit (behaviour, locale) and implicit (values) levels; (v) technical competence, denoting the knowledge, abilities and skills required to use translation-enhancing technical resources (tools and IT systems); and (vi) domain competence, which permits one to comprehend SL content and translate it into TL using the appropriate style and terminology.

The profile of translator competence provided in the standard for translation projects (ISO 11669, 2012) contains two major components: (i) SL and TL competence and (ii) translation competence. The former competence entails the ability to read in SL and write in TL, university-level study in SL and TL and immersion or residence in SL/TL countries, to name a few. It is worth noting that the competence reaches beyond mere language and also covers the subject area (domain). The other major competence (translation competence) refers to translation in the relevant direction within the SL/TL language pair and is validated by parameters such as length of experience providing professional translation service provision in the relevant languages, a university degree in translation, professional certification and evidence of previous work (e.g. references and sample translations).

The other competences defined in ISO 11669:2012 are those which distinguish revisers from translators. There are six of them in all, but the five which are pertinent to the present discussion refer to: (i) the ability to proficiently use the technology required by the project specifications, (ii) the ability to interact with stakeholders in the translation process, (iii) research skills useful for finding domain information and TL terminology, (iv) social skills facilitating effective teamwork and – at least to some extent – (v) an understanding of the SL and TL cultures.

Although one might be tempted to believe that reviser competences are irrelevant to translator education, the assumption would be unwarranted, as today's translation market is so dynamic that translation students must not be prepared for a single role only. In fact, in professional life, they can be expected to adapt and take on multiple roles, depending on the context and immediate needs (cf. Ehrensberger-Dow & Massey, 2022).

To investigate whether the models of translator (and reviser) competence delineated in professional translation standards relate – at least implicitly – to telecollaboration, their components need to be analysed for traces of computer-mediated teamwork or tools relevant to it. To aid the analysis, Table 3.2 was designed where the competence models described in ISO17100:2015 and ISO11669:2012 are aligned to the generic competences proposed by the present author, with the constituents of particular competences indicated as those that do (●) or do not (○) entail telecollaboration.

As the table demonstrates, three competences seem most amenable to development through telecollaboration: (i) *cultural competence,* (ii) *technology/technical competence* and (iii) *interpersonal competence.*

As far as cultural competence goes, ISO17100:2015 contains extra-linguistic competence, which involves (inter)cultural knowledge (information), the resulting skills to use that information in translation. If one realises that translation constitutes a form of intercultural mediation between SL and TL cultures and that this mediation requires explicit (behaviour, locale) and implicit (values) (inter)cultural knowledge, it becomes clear that telecollaboration may be very helpful in exploring the aforementioned areas of competence and practising intercultural mediation via genuine interaction with representative of other languacultures.

By the same token, ISO11669:2012, which features understanding of SL/TL cultures, can be viewed as a standard which calls for the implementation of telecollaboration in translator education, as the general wording of the relevant descriptor implies the learning of (inter)cultural knowledge, skills, attitudes and awareness, which, for example, OIEs and e-tandems can be used to foster (cf. Byram, 1997).

Table 3.2 Telecollaboration *vis-à-vis* professional translation standards

Generic competences	ISO17100:2015	ISO11669:2012	Telecollaboration as a component
Translation competence	Translation competence	Translation competence	○
Linguistic competence	Linguistic and textual competence	Source- and target-language competence	○
Cultural competence	Extra-linguistic sub-competence	Understanding of SL/TL cultures	●
Technology/ technical competence	Technical competence	Ability to proficiently use technology required by project specifications	●
(Domain) research competence	Competence in research, information finding and processing	Research skills for finding domain information and TL terminology	○
Interpersonal competence	–	Social skills for interaction within a translation team and with stakeholders in translation	●

The second competence is in ISO17100:2015, represented by technical competence, comprising "the knowledge, abilities and skills required to perform the technical tasks in the translation process by employing technical resources including the tools and IT systems that support the whole translation process" (ISO 17100, 2015), while in ISO11669:2012, it is one of the reviser competences, defined as "proficiency in using the technology that is required by the project specifications" (ISO 11669, 2012, p. 7). In both cases, the general wording warrants the conclusion that telecollaboration may be used to develop these components of both ISO standards. After all, translation technology or technical resources – regardless of the name – are very likely to include CAT tools and TMSs with functionalities for online team translation or resource management, which telecollaboration translation projects would inevitably involve.

Interestingly, the content of ISO 11669:2012 seems to corroborate the previous conclusion through its description of translation parameters defining the conditions of the translation process with regard to – *inter alia* – translation-enhancing technology and product delivery functionalities which the technology integrates at times. It is by no means an overstatement that the technology is most likely to be telecollaborative, as product delivery mechanisms are often built into telecollaborative translation tools such as the aforementioned TMSs (e.g. Transifex) or cloud CAT tools (e.g. Phrase).

Finally, ISO 11669:2012 also features elements of interpersonal competence, entailing social skills for interaction within a translation team and with stakeholders in translation. Through the reference that the definition of this competence makes to teamwork and interaction with various parties involved in the translation process, it implicitly comprises (business) online collaboration, which telecollaborative translation projects will foster through team effort and in-project communication.

References

Byram, M. (1997). *Teaching and assessing intercultural communicative competence.* Clevedon: Multilingual Matters.

Campbell, S. (1998). *Translation into the second language. Applied linguistics and language study.* London: Longman.

Dybiec-Gajer, J. (2013). *Zmierzyć przekład? Z metodologii oceniania w dydaktyce przekładu pisemnego.* Kraków: Towarzystwo Autorów i Wydawców Prac Naukowych Universitas.

Dybiec-Gajer, J. (2014). *Going professional: Challenges and opportunities for the contemporary translator educators.* Intralinea, Special issue: Challenges in Translation Pedagogy. Retrieved from http://www.intralinea.org/specials/article/ going_professional_challenges_and_opportunities_for_translator_educators

Ehrensberger-Dow, M., & Massey, G. (2022). *The changing (inter)face of professional translation: Lecture delivered on 8th December 2021 as part of the centre for translation studies' convergence lecture series.* Retrieved from https://www. youtube.com/watch?v=Hzw6TR-Rah8

EMT. (2009). *European master's in translation – Competences for professional translators.* Retrieved from https://ec.europa.eu/info/sites/info/files/emt_competences_ translators_en.pdf

EMT. (2017). *European master's in translation competence framework 2017.* Retrieved from https://ec.europa.eu/info/sites/info/files/emt_competence_fwk_ 2017_en_web.pdf

EMT. (2022a). *European master's in translation competence framework 2022.* Retrieved from https://commission.europa.eu/system/files/2022-11/emt_ competence_fwk_2022_en.pdf

EMT. (2022b). *List of EMT members 2019–2024.* Retrieved from https://com-mission.europa.eu/resources-partners/european-masters-translation-emt/list-emt-members-2019-2024_en

EMT Board. (2017). *European master's in translation. Competence framework 2017*. Retrieved from https://commission.europa.eu/system/files/2018-02/emt_competence_fwk_2017_en_web.pdf

Göpferich, S. (2009a). Adding value to data in translation process research: The transcomp asset management system. In I. M. Mees, F. Alves, S. Göpferich, & A. L. Jakobsen (Eds.), *Copenhagen studies in language, 0905–9857: Vol. 38. Methodology, technology and innovation in translation process research: A tribute to Arnt Lykke Jakobsen/edited by Inger M. Mees, Fabio Alves, Susanne Göpferich* (pp. 159–182). Frederiksberg: Samfundslitteratur.

Göpferich, S. (2009b). Towards a model of translation competence and its acquisition: The longitudinal study of TransComp. In S. Göpferich, A. L. Jakobsen, & I. M. Mees (Eds.), *Copenhagen studies in language: Vol. 37. Behind the mind: Methods, models and results in translation process research* (pp. 11–37). Frederiksberg: Samfundslitteratur.

Göpferich, S., & Jääskeläinen, R. (2009). Process research into the development of translation competence: Where are we, and where do we need to go? *Across Languages and Cultures, 10*(2), 169–191. https://doi.org/10.1556/Acr.10.2009.2.1

Grucza, S. (2005). Adaptacja tekstów specjalistycznych w dydaktyce przekładu. In M. Piotrowska (Ed.), *Język trzeciego tysiąclecia III: Tom 2. Język a komunikacja 8: Konteksty przekładowe* (pp. 407–417). Kraków: Tertium.

Harris, B., & Sherwood, B. (1978). Translating as an Innate skill. In D. Gerver & W. Sinaiko (Eds.), *Language, interpretation and communication* (pp. 155–170). Oxford: Plenum Press.

Hejwowski, K. (2012). *Kognitywno-komunikacyjna teoria przekładu* (Wyd. 1, 4 dodr). Przekład, Mity i Rzeczywistość. Warszawa: Wydawnictwo Naukowe PWN.

Hönig, H. G. (1988). Wissen Ubersetzer eigentlich, was sie tun? *Lebende Sprachen, 33*(1), 10–14.

Hurtado Albir, A. (2007). Competence-based curriculum design for training translators. *The Interpreter and Translator Trainer, 1*(2), 163–195.

Hurtado Albir, A. (2017). *Researching translation competence by PACTE group. Benjamins translation library, 0929–7316: Vol. 127.* Amsterdam & Philadelphia: John Benjamins Publishing Company.

ISO. (2019). *Guidance on the Systematic Review process in ISO.* Retrieved from https://www.iso.org/publication/PUB100413.html

ISO. (2022a). *About us.* Retrieved from https://www.iso.org/about-us.html

ISO.(2022b).*Developingstandards.*Retrievedfromhttps://www.iso.org/developing-standards.html

ISO 11669. (2012). *Translation projects – General guidance* (ISO, 11669:2012). Switzerland: ISO.

ISO 17100. (2015). *Translation services – Requirements for translation services* (ISO, 17100:2015). Switzerland: ISO.

Kelly, D. (2005). *A handbook for translator trainers: A guide to reflective practice.* Manchester: St. Jerome.

Kelly, D. (2007). Translator competence contextualized, translator training in the framework of higher education reform: In search of alignment in curricular design. In D. Kenny & K. Ryou (Eds.), *Across boundaries: International perspectives on translation studies/edited by Dorothy Kenny and Kyongjoo Ryou* (pp. 128–142). Newcastle: Cambridge Scholars Pub.

Kielar, B. (1988). *Tłumaczenie i koncepcje translatoryczne*. Wrocław: Zakład Narodowy im. Ossolińskich.

Kiraly, D. C. (1995). *Pathways to translation: Pedagogy and process*. Kent, OH & London: Kent State University Press.

Kiraly, D. C., & Hofmann, S. (2016). Towards a postpositivist curriculum development model for translator education. In D. C. Kiraly (Ed.), *V&R academic. Towards authentic experiential learning in translator education* (pp. 67–88). Göttingen: V & R Unipress; Mainz University Press.

Klimkowski, K. (2015). *Towards a shared curriculum in translator and interpreter education. Languages in contact: Vol. 3*. Wrocław & Washington, DC: Wydawnictwo Wyższej Szkoły Filologicznej; Polska Akademia Nauk. Oddział we Wrocławiu; International Communicology Institute.

Lörscher, W. (1991). *Translation performance, translation process, and translation strategies: Psycholinguistic investigation. Language in performance: Vol. 4*. Tübingen: Narr.

Massey, G. (2021). Re-framing conceptual metaphor translation research in the age of neural machine translation: Investigating translators' added value with products and processes. *Training, Language and Culture*, 5(1), 37–56. https://doi.org/10.22363/2521-442X-2021-5-1-37-56

Massey, G., & Kiraly, D. (2021). The dreyfus model as a cornerstone of an emergentist approach to translator expertise development. In E. M. Silva Mangiante, K. Peno, & J. Northup (Eds.), *Adult learning in professional, educational, and community settings. Teaching and learning for adult skill acquisition: Applying the Dreyfus and Dreyfus model in different fields* (pp. 237–266). Charlotte, NC: Information Age Publishing, Inc.

Orlando, M. (2016). *Training 21st-century translators and interpreters: At the crossroads of practice, research and pedagogy. Transkulturalität – Translation - Transfer*. Berlin: Frank & Timme.

PACTE. (2000). Acquiring translation competence: Hypotheses and methodological problems in a research project. In A. Beeby, D. Ensinger, & M. Presas (Ed.), *Investigating translation* (pp. 99–106). Amsterdam: John Benjamins.

PACTE. (2002). Exploratory tests in a study of translation competence. *Conference Translation and Interpretation*, 4(4), 41–69.

PACTE. (2003). Building a translation competence model. In F. Alves (Ed.), *Triangulating translation: Perspectives in process-oriented research* (pp. 43–66). Amsterdam & Philadelphia: John Benjamins Publishing Company.

PACTE. (2005). Investigating translation competence: Conceptual and methodological issues. Übersetzungskompetenz. *Meta*, 50(2), 609–619.

PACTE. (2008). First results of a translation competence experiment: 'Knowledge of translation' and 'efficacy of the translation process'. In J. Kearns (Ed.), *Translator and interpreter training: Issues, methods and debates* (pp. 104–126). London & New York: Continuum International Publishing Group.

Pieńkos, J. (2003). *Podstawy przekładoznawstwa. Od teorii do praktyki*. Kraków: Kantor Wydawniczy Zakamycze.

Pietrzak, P. (2020). Inside and outside the translation classroom. *Research in Language, 18*(2), 109–117. https://doi.org/10.18778/1731-7533.18.2.07

Pietrzak, P. (2022). *Metacognitive translator training: Focus on personal resources/ Paulina Pietrzak. Palgrave studies in translating and interpreting.* Basingstoke: Palgrave Macmillan.

Piotrowska, M. (2007). *Proces decyzyjny tłumacza: Podstawy metodologii nauczania przekładu pisemnego.* Kraków: Wydawnictwo Naukowe Akademii Pedagogicznej.

Piotrowska, M. (2022). *Translation: Inspirations we live by.* Kraków: Księgarnia Akademicka Publishing.

Popiołek, M. (2020). ISO 20771:2020 overview and legal translator competence requirements in the context of the European Qualifications Framework, ISO 17100:2015 and relevant research. *Lingua Legis, 28*, 7–40.

Pym, A. (2003). Redefining translation competence in an electronic age: In defence of a minimalist approach. *Meta: Translators' Journal, 48*(4), 481–497. Retrieved from www.erudit.org/revue/meta/2003/v48/n4/008533ar.pdf

Risku, H. (2002). Situatedness in translation studies. *Cognitive Systems Research, 3*(3), 523–533.

Schäffner, C., & Adab, B. J. (Eds.). (2000). *Developing translation competence. Benjamins translation library: Vol. 38.* Amsterdam & Philadelphia: J. Benjamins Pub. Co.

Shreve, G. M. (1997). Cognition and the evolution of translation competence. In J. H. Danks, G. M. Shreve, S. B. Fountain, & M. K. McBeath (Eds.), *Cognitive processes in translation and interpreting* (pp. 120–136). Thousand Oaks: Sage Publications.

Tabakowska, E. (1999). *O przekładzie na przykładzie: Rozprawa tłumacza z "Europą" Normana Daviesa.* Kraków: Znak.

Tabakowska, E. (2003). *O przekładzie na przykładzie.* Kraków: Znak.

Toury, G. (1984). The notion of "native translator" and translation teaching. In W. Wills & G. Thome (Eds.), *Translation theory and its implementation in the teaching of translating and interpreting* (pp. 186–195). Tübingen: Gunter Narr Verlag.

Toury, G. (2012). *Descriptive translation studies – and beyond. Benjamins translation library: v. 100* (2nd expanded ed.). Amsterdam & Philadelphia: John Benjamins Pub. Co.

UniGraz. (n.d.). *TransComp: The development of translation competence.* Retrieved from https://gams.uni-graz.at/transcomp

Waddington, C. (2001). Should translations be assessed holistically or through error analysis? *Hermes (Denmark), 14*(26), 15–37.

Whyatt, B. (2012). *Translation as a human skill: From predisposition to expertise. Seria Filologia Angielska/Uniwersytet im. Adama Mickiewicza w Poznaniu: nr 38.* Poznań: Wydawnictwo Naukowe UAM.

Wills, W. (1996). *Knowledge and skills in translator behavior. Benjamins translation library: Vol. 15.* Amsterdam: Benjamins.

4 Pedagogical foundations of telecollaboration

The idea of implementing telecollaboration in translator education constitutes an attempt to transfer the teaching mode and the rationale behind it from the field of language education, where it has been used and researched – both conceptually and empirically – for nearly three decades now. In that sense, it is a response to Kiraly's (2015) concern about the fact that translation education seems to have been developing in isolation from research on language education, despite the abundance of the latter. However, this chapter also aims to respond to yet another – even graver – problem which Kiraly (2015) finds disconcerting, namely, the fact that although various teaching solutions have been experimented with in the translation classroom, there has been little reflection on their epistemological underpinnings. To remedy the problem, a discussion follows on the pedagogical foundations on which telecollaborative translator education could be based. First, three major epistemological perspectives on education at large and the corresponding pedagogical approaches to (translator) education will be reviewed to illustrate how possible stances on education and its goals are rooted in more generic worldviews. Subsequently, the concept of telecollaboration will be juxtaposed with the aforementioned pedagogies to demonstrate how the former seems to be compatible with – and applicable to – the latter. By linking the generic characteristics of telecollaboration to particular pedagogies, the analysis will help translation teachers establish the extent to which they can implement telecollaboration while pursuing the tenets of those pedagogies in their instructional practices.

4.1 Major epistemological perspectives and pedagogies

The three major educational epistemologies selected for discussion here are empirico-rationalism, constructivism and emergentism. Although other categorisations are possible (e.g. empiricism and rationalism could be treated as separate epistemologies, while constructivism could be broken

DOI: 10.4324/9781003424932-5

down into constructivism, social constructivism and radical constructivism), the typology presented here is only to outline the epistemological streams which have led to the emergence of the corresponding pedagogical approaches: transmissionist, transformative and situated, praxis oriented. The aim of the discussion is to illustrate how particular worldviews translate into specific approaches to pedagogical practices and to what extent the latter seem to permit the implementation of telecollaborative work modes.

4.1.1   Empirico-rationalism

Empiricism is a philosophical movement primarily – though not exclusively – linked to the period of Enlightenment and the views and writings of its major proponents, such as Bacon, Berkeley, Hume, Locke, Galileo and Newton. Empiricists considered knowledge to come from the senses (Fuller, 2016), and they perceived it as *a posteriori* in nature (i.e. dependent on, and deriving from, the sensory experience of the world around). Hence, they believed that at birth, the human mind is a *tabula rasa* – a blank slate to be written upon by experience. It is through this concept that empiricism may also be related to Stoic epistemology and its representatives, for example, ancient Greek philosophers Epicurus or Democritus (Long & Sedley, 1987), who could – at least to a degree – be regarded as the forerunners of the movement. Since empiricists attributed an essential role in knowledge development to both observation and measurement, consequently, as Markie (2017) states, they rejected the idea that knowledge may be preconceived in the mind, or that it is innate. To empiricists, intuition or deduction cannot be used to develop knowledge, hence, their rejection of the superiority of reason. Gergen (1985) calls this an exogenic perspective on knowledge construction, which makes knowledge independent of the human being.

Rationalism, whose main underpinnings were laid out by Comte, Descartes, Leibniz and Spinoza, as well as ancient Greek philosophers such as Socrates or Plato, conceived of the nature of knowledge as derived from the intellect (Fuller, 2016) and as *a priori* (i.e. discoverable through the use of mental powers). To rationalists, logical reasoning supersedes experience in that the latter may only provide ideas – food for thought, as it were – yet it is reasoning that is the source of knowledge. Intuition and deduction are viewed as instruments which render experience redundant; some propositions can be knowable by intuition per se, while others can be deducted from what has already been intuited. What is more, rationalists do not accept the idea that the mind at birth is a *tabula rasa*. On the contrary, they believe that the mind is innately equipped with knowledge, which only needs to be externalised. Hence, Gergen's (1985) suggestion that in rationalism, knowledge construction is viewed as endogenic (i.e. "endemic to the organism") (Gergen, 1985, p. 269).

Although empiricism and rationalism are often distinguished as disparate philosophical thoughts, there are at least two reasons for which they can be considered together, particularly in discourse on pedagogical epistemologies. Firstly, Markie (2017) observes that empiricist and rationalist worldviews need not be mutually exclusive. From an ontological perspective, when applied to the same concepts, empiricist and rationalist worldviews indeed seem irreconcilable, but it is possible for the same person to be a rationalist in relation to a specific body of knowledge and an empiricist in relation to another. Even Locke himself was a case in point, as while generally rejecting the concept of the innateness of knowledge, he accepted the role of intuition and deduction in knowing the existence of God. In the same vein, the three major rationalists, Descartes, Spinoza and Leibniz, all recognised the importance of empirical science. As if, in recognition of that fact, another rationalist – Kant, who delved into metaphysical considerations – had synthesised traditional rationalist and empiricist views into his own version of rationalism, which is succinctly encapsulated in his claim that "The understanding can intuit nothing, the senses can think nothing. Only through their unison can knowledge arise" (Fuller, 2016, p. 356).

Secondly, as Kiraly (2006) points out, whether knowledge is perceived in empiricist or rationalist terms (i.e. as discoverable through observation or reasoning respectively), it nevertheless seems to be the same kind of objectivised reflection of the real world, a mirrored version of an objective truth. Empiricism and rationalism differ only in the means by which the knowledge is arrived at – or the point of departure, as one might add. Irrespective of whether the top-down approach, where all starts with reason, or the bottom-up approach, where experience is the beginning, is followed, the ultimate outcome is always a truth which seemingly lies out there to be discovered. From the pedagogical vantage point, it is this concept of knowledge as set, objective and universal that brings both empiricism and rationalism to the common denominator.

The two arguments cited earlier demonstrate why the philosophical worldviews are being considered under the umbrella term of empirico-rationalism. Far more important than the terminology, though, is the influence that the positivist belief that knowledge is objective – derived more or less consciously from empirico-rationalist epistemology – has exerted on pedagogical approaches. The writings of ancient Greek scholars, to whom the roots of empirico-rationalism can be traced, including Democritus, Epicurus, Socrates and Plato, but also publications by the advocates of this epistemology at its peak (e.g. Bacon, Berkeley, Hume and Locke), have instilled in people the concept of knowledge as objectivised, disconnected from human experience, hence, abstract. That in turn inspired numerous

19th- and 20th-century innovators and writers to provide solid foundations for education compatible with the empirico-rationalist perspective.

In the realm of glottodidactics, towards the end of the 18th and the beginning of the 19th century, a *group* of German scholars, including Johann Seidenstücker, Karl Plötz, H. S. Ollendorf and Johann Meidinger (Richards & Rodgers, 2014), laid out the principles of the Grammar-Translation Method (GTM) – due to its provenance also known as the Prussian Method – which translated empirico-rational philosophy into a set of prescribed classroom practices to be used by language instructors.

In general education, a 20th-century American inventor and innovator, Frederick Taylor, proposed a system of scientific management aimed to maximise factory workers' *productivity*, which first guided American engineering education (Gibson, 1992) and later inspired Ralph Tyler to develop a framework for an education system which relied on the identification of clear-cut goals, compatible means and adequate assessment as its main pillars (Finder, 2004).

In the late 1950s, neo-behaviourist Skinner (1957) contributed to yet another important development in glottodidactics by publishing his book *Verbal Behaviour*, where he advocated the integration of behaviourist psychology into language teaching pedagogy, which led to the development of the Audiolingual Method (ALM) (Richards & Rodgers, 2014), based on mechanical repetition and rote learning.

A natural consequence of the representation of knowledge as objective truth was the tendency to treat the former as external, recorded, storable and – most importantly – passable, or transmittable. How that has impacted education can be seen by examining the two language teaching methods mentioned earlier, which illustrate the workings of transmissionist pedagogy.

Transmissionist pedagogy. As the principles of both aforementioned methods indicate, in transmissionist pedagogy, knowledge is compartmentalised and stored externally (e.g. in GTM initially in scripts but later also in reference materials such as dictionaries, encyclopaedias or grammar books). Interestingly, it is also believed that knowledge can also be stored in a person's mind, including that of the teacher (GTM, ALM) (Larsen-Freeman & Anderson, 2018). Consequently, the primary concern of the instructors is to identify the right method through which to effectively transmit that knowledge to the learners. As the alternative name for transmissionism (reductionism) indicates, the view of knowledge here is highly restricted in that knowledge to be transmitted is supposedly objective and reflective of reality; thus, it is not to be questioned or negotiated. It only needs to be predetermined, compartmentalised and packaged to ensure that is it accurately assimilated.

Since the teacher is an expert, an unquestionable source of knowledge, or *knower* (Larsen-Freeman & Anderson, 2018), the teaching procedures are heavily teacher-controlled, which is epitomised by the names which the teacher goes by – that is, authority (GTM) and orchestra leader (ALM). In the Audiolingual Method, for ethical reasons, the latter has replaced the term even more reflective of the theoretical provenance of the method – *dog-trainer*, to which a reference is made in Brown (2006). What draws attention is the highly undemocratic nature of transmissionist teaching. In GTM, the teacher instructs, nominates, asks questions, collects and validates answers or requires students to recite what they have learnt mechanically. Similarly, in ALM, only the teacher asserts power by different means (e.g. by modelling language behaviour, eliciting accurate imitation and providing positive or negative reinforcement to consolidate correct responses or prevent the development of wrong habits, respectively – all along the lines of the *stick-and-carrot* methodology) (Larsen-Freeman & Anderson, 2018).

The transmissionist approach simultaneously reduces the role of learners, who have no say over what is being learnt, how it is being learnt and what outcomes are being targeted. What is more, learners practically do not interact with one another. Since classes are teacher-centred, the prevalent interaction pattern is teacher-student-teacher, where the teacher initiates interaction by asking questions, while the learners provide answers. It is the teacher, though, who has the final say, as (s)he provides feedback. It is striking that even in ALM, where learners develop verbal habits by mechanically producing dialogue lines, it is hard to say there is much student-student interaction. Technically, students perform dialogues, but the lines they produce are preset and rigidly controlled and performance is teacher-directed. Relinquishing that control could lead to an increased number of errors, the repetition of erroneous language forms and, in the long run, the formation of bad habits (Larsen-Freeman & Anderson, 2018).

Characteristically for transmissionist pedagogy, both methods emphasise accuracy as the major goal of learning. In GTM, learners first mechanically learn language rules and vocabulary and then apply this knowledge in controlled activities, mostly gap-filling tasks. However, in case of errors, the teacher insists that learners recite explicit grammar rules. In ALM, learners are only expected to imitate the teacher-modelled language performance and progress through the cycle of stimulus-response-reinforcement (Richards & Rodgers, 2014) until they can perform automatically. To augment habit formation, learners repeat language chunks (i.e. relatively short and manageable dialogue lines). This idea resounded in the propositions of Taylor (Gibson, 1992), who – inspired by Skinner's work – proposed that engineering practise be based on little attention to humans and their needs, step-by-step progression from simple to more complex tasks and the granting of individual rewards as incentives. As the works modes discussed earlier demonstrate, transmission is applicable to the development of two kinds of knowledge. While GTM involves the internalisation of theoretical, declarative knowledge, which is supposed to result in accurate language performance, ALM focuses on procedural knowledge and emphasises correct language performance without overt rule learning.

Finally, transmissionist teaching involves rigid assessment, where learners' performance can be judged either on the accuracy of the declarative, factual knowledge through formalised tests (GTM) or – in the case of procedural knowledge – the quality of performance in less formal discrete-point tests requiring near-perfect accuracy.

4.1.2 *Constructivism*

Constructivism is an educational philosophy which arose in opposition to the empirico-rationalist view of knowledge as objective truth and a representation of the real world in the learner's mind. Its roots can be traced back to Jean Piaget, who is considered to be "the great pioneer of the constructivist theory of knowing" (Glasersfeld, 1990, p. 22), John Dewey or Lev Vygotsky in the first half of the 20th century but also Jerome Bruner and Ernst von Glaserfeld (Walshe, 2020). By and large, constructivist thought recognises the fact that in lieu of assimilating predetermined knowledge, learners construct their own and integrate it with what they already know. Therefore, it dismissed the idea that knowledge needs to match reality.

Constructivism is an umbrella term for a concoction of various theories which revolved around the concept of knowledge construction but explained the nature of the process in disparate ways. For the purpose of the present discussion, three types of constructivism will be discussed, including trivial, social and radical constructivism, as those which sufficiently illustrate constructivist epistemology at large.

As Jordan, Carlile, and Stack (2018) explain, *trivial constructivism* bases on the concept of individualised knowledge construction which is affected by an individual's mental build and processing mechanisms but produces different, yet overlapping, outcomes. Briefly speaking, people are believed to develop an understanding of the world through the constructs which they individually develop while accommodating new information to the constructs they have created before. Transplanted into the learning context, it means that learners build knowledge cyclically by building, dismantling and reassembling constructs, which are in a state of perpetual flux, with each iteration of the cycle leading to increased understanding.

The main representatives of trivial constructivism were Piaget and Bruner. Piaget developed a theory of cognitive development which explained that children learn effectively through play and interaction with the outside world, whereby they construct meaning. The process inevitably involves cognitive conflict with the views of others but that stimulates individuals to synthesise disparate views and reconfigure theirs accordingly (Jordan et al., 2018). Bruner (1966) proposed – *inter alia* – the structuring and sequencing of content to help learners accommodate new knowledge to the constructs they have already developed, but he can also be viewed as a link between trivial and social constructivism in that he had himself begun to emphasise the importance of culture as a framework for learning based on prediction making.

The views of Piaget and Bruner had a number of implications for pedagogy, including the popularisation of learning based on play and discovery, natural learner curiosity, learner autonomy, peer-to-peer interaction and discussion, limited teacher intervention and the use of the spiral syllabus, which offers learners opportunities to develop constructs cyclically, with each iteration involving increased cognitive challenges (Jordan et al., 2018).

Social constructivist thought, as the very name indicates, is grounded in the assumption that knowing is a social phenomenon. Therefore. it adds the impact of societal and cultural factors to the constructive equation. This strand of constructivism, represented, for example, by Lev Vygotsky, was reflective of the idea that individual impressions, interpretations and meanings are affected by those with whom individuals interact linguistically and socially. Especially, the recognition of linguistic interaction is important here, as it suggests that discussion helps people develop shared – not individual – understandings (Jordan et al., 2018).

The most outstanding was Vygotsky's (1978) concept the Zone of Proximal Development (ZPD), whereby he demonstrated that the potential development of a child aided by an adult is likely to be greater than that of an unaided child. Through ZPD, which is an imaginary zone of teacher-learner interaction, he advocated that teacher support is crucial to learner development. Moreover, in a similar vein, support from more knowledgeable peers can add to that effect, as "what a child can do with assistance today, she will be able to do be herself tomorrow" (Vygotsky, 1978, p. 89).

Pedagogically, social constructivism induced the introduction of two important classroom solutions: (i) guided learning, which involves social knowledge construction facilitated by teacher-guided discussion, and (ii) scaffolding, which "refers to the steps taken to reduce the degrees of freedom in carrying out some task so that the child can concentrate on the difficult skill she is in the process of acquiring" (Bruner, 1978, p. 19).

Radical constructivism was developed by Glasersfeld (1995), who in his radical view of the relation between knowledge and reality proposed that the former is functionally adapted to the latter. It denotes that although knowledge derives from perception, perception in itself is limited, which renders reality inaccessible in a direct manner. Consequently, the knowledge one develops is not validated against an objective world but rather the extent to which it permits one to make predictions and achieve concrete goals (e.g. by causing or avoiding specific situations).

As Walshe (2020) sums up, from the pedagogical perspective, radical constructionism subordinates teaching to learning in that the former is to promote the latter. It also views learners as constructing knowledge on the basis of their own thoughts and reflections, which are more potent carriers of concepts than language, which may be subject to misinterpretation. Therefore, although learners are to be encouraged to verbalise their constructs, the teacher needs to stimulate discussion in a way which would not permit learners to arrive at incorrect conceptions.

A discussion of the pedagogical implications of constructivism, also those stemming from the provisions of its radical strand, will not be complete without a reference to the views of John Dewey, a representative of the 19th century's Progressive Education Movement. Dewey's propositions are important for at least two reasons. On the one hand, some of his views were congruent with constructivist thought at large, and in this sense, he may be regarded as the forerunner of constructivism (Williams, 2017). On the other hand – quite astoundingly – despite the passage of time, his educational propositions continue to inform curriculum design (e.g. in 21st-century science education in the United States) (Walshe, 2020).

He advocated democratic education, suggesting that each learner must be offered a chance to develop their full potential so that they could themselves effect social change. He believed that knowledge is constructed on the basis of learners' own knowledge through experience, communicative interaction and reflection, which clearly positions him as a social constructivist. Most significantly, though, he recommended that learning be enquiry based, which not only dovetails with the practical application of radical constructivism to science education but also finds reflection in contemporary US education programmes in that field. In some contemporary incarnations, the programmes promote learning through enquiry-driven learning, which involves observation, consultation of information sources, experimentation, questioning, explanation or prediction (Walshe, 2020).

The difference between empirico-rationalist and constructivist epistemologies represents contrasting views of education which Miller and Seller (1985) label as transmission and transformation respectively. Hence, while empirico-rationalism provides the underpinnings of transmissionist pedagogy, constructivism underlies the tenets of what is known as transformative pedagogy.

Transformative pedagogy. Again, the characteristics of this pedagogical approach can be illustrated by analysing how it has been implemented in glottodidactics, where – as Richards and Rodgers (2014) purport, it has penetrated several teaching methods, including Communicative Language Teaching (CLT), Community Language Learning (CLL), or Cooperative Language Learning (CoopLL). For the purpose of brevity, the methods will be further referred to by corresponding acronyms, with the caveat that for clarity, the acronym CLL, which is rather confusingly used for either Community Language Learning or Cooperative Language Learning, has been modified into CoopLL to denote the latter method.

Knowledge in this approach is viewed as constructed and needs to be arrived at, but its nature may be mixed. Although in CLL, it is not usually predetermined and learners decide on what they would like to learn, it defers in this respect from the other two methods. In CLT, the goal is for students to develop native-like communicative competence in the target language. And although learners analyse and interpret texts and authors' intentions, which means that they build their knowledge by processing information on their own, they nevertheless are to build competence modelled on native speakers' language performance (Larsen-Freeman & Anderson, 2018). Similarly, in CoopLL (Richards & Rodgers, 2014), although learners enjoy a degree of freedom while interacting with materials and peers, consult and review information sources and are encouraged to synthesise knowledge by using critical thinking skills to increase learning effectiveness, content may be pre-set in that specific lexical items, language structures or communicative functions may be targeted for development. Overall, it may be stated that knowledge in transformative teaching is treated as private and individual; however, as it will be demonstrated later, it does not mean that learning occurs in isolation.

The teacher's role in transformative pedagogy is to support learning. In CLT, the teacher facilitates communication, involves students in communicative situations, acts an adviser and monitors learners' language performance. In CLL, the teacher provides support and reassurance to students, attempts to reduce stress levels in learning situations and gradually relinquishes initial control to increase learners' independence (Larsen-Freeman & Anderson, 2018). In CoopLL (Richards & Rodgers, 2014), the teacher is perceived as a facilitator, organiser of group work and one who encourages learners to use critical thinking skills. All in all, the teacher is no longer an authority.

Contrary to the tenets of transmissionist pedagogy, in the transformative approach, the learners' position has been recognisably elevated. The learner is no longer the object but subject of the education process. Symptomatic of that is the treatment of the learner in CLL, where (s)he is perceived as a whole person, whose individual inhibitions and limitations can be openly expressed and need to be respected. In fact, both teachers and students are supposed to regard one another's thoughts and feelings. Quite similarly, in CLT, teachers need to ensure that learners feel comfortable in the classroom, are motivated by the usefulness of what they are learning and have opportunities to express themselves openly (Larsen-Freeman & Anderson, 2018). In CoopLL (Richards & Rodgers, 2014), learners are viewed as socially active, involve in interaction with peers and enjoy a status equal with that of the teacher.

A synthesis of the teaching goals of the aforementioned methods, as delineated by Richards and Rodgers (2014) and Larsen-Freeman and Anderson (2018), reveals that the transformative approach aims at focused attention to specific content (CoopLL), the promotion of learners' transformation, for example, from teacher-dependent to independent learners (CLT), facilitation of learning through a learner-friendly and supportive atmosphere, peer support with varying degrees of directness, interaction and group work (CLT, CLL, CoopLL), as well as the elevation of the learners' status in the classroom (CLT, CLL, CoopLL), with the latter reflecting Dewey's (1916) views.

Transformative pedagogy does not involve formalised testing, which is pervasive in transmissionist teaching since errors tend to be seen as inherent to learning (e.g. in CLT). Consequently, perfect accuracy is not expected. In addition, students' well-being is emphasized; thus, assessment is rather informal, unobtrusive and respectful in manner, with the teacher providing general feedback (CLT), repeating the correct forms (CLL) or encouraging peer assessment (CoopLL).

It must be underlined that, although the teaching methods analysed earlier all contain elements of constructivist thought (Richards & Rodgers, 2014), not all of their characteristics are illustrative of transformative pedagogy. It is particularly pertinent to CLT, which does involve student-student interaction and permit peer-to-peer learning, but given the fact that the communicative competence which it aims to develop is largely predetermined, the method is skewed towards yet another pedagogical approach, namely, *transactionist pedagogy*. As Klimkowski (2015) rightly observes, the CLT teacher must technically be viewed as a trainer rather than true facilitator – a role much closer to that of an instructor in the transmissionist approach. At the same time, in CLT, learners do enjoy a changed status, but they convert from novices (transmissionist pedagogy) to apprentices (transactionist pedagogy), who develop knowledge modelled – albeit indirectly – by the trainer. The reason for which transactionist pedagogy has been left outside the scope of this publication is that although transactionist teaching can be seen as an attempt to move beyond transmissionist instruction, it nevertheless contrasts with the latter much less significantly than transformative pedagogy.

4.1.3   *Emergentism*

Emergentist epistemology is founded on the premises of complexity theory, which Morrison (2008) defines as "a theory of change, evolution, adaptation and development for survival" (Morrison, 2008, p. 16). It emerged in response to the Newtonian perspective on the universe as a stable, linear, predictable, closed and orderly clockwork-like system which can be objectively described through laws by which it is governed (e.g. the laws of causality).

The complexity theory builds on process philosophy, substantially developed by American scholar Alfred Whitehead, who – as he openly admits in *Process and Reality* (Whitehead, 1929) – had in turn been inspired by the writings of Dewey and Bergson. In its essence, process philosophy questioned stability at both macro and micro level. On the one hand, it claimed that "There is nothing in the real world which is merely an inert fact. Every reality is there for feeling: it promotes feeling; and it is felt" (Whitehead, 1978, p. 310). On the other hand, quite consistently, it explained that conventional objects, including even the molecules they are built of, are mere occasions of experience. Overall, process philosophers perceived the world as a very dynamic entity which undergoes constant – albeit evolutionary – change.

Advocates of the complexity theory regard change, which is a feature of open, ever-evolving systems, as a *condition sine qua non* of survival, purporting at the same time that "Equilibrium is the precursor to death" (Pascale, 1999, p. 85). Closed and stable systems are thus bound to disintegrate and cease to exist, as the only state that warrants survival is that of disequilibrium. Systems survive because in response to changes in the environment and through the interaction of their members, they undergo *autopoiesis* – a term introduced by biologists Maturana and Varela (1929) – which denotes constant self-creation, or self-production. It is through autopoiesis that systems emerge as new, thus better fit for survival. Examples of autopoietic development are termite hills or beehives (Hölldobler & Wilson, 1990) or the emergence of social institutions (Padgett & Powell, 2012), which means that it autopoietic change is observable on various planes: biological, social or economic.

The process of self-organisation, on which the complex world relies, is founded on adaptability, openness, learning, which have been discussed earlier, as well as feedback, communication, interconnectedness, knowledge distribution and emergence (Turner & Baker, 2019). Feedback is necessary in that it regulates interaction between the elements of a system while permitting self-regeneration and self-perpetuation, which ultimately stimulate progress towards more advanced complexity levels until modified versions of the system finally emerge. It is interesting how these *complex adaptive systems* (Turner & Baker, 2019) by self-organising dynamically, with little or no external control, emerge in a manner which is completely unpredictable *a priori*. Hypothetically, a corollary of that could – sooner or later – be the descent of an ever-evolving system into chaos due to lack of a set path which would guide its reiterative emergence. Yet while emergent systems operate at the "edge of chaos" (Borzillo & Kaminska-Labbé, 2017, p. 356), they themselves are not chaotic. As Kauffman (1995) explicates, complex systems function "in a kind of liquid regime located between order and chaos" (Kauffman, 1995, p. 26), where they are neither too rigid nor too chaotic. Rigidity would make it difficult to coordinate further development, as the system would be too set. On the other hand, chaos would render the system too disorderly and thus susceptible to collapse. The optimal way is the aforementioned balancing act between the two extremes, where system elements neither completely fall into place, which allows change, nor disperse too much, which prevents disintegration. Consequently, systems at the edge of chaos tend to retain integrity and internal identity (Wheatley, 1999), as internal knowledge – necessary to resolve problems (Turner, Baker, & Morris, 2018) – is distributed, decentralised, shared and constantly exchanged via intensive communication and collaboration (Cilliers, 1998; Turner et al., 2018).

The educational implications of emergentist epistemology are far-reaching, as it seems to reject the linear programming which education has long been dominated by due to the lasting impact of the objectivist, reductionist perspective. Simultaneously, it elevates the role of education and learning to that of a prerequisite for development, change and survival. It is learning with inward and outward orientation, so to speak, in that the complexity theory calls for any evolving systems to learn about themselves while also exploring the outside environment which perpetrates their evolution. Learning must involve initiative-driven, bottom-up development, where learning needs and goals are determined in response to circumstances.

At curricular level, emergentism means a further breakaway from the prescriptive tradition of linear design, rigidly pre-set goals or compartmentalisation of knowledge (e.g. under the guise of disciplines) and evolution towards interdisciplinary learning, which would stimulate the emergence of knowledge. It is a process-focused rather than product-oriented view of education, motivated by the belief that "Emergence and self-organization require room for development; tightly prescribed, programmed and controlled curricula and formats for teaching and learning, and standardised rates of progression are anathema to complexity theory" (Morrison, 2008, p. 23).

The emergent perspective on education requires that learning be viewed as an interplay of a complex network of interrelations within a class, school, local community and society which fosters the evolution of all the parties involved. Just as learners' minds will be reiteratively emerging, so will be classes, schools, teachers, communities and societies in response to changes in each of them. That conjures up a very dynamic image learning and knowledge, which are both decentralised, shared and distributed. If what individuals know is situated, socially and culturally contextualised, the teacher cannot pose as an expert but must rather be recognised as co-learner or co-constructor, whose mind also evolves alongside the minds of the learners. The pedagogical approach compatible with emergentist epistemology could be referred to as situated, praxis-oriented instruction (Kiraly, 2016; Risku, 2010).

Situated, praxis-oriented pedagogy cannot be illustrated through the tenets of specific language teaching methods, which was possible in the case of transmissionist and constructivist pedagogy. The major reason for that is ontological in nature. It is the very nature of emergentist episte-mology, from which situated and praxis-oriented pedagogy derives, that precludes the use of any *method* with which to develop knowledge. The development of teaching methods was a consequence of the reductionist belief that knowledge, which is a one-to-one reflection of the real world, can be distilled, simplified and transmitted. Consequently, it was criti-cally important to find procedures – methods permitting the most effective transmission. However, the further away one escapes from the transmis-sionist paradigm, realising that knowledge is a complex, unpredictable, emergent entity, the more evident it becomes that there can be no *method*, or panacea, for the complexity of knowing. Hence, the gradual transition of foreign language teaching to the post-method era, discernible at least since the onset of the current millennium (Galante, 2014), in which teach-ers need to "invite learners to embark on a journey where their contexts, identities, affective and cognitive variables merge with critical practices in ELT" (Galante, 2014, p. 61). In the light of the emergentist perspective, the devaluation of *method* holds true for any other area, including trans-lator education, which has nevertheless been primordially characterised by scarcity of teaching methods. That is why the basic elements of situ-ated, praxis-oriented pedagogy will need to be derived from the writings of – *inter alia* – Kiraly (2014, 2015, 2016) or Risku (2010), who have advocated the implementation of this kind of pedagogy with a view to enhancing translation education.

In this approach, knowledge is not pre-defined for teaching. Consequently, knowledge is viewed as a process in which learners need to actively delve rather than a product which needs to be generated, hence, the gerund form (knowing) used for it. In Kiraly's words, knowing is explained:

> a nonlinear process of context-dependent embodied and enactive meaning-creation involving myriad interrelated knowing systems, from neurons to brains to individual minds through communities of prac- tice and on to cultures and societies (and in fact the environment as a whole).
>
> (Kiraly, 2015, p. 14)

As Kiraly (2013) describes it, since translator competence is an instance of embodied and socially-situated cognition, it will emerge unpredictably from an interplay of cognitive processes (e.g. past experiences, intuitions and learning outcomes), material and human resources, personal and interpersonal dispositions, as well as the affordances of the learning envi- ronment. Analogically to how life emerged on earth from a solution of organic compounds, it is out of the previously cited cocktail that transla- tion competence will emerge in what Kiraly (2013) refers to as a transla- tory moment.

It may be posited that in situated and praxis-based pedagogy, knowing will involve as a series of recurrent translatory moments, through which learners will have a chance to learn, unlearn and relearn. The concept of learning, unlearning and relearning seems to fit perfectly into emergent learning in that, as Davidson (2012) reports, it requires cultivated distrac- tion, which would permit learners to lose sight of what they are currently concentrating on so that they can notice what otherwise would be missed. Apparently, learning which occurs at the edge of chaos is very likely to involve this kind of facilitative distraction.

Finally, Kiraly (2013) posits that situated knowledge will not only be emergent but co-emergent since the complex emergence universes of indi- vidual students will inevitably interact with those of their co-learners. Thus, knowledge will be socially embedded and inter- rather than intrac- ranial. And if that knowledge reaches a critical level of complexity, it will be synergic in nature. In other words, as Mason (2008) argues, the whole will become more than the sum of its parts.

In congruence with the previous example, Kiraly (2015) defines the role of the teacher in situated pedagogy through the concept of *occasioning* knowledge, originally developed by Davis and Simmt (2003). Occasioning reflects the emergentist rejection of causality – as reported by Morrison (2008) – as a remnant of the rationalistic worldview and denotes the expectation that the teacher will facilitate learning by creating opportu- nities for the emergence of knowledge (e.g. through the orientation or scaffolding of learning situations). As Davis and Simmt (2003) explain, emergence cannot be caused, it might only be occasioned. Taking into account that, as Stacey (2016) suggests, chaos requires systems to revisit and reformulate their assumptions, it would be reasonable to say that emergence may be facilitated by the teacher creating learning situations characterised by a high degree of complexity. An example could be authentic, or near-authentic, translation projects, which as Risku (2010) explains, require students not only to handle varied translation-related tasks such as "information research, terminological work, project management and teamwork" (Risku, 2010, p. 105) but also to "organise their working environments and to claim their place in it" (Risku, 2010, p. 105). At the same time, the teacher is also a co-learner, or co-constructer of meaning; thus, (s)he has both a facilitative and participatory role to play. After all, since emergent knowledge is impossible to define *a priori*, learning is a journey into the unknown, where the teacher is as likely to learn as the learners.

The pedagogy in question brings the status of the learner much closer to that of the teacher than in the transmissionist classroom. It aims to involve learners in joint exploration of complex situations with a view to occasioning emergence. Thus, learners need to be self-directed, responsible and autonomous, as their learning paths are not predetermined and reflexive. They are supposed to do precisely the opposite of what Kiraly (2015) describes as the falsity of transmissionist teaching, according to which "learners do not need to experience the messy, complicated real world for themselves" (Kiraly, 2015, p. 13). In fact, learners do need this kind of experience because it is likely to help them move towards the edge of chaos, which is conducive to emergence. They need to learn through enquiry and exploration, which will foster the emergence of knowledge, provided that learners display the right attitude, which Doll (2008) describes as "opening oneself, as teacher or learner, to experiencing the situation at hand; . . . immersing oneself in the situation fully enough for experiencing to happen" (Doll, 2008, p. 197). Essential is a learner's open mind in interpreting the results of own enquiries. Learners must not lose sight of the dynamic nature of knowledge; thus, they must allow for further modifications to the knowledge emergent in a particular situation – re-emergence of it in future instances of learning.

The goals of situated, praxis-oriented pedagogy need to account for the fact that learning outcomes are as unpredictable as the very emergence of knowledge. Since "Emergence means that there is no blueprint, plan or programme for the whole system" (Stacey, 2016, p. 236) and the emergentist perception of knowledge is processual, goals need to be defined proscriptively rather than prescriptively. Davis and Simmt (2003) explain it by claiming that "decisions around planning are more about setting boundaries and conditions for activity than about predetermining outcomes" (Davis & Simmt, 2003, p. 147). This kind of goal setting makes the learning process an open plan, where teachers are expected to occasion experiential, enquiry-based learning which will emancipate learners. While the teacher needs to inform learners about what is forbidden, (s)he also needs to tell them that they are permitted to do all beyond that.

As process is emphasised over product, process-oriented evaluation will dominate within this pedagogical approach. Just as the teacher's efficacy here will be judged on the extent to which (s)he manages to occasion the (co-)emergence of knowledge, to use Kiraly's (2013) concept, so will learners be assessed on the basis of how actively they engage with the learning situations, how responsive, open and interactive they are and how they contribute to the social development of knowledge. Engagement must be a crucial element of a pedagogy based on emergentist epistemology, which Morrison (2008) explains claiming that in the light of the complexity theory, "The curriculum and learning bind cool reflection with passion and humanity" (Morrison, 2008, p. 22); thus, "The natural consequence of this view of learning is an emphasis on the *conditions* to promote emergence, including motivation, enjoyment, passion, cooperative and collaborative activity" (Morrison, 2008, p. 22).

In addition, learners also need to be assessed with regard self-direction – that is, how much responsibility they take for their own and colleagues' learning, how introspectively, retrospectively and globally reflective they are on experience and how they self-set their learning goals, which, as Kiraly (2013) demonstrates, could encompass elements of personal, social and translation competence.

4.2 Telecollaboration vis-à-vis pedagogical approaches

The three major epistemologies and ensuing pedagogical approaches discussed so far are by no means to be treated as mutually exclusive. Neither should any one of them be considered as superior in an *a priori* fashion to the remaining two. They are rather to be treated as illustrative of the perspectives and pedagogical solutions that can possibly be adopted with a view to augmenting translator education. The decision on the extent and manner in which they will be implemented, though, lies with the teacher, who needs to make pedagogically sound and methodologically informed choices with regard to the options at hand. There are several reasons for that.

Firstly, González Davies (2004) remarks that "different pedagogical approaches can be effective depending on the teaching circumstances" (González Davies, 2004, p. 3) and calls an attempt to prioritise any particular teaching approach over others an absurdity. She rightly indicates that the most desirable educational outcomes are apparently produced by a blend of context-dependent factors, including instructional goals, approach, materials and people involved in the learning process.

Secondly, in the post-method era, which education entered over two decades ago, it would be unreasonable to recourse to the idea that a single approach or method is a panacea with which to cure all educational ills. After all, as Richards and Rodgers (2014) note, a more productive solution may be what they call *principled eclecticism*, through which individual teachers develop their own methods.

Thirdly, it would be extremely hard – if not downright impossible – to teach with the implementation of a single approach or method exclusively. Given the dynamics of the teaching-learning process, it is highly likely that alterations will occur, be it as a result of the teacher's decision or learners' intuitions. Baumgarten, Klimkowski, and Sullivan (2010) provide an example of how in a translation project which was planned and launched in transgressionist mode, epistemological regression from transgression to transaction became necessary when, due to variation in the level of students' skills, the teacher needed to intervene through guidance on information retrieval and task organisation to ensure project completion. This demonstrates that eclecticism may function not only across but also within tasks.

On an ontological note, it could be claimed that eclecticism – irrespective of whether it is principled or unprincipled – could also be perceived as a *method*; thus, the idea of discarding *method* as a concept seems to run in the face of both logic and practice. An answer to this, though, is that as long as teaching involves a sound amalgam of different elements which have been derived from various methods, learning is likely to be more effective than in a context where one method only is being rigidly used. That is precisely how teaching is perceived in the post-method era, hence, the secondary importance of the ontological dispute over its branding.

What follows is an attempt to demonstrate to what extent telecollaboration seems compatible with the transmissionist, transformative and situated, praxis-oriented pedagogical approaches with regard to selected characteristics, including instructional goals, the nature of knowledge, teacher and learner status, as well as assessment. Again, the analysis will be undertaken not to help translator educators make a definitive choice between these approaches but to increase their awareness of how telecollaboration lends itself to particular pedagogies and inform the (re)construction of their own methods in different educational settings.

At first, the generic affordances of telecollaboration regarding the aforementioned characteristics will be discussed. Subsequently, the three pedagogical approaches in question will be discussed in the context of translator education courses, with particular attention to the kinds of content, including elements of selected TS theories, for the teaching of which the approaches seem to be suitable and related examples of instructional practices. The TS theories to which the pedagogical approaches will be aligned are those which both González Davies (2004) and Baumgarten et al. (2010) believe to be tackled in the translation classroom – that is, the linguistics-based approach, the cognitive approach, the cultural studies approach and the functionalist approach, as well as the two approaches (philosophical and poetic) additionally discussed by González Davies (2004).

Telecollaboration. At its most general, telecollaboration aims to facilitate the exploration, discovery, (co-)construction or (co-)construal of knowledge, not memorisation. Telecollaboration does not foster learning where knowledge would be definable *a priori.* On the contrary, its rationale rests upon the idea that knowledge will be worked out or that it will emerge dynamically. In telecollaborative tasks, learners are not to imitate ready-made procedural models but rather induce or infer desirable procedures or behavioural patterns, which they can later implement or further refine through trial and error.

Telecollaboration decentres the teacher and enhances the status of the learners. While the teacher organises, facilitates and guides learning or offers advice, with time, his or her role diminishes to develop learners' teacher independence. Thus, telecollaborative learning might be said to take place through three types of technology-mediated interaction: *learner-learner, learner-learner-teacher* or *learner-learner-teacher-learner.*

The *learner-learner* pattern seemingly implies that the teacher is completely excluded from the learning process, which is not the case in telecollaboration. The teacher may be sidestepped, as (s)he is mostly a facilitator, guide, advisor or even observer, but those roles do not preclude learner-teacher interaction. Consequently, the *learner-learner-teacher* interaction pattern seems more adequate, as it denotes that, first and foremost, learners interact with one another, and only then do they occasionally consult the teacher. However, the teacher's terminal position in the sequence may imply that the teacher provides final verdicts on learning outcomes or learner performance. Hence, the extended interaction pattern (*learner-learner-teacher-learner*), which is the present author proposes to underline the learner-centredness of telecollaboration and its learner-empowering nature. It highlights the primary role of learner-learner interaction and entails possible teacher support while indicating learners' final say in knowledge development. Moreover, positioning the teacher inside the latter sequence additionally reflects that (s)he can also co-learn.

Finally, telecollaboration usually involves informal, self- or peer assessment based on retrospective reflection, which will be further discussed in Chapter 5.2.

4.2.1 Transmissionist approach

As it has been demonstrated, transmissionist pedagogy is curriculum-driven, and its major goal is to ensure that learners effectively memorise declarative, factual or procedural knowledge through intensive mechanical repetition, or *rote learning*. The knowledge to be developed consists of learnable, recitable rules, paradigms or models of behaviour which learners follow. Since transmissionist pedagogy emphasises accuracy, assessment will tend to involve formal testing, the measurement of learning progress and judgement against an idealised knowledge model on which instruction is based, with little tolerance of errors, which are perceived as a sign of failure, or non-learning.

An account of a typical teacher-controlled translation class is provided by Nord (1996), who distinguishes three major steps on which the teaching procedure is based: (i) the teacher provides a text to be translated, nominates a student or asks for volunteers, (ii) the nominee or volunteer student delivers the translation and (iii) the teacher provides accuracy-focused feedback on the student's translation. This procedure could be encapsulated as the *ask question – nominate – provide feedback* sequence, where the teacher initiates, directs and assesses learning. However, it need not apply to translation-focused work, exclusively. In translation courses, the same procedure can be utilised for a plethora of purposes other than translation *per se*, e.g. to refine students' general linguistic knowledge, or increase their explicit knowledge of both the native and foreign language and its subsystems, including phonology, morphology, syntax, and lexis. That can be effectively complemented with teaching along the lines of the linguistics-based approach, which – as Baumgarten et al. (2010) and González Davies (2004) state – in translator education is typically used to compare and contrast different language systems, teach about text genres and types, or explore the pragmatic, semiotic or semantic dimensions of language. This kind of teaching relies heavily on text analysis and referential sources, e.g. grammar books and dictionaries, which implies that it tends to be dominated by *chalk-and-talk* (Kiraly, 2014) or *stand-and-deliver (Newell, 2003)* methodology, where the teacher occupies the central position in the classroom and controls knowledge internalisation. Regardless of the instructional content, learners will be expected to either accurately recite or reproduce what they have learnt, or use the knowledge in teacher-controlled tasks, preferably following the teacher's model.

Although transmissionist pedagogy has been criticised on epistemological, pedagogical and practical grounds, it is still being used in some contexts, as is the case with both GTM and ALM (Richards & Rodgers, 2014) in foreign language education. The same applies to translator education, where transmissionist teaching and its controlled environment may be used to foster learning "particularly [in] early stages of learning within an institutional setting" (Kiraly, 2016, unpaginated). For instance, GTM-modelled recitation of language rules could be used to increase students' metalinguistic competence and perfect performance in activities involving sentence translation into and from the students' native language.

The previous example may be one of the reasons for which – as Kiraly (2014) and Hofmann (Kiraly & Hofmann, 2016) maintain – transmissionist practices have been quite pervasive and have become part of folk peda-gogy, willingly adopted by numerous translation teachers.

Other reasons which seem to plausibly explain the continued use of trans-missionist pedagogy have been offered by Richards and Rodgers (2014), who – while analysing the possible advantages of GTM – admit that teacher-controlled instructional modes may be convenient to the instructor, as they limit the scope of instruction, increase the teacher's sense of security and are easy to mimic by those who themselves have been taught in that man-ner. Hence, for many transmission-based instruction is a well-entrenched *modus operandi*, which Kiraly (2016) corroborates, observing that Nord's method intended to systematise translation education did not divert far from transmissionism involving the pre-determination of teaching content, teacher-controlled practice and teacher feedback. Simultaneously, in an attempt to do justice to Nord – and transmissionist teaching *per se* – Kiraly (2016) admits that in particular circumstances, transmissionist teaching need not be rejected. Richards and Rodgers (2014) also seem to subscribe to the viewpoint despite their rather adamant rejection of the GTM as a language teaching method due to the lack of adequate rationale.

To do justice to GTM, it must be underlined that although the method has been heavily criticised for transmitting knowledge about language rather than teaching the target language itself for genuine communica-tion, it had never been intended for the former. In fact, the goal of the method was to create opportunities for intellectual development and men-tal exercise, which it did offer to students through transmission-oriented procedures.

As it will be further illustrated in Chapters 4.2.2 and 4.2.3, teaching focused on the other TS theories – that is, the cultural studies approach, the functionalist approach, the cognitive approach and the philosophical and poetic approaches – seems less likely to be transmissionist in nature; however, it is only a generalisation, and as such, it must not be taken as a given. After all, it is possible to isolate theoretical dimensions of knowl-edge pertinent to all those approaches (e.g. the concepts of *postcoloni-alism, functional equivalence, priming* or *hermeneutics* respectively) and package them for explicit transmission. Just as it is possible to envisage the teaching of linguistic aspects of translation through multimodal texts other than the traditional printed copy (e.g. Web pages, whose dynamic, non-linear structure, perpetrated by hyperlinks and multimedia, would render the study of translation-related linguistic phenomena much more suitable for constructed, or enquiry-based, learning rather than overt instruction). This juxtaposition of three different modes (transmissionist, constructivist and enquiry based) in which components of the functional and linguistics-based TS theories could be taught illustrates what has been suggested before; namely that irrespective of whether specific instructional content seems more or less suited for a given pedagogy, ultimately, it is the teacher who decides how teaching will actually be administered.

The generic characteristics of telecollaboration and the possible implementations of transmissionist pedagogy in translator education discussed so far are summarised in Table 4.1, which additionally indicates to what extent telecollaboration and transmissionist pedagogy are mutually compatible.

As it can be seen in Table 4.1, out of the three degrees of compatibility (high compatibility [+], limited compatibility [–/+] and no compatibility [–]) which were considered, only the no compatibility option (–) was applicable across all levels of comparison, which indicates that, generally, telecollaboration is rather ill-suited for transmissionist instruction, and – if at all – the latter is likely to be integrated in telecollaboration tasks only to a limited extent, as it is presented next.

First, it must be borne in mind that, as Furstenberg and Levet (2010) underline, telecollaboration does not occur in a void and is usually delivered in a blended mode, where online teaching is accompanied by more conventional classroom instruction. It is corroborated by Jauregi and Bañados (2010), who describe a telecollaborative project as a component built into a regular study programme, with the participants of the project receiving regular classroom instruction in several related courses. Dooly (2010) remarks that when telecollaborative learning occurs in a blended mode, students are likely to be involved in coursebook and workbook activities, by which she implies that explicit teaching may be part of the experience.

Interestingly, when the New London Group (2000) admits that telecollaboration may involve forms of what it refers to as *overt instruction*, it immediately adds that the instruction does not entail direct transmission. However, if this overt instruction is defined as "all those active interventions on the part of the teacher and other experts that scaffold learning activities; that focus the learner on the important features of their experiences and activities within a community of learners; and that allow the learner to gain *explicit information* at times when it can *most*

Table 4.1 Transmissionist pedagogy *vis-à-vis* telecollaboration

Element	Transmissionist pedagogy	Compatibility	Telecollaboration
Goals	Memorisation, rote learning of factual, declarative and procedural knowledge, accurate recitation and reproduction	–	Working towards a shared goal, co-construction, co-construal of knowledge, development of digital and online literacies, intercultural competences and social agency
Knowledge	Sets of learnable, recitable rules, models, paradigms, pre-set patterns (e.g. translation methods and strategies, language rules, cultural knowledge)	–	Knowledge as explored inferred, discovered, co-constructed, emergent
Teacher	Authority, controller, orchestrator, knower, model, director of learner behaviour, assessor, final judge	–	Organiser, facilitator, guide, adviser, observer
Learners	Objects of teaching, disciples, imitators, prospective copies of the teacher	–	Independent, knowledge constructors, explorers, discoverers
Assessment	Formal testing, accuracy-focused tasks, measurement of learning progress, with results judged against an idealised model, little tolerance of errors	–	Informal, self-assessment, peer assessment, reflection based

usefully organize and guide practice" (New London Group, 2000, p. 33, emphasis added), one may suspect that at least in part, the term covers situations in which portions of knowledge necessary for more productive telecollaboration are transmitted to students (e.g. due to time constraints). And that must not, by any means, be seen as downgrading the value of telecollaboration.

In Panichi, Deutschmann, and Molka-Danielsen's (2010) view, telecollaboration "is not about creating dichotomies between opposing views of learning but about enabling affordances and providing a variety of educational options" (Panichi et al., 2010, p. 165). After all, it is reasonable to assume that students may not be able to build all the knowledge they need to engage in telecollaboration; some of it may need to be transmitted, for example, at the introductory stage, where the project setup must be introduced, as was the case in an intra-university translation project described by Paradowska (2021), or even when telecollaboration is in progress and it occurs that students need to urgently familiarise themselves with declarative knowledge which happens to be indispensable to them at a given project stage. Resorting to knowledge transmission might be perceived as an advantage since thanks to it, students will have more time to focus on building knowledge in other areas.

In addition, it must be noted that the very concept of telecollaboration must first be presented to students, or even promoted among them, so that they are eager to participate in it, which will also conventionally be done via transmission. As an aside, the latter constitutes an interesting epistemological issue in that, from the postpositivist perspective – which telecollaborative learning relates to – work modes should not be imposed. Ideally, students should themselves explore the learning mode and construe its validity independently of the teacher.

4.2.2 Transformative approach

Transformative pedagogy takes the real world and learners' interests as its point of departure and aims to involve students in project work, through which they will attempt to make sense of the problems which they experience while completing specific tasks. The learning process is less rigidly frameworked than in transmissionist pedagogy. Knowledge is viewed as synthesised from various information sources, including colleagues, and developed in cooperation. The teacher facilitates and organises group work, provides advice, motivates and counsels the students in case of challenge. Learners are viewed as whole persons, (co-)constructors of knowledge and partners. Due to the lack of emphasis on knowledge memorisation, students' problem-solving, critical thinking, self-learning and knowledge-construction skills are assessed informally and unobtrusively not to impede involvement.

Transformative teaching in translator education may be integrated with the implementation of the cognitive, functionalist, cultural, as well as philosophical and poetic approaches to Translation Studies. For instance, Baumgarten et al. (2010) suggest that the thought processes and competences underlying translation performance, which fall within the scope of the cognitive approach, may be explored by learners through think-aloud protocols (TAPs), to which one might add other relevant instruments or procedures, such as translation logs or Gile's (2004) Integrated Problem and Decision Reporting (IPDR). Since these are valid translation process research instruments, they are applicable to teaching which relies on discovery and experimentation. Similarly, the strand of the cognitivist approach which deals with the implementation of various translation strategies or procedures to solve specific problems will be perfectly fit for transformative learning – the more that it involves testing practical solutions and is likely not only to involve but also to foster a range of transferable skills.

The functionalist approach, which explores translation through the prism of the possible function(s) of the target text in relation to the client or end users, also seems to be suitable for transformative learning, where – through trial and error – students would be able to not only experiment with alternative translations but also work out a justification for each of them. That learning mode would help students develop translation competence in Pym's (2003) minimalist sense.

The cultural approach, which deals – *inter alia* – with the cultural context of translation, implicit and explicit author intentions or power relations traceable in texts, also seems to lend itself to transformative learning, as the study of issues which fall within its scope would best be facilitated through knowledge construction rather than transmission (if only for ethical reasons, lest the teacher should be accused of indoctrinating students by imposing particular worldviews on them). The latter approach in particular is likely to result in students' transformation on both a cognitive and social level.

Transformative pedagogy can also involve themes relating to the philosophical and poetic approaches to TS, with the latter embracing the hermeneutic perspective on translation. In Stolze's (2012) view, the hermeneutical approach covers the intricacies of text comprehension, the role of the translator as a co-author who attempts to transfer the meaning universe of the source text into the target text, and hermeneutical translation competence, which is necessary for the latter to materialise. The suitability of transformative, (co-)constructive learning for the hermeneutical approach finds illustration in Stolze's definition of hermeneutical translation competence, whose components – such as "the readiness for self-critical reflection, the openness for constant learning, the ability to integrate new cognitive input, the courage for linguistic creativity, and an empathetic identification with the message" (Stolze, 2012, p. 30) – apparently overlap with the competences involved in transformative work modes.

Examples of the implementation of transformative pedagogy, within the framework of socio-constructive epistemology, have been extensively discussed by Kiraly (2000). For instance, he reported on how he taught an introduction to TS course along the lines of social constructivism. Discussing the procedures used in their entirety is far beyond the scope of this publication, but an overview of how the course content was decided upon will suffice to shed light on the nature of the coursework. At first, to create a relaxed atmosphere conducive to cooperation and collaboration, the teacher ran preliminary activities through which the course participants got to know one another. Subsequently, the course content was established by paired students offering their ideas for it and the teacher providing his. This initial stage Kiraly (2000) saw as the establishment of his local version of Vygotskyan Zone of Proximal Development, on the basis of which the students, paired differently this time, could explore the specific skills and knowledge which they regarded as necessary for the professional translator. Their lists were further used to select the core skills and knowledge targeted in the course, which were appended with the teacher's propositions, but only as long as the students found them relevant. By appropriating, that is, interpreting the students' ideas, the teacher had provided scaffolding but also empowered the students signalling that their voice was as important as the teacher's.

The implementation of transformative pedagogy in translator education described previously reveals an important truth about learning based on (socio-)constructivist epistemology, which – with the benefit of hindsight – Kiraly (2016) himself observed when he had shifted his pedagogical interests towards emergentist epistemology. Namely, he underlined that, although students collaborate and the teacher permits them to construct knowledge, rather than simply internalising it, "the *construction* metaphor still emphasizes the reification of knowledge and the understanding that the processes at work are largely mechanical" (Kiraly, 2016, p. 58). In other words, although transformative pedagogy was indeed a step away from transmissionist pedagogy, remnants of the reductionist perspective continued to reverberate in it as, although course content to be socially constructed was only provisionally outlined, it was nevertheless pre-set.

Another example of transformation-oriented translator education which Kiraly (2000) cites is a collaborative translation project in which his students participated. The idea behind it was to involve students in authentic translation for a genuine client, where – faced with the real-world task of translating fragments of a book from German into English – they themselves needed to identify the sub-tasks to be performed to warrant project completion in keeping with professional standards. Interestingly, no formal introduction to the basics of collaborative work was made; instead, the general concept of the project was presented, the students were distributed relevant fragments of the source text and the project was launched. As the project unfolded, the students were free to consult any reference sources they deemed useful. In addition, they also discussed language issues with two native speakers of English, who were available *in situ* as language consultants. At the students' request, aspects of the translation, for example, the need to reflect the author's style or target text formatting and layout, were also discussed in class, but no particular procedures were imposed.

The students worked in groups of three or four; the project spanned a total of six sessions and was completed on time. Having action-researched the project, Kiraly (2000) made important observations regarding group size, student roles or motivation and attrition levels and offered several important implications, urging teachers:

- introduce students to collaborative work;
- tacitly intervene to ensure positive in-group relations;
- provide for student accountability to preclude social loafing;
- sensitise students to the desirability of non-authoritarian feedback provision;
- simulate authentic translation to provide varied tasks; and
- systematise work on translation problems, for example, appropriateness or style, while maintaining its student-centredness;

Both examples of socio-constructivist learning involved collaboration, which – apart from the affordances discussed previously – also provided students with opportunities for (co-)constructing transferrable skills (e.g. time management, the ability to work under the pressure of time, interaction skills, interpersonal skills or conflict management skills).

And here, another important observation made by Kiraly (2016) needs to be brought to light. Although students who are involved in collaborative translation projects work towards a common goal and seemingly have multiple opportunities for the joint construction of knowledge, ultimately, the knowledge which they develop will be stored in individual minds. Consequently, knowledge is socially constructed on a procedural level, yet it is nevertheless individual on a cognitive level. In Piagetian terms (Piaget, 1959, 1977), it means that as students experience a cognitive conflict between their own knowledge and that of their colleagues, they seek to adjust what they know to avoid similar cognitive conflicts in the future. Child and Shaw (2018) view it as "disequilibrium, caused when there is an imbalance between what was understood and what was encountered . . . [which] instils a challenge to [learners'] cognitive schemas" (Child & Shaw, 2018, p. 277) and thus promotes individual knowledge construction. From the Vygotskyan (Vygotsky, 1978) perspective, collaborative work may also involve social interaction which will help students go beyond individual learning and construct shared meaning based on students' shared semiotic systems. Should that happen, collaboration will promote social knowledge construction which will be enriched with new information. The fact that in transformative pedagogy, collaborative assignments may entail cooperation does not, by any means, discredit the pedagogy, but it may be helpful in discerning the difference between transformative setups, which are conducive to knowledge construction, and situated, praxis-based setups, which are more likely to foster knowledge emergence.

The instances of transformative teaching reported by Kiraly (2000) involved in-class collaboration, not telecollaboration, but they could be easily transformed into telecollaborative work if interaction between students and the teacher were mediated by computer technology, which in team translation projects would entail the use of not only online communication tools but also CAT software with teamwork functionalities.

In fact, despite technical and infrastructural limitations and challenges faced by translator educators and translator education institutions back in the year 2000, Kiraly (2000) himself advocated a move towards the introduction of computer technologies to translator education to further increase the authenticity of project-based translation learning. Over 20 years later, with the proliferation of online technologies and the particularly intensive digitalisation of the teaching and learning process in the wake of the COVID-19 pandemic, technical limitations have practically disappeared. At present, telecollaboration, which has penetrated not only the translation service provision market (see Chapter 2) but also numerous areas of education such as language learning, mathematics, engineering or health education (see Chapter 1), is now being increasingly used in translator education programmes as part of what Żmudzki (2018) calls a clearly marked trend to make students learn within project teams. Examples of telecollaboration practices in translator education have been cited by Mastela (2022), Paradowska (2021), Kodura (2019) or Marczak (2019).

In the light of the previous example, it is evident that telecollaboration is more suitable for transformative than transmissionist pedagogy, both due to the areas of Translation Studies and the work modes which the former kind of pedagogy is likely to involve. What is more, the digital technologies which telecollaboration involves have the potential to enhance transformative teaching creating opportunities for students to additionally develop generic computer skills, as well as digital and online literacies, thus equipping students better for the realities of the translation market.

The compatibility of telecollaboration with transformative teaching, depicted with regard to three degrees – compatibility (+), limited compatibility (–/+) and no compatibility (–) – is summarised in Table 4.2.

Table 4.2 Transformative pedagogy *vis-à-vis* telecollaboration

Element	Transformative pedagogy	Compatibility	Telecollaboration
Goals	Promotion of cooperative learning, learner transformation from teacher dependence to independence	+	Working towards a shared goal, co-construction, co-construal of knowledge, development of digital and online literacies, intercultural competences and social agency
Knowledge	(Socially) constructed, learner or teacher determined, developed through cooperative tasks, scaffolded, synthesised from information sources	+	Knowledge as explored, inferred, discovered, co-constructed, emergent
Teacher	Facilitator, guide (provider of scaffolding), organiser of group work, motivator, counsel	+	Organiser, facilitator, guide, adviser, observer
Learners	Subjects of teaching, apprentices, whole persons, co-learners, interactants	+	Independent knowledge constructors, explorers, discoverers
Assessment	Informal, unobtrusive testing, formative assessment, depersonalised feedback	+	Informal, self-assessment, peer assessment, reflection based

4.2.3 *Situated, praxis-based approach*

Situated, praxis-based pedagogy aims to occasion learning which will eventually lead to the emergence of knowledge; however, it does not specify the scope of that knowledge *a priori*. The idea behind it is to involve learners in collaborative, experiential, hands-on learning at the edge of chaos. Within this pedagogical approach, knowledge is perceived as a process rather than a product due to its dynamic, ever-evolving, complex and socially situated nature. The teacher mostly facilitates emergence, outlines task boundaries or otherwise co-learns through autonomous exploration, enquiry and research in an attempt to co-construe knowledge. Learning within this approach is process oriented, focused on levels of learner engagement, participation, contribution and collaboration, self- and co-organisation of the learning process, reflection on experience and self-directedness.

Situated pedagogy is as suitable for teaching translation along the lines of the various approaches to TS as transformative pedagogy, with the caveat that the former seems to offer new affordances. For instance, translator education based on the cognitive approach could be particularly amenable to the exploration of mental processes and competences involved in the translation process or the strategies and procedures used to resolve translation problems – the more that this exploration can be performed with the use of the aforementioned genuine research instruments, such as TAPs, translation logs or IPDR. The implementation of situated learning in this context will answer Orlando's (2016) call for translation students to act as *practisearchers*, with two potentially major advantages. One of them is that students' realisations in the subject area may be novel, as emergent knowledge is unconstrained, and it does not need to lead to pre-set outcomes. Co-emergent amalgamation is more likely to produce a complex picture of the translation process rather than a simplified version of it, which students could find in transmission-oriented instructional materials. The other advantage relates to the fact that emergent knowledge will derive not only from the interstices of interpersonal interaction but also students' interaction with the physical environment in which they will be translating. Consequently, they will be able to go beyond the mental dimension of cognition and tap into what Massey (2017) and Risku (2014) refer to as situated cognition, which Risku (2002) exemplifies claiming that "Translation is done not only by the brain, but also by complex systems, systems which include people, their specific social and physical environments and all their cultural artefacts" (Risku, 2002, p. 529).

The open nature of emergent learning, which situated pedagogy promotes, is also suitable for teaching elements of the functionalist approach, where students will be able to experientially examine the function(s) of the target text from the perspective of the client, or end users. As Baumgarten et al. (2010) suggest, the functional approach lends itself to different teaching modes from transactionist to transgressionist ones. One of the greatest affordances created by the implementation of situated learning is that students will not need to only simulate translation situations to explore various dimensions of text functions but they will also be able to do it through real-life translation projects, which they can manage and complete all by themselves, perhaps with a very little teacher intervention when need be.

The same applies to the implementation of emergent learning with a view to exploring cultural issues in translation, such as author intentions or power relations implicitly carried by texts. Through genuine translation experience, students will be able inspect that dimension of text in a situated learning context (i.e. with a particular context in mind).

In the same manner, they will be able to explore the role of the translator in mediating – and the processes involved in – text comprehension, which are studied within the philosophical and poetic approach. The functional, cultural approach and philosophical and poetic approaches are well suited for situated pedagogy, as they all require a high dose of in-depth reflection, which emergent learning entails. Thus, the latter is not only a suitable pedagogical solution for teaching based on these approaches but – in the wake of the situated experience – it is also likely to make students far more reflexive than they otherwise would have been. Consequently, in their professional practices, students could be more likely to involve in reflective practice and thus self-learn to flexibly deal with novelty or challenges caused by the dynamics of the translation market.

Situated, praxis-oriented pedagogy is founded on the concept of complexity. Moreover, as it has already been demonstrated in this chapter, the greater the degree of complexity, the greater the chance for knowledge emergence. By delivering situated, praxis-oriented teaching as telecollaboration, the complexity of the learning environment will inevitably increase, thus pushing students towards the edge of chaos, where systems become autocatalytic – that is, as Wheatley (1999) posits, they induce self-regeneration and self-perpetuation of permanent change. There is an interesting correspondence between the emergentist view of learning in this respect and O'Dowd's (2021) perspective on conditions which best facilitate effective telecollaborative learning, in the light of which learner challenge breeds development. The more learners are forced – as it were – to leave their comfort zone and overcome barriers to collaboration and communication, the more likely it is that they will develop skills and attitudes. Just as systems which find themselves at the edge of chaos need to adjust and recreate to warrant survival, so do learners seem to readjust when facing challenge or difficulty.

Consequently, it might be stated that emergent learning and telecollaboration are mutually complementary. The former provides challenges which enhance the learning outcomes of the latter, while the latter even increases the degree of complexity which the former inherently involves, thus enriching the learning environment. This enrichment is particularly conducive to emergent learning, as the complexity theory – in contrast to socio-constructive thought, which underlies transformative pedagogy – emphasises the intricacy and unpredictability of knowledge which emerges not only through interpersonal interaction but also learners' interaction with the learning environment.

Table 4.3 Telecollaboration *vis-à-vis* situated, praxis-oriented pedagogy

Element	Situated pedagogy	Compatibility	Telecollaboration
Goals	Occasioning of learning and emergence of knowledge, outlining activity boundaries, creating opportunities for collaborative, experiential, hands-on learning	+	Working towards a shared goal, co-construction, co-construal of knowledge, development of digital and online literacies, intercultural competences and social agency
Knowledge	Process, not product (knowing), undefined, non-linear, emergent, complex, dynamic, socially situated, recursive	+	Knowledge as explored inferred, discovered, co-constructed, emergent
Teacher	Facilitator, responsible for occasioning learning, outlining task boundaries, co-learner, co-construer	+	Organiser, facilitator, guide, adviser, observer
Learners	Autonomous explorers, enquirers, *practisearchers* (Gile, 1995; Orlando, 2016), co-learners, co-construers, organisers of (self-)learning	+	Independent knowledge constructors, explorers, discoverers
Assessment	Process oriented, focused on levels of learner engagement, participation, contribution and collaboration, self- and co-organisation of the learning process, reflection on experience, self-directedness	+	Informal, self-assessment, peer assessment, reflection based

The compatibility of telecollaboration with praxis-oriented pedagogy with regard to three degrees of it, compatibility (+), limited compatibility (–/+) and no compatibility (–), is summarised in Table 4.3.

It has been demonstrated to what extent telecollaboration lends itself to translation teaching administered in compliance with the tenets of three basic pedagogical approaches: transmissionist, transformative and situated, praxis oriented. It needs to be reiterated, though, that the pedagogies discussed earlier are not to be treated as mutually exclusive alternatives.

Neither should it be understood that the use of telecollaborative work modes in translator education by definition precludes the use of any other means of instruction. Instructors have always been in pursuit of more effective modes of delivery, hence, the evolvement of varied pedagogies, from teacher-centred transmissionism, through transactionism, to more emancipatory transformatism and further towards even more liberating emergentism. However, it would be an ungrounded interpretation of the entire history of education if teachers navigated only *between* different pedagogies and if they did it in a linear fashion to reflect the chronological order in which these pedagogies have developed. Pedagogical choices need to be made with the educational setting in mind and in response to set goals, infrastructural conditions and teachers' or students' dispositions.

In the light of the argument that eclectic solutions seem to work best, as it has already been elucidated, collaboration need not exclude knowledge transmission, neither need it eliminate offline working modes. Kiraly (2006) rightly remarks that it may be as difficult for teachers experienced in instruction-based methodology to suddenly adopt to collaborative work as it would be for students inculcated into teacher dependence to swiftly involve in collaboration and social-constructivist learning. Hence, the need for teachers to work out their own individual methodologies which would be likely to produce optimal outcomes; telecollaboration is only yet another component which could possibly go into the mix.

References

Baumgarten, S., Klimkowski, K., & Sullivan, C. (2010). Towards a transgressionist approach: Critical-reflexive translator education. *T21N*, *5*, 1–32. Retrieved from www.t21n.com/homepage/articles/T21N-2010-05-Baumgarten,Klimkowski, Sullivan.pdf

Borzillo, S., & Kaminska-Labbé, R. (2017). Unravelling the dynamics of knowledge creation in communities of practice though complexity theory lenses. *Knowledge Management Research & Practice*, *9*(4), 353–366. https://doi.org/10. 1057/kmrp.2011.13

Brown, H. D. (2006). *Principles of language learning and teaching* (5th ed.). White Plains, NY: Longman.

Bruner, J. (1966). *Toward a theory of instruction.* Cambridge, MA: Harvard University Press.

Bruner, J. (1978). The role of dialogue in language acquisition. In A. Sinclair, R. J. Jarvelle, & W. J. M. Levelt (Eds.), *The child's concept of language.* New York: Springer-Verlag.

Child, S. F. J., & Shaw, S. (2018). Towards an operational framework for establishing and assessing collaborative interactions. *Research Papers in Education*, *34*(3), 276–297. https://doi.org/10.1080/02671522.2018.1424928

Cilliers, P. (1998). *Complexity and postmodernism: Understanding complex systems.* London & New York: Routledge.

Davidson, C. (2012). *Now you see it: How technology and brain science will transform schools and business for the 21st century*. New York: Penguin.

Davis, B., & Simmt, E. (2003). Understanding learning systems: Mathematics education and complexity science. *Journal for Research in Mathematics Education*, *34*(2), 137. https://doi.org/10.2307/30034903

Dewey, J. (1916). *Democracy and education: An introduction to the philosophy of education*. New York: Macmillan.

Doll, W. E. (2008). Complexity and the culture of curriculum. In M. Mason (Ed.), *Complexity theory and the philosophy of education* (pp. 181–203). Malden, MA & Oxford: Wiley-Blackwell.

Dooly, M. (2010). Teacher 2.0. In S. Guth & F. Helm (Eds.), *Telecollaboration 2.0: Language, literacies and intercultural learning in the 21st century* (pp. 277–304). Bern, Berlin, Bruxelles, Frankfurt am Main, New York, Oxford, & Wien: Peter Lang.

Finder, M. (2004). *Educating America: How Ralph W. Tyler taught America to teach*. Westport, CT: Praeger.

Fuller, S. (2016). The social construction of knowledge. In L. C. McIntyre & A. Rosenberg (Eds.), *Routledge philosophy companions. The Routledge companion to philosophy of social science* (pp. 351–361). London: Routledge.

Furstenberg, G., & Levet, S. (2010). Integrating telecollaboration into the language classroom: Some insights. In S. Guth & F. Helm (Eds.), *Telecollaboration 2.0: Language, literacies and intercultural learning in the 21st century*. Bern, Berlin, Bruxelles, Frankfurt am Main, New York, Oxford, & Wien: Peter Lang.

Galante, A. (2014). English language teaching in the post-method era. *Contact Magazine*, *40*(4), 57–62.

Gergen, K. J. (1985). The social constructionist movement in modern psychology. *American Psychologist*, *40*(3), 266–275.

Gibson, J. E. (1992). Taylorism and professional education. In National Academy of Engineering (Ed.), *Manufacturing systems* (pp. 149–157). Washington, DC: National Academies Press.

Gile, D. (1995). Interpretation research: A new impetus? *Hermes, Journal of Linguistics*, *14*, 15–29.

Gile, D. (2004). Integrated problem and decision reporting as a translator training tool. *JoSTrans*, *02*, 2–20. Retrieved from https://jostrans.org/issue02/art_gile.pdf

Glasersfeld, E. von (1990). Chapter 2: An exposition of constructivism: Why some like it radical. *Journal for Research in Mathematics Education. Monograph*, *4*, 19. https://doi.org/10.2307/749910

Glasersfeld, E. von (1995). *Radical constructivism: A way of knowing and learning*. London & Washington, DC: The Farmer Press.

González Davies, M. (2004). *Multiple voices in the translation classroom: Activities, tasks, and projects. Benjamins translation library: Vol. 54*. Amsterdam & Philadelphia: J. Benjamins Pub.

Hölldobler, B., & Wilson, E. O. (1990). *The Ants*. Cambridge, MA: Belknap Press of Harvard University Press.

Jauregi, K., & Bañados, E. (2010). An intercontinental video-web communication project between Chile and The Netherlands. In S. Guth & F. Helm (Eds.), *Telecollaboration 2.0: language, literacies and intercultural learning in the 21st century* (pp. 427–436). Bern, Berlin, Bruxelles, Frankfurt am Main, New York, Oxford, & Wien: Peter Lang.

Jordan, A., Carlile, O., & Stack, A. (2018). *Approaches to learning: A guide for teachers/Anne Jordan, Orison Carlile, Annetta Stack.* Maidenhead: Open University Press.

Kauffman, S. A. (1995). *At home in the universe: The search for laws of self-organization and complexity/Stuart Kauffman.* London: Viking.

Kiraly, D. C. (2000). *A social constructivist approach to translator education: Empowerment from theory to practice.* Manchester: St. Jerome.

Kiraly, D. C. (2006). Beyond social constructivism: Complexity theory and translator education. *Translation and Interpreting Studies, 6*(1), 68–86.

Kiraly, D. C. (2013). Towards a view of translator competence as an emergent phenomenon: Thinking outside the box(es) in translator education. In D. C. Kiraly, S. Hansen-Schirra, & K. Maksymsk (Eds.), *New prospects and perspectives for educating language mediators* (Translationswissenschaft, pp. 197–224). Tübingen: Narr Verlag.

Kiraly, D. C. (2014). From assumptions about knowing and learning to praxis in translation education. *Intralinea* (Special Issue: Challenges in Translation Pedagogy). Retrieved from www.intralinea.org/specials/article/2100

Kiraly, D. C. (2015). Occasioning translator competence: Moving beyond social constructivism. Toward a postmodern alternative to instructionism. *Translation and Interpreting Studies, 10*(1), 8–32.

Kiraly, D. C. (2016). Authentic project work and pedagogical epistemologies: A question of competing or complementary worldviews? In D. C. Kiraly (Ed.), *V&R academic. Towards authentic experiential learning in translator education* (pp. 53–65). Göttingen: V & R Unipress; Mainz University Press.

Kiraly, D. C., & Hofmann, S. (2016). Towards a postpositivist curriculum development model for translator education. In D. C. Kiraly (Ed.), *V&R academic. Towards authentic experiential learning in translator education* (pp. 67–88). Göttingen: V & R Unipress; Mainz University Press.

Klimkowski, K. (2015). *Towards a shared curriculum in translator and interpreter education. Languages in Contact: Vol. 3.* Wrocław & Washington, DC: Wydawnictwo Wyższej Szkoły Filologicznej; Polska Akademia Nauk. Oddział we Wrocławiu; International Communicology Institute.

Kodura, M. (2019). Wikipedia-based activities and translation competence development. *Current Trends in Translation Teaching and Learning E, 6,* 193–231.

Larsen-Freeman, D., & Anderson, M. (2018). *Techniques & principles in language teaching* (3rd ed.). Oxford [i pozostałe]: Oxford University Press.

Long, A. A., & Sedley, D. N. (1987). *The Hellenistic philosophers.* Cambridge: Cambridge University Press.

Marczak, M. (2019). Successful e-learning: Intercultural development in GPE's global understanding project. In E. Smyrnova-Trybulska (Ed.), *E-learning: Vol. 11. E-leaming and STEM education* (pp. 233–254). Katowice-Cieszyn: Studio Noa for University of Silesia.

Markie, P. (2017). Rationalism vs. Empiricism. In E. N. Zalta (Ed.), *The Stanford encyclopedia of philosophy* (Fall 2017 ed.). Retrieved from https://plato.stanford.edu/archives/fall2017/entries/rationalism-empiricism/.

Mason, M. (Ed.). (2008). *Complexity theory and the philosophy of education.* Malden, MA & Oxford: Wiley-Blackwell.

Massey, G. (2017). Translation competence development and process-oriented pedagogy. In J. W. Schwieter & A. Ferreira (Eds.), *The handbook of translation and cognition: First edition* (pp. 496–518). Hoboken, NJ: John Wiley & Sons, Inc.

Mastela, O. (2022). Zaangażowana dydaktyka akademicka i jej wpływ na jakość kształcenia tłumaczy. In J. Bugaj & M. Budzanowska-Drzewiecka (Eds.), *Jakość kształcenia akademickiego* (pp. 182–198). Kraków: Wydawnictwo Uniwersytetu Jagiellońskiego.

Maturana, U. R., & Varela, F. J. (1929). *Autopoiesis and cognition: The realization of living.* Dordrectht, Holland, Boston, & London: D. Reidel Publishin Company.

Miller, J. P., & Seller, W. (1985). Transmission position: Educational practice. In J. P. Miller & W. Seller (Eds.), *Curriculum perspectives and practice* (pp. 37–61). New York: Addison-Wesley Longman.

Morrison, K. (2008). Educational philosophy and the challenge of complexity theory. In M. Mason (Ed.), *Complexity theory and the philosophy of education* (pp. 16–31). Malden, MA & Oxford: Wiley-Blackwell.

Newell, R. (2003). *Passion for learning.: How project-based learning meets the needs of 21st-century learners.* Lanham, MD, Toronto, & Oxford: Scarecrow Education.

New London Group. (2000). A pedagogy of multiliteracies: Designing social futures. In B. Cope & M. Kalantzis (Eds.), *Multiliteracies: Literacy learning and the design of social futures* (pp. 9–37). London: Routledge.

Nord, C. (1996). Wer nimmt denn mal den ersten Satz? Überlegungen zu neuen Arbeitsformen im Übersetzungsunterricht. In A. Lauer, H. Gerzymisch-Arbogast, J. Haller, & E. Steiner (Eds.), *Translationwissenscha im Umbruch. Festschri für Wolfram Wilss* (pp. 313–327). Tübingen: Gunter Narr Verlag.

O'Dowd, R. (2021). Virtual exchange: Moving forward into the next decade. *Computer Assisted Language Learning, 34*(3), 209–224.

Orlando, M. (2016). *Training 21st-century translators and interpreters: At the crossroads of practice, research and pedagogy. Transkulturalität – Translation – Transfer.* Berlin: Frank & Timme.

Padgett, J. F., & Powell, W. W. (2012). *The emergence of organizations and markets.* Princeton: Princeton University Press.

Panichi, L., Deutschmann, M., & Molka-Danielsen, J. (2010). Virtual worlds for foreign language learning and intercultural exchange: Is it for real? In S. Guth & F. Helm (Eds.), *Telecollaboration 2.0: Language, literacies and intercultural learning in the 21st century* (pp. 165–195). Bern, Berlin, Bruxelles, Frankfurt am Main, New York, Oxford, & Wien: Peter Lang.

Paradowska, U. (2021). Benefits and challenges of an intra-university authentic collaborative translation project. *New Voices in Translation Studies, 24,* 23–45.

Pascale, R. T. (1999). Surfing the edge of chaos. *Sloan Management Review, 40*(3), 83–94.

Piaget, J. (1959). *The language and thought of the child. International library of psychology, philosophy and scientific method* (3d ed. rev. and enl.). New York: Humanities Press.

Piaget, J. (1977). *The development of thought: Equilibration of cognitive structures/Jean Piaget; translated by Arnold Rosin.* New York: Viking Press.

Pym, A. (2003). Redefining translation competence in an electronic age: In defence of a minimalist approach. *Meta: Translators' Journal, 48*(4), 481–497. Retrieved from www.erudit.org/revue/meta/2003/v48/n4/008533ar.pdf

Richards, J. C., & Rodgers, T. S. (2014). *Approaches and methods in language teaching* (3rd ed.). New York: Cambridge University Press. Retrieved from www.loc.gov/catdir/enhancements/fy1403/2013041790-d.html

Risku, H. (2002). Situatedness in translation studies. *Cognitive Systems Research, 3*(3), 523–533.

Risku, H. (2010). A cognitive scientific view on technical communication and translation. DO embodiment and situatedness really make a difference? *Target, 22*(1), 94–111.

Risku, H. (2014). Translation process research as interaction research: From mental to socio-cognitive processes. *MonTI. Monografías de Traducción e Interpretación,* 331–353. Retrieved from www.redalyc.org/articulo.oa?id=265134676012

Skinner, F. B. (1957). *Verbal behavior.* Acton, MA: Copley Publishing Group.

Stacey, R. D. (2016). *Strategic management and organizational dynamics: The challenge of complexity.* In D. S. Ralph, (Ed.), *Strategic management and organizational dynamics.* Harlow, Essex: Pearson Education Limited.

Stolze, R. (2012). The hermeneutical approach to translation. *Vertimo Studijos, 5,* 30–42.

Turner, J. R., & Baker, R. M. (2019). Complexity theory: An overview with potential applications for the social sciences. *Systems, 7*(1), 4. https://doi.org/10.3390/systems7010004

Turner, J. R., Baker, R. M., & Morris, M. (2018). Complex adaptive systems: Adapting and managing teams and team conflict. In A. A. Vilas Boas (Ed.), *Organizational conflict* (pp. 65–94). London: IntechOpen.

Vygotsky, L. S. (1978). *Mind in society: The development of higher psychological processes.* Cambridge, MA: Harvard University Press.

Walshe, G. (2020). Radical constructivism – von Glasersfeld. In B. Akpan & T. J. Kennedy (Eds.), *Science education in theory and practice* (pp. 359–371). Cham: Springer International Publishing.

Wheatley, M. (1999). *Leadership and the new science: Discovering order in a chaotic world* (2nd ed.). San Francisco: Berrett-Koehler Publishers.

Whitehead, A. N. (1929). *Process and reality.* New York: Macmillan.

Whitehead, A. N. (1978). *Process and reality: An essay in cosmology.* New York: The Free Press.

Williams, M. K. (2017). John Dewey in the 21st century. *Journal of Inquiry & Action in Education, 9*(1), 91–102.

Żmudzki, J. (2018). Kilka refleksji nad aktualnym stanem nauki o translacji. *Orbis Linguarum, 51.* https://doi.org/10.23817/olin.51-28

5 Telecollaborative work modes in translator education

As it has already been demonstrated (see Chapter 1), telecollaboration is an umbrella term for a large number of designs, which renders it difficult to define in an exhaustive manner while making it adaptable to numerous educational settings, including translator education. Thus, it needs to be elucidated what exactly telecollaboration entails in the latter context. A possible definition can now be derived from the myriad of definitions of telecollaboration of varied authorship which have been analysed in Chapter 1. They were largely definitions of telecollaboration as it is interpreted in the field of language education, where it has been in used for nearly four decades now, but some were generic rather than subject dependent. A common dominator for the definitions of telecollaboration of both types will now be established by selecting the elements which seem applicable to translator education while omitting those which seem completely irrelevant.

Undeniably, telecollaboration involves a *group of students* (Harris, 1999; cf. Merriam-Webster, n.d.; O'Dowd, 2011) operating from *different locations* (cf. Belz, 2003; Harris, 1999; O'Dowd, 2011) and using synchronous and asynchronous forms of *online communication* (cf. Dooly, 2008; Guth & Helm, 2010; O'Dowd, 2011) in order to *work together* (Harris, 1999; cf. Merriam-Webster, n.d.), also with *other parties* (cf. Narayan, 2013), towards a *shared goal* (Lamy & Goodfellow, 2010; cf. Lamy & Goodfellow, 2010), which usually involves the creation of a *joint product* (cf. Lamy & Goodfellow, 2010). Certain elements of this definition, italicised for ease of recognition, need to be elaborated upon to ensure their clarity.

Firstly, although the participation of a group of students in telecollaboration seems to be an inherent feature of it, it must be remembered that the smallest student grouping is a pair. Since as O'Dowd (2011) reports, one of the possible telecollaborative setups is that of an e-tandem model, the word *group* in the previously cited definition of telecollaboration is inclusive of teams of two students.

DOI: 10.4324/9781003424932-6

Secondly, contrary to what definitions offered within the area of inter-cultural learning suggest (cf. Harris, 1999), telecollaboration need not always involve students working in geographically distant positions. It may be important in intercultural learning settings, where telecollabora-tion gives students an opportunity to interact with representatives of other languacultures; although even then, it is not unconditionally required – a point which will be elaborated on when OIEs will be discussed. In transla-tor education, geographical distance does not matter so much, although it is not an obstacle either. It is important that students involve in telecol-laboration to mediate teamwork which due to the distance between the participants would otherwise be impossible, but the actual distance is far less important. It may happen that students who collaborate are located in different countries or even on different continents, but they may equally be located within the same city, quarter or even residential area. It does not matter whether they are thousands of kilometres apart or whether they are literally two blocks away from one another. What does matter, though, is that telecollaboration permits students to work jointly while it is impos-sible for them to meet in the same location in person. Hence, in translator education, it seems more reasonable to talk about different, rather than distant, locations.

Thirdly, what needs emphasising in the aforementioned definition of tel-ecollaboration is that collaboration need not be limited only to student participants, but it may also involve third parties that could possibly con-tribute to students' learning or project outcomes. Narayan (2013) suggests that students use the affordances of telecollaboration to reach the world beyond their immediate learning environment and contact, for example, scholars and researchers, scientists or industry leaders. It is particularly pertinent to the area of translator education, where they have been so many initiatives, and calls for, involving market representatives, transla-tion experts, genuine clients and other stakeholders in the translation pro-cess in the didactic process (cf. ALTA, 2015; Bondarenko, Bondarenko, Andrienko, Potapenko, & Slavova, 2021; Elia Exchange, 2014; Orlando, 2016; Saldanha, 2019) and translation research (cf. Schäffner, 2019).

Fourthly, telecollaboration, which is driven by a shared goal – usually, the creation of a clearly definable end product, such as a presentation, an online/offline publication, a term base, a translation or a book/film adap-tation – must involve interaction. The need to emphasise the interactivity of telecollaborative tasks is best exemplified by an assignment requiring learners to find specific information online. If each of the learners runs their own search without interacting with the others and subsequently contributes their findings to a wiki mechanically compiled from student-provided entries, the assignment will hardly qualify as telecollabora-tion. Although the project involves a shared goal (the creation of the wiki), each student will have, in fact, done their share of the work alone, unaided by colleagues. Demonstrably, group work does not in its own right entail shared work. On the contrary, the example in question shows that certain instances of group work may not involve telecollaboration at all. Hence, it is critically important to underline that working together does not mean the shared distribution of work but interaction-enhanced performance.

Now that the concept of telecollaboration in translator education has been largely characterised, it is important to consider how it could possibly convert into pedagogical practices. However, as planning for telecollaboration will need to factor a greater level of context-specific detail, it seems advisable to delve into the intricacies of telecollaboration with regard to concrete telecollaborative tasks and projects.

The distinction between these two units becomes clear when one looks at the particulars of the now-historic Bangalore project, administered at the turn of the 1970s and 1980s to examine the practicability of task-based learning in foreign language education, where – as Prabhu (1987) reported – three major task types were used: information gap, reasoning gap and opinion gap. The difference between the task types is of little importance at this point, but it indicates that a project is a more general unit than a task; that is why the latter will normally constitute the fabric of the former. In line with that, Nunan (2004) defines a project as a *maxitask*, which consists of a number of sequenced subsidiary tasks.

González Davies (2004) distinguishes several features which are helpful in telling projects apart from tasks, and although she refers to collaborative projects, in the light of the definition of telecollaboration in translator education proposed in this chapter, it is clear that the characteristics she offers also fully apply to telecollaboration projects.

She believes that projects differ from tasks in duration, student involvement, structure and work mode. In her view, projects tend to last relatively long (two weeks – two months), while tasks are shorter. Projects require active student participation throughout, including decision taking and assessment, whereas tasks may be more set in that certain decisions and assessment may be at the teacher's discretion. Projects comprise a sequence of loosely sequenced teacher- or student-initiated tasks and involve students in teamwork characterised by joint effort, while tasks are not only smaller in scope but also involve less student-student collaboration.

The last feature of tasks might paradoxically undermine the idea of telecollaboration projects as consisting of tasks; if tasks may involve no collaboration, then projects into which those tasks fall cannot be collaborative either. However, this argument is rebuttable on the following grounds: while task design and task choice are critical for ensuring the collaborative nature of projects, if a project involves a task sequence, some tasks need not involve collaboration, or they may involve less of it, without affecting the overall nature of the project work.

As it has been explained, a task is a project constituent, which in FL pedagogy, Ellis (2003) has defined:

> a workplan that requires learners to process language pragmatically in order to achieve an outcome that can be evaluated in terms of whether the correct or appropriate propositional content has been conveyed. To this end, it requires them to give primary attention to meaning and to make use of their own linguistic resources, although the design of the task may predispose them to choose particular forms. A task is intended to result in language use that bears a resemblance, direct or indirect, to the way language is used in the real world. Like other language activities, a task can engage productive or receptive, and oral or written skills and also various cognitive processes.
>
> (Ellis, 2003, p. 16)

The previously cited definition highlights several pivotally important points. Firstly, in a task, pragmatic language processing is subordinate to outcome achievement. Secondly, students are at liberty to use the language resources which they deem adequate for the set purposes. Thirdly, students are expected to use their language resources in a way which will reflect real-world language use. Fourthly, a task is likely to involve various language skills and cognitive processes.

If task elements were to be tailored to the context of translator education, the concept of a task could be redefined as follows: in a task, emphasis is placed on the pragmatic manipulation of adequate translation-related resources with a view to realising specified goals. To that end, students are entitled to use any resources they find adequate, but they are expected to use their translator competence in a way reflective of real-world settings. A task is likely to involve a range of competences and cognitive processes.

A concise definition of a task comes from Nunan (2004), who describes it as "a piece of classroom work" (Nunan, 2004, p. 4) that involves TL comprehension, manipulation, production or interaction and focuses on conveying meaning. Transplanted to translator education, it could be modified to denote a piece of classroom work involving the use of various components of translator competence towards the realisation of set goals, with the caveat that in the case of telecollaboration *classroom work*, which by the way denotes the pedagogical tilt in his definition, would rather be understood as *coursework*, as telecollaboration often happens outside the classroom. It is interesting how Nunan (2004) adds that a task constitutes a complete communicative act, with a clear-cut beginning, middle and end, which has two important implications for use and design. Firstly, tasks can be used in a sequence, but they might equally function as stand-alone units. Secondly, Nunan's (2004) distinction of three basic task phases indicates that each task should be planned to involve a pre-, while- and post-task stage so that it genuinely can be used as a pedagogical unit in its own right.

5.1 Design types

What follows is a discussion of the possible implementations of telecollaboration in translator education. However, due to the wide range of design options, which – as O'Dowd and Ware (2009) imply – could practically be listed *ad infinitum*, the solutions presented here are by no means to be treated as exhaustive. Neither should they be viewed as prescriptive because they are inevitably open to interpretation and modification in response to specific educational circumstances. They should rather be perceived as generic and are only to demonstrate the lines along which telecollaboration can be designed. Since the design modes will be presented in a top-down fashion, that is, from the more general towards the detailed, three major categories of telecollaboration projects will be distinguished:

1 Online Intercultural Exchanges (OIEs)
2 telecollaborative translation projects
3 miscellaneous projects

It needs to be stressed that although these projects are intended for use in translator education and foster the development of various components of translator competence, including translation competence, it does not automatically imply that each of them needs to involve translation per se. Especially projects from the first and third categories proposed earlier may not require students to translate at all, but they may nevertheless involve activities promoting the development of translation-related knowledge, skills and awareness. First, the key features of each project type will be identified. Afterwards, a number of suggestions will be made with regard to the tasks which the projects can possibly involve.

5.1.1 Online Intercultural Exchanges

A major project type to be used in translator education comprises Online Intercultural Exchanges (OIEs), which have an established position in FL education. The relevance of OIEs to translator education is evidenced by the fact that, as research reveals, they promote the development of various competences targeted for development in models of translator/translation competence, including intercultural competence, language competence, digital literacy, disciplinary skills and knowledge, as well as transversal competences.

(Inter)cultural competence is a permanent component of most models of translation competence, irrespective whether they have been proposed by individual researchers, for example, Kelly's model (Kelly, 2005) and Kiraly's model (Kiraly, 2006), or by research teams, for example, the PACTE model (PACTE, 2003), the TransComp model (Göpferich, 2009) and the EMT model (EMT, 2009, 2017, 2022b).

These projects primarily aim to foster the development of intercultural communicative competence, which, for example, in Byram's (1997) classic view of it, encompasses two constituent sub-competences: communicative competence and intercultural competence. While the former comprises linguistic competence (receptive and productive language performance), sociolinguistic competence (sociopragmatic skills) and discourse competence (ability to construct or create text types), the latter consists of (i) affective competence (attitudes), cognitive competence (knowledge), action-oriented competence (skills) and educational competence (critical cultural awareness). A thorough delineation of the model falls beyond the scope of this publication; the more that it has been discussed extensively in the professional literature (cf. Byram, 1997, 2008, 2014; Byram & Zarate, 1998), but what merits note is that some of the elements of the model are particularly pertinent to the use of translation skills in intercultural situations, for example, the ability to "use in real-time knowledge, skills and attitudes for mediation between interlocutors of one's own and foreign culture" (Byram, 2008, p. 233) or "interact and mediate in intercultural exchanges in accordance with explicit criteria, negotiating where necessary a degree of acceptance of them by drawing upon one's knowledge, skills and attitudes" (Byram, 2008, p. 233).

Digital literacy skills are also a perennial component of translation competence models, only they have been placed there under different names. In Kelly's (2005) model, they are labelled as instrumental sub-competence and involve the ability to use documentation sources and information technologies applicable to translation. In Kiraly's (2006) model, the component called *technology* falls into translation competence, which along with social and personal competence constitutes translator competence. The PACTE (2003) model places digital literacy skills within the broader instrumental sub-competence, which it defines as "predominantly procedural knowledge related to the use of documentation sources and information and communication technologies applied to translation: dictionaries of all kinds, encyclopaedias, grammar books, style guides, parallel texts, electronic corpora, search engines, etc." (PACTE, 2003, p. 59). In the original version of the EMT model, digital literacies are integrated with two sub-competences, information mining competence and technological competence. The former refers to the ability to effectively use search engines and other information mining tools (e.g. terminology software, electronic corpora or electronic dictionaries), while the latter denotes the ability to use text-processing software, databases or machine translation to enhance the translation of documents in different formats, as well as the ability to adapt and learn new CAT tools. In the newer EMT (2017, 2022a, 2022b) models, digital literacies are identifiable in the technology component, which entails file management skills, information searching skills, as well as the ability to use CAT tools, MT systems and translation workflow management software.

Disciplinary skills are most often incorporated into competence models under the names of (i) subject knowledge in special areas, which in the PACTE (PACTE, 2003) model is subsumed under the more general extra-linguistic sub-competence; (ii) subject area competence (Kelly, 2005); (iii) domain competence, as in the TransComp (Göpferich, 2009) model; and (iv) thematic competence, which is part of all the EMT (2009, 2017, 2022a) models, with the latest version (EMT, 2022a) describing it as thematic/domain-specific knowledge and the ability to translate varied domain-specific content.

Last but not least, TS researchers have also advocated the need to develop students' transversal skills, which are also referred to as transferable skills (cf. Kearns, 2006). It is particularly vital at university level, where – as Kearns (2006) posits – the skills "form part of the tertiary education sector's mission to help individual's attain personal fulfilment and development, inclusion and employment; the second play a role more specific to their own respective fields" (Kearns, 2006, p. 137). The transferrable skills, which Kearns (2006) found to be recognised as crucial to a graduate's career, comprise – *inter alia* – time management, teamwork skills, presentation skills or the ability to cope with multiple tasks. Other equally important skills are those listed by Piotrowska (2007), who additionally emphasised the importance of flexibility, a person's intellectual capacities or the ability to swiftly respond to changes in the professional environment. Overall, Kearns (2006) concisely justifies the value of transferable skills claiming that they facilitate mobility between jobs, which means that they are subject- and vocation-independent, universal skills which seem indispensable, especially in the light of the volatility of today's translation market. Simultaneously, his concept of *mobility between jobs* could also be interpreted more literally to mean the ability to move from translation job to another (i.e. cope successfully with various translation commissions, each of which will make different requirements on the translator). This idea reverberates in the words of Piotrowska (2007, 2022), who – in agreement with concerns voiced by Kiraly (1995) – questioned the feasibility of predetermining relevant competences in translator education or professional contexts without knowing their exact specifications.

As it has been mentioned, OIEs are a pedagogical response to the need for developing the aforementioned competences and may be implemented within various scenarios: as part of core or elective university-level TS courses, designed as in FL education – with analogical tasks – or geared towards translation. To learn how they can work in the latter context, three main OIE task types – information exchange tasks, comparison and analysis tasks and collaborative tasks – as identified by O'Dowd and Ware (2009) in over 40 publications on telecollaborative exchanges, will be briefly characterised and reviewed for the possibility of orientating them more towards translation *per se*, or the development of translation-related competences. O'Dowd and Ware's (2009) list is a synthesis of task designs, not a random choice; hence, they can be regarded as a firm foundation for OIE task adaptation.

Information exchange tasks correspond to what in language teaching methodology is known as information gap (Nunan, 2004; Prabhu, 1987) tasks, where typically one person possesses information the other person misses, with the caveat that the reverse is also true. To compete the task, both parties – individuals or student groups – are supposed to exchange the information that they have to bridge the initial information gap between them, hence, the task's name. The content to be exchanged can be freely decided; thus, it may involve personal information, one's languacultural background (language, social/cultural/ethnic group) or physical bearings (city, region, country). This kind of task, as any other, can be potentially performed in numerous ways. Yet whatever decisions are taken, one must be cognisant of the nature of interaction they will involve and the competences which they will – or will not – foster.

For instance, within the *monologic* (O'Dowd & Ware, 2009) design, the task may be limited to mere information exchange, which will involve limited interaction between the participants. Consequently, although person A and B mutually relay information, genuine communication is not established, and the task hardly qualifies as telecollaboration. However, it does not render the task useless for telecollaborative exchanges, where it could be used as only one of a sequence of tasks, with interactive follow-up tasks supplementing the information exchange with proper communication or negotiation.

Alternatively, this task can be planned as deeply interactive and require students to exchange information beyond generalities. If students need to obtain details, they will need to involve in the negotiation of meaning (e.g. asking for repetition, clarification or exemplification), thus taking more communicative turns. O'Dowd and Ware (2009) suggest that the same effect could be obtained if the task were set as a mutual ethnographic interview, while Prabhu (1987) states that the task could require students to use the information they exchange to create a joint product (e.g. a text summary table).

Information exchange tasks set within OIEs could be adapted in multiple ways to foster the development of translator competence. An example would be an interview held mutually by both parties involved in the project – be they groups or individuals – to obtain information about the CAT tools, MT systems or other digital aids while performing translation assignments. This task design presumes that the OIE partners are all TS students, but if that is the case, students will be able to practise communication skills, negotiate meaning and expand or consolidate knowledge of translation technologies.

Another example is an adaptation of a task described by O'Dowd and Ware (2009) in which in the original version two groups of students collect legends, folk tales or accounts of historical events and exchange with them with each other to produce a class magazine or website. A modified version of the task might require students to team-translate the content in question (e.g. in a cloud CAT tool) while negotiating the most adequate translation solutions which would help them render the target content both understandable to foreign partners but also functionally equivalent so that it has the same air and impact on the recipients as the original. After the exchange, both groups would jointly produce a magazine or website negotiating the choice of content. In this way, the task would involve significant information processing, the use of translation technologies, techniques ensuring functional equivalence and negotiation skills.

Comparison and analysis tasks are another category identified by O'Dowd and Ware (2009), who explain that within this design, students go beyond mere information exchange and compare or critically analyse content, including the products of what Tomalin and Stempleski (1993) label as *big C culture* (e.g. books or films) and *low c culture* (e.g. surveys or newspaper articles). The comparison and analyses, which can be linguistic or cultural in focus, are to induce a communicative exchange through which cultural similarities or differences could be discovered. Tasks within this category permit the development of Byram's (1997) *skills of interpreting and relating*, which involve interpreting cultural documents or events from other cultures and relating them to equivalents from one's native culture, thus fostering reflection on both cultures.

A comparison and analysis task cited by O'Dowd and Ware (2009) consists in partner students comparing their responses to an independently completed questionnaire. Another two tasks involve translation *per se*. In one, students compare parallel versions (i.e. the original and its translation) of literary pieces or films based on a common theme, while in the other students from one group translate a text from their native language into the language of their exchange partners to have the translation refined and corrected by the latter.

Again, comparison and analysis tasks can be adapted for translator education. For instance, if the partner groups in the translation task happen to know each other's languages, they could perform mutual L1 to L2 translation and exchange the texts to work on possible inadequacies. This design would enable both groups to revise the translations they receive against the source text. That would create room not only for the development of language awareness and linguistic competence, which the original version of the task was limited to, but also for learning about cultural issues in translation and developing translation competence.

Another adaptation could involve the questionnaire-based task described earlier, where the questions which the exchange students are supposed to answer could cover translation (processes). Options are limitless, but sample themes – additionally aimed at personalising the activity to increase student involvement and contribution to the ensuing comparison and analysis – could comprise the students' translation experience, employability prospects, learning preferences or views on the most useful transferrable skills in the local translation market.

One more example could be an extended version of the task involving the exchange of legends, folk tales and accounts of historical events, which comes from the previously discussed category of tasks. The original could be modified by requiring students to publish a magazine or website featuring only stories or folk tales with a degree of correspondence between them. In that way, students would need to focus on the differences and similarities between their outputs not only as output characteristics but also as selection criteria for the publishable content. Alternatively, students could publish accounts of the same historical event from both partners and report on differences and similarities and the underlying reasons for them, which would require an in-depth joint analysis. This example illustrates the openness and flexibility of OIE task formats, which teachers can use to their own and students' advantage.

Collaborative tasks are those which O'Dowd and Ware (2009) define with three important characteristics: (i) working towards a joint product, (ii) extensive planning and coordination and (iii) increased levels of negotiation. This definition reveals the putative nature of task categorisation by any authors and thus the need to approach such categorisations with caution. The reason for that is the thin line demarcating the difference between *collaborative tasks* and *comparison and analysis tasks*. Tasks from the latter category may undeniably share certain elements with those from the former group, as – even prior to adaptation – they may involve working towards a joint product (e.g. a magazine or a website). Examples of *collaborative tasks* cited by O'Dowd and Ware (2009) comprise the joint writing of an essay or the creation of a website, the inter-genre conversion of texts or the appropriate translation of a product for another culture. In fact, each of those tasks bears close resemblance to the tasks exemplifying the other two categories, while the task involving the production of a culturally appropriate translation resembles the modified, more translation-centred version of the task which involved the exchange of legends, folk tales and accounts of historical events.

To some extent, the demarcation of *collaborative tasks* may also be difficult due to the very name they have been given. O'Dowd and Ware (2009) set out to delineate different categories of telecollaborative tasks; hence, giving nearly the same name to one of the task categories which they have identified breeds confusion. It has already been demonstrated that tasks within the other two categories (information exchange tasks and comparison and analysis tasks) may also involve collaboration; thus, the name of the third category might be misinterpreted as an overarching category to which the other two belong.

The previous example by no means devalues O'Dowd and Ware's (2009) categorisation or naming of tasks. One must be cognisant that the category names simply denote the focus of the tasks within them, not the elements the tasks are likely to involve. Consequently, while *information exchange tasks* or *comparison and analysis tasks* may – *mutadis mutandi* – involve collaboration or negotiation, *collaborative tasks* are inherently characterised by both, hence the difference in levels of collaboration and negotiation, which O'Dowd and Ware (2009) stress in their definition of the latter task category. The difference within particular categories is clearly noticeable in that in *information exchange tasks* or *comparison and analysis tasks,* students from each partner group first work independently from their telecollaboration partners and only then begin to interact. In contrast, *collaborative tasks* require partners to interact and collaborate on a product from day one, thus stimulating joint negotiation and intensive coordination.

The conclusion that teachers can draw from the previous discussion is that although telecollaborative tasks are easily adaptable – even within the aforementioned three task categories, the number of possible designs and adaptations is potentially large – decisions on which design to select or what modifications to introduce must be made with deliberation, as even seemingly insignificant alterations may have a significant impact on the task focus, work modes and outcomes.

As far as possible adaptations of *collaborative tasks* for translation students go, multiple options are possible. For instance, the original task where students work jointly on the creation of a document or a multimedia product could require students to work on a joint translation of an essay, article, book excerpt or presentation from the *lingua franca* of the exchange to a third language which both partner groups can use. Not only would the task have all the three features of a collaborative endeavour, it would also involve a great deal of translator competence, including (inter)cultural componence, translation competence and transversal skills.

Another adaptation could involve a task which in its original form O'Dowd and Ware (2009) describe as the joint rewriting of a TL text in a different genre. If the choice of the target genre is carefully considered, it could additionally require changes to the modality of the content. For example, if a text is to be converted into a poster or infographic, at least some of its content will need to be visualised. Consequently, students would not only practise the intralanguage translation conventions relevant to a given genre, but they would also develop intersemiotic translation skills, which could be useful preparation for jobs in transcreation or localisation.

5.1.2   Telecollaborative translation projects

Virtual collaboration project. Tsai (2020) reports on a translation project administered in the mode of virtual collaboration as part of an elective course in Specialised Translation for students on an undergraduate programme in translation and interpreting programme at National Taiwan University. The project was a one-day event and involved a team of 27 students in the translation of technical news reports, technical texts, and travel texts of roughly 500 words each, from English to Chinese Mandarin.

The students operated in teams of three and had three hours to complete their translations. They worked from various locations outside university and performed translation in a cloud-based CAT tool called *Termsoup* (https://termsoup.com). Developed by a Web designer who happens to also work as a translator and translation project manager, *Termsoup* has a simple graphic interface and offers various functionalities, including a shared translation memory, machine translation, term base, Web-based term look-up options, Netspeak, which is a tool for searching words in context, and a panel with project metadata and productivity statistics. The main channel for communication in the program is a comment tool, complete with instant messaging, but interaction between project participants is additionally enhanced by an edit history (Tsai, 2020).

For in-project communication, the students did not need to rely on *Termsoup* functionalities exclusively. As a result, they chiefly communicated via Facebook Messenger, with very few students using the *Termsoup* chat, or LINE – yet another messaging app. Emphasis was placed on student-student live interaction, joint proofreading and mutual feedback provision. The project work involved the following stages: discussion of working arrangements, collaboration on *Termsoup*, proofreading and project submission (Tsai, 2020).

Trans-Atlantic Project. Maylath et al. (2013) report on two multilateral international collaboration projects completed in 2010 under the common name of the Trans-Atlantic Project. A total of five tertiary-level institutions were involved in it, including Aarhus University from Denmark, University College Ghent from Belgium, North Dakota State University from the United States, Vaasa University from Finland and Paris Diderot University from France. The projects were complex in design and required students to perform various actions, including text authoring, usability testing and translation.

In one of the projects, for the purpose of distinction referred to as the EU→USA project, students translated news articles from Danish and Dutch into English, and their translations were subsequently edited by foreign partners into American English. The translations from Danish and Dutch were performed by Danish and Belgian students respectively, while the editing was done by US students. Maylath et al. (2013) do not specify in what mode exactly the translations were performed, but they make it explicit that at least while editing, the US students closely collaborated with the their Danish and Belgian partners.

The other project, analogically called the USA→EU project, involved the same student groups, with the addition of a group of Finnish students. Within this project, the US students first produced texts on various topics, conducted usability tests on local subjects, but they also had another battery of usability tests run by their project partners from Finland. Afterwards, the US students sent the finalised versions of their texts, prepared for localisation, to TS students from Belgium and France for translation into Dutch and French respectively.

In both projects, communication was mostly mediated via email and Facebook, but the final round-up session was held as a joint Skype videoconference for the all the EU→USA and USA→EU project participants. From the perspective of the present discussion, it is important to what extent telecollaboration was involved in the translation process within the aforementioned projects. Although Maylath et al. (2013) claim that the project was collaborative, with the source texts chunked and fragments distributed among individuals who collaborated to translate, revise and review the texts, they do not clarify whether telecollaboration was used. Simultaneously, the Trans-Atlantic Project must have been at least partly telecollaborative (e.g. whenever translations or translation-related issues required consultation with foreign partners).

The Trans-Atlantic project demonstrates several interesting truths about telecollaborative project design. Firstly, such projects need not always involve students of translation on both sides. It is possible that TS students collaborate with partners majoring in areas outside translation per se, but the design may nevertheless be mutually beneficial. For instance, in the

EU→USA project, while the Danish and Belgian students performed translation, their American partners, who were on a technical writing course, edited the translations into American English. Consequently, the project partners on either side could pursue their line of study and develop competences relevant to their academic – and potentially professional – interests.

Secondly, students need not telecollaborate throughout the project; telecollaboration may constitute a possible work mode, which is likely to increase students' professional flexibility. Hence, although the Danish and Belgian translation students may not have produced their original target texts via telecollaboration, they telecollaborated on them with their US partners at the editing stage, at which the final versions were produced. This duality of work modes, involving collaborative and telecollaborative translation, may be an opportunity for students to compare both setups and reflect on the potential affordances and shortcomings of each.

In an attempt to summarise the first batch of telecollaborative projects discussed so far, the most important characteristics of the projects, including time, duration, project task, content type, client/requester, geographical range, participants, collaboration mode, translation technologies and communication channels, have been juxtaposed in Table 5.1.

Jacob of Paradies University project. Another example of a telecollaborative translation project has been reported on by Paradowska (2021). The project was administered at the Jacob of Paradies University, Gorzów Wielkopolski, Poland, where 12 undergraduate students of translation – members of two simulated translation bureaus, Morenzza and Eng-Pol, established prior to the project – were commissioned to provide translation services for the university's Promotion and Information Department.

At the outset, it was agreed that the source texts would comprise the university's candidate information booklet and the official university website, both constituting publishable content, with the former to be published in print and online. However, as the project progressed, the client also submitted other non-publishable content for translation, including press articles. Two students in the project were project managers, while the others acted as terminologists, translators and revisers, subject to personal preferences. Prior to publication, the target texts were reviewed by the course instructor. The translation process was managed through Memsource Cloud (currently known as Phrase), which was used to assign roles, set deadlines, manage the project resources (e.g. a shared translation memory and term base) and perform the translation. In addition, MS Excel Online was used to pre-process terminology before it was uploaded to the official project term base, while the Moodle learning management system was utilised as a platform for project managers to reflect on the project challenges and solutions (Paradowska, 2021).

Table 5.1 Translation project setups (1)

Design/Project	Virtual collaboration (Tsai, 2020)	Trans-Atlantic Project EU→USA (Maylath et al., 2013)	Trans-Atlantic Project USA→US (Maylath et al., 2013)
Time	2020	2010	2010
Duration	One day		
Project task	Translation of technical news reports, technical texts and travel texts of roughly 500 words each from English to Chinese Mandarin	Translation of GPL texts from Danish and Dutch into English and editing the target texts into American English	Writing, usability testing and translation from English into Dutch and French
Content type	Non-publishable	Non-publishable	Non-publishable
Client/requester	Simulated: students	Simulated: teacher	Simulated: teacher
Geographical range	Taiwan	Belgium, Denmark, USA	Belgium, Finland, France, USA
Participants	27 Taiwanese students working in teams of 3	9 Danish students, 37 Belgian students, 11 US students	11 US students, 37 Belgian students, 8 Finnish students, 61 French students (2 groups: 25 and 36)
Collaboration mode	Online	Hybrid (on-site and online)	Hybrid (on-site and online)
Translation technologies	*Termsoup* (SaaS)	None	None
Communication channels	Facebook Messenger, LINE (messenger), *Termsoup* comments (instant messaging)	Email, Facebook, Skype for an all-student videoconference	Email, Facebook, Skype for an all-student videoconference

University Pablo de Olavide project. In 2013, Prieto-Velasco and Fuentes-Luque (2016) conducted a telecollaborative translation project at University Pablo de Olavide in Seville, Spain, which involved 56 students on an English-Spanish translation course, who worked in teams of four. Within all teams, individual students were appointed one of the four roles: project manager, translator, documentalist or reviser.

The project managers were charged with ascertaining the time needed for project completion and delivery, pre-configuring the online collaborative environment in accordance with the project metadata, delegating tasks and responsibilities to team members, setting deadlines and coordinating project work. The translators rendered assigned text fragments into Spanish, deciding on most relevant strategies and, most importantly, coordinating their efforts with colleagues to ensure terminological or cultural consistency across all the target text. The documentalists analysed the source text, identified terms, created a glossary, searched for adequate reference sources and compiled a project reference list, while the revisers ensured the final version of the target text met appropriate language standards and formal specifications (e.g. regarding layout) (Prieto-Velasco & Fuentes-Luque, 2016).

The project task involved translating excerpts from seven selected chapters of Steve Colbert's book entitled *I am America (And So Can You!)* from English into Spanish. The task was original, as no Spanish translation of the book had been produced, and the translation was commissioned by the course teachers, but it was worded as if it had come from the publisher. Prieto-Velasco and Fuentes-Luque (2016) characterised the source text as linguistically and culturally challenging due to – *inter alia* – the presence of verbal and visual humour, wordplay, taboo language and cultural references.

Before the students embarked on the project, instruction was delivered on the use of relevant telecollaboration and translation tools, the work involved in the translation process (preparation of materials, pre-translation and revision) and the responsibilities of those appointed to specific roles, such as project manager, translator, documentalist and reviser. Once the project began, monitoring and support were ensured via continuous feedback flow between the students and the teacher (Prieto-Velasco & Fuentes-Luque, 2016).

As Prieto-Velasco and Fuentes-Luque (2016) reported, the students worked in a rich collaborative environment using tools which augmented project management, information and documentation, text revision and translation *per se*. In-project synchronous and asynchronous communication was mostly facilitated by Google Hangouts and Google Groups. The main translation software was the now discontinued Google Translator Toolkit, which was also used for managing terminology. ErrorSpy was used to facilitate language quality assessment, Google Sites or Google Blogger were used for publishing and comparing source and target text versions, while Google Drive served as storage for the project content.

FTSK 2013 project. One more example of a telecollaborative translation project is that administered in the academic year of 2013–2014 by Kiraly (Kiraly, Rüth, Signer, & Stederoth, 2019) at Fachbereich Translations-, Sprach- und Kulturwissenschaft (FTSK) in Germersheim, Germany. As part of an authentic translation project integrated into an MA course in TS, 37 students were commissioned to translate two issues of an economic online journal entitled *Magazine for Economic Sustainability*. The project, which was completed for a genuine external client, spanned a semester and was conducted in a semi-blended mode in that the students met the course instructor at three points in the semester: for an introductory meeting at the beginning, in the middle of the semester (to finalise the first part of the project) and at the end (to conclude the second part and collect feedback).

The source texts were supposed to have publishable quality, as they were to be published online, appended with translators' names. The main project tool was the Moodle learning management platform, which was used for translation, in-project communication and sharing relevant parallel texts, which the students had collected online prior to translation. A shared glossary was also prepared by extracting and researching terminology from the source texts. The project procedure had students translate their source texts on a segment-by-segment basis and post drafts to Moodle for the team editing, with the original translators introducing revisions suggested by their colleagues. The process was cyclical, as the revised versions were proofread by colleagues and finalised in line with the feedback obtained. The final versions of the text were proofread and submitted to the client by the course instructor.

The FTSK project is important for several reasons. Firstly, although it involved the use of a rather teacher-controlled online environment, Kiraly et al. (2019) reported that the need for students to work in interdependent teams and take responsibility for the completion of the project was emphasised. Secondly, although Moodle – as a commonly used e-learning platform at the time – was used for in-project collaboration, over time, the project evolved to involve other tools in future iterations in the years 2014–2018. For instance, Slack, a business communication platform, gradually replaced Moodle for communication, while Memsource Cloud (Phrase) was introduced to facilitate the translation process. Thirdly, due to Kiraly's significant contribution to the promotion of project-based learning in translator education, it has certainly inspired other (tele)collaborative translation projects.

An overview of the second batch of telecollaborative projects discussed earlier, with regard to the characteristics included previously, is presented in Table 5.2.

Although the six projects discussed earlier cannot be treated as an exhaustive representation of possible implementations modes, they provide a useful insight into the characteristics of telecollaborative translation projects in translator education courses, as summarised next:

- Duration: one day – entire semester
- Level of study: undergraduate, postgraduate

Table 5.2 Translation project setups (2)

Design/Project	Jacob of Paradies University project (Paradowska, 2021)	University Pablo de Olavide project (Prieto-Velasco & Fuentes-Luque, 2016)	FTSK WS 2013-SS 2014 project (Kiraly et al., 2019)
Time	2019	2013	2013–2014
Duration	3 months	8 weeks	2 semesters
Project task	Translation of the university's candidate information booklet, official university website and press articles (non-publishable) from Polish into English	Translation of excerpts from Steve Colbert's book *I Am America (And So Can You!)* from English into Spanish	Translation of two issues of an online economic journal
Content type	Publishable/ non-publishable	Non-publishable	Publishable
Client/requester	Real: Promotion and Information Department, the Jacob of Paradies University, Gorzów Wielkopolski, Poland	Teacher	Journal editing team
Geographical range	Poland	Spain	Germany
Participants	12 students working as two simulated translation bureaus	56 students	37 students
Collaboration mode	Hybrid (on-site and online)	Online	Online (at translation phase)
Translation technologies	*Memsource Cloud* (SaaS)	Google Translator Toolkit, ErrorSpy	None (Memsource Cloud introduced in future iterations)
Communication channels	Email	Google Hangouts, Google Groups, Google Sites, Google Blogger, Google Drive	Moodle (Slack introduced in future iterations)

- Content type: publishable, non-publishable
- Client/requester: real-world, teacher, student partners
- Geographical range: 1–6 countries
- Participants: 12–117 students
- Collaboration mode: online, hybrid (on-site and online)
- Translation technologies: none, Termsoup, Memsource Cloud (SaaS), Google Translator Toolkit, ErrorSpy
- Communication channels: Facebook Messenger, LINE (messengers), Google Hangouts, Google Groups, Google Sites, Google Blogger, Google Drive, Moodle, Slack

As it has been demonstrated, projects can significantly vary in length, from extremely short, one-day courses to those spanning a whole semester. Projects can be conducted at undergraduate and postgraduate levels, and they can involve student groupings varying from 12 to 117 students. They can be national, involving students from a single country, or international, with participants from as many as six countries. Project translations may be commissioned by different parties, including an external, real-world client, the course instructor or even partner students, as was the case in the Trans-Atlantic Project. The collaboration may be held entirely online or on-site and online, depending on the project phase. Communication can be mediated via multiple tools, from internationally or locally used online synchronous communicators (Facebook Messenger or LINE respectively) to asynchronous communication tools (Google Hangouts, Google Groups), content publishing tools (Google Blogger, Google Sites), file storage/sharing software (Google Drive) and business communication platforms (Slack). What draws attention is the choice of cloud and generic tools rather than business software. Interestingly, some projects may not involve the use of any translation tools, while others rely on cloud-based and toll-free solutions in three versions: full (Google Translator Toolkit), trial (Termsoup) or academically licensed (Memsource Cloud/Phrase). As an aside, it must be underlined that the two projects which did not involve translation technologies were those most distant in time, which implies restricted tool availability or limited trust in their usefulness at the time.

5.1.3 Miscellaneous projects

Apart from the now-well established – particularly in FL education – OIEs and telecollaborative translation projects, other project types are applicable to translator education. They differ from the other two types in the extent to which they involve telecollaboration, but translation teachers can consider them as alternative instructional options. Due to their open nature, miscellaneous projects potentially comprise various formats, which are difficult to define *a priori*; hence, three sample designs will be discussed here for illustrative purposes, with the caveat that numerous others are possible. As an aside, Chapter 6.3.1 contains an account of research based on yet another possible design from this project category, which implements the idea mentioned by Weigt (2012), who talks about projects where students who study specialised texts expand their lexical resources by jointly preparing glossaries.

Translator-client communication task. One of them has been discussed by Chodkiewicz (2016), who taught two groups of undergraduate translation students enrolled in a programme in applied linguistics through tasks simulating CMC with the client. The instructor's intention was to develop the students' *knowledge about translation* and *strategic competence* as components of the PACTE (2008) model.

The client was impersonated by the course instructor, and communication was practised via two channels: a Moodle-based forum and email. Throughout the course in Non-Specialised Translation, in which the task was used, the students were given several translation assignments under the guise of client-ordered translation jobs. Prior to translation, the students needed to collect or infer all the information necessary for them to deliver a functionally good translation and ensure target text usability. Whenever they believed they were missing important details, they had the liberty to contact the client. The translator (student)-client (teacher) communication was performed via telecollaboration out of class, and the students worked from home. In one of the groups (54 members), students communicated with the client on a Moodle discussion forum, while in the other (39 students), email was used exclusively. The latter was motivated – *inter alia* – by students' perception of a discussion forum as a tool unlikely to be used for translator-client communication in real life (Chodkiewicz, 2016).

Interestingly, although translation was not performed in telecollaborative mode, telecollaboration skills were nevertheless practised regarding translator-client communication, which demonstrates that even if telecollaboration is not at the core of translation assignments, it may facilitate translation-related competences. This conception was corroborated by the findings of the accompanying research which Chodkiewicz (2016) conducted to exame the students' performance and perceptions of the task. Not only had the relevance of students' questions to the client significantly increased on the final assignments but the students also declared that they perceived the task as professionally useful. For a detailed account of the task setup and an analysis of the research results, see Chodkiewicz (2014, 2016).

Simulated translation bureaus. Another setup which promotes telecollaborative translator education is that of student-run simulated translation bureaus (STBs), where professional service provision practices can be emulated. As van Egdom et al. (2020) explain, this work mode is elaborate and involves varied tasks. First, students consider the profile of the business, their roles and targeted customers and prepare a business plan. The planning stage is demanding, as it requires students to research the translation market, analyse the possible business models, choose their own and decide on what services to offer. Afterwards, students need to consider the financial aspects of the enterprise, including the costs to be incurred, revenue and tax issues and service pricing. Finally, elements relating to the bureau's market position and publicity need to be decided upon, including the name, logo, motto and website.

This pedagogical solution can potentially make students develop complex near-real organisational structures, or international networks, which finds illustration in the fact that STBs may even join the International Network of Simulated Translation Bureaus (INSTB), which promotes and facilitates "translation company simulation pedagogy" (van Egdom et al., 2020, p. 82). What is more important, however, is the complexity of STBs' working environment, which requires high levels of coordination, decision making and permanent communication to ensure proper workflow management and feedback loops, with the active involvement of relevant stakeholders.

In fact, an STB can be perceived as macro-scale project, much larger than telecollaborative translation projects, given that the latter involve only some of the responsibilities students need to handle while operating STBs. Consequently, the scope of the workload requires students to work out of class, from physically dispersed locations, be it from home or students' accommodation, which naturally stimulates telecollaboration. However, the reasons for telecollaboration in STBs go far beyond restrictions imposed by the rigidity of the university timetable. As Jiménez-Crespo (2017) maintains that telework mirrors professional reality, it might be stated that running an STB without it would render the work mode questionable.

With that in mind, perhaps, van Egdom et al. (2020) deem communication as an essential prerequisite for numerous student activities, including the finding and retaining of clients through social media marketing, building e-reputation or online/offline networking. However, communication in STB translation projects is equally vital, as it is monitored and evaluated. For instance, at the University of Lille – an INSTB member institution – in-project online communication, mediated via Slack, is recorded for analysis and feedback provision.

The choice of telecollaboration and other tools that the project work will potentially require (e.g. content management systems for designing and administering bureau websites, translation and workflow management tools or file storage systems) is very large. So is the scale of STB projects, which course instructors – perhaps in liaison with students – need to decide upon. Consequently, opportunities arise to develop a situated and challenging learning context which, due to its complexity, is likely not only to mimic professional reality but also, above all, foster the emergence of translator competence. With informed design and systematic feedback flows, this kind of learning might be truly effective, which finds preliminary corroboration in the findings of quasi-experimental (Cohen, Manion, & Morrison, 2011, 2017) research conducted by van Egdom et al. (2020). As the authors report – albeit with a great deal of design-related caution – the pre- and post-test data they had collected revealed a positive effect of a STB experience on students' perceived entrepreneurial competence and self-efficacy in planning, setting up and managing a translating business.

Crowdsourcing-mediated projects. Another type of task involving tel-ecollaborative translation may be those which integrate crowdsourcing in translator education. Jiménez-Crespo (2017), who wrote extensively on crowdsourcing and collaborative translation, defines the former as an umbrella term for various technological solutions developed with a view to "harnessing the wisdom of the crowd" (Jiménez-Crespo, 2017, p. 82). Among them, there are crowdsourcing platforms, which permit volunteers with varying levels of translation experience, including ama-teurs, translation students or translation professionals, to team up and deliver translations of desired content.

Crowdsourcing is facilitated by Web-based platforms permitting the source and target content can be stored, shared or commented and voted on. Some platforms may be quite elaborate and resemble MT-based CAT tools, but they are geared towards crowdsourced work. A discussion of the tools is beyond the scope of this publication, but the types of crowd-sourced translation models are pertinent to crowdsourcing-mediated pro-jects, whose concept will be introduced further. A synthesised typology of the models, originally proposed by Morera-Mesa (2014), has been out-lined by Jiménez-Crespo (2017), who distinguishes: colony translations, wiki translations, translations for engagement and the crowd translation-edit-publish model. In the colony model, specific segments of the source content are translated by multiple translators, and the best options are selected – be it automatically or through human assessment – for the final version. In translations for engagement, volunteers translate specific seg-ments, which after further editing – by the original crowd translators or other volunteers – are compiled into the final version. In the wiki model, volunteers translate selected segments of the source content, and their translations are voted on; those preferred by the largest number of voters are integrated into the final version. Finally, in the crowd translation-edit-publish model, volunteers translate whole texts, which are later edited and integrated in the final product to be published online.

The aforementioned characteristics of crowdsourced translation demonstrate that although crowdsourcing by definition involves a team, it may involve surprisingly little collaboration. Volunteer translators interact with the content, but their interaction with others is minimal.

Having said that, the concept of crowdsourcing-mediated translation projects can now be introduced. As the name indicates, in such projects, student translators will be encouraged to volunteer to join a translation crowdsourcing project and contribute their translations to it. However, as the project may involve little or no telecollaboration, the students will simultaneously join a purpose-created online communication platform (e.g. Slack), where they will be able to comment jointly on attention-worthy segments of their own and others' authorship. Consequently, they will involve in genuine telecollaboration, finalise translations jointly, comment on them or reflect on translation problems while working towards a genuine cause and developing social agency (Massey, 2023). The latter is possible, as crowdsourcing initiatives frequently originate from disadvantaged social groups or charitable, non-profit organisations working in support of important social causes.

A case in point – albeit with limited correspondence – is the Global Voices project, described by Hagemann (2016). The project was set up at FTSK in Germersheim, Germany, and consisted in students working in teams to translate website content for the Global Voices (https://global-voices.org) – an international non-profit foundation supporting a volunteer community of activists intent on promoting the voices of communities and people underrepresented in mainstream media. From Hagemann's (2016) description, it is unclear how exactly the translation team members worked (i.e. whether they collaborated on-site or online), but the project participants created an online forum where they could share content and exchange information in asynchronous mode. Occasionally, the team project managers also contacted a Global Voices editor to consult him or her on important translation-related issues.

The Global Voices project illustrates a step towards the administration of crowdsourcing-mediated projects, where teachers need to make provisions for telecollaboration, insisting that an online forum is to be used not only for content and information sharing but also for fully-fledged negotiations on translation problems, whereby the final versions of particular segments would be a synergy of the team members' contributions. Additionally, the client's editor(s) could also be invited to partake in the forum interactions, thus enriching the scope of telecollaboration and the students' learning experience at large. Within the proposed mode, crowdsourcing is not the mainframe for telecollaboration but rather the springboard for it. It provides a real-world context for the translation work while anchoring it within the client's specifications. At the same time, the addition of the communication platform will create opportunities for the commission to be delivered in a truly telecollaborative manner.

5.2　Assessment

5.2.1　*Areas of assessment*

Assessment is an inherent component of education, and even when the learning outcomes appear too implicit to measure (e.g. students' openness to novelty) or when assessment is likely to raise ethical questions (e.g. while assessing students' behaviour in intercultural communicative interactions), it is nevertheless undertaken. The tendency to estimate, measure and assess usually derives from the rigidity of formal institutional requirements, whereby teachers are obliged to produce tangible evidence of their instructional efficacy and the ensuing students' learning – often in the form of numerical scores or grades. However, it is also true that teachers themselves have a vested interest in administering various forms of assessment to obtain feedback on the applicability of the pedagogical solutions they use, as well as their learners' progress or achievement. Perhaps that is why, while referring to the intercultural competence, which is a challenge to assess, Byram (2000) made the claim that "If it isn't tested, it's not taught" (Byram, 2000, p. 8). Last but not least, it must be remembered that students themselves are also likely to share Byram's (2000) stance on assessment; hence, they will often insist on feedback regarding the teaching and learning process, as well as its outcomes.

As it will be demonstrated later, there are various forms of assessment which could potentially be used for assessment in telecollaboration-based instruction. However, to ensure that assessment works effectively and meets teachers' and students' expectations, the choice of its types must be based in congruence with the intended focus, depending on beliefs about the nature of (tele)collaboration per se. Thus, it is critically important that teachers decide whether they perceive collaboration as a means towards an end vs. a skill to be demonstrated – a distinction made by Child and Shaw (2018) – or perhaps, as both. As Child and Shaw (2018) explain, the historically dominant pedagogical tradition has been to regard collaboration as a means of achievement, such as knowledge/skill development, problem resolution or the creation of tangible products. As they note, this understanding of collaboration clearly reverberates with the (socio-)constructivist views of learning (Piaget, 1959; Vygotsky, 1978) (see Chapter 3). In the eyes of the former, collaboration challenged individual learners' cognitive schemas and led to knowledge reconstruction, while according to the latter, social interaction spawned knowledge negotiation and thus its social construction. The more recent tradition which Child and Shaw (2018) discuss involves understanding collaboration as a skill in itself, an observable and measurable asset listed among the skills prioritised for development within 21st-century education systems (National Education Association, 2016).

Telecollaboration-based instruction, orientated towards either of the two traditions, will be based on different sets of goals. While in the means-towards-an-end tradition, emphasis will be placed on outcomes generated through students' telecollaboration, within the skill-to-be-demonstrated tradition, the focus will be largely on the collaboration process itself. Thus, the former telecollaboration setup could be referred to as product oriented, while the latter could be deemed process oriented. As the very names imply, each of the setups will prioritise different areas of assessment. It is essential to elucidate that in product-oriented collaboration, the notion of product extends beyond the physical dimension to comprise not only what is immediately presentable (e.g. a jointly composed piece of writing – possibly a translation, multimedia presentation, podcast or website) but also less tangible, albeit observable and measurable, products of learning such as an increased understanding of a problem or newly acquired declarative or procedural knowledge.

Therefore, assessment in product-oriented collaboration will seek to establish what it is, on a physical or cognitive level, that has come to existence through collaborative work. Hence, Child and Shaw's (2018) conceptualisation of products as outcomes, which cover artefacts and the "'before' and 'after' of student knowledge and understanding" (Child & Shaw, 2018, p. 281). In telecollaboration skewed towards translator education, the physical outcomes to be assessed could be content translated through teamwork (e.g. written documents, localised websites or software), collaboratively compiled databases (e.g. translation memories, parallel corpora) or products demonstrating declarative TS knowledge (e.g. essays, terminology wikis or learning apps) – a very interesting example of the latter is an all-round Memrise-based (app.memrise.com) learning course on research methodology for Translation Studies, prepared by students of the Institute of English Studies, University of Warsaw, Poland, under the guidance of Piotr Szymczak, PhD (see https://app.memrise.com/course/1001236/research-methodology-for-translation-studies/).

The assessment of cognitive outcomes, mostly regarding components of translation competence, are delineated in numerous competence models, where they are grouped into the core competences, which are linguistic (communicative, bilingual) competence (EMT, 2009, 2017, 2022a; Fox, 2000; Göpferich, 2009; Kelly, 2005; Massey, 2023; PACTE, 2003), technological (instrumental) competence (EMT, 2009, 2017; Fox, 2000; Göpferich, 2009; Kelly, 2005; PACTE, 2003), (inter)cultural and socio-cultural competence (EMT, 2009, 2017; Fox, 2000; Göpferich, 2009;

Kelly, 2005; PACTE, 2003), domain (subject area) competence (EMT, 2009, 2017; Fox, 2000; Göpferich, 2009; Kelly, 2005; PACTE, 2003), methodological (strategic) competence (EMT, 2009, 2017; Fox, 2000; Göpferich, 2009; Kelly, 2005; PACTE, 2003) or service provision competence (EMT, 2022a).

In OIEs, models of intercultural (communicative) competence could be used to operationalise the knowledge, skills and attitudes to be assessed. One of the models which could be used for that purpose is Byram's (1997) intercultural communicative competence, which has gained international recognition (Liu, 2019) informing educational policies, course design, instructional materials and classroom practices worldwide. For instance, in Europe, it has been integrated into two seminal documents shaping teaching programmes and assessment procedures within the educational systems of the Council of Europe member states: the Common European Framework of Reference for Languages (CEFR) (CUP, 2001) and the Reference Framework of Competences for Democratic Culture (RFCDC) (CoE, 2018). Outside Europe, the model has been very influential in South and East Asia or the United States of America (Kramsch & Whiteside, 2015).

Byram's (1997) competences fall into two major areas, communicative competence and intercultural competence, which break down into numerous sub-competences. Communicative competence covers linguistic competence, sociolinguistic competence and discourse competence, while intercultural competence comprises attitudes, knowledge, skills of interpreting and relating, skills of discovery and interaction, as well as critical cultural awareness/political education. They are further delineated as savoirs:

- *savoir être* (including attitudes of curiosity and inquisitiveness);
- *savoirs* (knowledge of life in a certain society, for example, work, education or traditions);
- *savoir comprendre* (skills of interpreting and relating);
- *savoir apprendre/savoir faire* (skills of discovery and interaction); and
- and *savoir s'engage* (critical cultural awareness).

The model may be a useful tool for assessment in translator education for at least three reasons. Firstly, it has been successfully used for operationalising the competence in question for teaching and assessment purposes in various educational contexts. Secondly, although the model is very extensive, its descriptors are clear and have been thoroughly discussed in Byram (1997), which makes it amenable to adaptation. Thirdly, the model embraces mediation in intercultural communicative situations, which is particularly relevant to translator education, where students are prepared precisely for that.

Other models of intercultural competence which could also be potentially used for assessment purposes include those proposed by Jandt (2001), Kohonen, Jaantinen, Kaikkonen, and Lehtovaara (2001) or Risager (2007a). Each of these models has something to offer with regard to translator/interpreter education. For instance, all three could be useful for interpreter training, as they comprise, for example, nonverbal communicative competence and the ability to cope with stress while trying to communicate in an unknown cultural environment (Jandt, 2001), the ability to cope with new, atypical situations without embarrassment (Kohonen et al., 2001) and the use of paralinguistic devices and kinesics in effective intercultural communication (Risager, 2007b). Risager's (2007a) model builds on Byram's (1997) while additionally emphasising the interplay of language and culture in plurilingual, pluricultural contexts through references to languacultural components (e.g. languastructural competence), which is a lexically, syntactically and morphologically rich repertoire of means of expression based on one's first and other languages, and languacultural translation and interpretation, understood as linguistic skills enhanced by the ability to mediate meaning and communication in intercultural situations.

Elements of these intercultural (communicative) competence models will overlap, but they provide multiple assessment areas. However, the actual choices will need to be made on a fit-for-purpose basis, depending on specific educational goals – analogically to the manner in which, within the Skopos Theory (O'Brien, 2012; Reiss, Vermeer, Nord, & Dudenhöfer, 2015), translations are judged with regard to how they meet their purpose.

Product-oriented assessment could also embrace more generic, domain-independent sub-competences, which equip students for life. Some are part of translator/translation competence models, for example, (inter)personal competence (EMT, 2022a; Kelly, 2005), metacognitive (learning how to learn) competence (Fox, 2000), problem-solving competence or competences relating to the psycho-physiological and attitudinal dispositions of a translator (Kelly, 2005; PACTE, 2003). Others – potentially complementary to those listed earlier – can be found in dedicated inventories, such as the tertiary-education-oriented list documented within the TUNING project (González & Wagenaar, 2008), the *Framework for 21st Century Learning*, issued by Partnership for 21st Century Skills to prepare learners "to thrive in today's digitally and globally interconnected world" (P21, 2016, p. 1), or the *Global Framework on Transferable Skills*, proposed by UNICEF (2019).

Although competences provided in the aforementioned documents partially overlap with those from translator/translation competence models, some are completely new. For instance, the TUNING project (González & Wagenaar, 2008) inventory contains cognitive abilities regarding the manipulation of ideas and thoughts (instrumental competences), ethical commitment (interpersonal competences) or leadership and concern for quality (systemic competences), while UNICEF's (2019) framework features perseverance (learning), influencing (employability), refusal skills (personal empowerment) and collaborative thinking (active citizenship).

Interestingly, process- and product-focused assessment of collaboration may apply to the same competences. For instance, although at first sight, some competences, such as interpersonal skills, teamwork skills or project design management skills, could appear as typically processual, thus worthy of assessment in collaboration-as-process educational contexts, Child and Shaw's (2018) perception of product as the before-and-after state of affairs also justifies the measurement of these competences as products of learning. If the perceptible level of these competences is measured before and after telecollaboration, an increase will represent the product of telecollaboration, provided that other intervening variables are carefully controlled. This demonstrates that the apparent product vs. process dichotomy is more of a continuum permitting assessors – be they teachers or students – to take arbitrary decisions on what and how to assess.

The discussion earlier mostly focused on product-oriented collaboration, or collaboration as outcome. Therefore, it is time now to have a closer look at assessment in process-oriented collaboration, which in lieu of products will concentrate on possibly observable or measurable aspects of social interaction involved in telecollaborative tasks. On purpose, this interaction has not been specified here as student-student because telecollaborative learning is highly likely to involve numerous third parties, including the client, translation or domain experts, translation technology support team members, editors, external project coordinators and the teacher.

In their framework for the assessment of collaborative interactions, Child and Shaw (2018) propose that process-oriented collaboration – or collaboration as process, as they call it – needs to be assessed with regard to its socio-cognitive aspects and actions indicative of attempts to maintain the state of collaboration. Socio-cognitive dimensions of collaboration involve the building of new meaning through dialogue and interaction; thus, they will be assessed with regard to students' actions, such as resource sharing, introducing new ideas or resolving conflicts. The maintenance of the state of collaboration is a concept developed by Brna (1998), who claims that collaboration is a state characterised by the participants' mutual agreement to collaborate, shared goals, a shared understanding of the problem in question and common vision, which needs to be maintained until the objectives of collaboration are met. Consequently, the assessment of this dimension involves evidencing social interdependence, communication and cooperation. In Child and Shaw's (2018) view, social interdependence means as state of mutual reliance where collaboration partners feel simultaneously compelled and motivated to work together. Communication denotes exchanges facilitating the clarification of viewpoints or explicitation of implicit ideas, which contribute to learning and task completion. Finally, cooperation signifies job sharing (i.e. delegating specific sub-tasks to individuals for them to take part of the workload), but it is critical that it constitutes only a stage of the collaborative project and is accompanied by consolidation and debate.

Although Child and Shaw's (2018) propositions of assessment areas formally concern collaboration, they also seem to implicitly extend to telecollaboration, with the authors acknowledging the existence of computer-supported collaborative learning (CSCL), which – as discussed by Stahl, Koschmann, and Suthers (2006) – involves computer and Web 2.0 technologies to enhance the collaboration of "individual learners [located] in different buildings or even different countries" (Stahl, Koschmann, & Suthers, 2014, p. 479), as well as content generation and assessment.

Kiraly et al.'s (2019) discussion of a team translation project illustrates how both product- and process-oriented assessment can indeed be implemented to judge student performance in telecollaboration. In the aforementioned project, student translators had their products (translations) assessed by means of a timeliness – completeness – quality (TCQ) assessment scheme featuring custom-developed criteria. However, student PMs' work was assessed as the management process, which was operationalised through a skill set, comprising communication, assumption of responsibility, effective teamwork and planning/scheduling, and evidenced by records of performance collected from Slack – the project communication platform.

Due to the adaptability of (tele)collaboration and the ensuing multitude of instructional scenarios motivated by various educational goals, it would be difficult to propose an all-purpose-all-context framework for product- and process-oriented assessment areas. Therefore, the details, including product assessment criteria and clear-cut operationalisations of the assessed process elements, will always need to be established in response to specific circumstances.

5.2.2   *Assessment modes*

What follows is an overview of modes suitable for assessing telecollaboration from the two perspectives delineated earlier (collaboration as outcome and collaboration as process) regarding the assessor and purpose of assessment.

Teacher assessment – or teacher-based assessment, as Eskelinen and Pakkala-Weckström (2016) name it – is the most traditional and has long prevailed in FL and translator education as a reflection of the positivist, reductionist epistemological perspective, which initially dominated both fields. As it was discussed in Chapter 3, in FL education, the mode supported the teacher's pursuit of accuracy in TL performance, which students were supposed to attain deducing linguistic rules (e.g. in Grammar-Translation Method) (Larsen-Freeman & Anderson, 2018; Richards & Rodgers, 2014) or intensively repeating language models (e.g. in the Audiolingual Method) (Larsen-Freeman & Anderson, 2018; Richards & Rodgers, 2014).

In translator education, positivist epistemology materialised in folk pedagogy (Kiraly & Hofmann, 2016), where teacher-centred instruction involved accuracy-focused work involving teacher assessment of students' translations. This assessment mode is so deeply inculcated that, when discussing how to measure the acquisition of translation competence, Orozco refers to it as "normal assessment" (Orozco, 2000, p. 208). She also exemplifies this assessment mode, citing a system proposed by Hurtado Albir (1995), where a student-translated text is initially allocated 20 points, to which the teacher subsequently adds a point for each correct translation solution or subtracts points for translation errors – one for a minor error and two for each major error.

Translation teachers will certainly recognise this assessment system and could offer their own modifications of it (e.g. based on predetermined error categories derived from professional translation quality metrics), such as SAE J2450 or LISA QA. The former was originally developed for quality assurance in translations of automotive service information, but over time, its use has extended to translations outside the original domain (Sirena, 2004). Similarly, the latter, which was originally designed by the Localization Industry Standards Association (LISA) to foster the quality of translation and localisation services, continues to be widely used, despite the formal discontinuation of its development in 2011 (Görög, 2017). Both metrics involve inventories of error types which could guide the construction of assessment criteria and scoring scales in translator education. SAE J2450 contains a list of language errors classified as wrong term, syntactic error, omission, word structure or agreement error, misspelling, punctuation error and miscellaneous, while LISA QA, which additionally covers errors in documentation and software formatting, lists language-related errors categorised as mistranslation, terminology, language, style and consistency.

Teacher assessment is typically product-oriented, hence, the discussion of criteria that can potentially be used in translation quality assessment, but any other instances of assessment involving pre-set, operationalised and scaled learning outcomes, such as elements of translation or intercultural competence, would lend themselves to this format.

A possible supplementation to teacher assessment could be assessment administered by a third party (*third-party assessment*) (e.g. the client for whom a telecollaborative translation project has been delivered, the client's domain editor or a translation/terminology expert). Kelly (2005) briefly discussed this possibility, and although she underlined that translation industry representatives might tend to issue overly strict verdicts on the quality of students' work, she admitted that this kind of assessment might benefit students familiarising them with professional assessment standards and the inevitable discrepancies between assessment criteria used in professional and academic settings.

Self-assessment consists in students assessing their own performance or learning outcomes; thus, it is part of a postpositivist perspective on education and learner roles. In Eskelinen and Pakkala-Weckström's (2016) view, this assessment mode has two major aims: one is to develop students' professional awareness, which helps them "to relate to the demands of professional work" (Eskelinen & Pakkala-Weckström, 2016, p. 324), while the other is to further their metacognitive competence, thanks to which they can build a better understanding of the learning process and have an opportunity to self-direct it. Iglesias Pérez, Vidal-Puga, and Pino Juste (2020) also add that it develops "critical skills in students, such as taking responsibility for their learning, . . . a better understanding of the subject's content, evaluation criteria and their values and judgments, . . . [as well as] critical reflection skills" (Iglesias Pérez et al., 2020, p. 2).

At the same time, Eskelinen and Pakkala-Weckström (2016) indicate that the reliability of self-assessment may be problematic due to its impressionistic nature, which in all likelihood affects its objectivity. A possible response to that argument, however, may be Nunan's (2004) observation that "While self-assessment has been criticized on the grounds that not all learners are accurate judges of their own ability, this criticism misses the point to some extent, which is to involve learners in their own learning processes" (Nunan, 2004, p. 149). In other words, rather than aiming at accuracy of assessment – which in positivist education is warranted by the teacher's status as classroom authority – self-assessment promotes learner empowerment. Consequently, its merit lies not in what exactly students establish about their learning success but in the sheer fact that they reflect on the cognitive (knowledge), performative (behaviour) or attitudinal (motivation, curiosity, openness to novelty) goals of their learning *vis-à-vis* their self-perceived level of attainment.

Self-assessment can be enhanced by self-reporting instruments, including checklists (Nunan, 2004), translation commentaries (Massey & Ehrensberger-Dow, 2014) or portfolios (Eskelinen & Pakkala-Weckström, 2016; Rico, 2017). Checklists can be defined as lists of can-do statements permitting learners to ascertain what they have already learnt or still need to learn. To illustrate the concept, Nunan (2004) cites a matrix of questions proposed by Cram (1995), which can be used to construct self-assessment checklists in FL education. The original matrix contained gains listed by level of achievement, including proficiency (overall gains), practice (functional gains), theory/structural gains (gains in knowledge and understanding) and affective gains (gains in motivation and confidence), which were delineated across four areas of achievement: general linguistic, sociocultural, vocational/academic and those relating to learning for life.

Table 5.3 contains a possible adaptation of that matrix for self-assessment to be used by students participating in a telecollaborative translation project. In the adapted version, the original achievement levels have

Table 5.3 A sample self-assessment checklist

Levels of achievement	Areas of achievement			
	General translation	Intercultural competence	Vocational/ Academic	Learning for life
Proficiency (overall gains)	Have I reached a higher level of proficiency in general and specialised translation?	Do I make a better intercultural mediator?	Am I able to cope better in TS and translation?	Am I a more self-reflective learner?
Practice (functional gains)	Can I co-edit a shared term base in a cloud-based CAT tool?	Do I know how to negotiate difference in intercultural communicative situations?	Can I do quality management in translation projects?	Have I improved my interpersonal skills, teamwork skills?
Theory/ structural (gains in knowledge, understanding)	Have I increased my knowledge of ISO standards for translation projects?	Have I increased my knowledge of the British legal system?	Have I increased my knowledge of current trends in the translation market?	Have I increased my knowledge of techniques in participant observation?
Affective (gains in motivation, confidence)	Am I more confident when translating?	Am I curious to learn about other cultures and explore otherness?	Am I confident that I can successfully enter the translation market?	Am I more motivated to continue learning after the course?

been retained, while the four areas of achievement have been slightly modified to reflect the nature of the learning in question, thus they now include translation competence at large, intercultural competence, vocational/academic development and gains relating to learning for life.

The questions proposed for each of the levels and areas of achievement are only to illustrate what students could potentially work on in a telecollaboration project aimed to develop translation competence, intercultural competence, vocational competence and competence relevant to lifelong learning, but dozens of alternative questions could easily be offered. As Table 5.3 shows, by answering this particular set of questions, students could self-assess their translation competence regarding the general level of proficiency in (non-)specialised translation, procedural knowledge relating to the use of CAT tools, theoretical knowledge of professional standards for translation projects and confidence in performing translation tasks.

As far as students' intercultural competence goes, students could self-assess their overall proficiency as intercultural mediators, procedural knowledge relating to the negotiation of intercultural differences in communicative situations, theoretical knowledge of the British legal system, as a typical element of national cultural studies which may augment intercultural communicative competence, curiosity about other cultures and readiness to explore otherness, which underlies successful intercultural learning (Byram, 1997). In terms of vocational development, students could self-assess their ability to successfully cope with the academic study of various TS areas and translation *per se*, practical knowledge of quality management in translation projects, declarative knowledge of the current trends in the translation market and confidence in dealing with the challenges which students can face when they graduate and enter the translation market to seek employment.

Finally, with regard to lifelong learning, students could self-assess their ability perform self-reflection as a permanent element of lifelong development, the practical knowledge of how to use interpersonal and teamwork skills, which are essential for (tele)collaboration, declarative knowledge of techniques in participant observation, which they could use for learning based on virtual ethnography (i.e. the observation of selected aspects of life by webcams) and the level of motivation to actively seek self-learning opportunities (e.g. through CPD formats, such as training sessions, workshops or webinars). As it has been stated, the previously cited sample questions have an illustrative function, but they can be modified at will to foster self-assessment in a concrete learning context.

Self-assessment could also be promoted by translation commentaries, with which students append their translations. As Eskelinen and Pakkala-Weckström (2016) explain, commentaries consist in students "discussing the challenges they have met during the translation process, along with successful outcomes and providing a summary of their information mining process" (Eskelinen & Pakkala-Weckström, 2016, p. 322). Commentaries could be used for specific translation tasks, or they could be written on a more regular basis over a longer period of time. In the latter case, they would involve student in "continuous self-assessment" (Eskelinen & Pakkala-Weckström, 2016, p. 322), which would focus students' attention not only on attainment in translation but also the learning process. In other words, it would simultaneously promote cognitive and metacognitive development.

Commentaries could be delivered in an open format (i.e. without specific guidelines on their structure), which Eskelinen and Pakkala-Weckström (2016) view as advantageous in that it permits students to experiment with various formats and ultimately decide on the one they find most useful. Alternatively, commentaries could be structured through guiding questions which could streamline students' reflections, as illustrated by Kelly (2005):

- What particular difficulties have you come up against in doing this translation?
- How have you gone about solving them?
- Are you satisfied with the solutions you have found?
- If not, what else could you have done (and what has prevented you from doing so)?

(Kelly, 2005, p. 143)

Kelly (2005) provides these questions to support self-assessment performed through short oral or written questionnaires or scripts, but they can easily be used to stimulate reflection in students' commentaries. It might even be said that the propositions of Kelly (2005) will nevertheless result in students producing commentaries, be it in oral or written form; thus, the questionnaires or scripts which she mentions appear to be forms of elicitation rather than separate formats of self-assessment.

As an aside, it must be underlined that commentaries as such are not inherently bound to self-assessment and student empowerment. McAlester's (2000) concept of their implementation demonstrates that they might equally be used within the framework of teacher-centred transmissionist pedagogy, as he proposed that students' translations be submitted with commentaries, where the choice of translation solutions would be explained in relation to the aims set by the student translators themselves. However, in his mind, the appropriateness of the aims and the adequacy of the solutions would subsequently be unilaterally assessed by the teacher acting as the ultimate judge.

One more format of self-assessment could be the portfolio, which Kelly (2005) defines as "A form of assessment whereby the student or learner submits a collection of items of evidence of learning. Originally developed in Fine Arts and similar fields, it is now relatively frequent in other disciplines" (Kelly, 2005, p. 159). It is a collection of materials which showcase students' best work (Rico, 2017) while also documenting their individual perspective on their own learning process and attainment in the light of the intended learning goals (Kelly, 2005). The merit of the (e-)portfolio lies in the fact that through it "a far-reaching degree of self-examination is carried out by students with regard to what exactly it is that they are learning and how" (Rico, 2017, p. 83). Consequently, it constitutes yet another powerful instrument with which to stimulate students' metacognitive development.

Kelly (2005) recommends that the format is first explicitly introduced to students, or even negotiated with them, and observes that the very discussion on the details (e.g. materials to be included in the portfolio or evidence of learning) is in itself an interesting activity which is likely to result in students' innovative contributions. In the case of Web-based learning, including telecollaboration, students can also prepare an electronic portfolio, or e-portfolio, as Rico (2017) refers to it. Portfolios may be structured depending on educational needs and goals, but in general, Kelly (2005) suggests that it needs to include an introduction featuring the objectives behind it, the materials which students decide to showcase, a brief explanation of the value of each item with a justification for its inclusion and an overall self-assessment statement. The range of content is potentially great, and according to Kelly (2005), it may include the following:

- translations;
- translation commentaries;
- glossaries with comment;
- students' translations assessed by experts; and
- small-scale market research results.

However, Rico (2017) also provides other content types particularly amenable to an e-portfolio:

- critical evaluations or comparisons of translation software;
- conceptual maps on syllabus-related topics;
- book reviews;
- social media threads on translation technologies;
- students' posts in classroom blogs; and
- multimedia presentations.

Although it is hard to predict what exactly a telecollaboration project for translation students will entail, materials for inclusion in a project-related (e-)portfolio could comprise the following:

- commentaries on in-project communication;
- comparisons of communication tools;
- reflections on project management;
- reflections on team-client communication;
- analysis of reference sources used in the project;
- SWOT analyses of the project work; and
- reflections on cognitive, attitudinal and metacognitive learning gains.

The merits of e-portfolio have been recognised by translator educators. Rico (2017) observes that the e-portfolio – alike its conventional counterpart, one might say – is a tool which fosters learner-centred education and learner autonomy, as it turns the teacher into a facilitator of the learning process, who promotes interactive knowledge construction while relinquishing responsibility for (evidencing) students' attainment. Most recently, Massey (2023) has underlined role of e-portfolio in stimulating constructive situated assessment which could foster the development of transferable skills, although he sees it as a cross-mode format, where content could be validated by peers (peer assessment), coaches or translation users (third-party assessment).

Peer assessment is an intermediate format between the other two formats discussed earlier (i.e. teacher assessment and self-assessment). That is why Kelly (2005), who defines it as "Assessment by fellow learners (peers)" (Kelly, 2005, p. 160), believes that it should be implemented as an introduction to self-assessment. It is often claimed that peer assessment is psychologically more acceptable, less obtrusive to students than teacher assessment; that is why it was used in language teaching methods based on the tenets of the Humanistic Approach (Larsen-Freeman & Anderson, 2018; Vygotsky, 1978). It also epitomises Vygotsky's (1978) concept of socio-constructivist learning, where learners benefit from scaffolding (Wood, Bruner, & Ross, 1976) and feedback provided by their colleagues. Through peer-to-peer interaction, more knowledgeable peers can gauge the learning process of novices, whereby creating the Zone of Proximal Development. Consequently, as Iglesias Pérez et al. (2020) observe, learners become responsible not only for their own learning but also that of others.

While discussing programme evaluation to be performed by teachers in less formalised contexts, Kelly (2005) also mentions peer assessment as a valuable option, and although she refers to teachers, her remarks also apply to peer assessment performed by students. In her mind, a peer assessor is a "critical friend" (Kelly, 2005, p. 147) who observes a colleague's classes and informally discusses areas for potential modification and improvement, thus gently preparing a peer for more formal assessment administered by a third party (e.g. a superior or a committee). Analogically, in student-performed peer assessment, students can mutually act as critical friends discussing, for example, the quality of each other's products (translations) or processes (in-project work) before assessment is provided by the teacher or an external party (e.g. the client for whom a telecollaborative translation project has been delivered).

Peer assessment may function as a gentle way in which to usher students into the world of professional practices through work in a friendly, facilitative environment. However, proper conditions must first be created, with emotional aspects of peer assessment taken into account, to counteract the side effects of this assessment mode, which – as Iglesias Pérez et al. (2020) and González de Sande and Godino-Llorente (2014) observe – can manifest in peer pressure, favouritism or the fear of disapproval. A solution to the problem could be anonymous peer assessment, which numerous scholars (Iglesias Pérez et al., 2020; Panadero & Alqassab, 2019) link to increased constructivity of peer-provided feedback, higher levels of comfort and ensuing motivation towards peer assessment. Interestingly, Iglesias Pérez et al. (2020) posit that the use of learning technologies permitting telecollaboration, such as Moodle, is likely to augment anonymity in peer assessment if appropriate tools are selected. In their research, they used the Workshop functionality of the platform (Moodle, 2021), which allows criteria-referenced peer assessment with the anonymisation of feedback sources.

The three assessment modes discussed earlier are not mutually exclusive. Depending on the characteristics of an educational setting, including teacher and learner needs, instructional goals and specific circumstances, such as time constraints, the modes can be selected for sequential or hybrid implementation to ensure optimal efficacy. Both implementation types may be facilitated by telecollaborative learning tools, such as the aforementioned Workshop on Moodle, where peer assessment may be performed on a stand-alone basis or triangulated through the provision of colleague- and teacher-provided feedback, thus creating opportunities for increased reflection and greater student involvement.

Table 5.4 summarises the aforementioned assessment modes by outlining their major characteristics and telecollaboration-related affordances. As it has been demonstrated previously, each of the assessment modes is justifiable and potentially beneficial. However, as research (González de Sande & Godino-Llorente, 2014; Iglesias Pérez et al., 2020) into their effectiveness in higher education indicates, they seem to constitute a peculiar hierarchy which ranks them from the most effective (peer assessment)

Table 5.4 Assessment modes and their affordances for telecollaborative learning

Features/Modes	Teacher assessment	Third-party assessment	Self-assessment	Peer assessment
Assessor	Course tutor	Client, domain editor, domain expert, external PM	Student himself/herself	Colleague
Possible implementations	Translation evaluation, possibly based on quality metrics	Evaluation or commentary on translation quality (e.g. language or terminological consistency)	Structured (self-check lists, questionnaires, guided translation commentaries, guided [e-]portfolio or unstructured, open translation commentaries or open [e-]portfolio)	Identified or anonymous peer assessment, written (possibly enhanced by Web-based learning tools, for example, VLEs such as Moodle, or oral, for example, discussions of peers' errors)
General advantages	Good for product-oriented assessment, legitimised by dint of teacher's authority	Usually product-oriented, feedback provided by stakeholders in the translation process or translation market representatives, illustrative of professional practices and evaluation criteria	Provides insight into TC as process, fosters students' responsibility for own learning, sense of self-directedness and metacognitive awareness, reduces stress levels	Provides insight into TC as process, fosters students' metacognitive awareness, peer support, responsibility for colleagues' learning, cooperation, collaborative learning and reduces stress levels

General drawbacks	Likely to be obtrusive, stress generating, makes learners teacher dependent	Likely to be obtrusive, stress generating, less pedagogical in nature, overly skewed towards professional assessment practices and standards	May require initial preparation, may be overly positive in absence of self-criticism	May require initial preparation, likely to involve peer pressure, favouritism and fear of disapproval if not performed in a constructive and supportive manner or if not anonymous
Affordances for telecollaboration	Likely to accelerate the learning of declarative background knowledge to leave more time for TC, may guide or complement self- and peer assessment	Professionalises TC, involves market representatives into the project experience, hence, potentially motivating	Likely to facilitate individual pre-TC (preparation stage) or post-TC work (reflection on experience or learning gains)	Potentially conducive to close collaboration and social learning; particularly fit for electronic formats when anonymous

through the less effective (self-assessment) to the least effective (teacher assessment).

5.2.3 *Purposes of assessment*

Assessment can be administered for various purposes (e.g. to diagnose the level of learners' knowledge or skills prior to a course), whereby establishing the point of departure (diagnostic assessment), to measure overall learner achievement at the end of a course (summative assessment) or to provide feedback to facilitate further learning (formative assessment). The latter two will be discussed in greater detail with a view to establishing their relevance for telecollaboration-based instruction.

Kelly (2005) defines summative assessment as "Any assessment activity designed to award grades, permit progression to a higher level, or award a diploma" (Kelly, 2005, p. 161), through which she depicts its three critical characteristics. Firstly, summative assessment usually involves grading, that is, generating a symbol (a numerical value or letter) which reflects the level of one's learning attainment in cognitive (declarative and procedural knowledge), behavioural (skills manifested through performance) or attitudinal (awareness) areas. Secondly, this kind of assessment is conventionally used at the end of one stage of the learning process, before progression to another (the end of a course, semester, academic year or graduation). Thirdly, it may relate to the issuance of a document, such as a certificate, diploma or accreditation, confirming a person's educational attainment and granting them formal qualifications.

By contrast, formative assessment is "Any assessment activity designed to give learners feedback on their progress and thus enhance learning" (Kelly, 2005, p. 158). In congruence with that, Wanner and Palmer (2018) rightly observe while summative assessment, which is outcome oriented, could be perceived as assessment *of learning*, formative assessment, which focuses on progress and aims to ameliorate the on-going learning progress, is assessment *for learning*. This seemingly subtle distinction has important repercussions for how assessment is administered. While summative assessment commonly involves the computation of grades – frequently in high-stakes contexts such as final examinations – formative assessment is founded on the provision of feedback. After all, students may expect to have their work graded so that they know how successfully they have been learning, but what they principally need is guidance on how to achieve the set learning outcomes. In the light of that, it is perfectly natural that "The lack of quality and timely feedback for their work is highlighted time and again in student satisfaction surveys" (Wanner & Palmer, 2018, p. 1035), as in the absence of feedback, students will find it difficult "to evaluate their own progress and improve on previous performance"

(González & Wagenaar, 2008, p. 147), which is what formative assessment is intended for. Consequently, it could be stated that formative assessment must be provided on a continuous rather than intermittent basis, as, if progress is to be made, the learning process needs to be systematically monitored.

Bold and Hutton (2007) have offered the following list of formative assessment activities for classes focused on the development of writing skills:

- **Reading and reflection activities.**
- **Tutors' modelling writing and referencing skills.**
- **Focused writing tasks, e.g. to reflect on and refer to a set reading.**
- **Paired sharing and evaluating writing.**
- **Tutor-led editing activities.**

(Bold & Hutton, 2007, p. 23, emphasis original)

However, their list may be easily adapted to exemplify activity types applicable to translator education contexts, as presented next:

- reading and reflection activities;
- tutor-led modelling;
- focused tasks (e.g. to target translation errors or strategies);
- paired translation sharing and evaluation; and
- tutor-led revision/reviewing activities.

Although both lists are hardly exhaustive and could be expanded to also contain other activities (e.g. in-class discussions, surveys or weekly quizzes), they suffice to demonstrate that formative assessment can be used in different modes, including teacher, peer and self-assessment. Interestingly, it is also true of its summative counterpart, which – although traditionally teacher centred – need not be the teacher's exclusive domain and might also involve learners. Deeley (2014) has reported that both summative and formative self-assessment are likely to be rather challenging to students, even those who have practised self-assessment beforehand. Her research findings indicate that while some students may be excessively modest and underrate their own while assessing their own learning attainment, others may feel confused about how self-assessment should be administered. Rather than discrediting the concept of self-assessment, the findings seem to indicate that at large, it will require educating students about how to establish clear-cut, objectivised assessment criteria (metacognitive knowledge and awareness) and how to use them in practice (metacognitive skills). Perhaps another step which could be taken to ease self-assessment would be to ask students to summatively or formatively assess one another so that they can negotiate uncertainties relating to the results – grades in summative assessment and conclusions in formative assessment – as well as the choice and implementation of specific assessment criteria.

An alternative solution, which might be a transition stage between teacher and student assessment is what Deeley (2014) refers to as summative/formative co-assessment, where a student assesses their learning process or outcomes together with the teacher. As Deeley (2014) maintains, co-assessment fosters a student's self-assessment skills through teacher feedback on the quality of his or her work and assessment of self. Her claim finds corroboration in her findings, which revealed that in students' view (e.g. summative co-assessment seems to be a fairer solution than summative self-assessment, as the former involves additional grade validation and the provision of complementary feedback by the teacher). In addition, some of the students examined by Deeley (2014) reportedly perceived co-assessment as an opportunity to develop various transferable skills or – quite interestingly – as a vital employability skill in itself, which is particularly pertinent to telecollaborative learning, which frequently targets transferable skills.

In conclusion, it could be said that the co-operative and collaborative modes of assessment discussed earlier, be they summative or formative, seem to represent a hierarchy of difficulty, with teacher-student co-assessment at the top as the relatively easy mode, through student-student co-assessment (or peer assessment) in the intermediate position, to self-assessment, which is apparently the most challenging format. Table 5.5 summarises the modes regarding the parties involved, major characteristics, advantages, possible challenges and telecollaboration-related affordances.

Particularly pertinent to the use of summative and formative assessment in telecollaborative learning is Bold and Hutton's (2007) perception of online learning as a format enhancing the provision of both types of assessment through Web-based learning tools. For instance, they observe that a virtual learning environment (VLE) such as Moodle (see Chapter 3) not only keeps an orderly record of students' submissions and sends out automated notifications of receipt to students and teachers but also permits the time-effective provision of personalised electronic feedback, including comments with which submissions may be appended.

With that in mind, several affordances of online summative and formative assessment can be distinguished. In the case of the former, they are the following:

- ease of content transfer (instantaneousness of task submission and feedback or a shorter delay in the provision of the latter);
- orderly documentation of assessment tasks (metadata, including submission dates, authorship and versioning);

Table 5.5 An overview of summative/formative assessment across different modes

	Teacher assessment	Co-assessment (S-T)	Co-assessment (S-S)	Self-assessment
Parties involved / *Characteristics*	Course tutor. Tutor alone assesses students' work or learning outcomes, provides final grade and feedback; students are recipients only	Student and course tutor. Student and tutor are co-assessors, negotiate final grade and jointly agree on feedback	Student colleagues. Student colleagues are co-assessors, negotiate final grade and jointly agree on feedback	Student alone. Student as sole assessor of self, comes up with final grade and self-addressed feedback
Major advantages	Student's recognition of final grade and feedback, which are authorised by teacher's expertise	Student's increased confidence in final grade and feedback due to teacher's validation of both	Student's increased sense of partnership due to students' equal status, increased confidence in final grade and feedback due to colleague's validation of both	Increased responsibility for own learning and self-directedness and independence
Challenges	Lack of triangulation, possible subjectivity of assessment, lack of opportunities for the development of metacognitive competence	Limited sense of partnership due to potentially intimidating influence of tutor as authority	Lack of validation by an authorised person	Higher risk of subjectivity, potential over- or underrating of outcomes, lack of confidence in final grade or validity of reflection
Affordances for telecollaboration	Acceleration of formal learning in preparatory stages, opportunity for students to learn from a third party (if administered by client or expert)	Development of student's metacognitive competence and employability skills	Potential mutual development of students' metacognitive competence and employability skills	Potential mutual development of own metacognitive competence, lifelong learning and other employability skills

- automated content management (storage and sharing, automated feedback for close-ended tasks); and
- enhanced archiving (easy access to a record of student-generated content, including in-project communication and peer or teacher feedback).

What comes to the fore as the primary affordance of online summative assessment is the possibility of archiving student-generated content (e.g. presentations, infographics, translations, commentaries, logs or portfolios), which can subsequently be analysed for evidence of cognitive, meta-cognitive, procedural or attitudinal learning outcomes.

The affordances of online formative assessment (e.g. administered through a VLE with a capacity for content archiving) are more progress oriented; thus, they are likely to comprise the following:

- identification of evidence of student involvement in records of in-project communication or indirectly also in products (e.g. presentations, translations or commentaries);
- observation of self-learning through records of information searching and reflection on experience; and
- tracking peer support in records of in-project communication, information sharing or instances of peer teaching.

On a final note, it must be underlined that the two purposes of assessment which are being discussed are not bipolar extremities but rather both ends of a continuum. Although Deeley (2014) states that "it is good practice to use both formative and summative assessment methods" (Deeley, 2014, p. 40), thus implying sequential implementation of the two methods, evidence can be found that they actually tend to overlap at times. For example, the definition of summative assessment – alike its very name – implies a sense of finality and the intention to recapitulate the extent to which the learner has achieved the expected learning outcomes; thus, it often takes the form of a final test or examination. However, Kelly (2005) observes that summative assessment may also involve forms of continuous assessment, whereby learners will be assessed cyclically, at various time intervals, to receive grades which will finally be accumulated to produce the final, end-of-course grade. On the one hand, continuous assessment involves the issuance of a grade, which is typical of summative assessment, but at the same time, each of the series of grades that learners continuously receive may be perceived as formative feedback, whose goal is to improve the quality of the learning process before another graded task is set.

By the same token, González and Wagenaar (2008) demonstrate that even typically achievement-focused evaluation methods, such as written, oral and practical tests or examinations, can perform both summative and formative functions. On the one hand, they help instructors measure learning outcomes, which is a summation of learning attainment, while on the other hand, they can help learners reflect on the learning process and plan for improvement, which constitutes formative assessment.

Apparently, the line between summative and formative assessment does not separate different tasks which are inherently suitable either purpose by design, but rather, it runs between two different perspectives from which assessment tasks and their end products (grades or feedback) can be approached. The clarity of the seeming divide depends on efforts made to keep the two perspectives apart. After all, grades may be viewed as the conclusion of learning, a means of diagnosis or indicators of progress in the same way as feedback may be taken for a verbal mode of grading or simply informative guidance towards improved learning.

5.3 Issues in project design: Cooperation/collaboration, online/ offline work, pedagogical functions, authenticity

Telecollaboration must not be implemented *ad hoc*, as it may produce outcomes substantially different from those intended. Consequently, instructors planning for telecollaboration need to consider several issues in project design, each with a potential impact on its nature and quality. Some of those issues, including the ratio of *cooperation* vs. *collaboration*, *online* vs. *offline learning* or *authentic* vs. *simulated work*, will be discussed next to illustrate the design choices which need to be made.

Cooperation vs. collaboration. A fundamental issue in telecollaboration is to what extent it involves cooperative and/or collaborative learning. Although at first sight, the question may seem tautological in nature, as the very term *telecollaboration* clearly denotes what kind of learning is inevitable, in reality, the answer is far less obvious and requires deliberation.

Cooperation and collaboration appear to be near synonyms and in certain contexts may even be used interchangeably. Yet on closer inspection, they denote two different kinds of learning. Hodge (2010) defines cooperative learning as an approach to teaching whereby groups/teams of mixed-ability students complete learning activities with a view to increasing their understanding of skills, tasks, strategies or content. He emphasises that learners who cooperate take responsibility for their own and colleagues' learning outcomes until all the students have successfully completed the tasks they have been assigned.

Panitz (1999) perceives cooperation as a practical teaching solution involving group work whose goal is to facilitate task completion, be it the creation of an end product or the attainment of a different goal. He associates cooperative learning with the development of what Bruffee (1995) refers to as foundational knowledge (i.e. a set of socially accepted beliefs which can be close-ended in nature, factual and approached as basics to be internalised through instruction provided by an unquestionable authority). In other words, although cooperative learning involves (sub-)tasks delegated to individual learners and work towards the accomplishment of a final goal, it tends to be teacher centred and teacher controlled, which brings it closer to the positivist perspective on education.

By contrast, Panitz (1999) maintains that collaborative learning "is a philosophy of interaction and personal lifestyle" (Panitz, 1999, p. 1), fostering the accomplishment of a shared goal through group work, which entails not only individuals' acceptance of responsibility for their share of the workload but also the sharing of authority. It is through the negotiation of authority within the group but also respect for group members and their contributions to the joint work at hand that collaboration is democratic and student centred. In addition, collaboration is linked to non-foundational knowledge, derived from the questioning of foundational knowledge and the very process of knowledge development.

An interesting reflection on the nature of knowledge which cooperative and collaborative learning are likely to promote in translator education comes from Kiraly et al. (2019), who maintain that cooperative learning can at best result in complicated knowledge, which – although intricate – resembles a multi-componential mechanism reducible enough for a competent technician to dis- and reassemble it at will. By contrast, they claim that collaborative learning, due to its open nature, fosters the development of complex knowledge, which is emergent, dynamic, unpredictable and unreducible due to its multi-componentiality and embeddedness in other complex systems.

Panitz (1999) cites the key features of collaboration, which could be summarised as follows:

1   increased understanding which derives from students' joint work and spoken/written interaction;
2   development of students' awareness of the link between social interactions and increased understanding;
3   idiosyncratic and unpredictable nature of the collaboration-induced understanding; and
4   voluntary participation.

If the generic characteristics of telecollaboration in translator education were to be extrapolated from previously cited features, they would be formulated as follows:

1   high-intensity computer-mediated multimodal students' interaction with multiple parties, including colleagues, translation professionals, domain experts or clients;

2   reflection on experience regarding in-project interactions, goal attainment and varied learning outcomes;
3   open-ended, unpredictable, dynamic or emergent learning outcomes, including understanding, awareness, declarative/procedural knowledge, skills and attitudes; and
4   active involvement due to increased motivation.

The first characteristic has been modified to emphasise the use of online communication tools through which interactions can be facilitated and the multimodality and nonverbal nature of those interactions, which computer technologies augment, as well as the fact that telecollaboration projects extend beyond the immediate classroom context, in contrast with collaboration, as it was described by Panitz (1999).

The second characteristic has not only been expanded to comprise reflection as a component of telecollaboration, which is necessary to promote increased awareness, but also other learning outcomes. The reason for that is twofold. Firstly, it is hard to believe that collaborative learning will develop awareness exclusively; thus, students need to reflect on all the other attained goals and outcomes, be they cognitive, behavioural or metacognitive in nature. Secondly, while it might be inferred from Panitz (1999) that the outcomes of collaborative learning, such as increased awareness, are developed by dint of students' engagement in collaboration, it seems more reasonable to assume that especially the development of metacognitive (awareness) and affective (attitudes) learning gains will require additional stimulation (reflection).

The third characteristic has been adapted to account more specifically for telecollaboration-induced outcomes other than metacognitive awareness, hence, the addition of cognitive (declarative and procedural knowledge), behavioural (skills) and affective (attitudes) components.

Finally, the fourth characteristic has been modified to integrate motivation as the driving force beyond students' active involvement in telecollaboration. It was done in response to Panitz's (1999) proposition that collaborative learning must be voluntary in nature. While very democratic at its core, the assumption seems rather ideological and unrealistic in educational contexts, where tasks are often set with limited regard to students' preferences. Ideally, students should be able to choose whether or not they wish to be involved in telecollaborative learning. However, even if the learning format is imposed on them, attempts can be made to kindle volunteerism through adequate motivation, be it intrinsic (Ness & Lin, 2013) or extrinsic (Jordan, Carlile, & Stack, 2018). The former stems from students' internal desire to participate in a project as an opportunity for self-development, intellectual growth or self-expression (Amabile, 1993; Kelly, 2005; Ness & Lin, 2013, 2013), whereas the latter is driven by the prospect of external compensation, such as a reward, admiration, recognition or feedback (Amabile, 1993; Jordan et al., 2018). Interestingly, since extrinsic motivation may be evoked by negative factors (e.g. the fear of low grades or failure to pass an examination), even in contexts where students partake in telecollaboration on a nonvoluntary basis, they may feel motivated to involve in the project work.

As Panitz (1999) rightly observes, while cooperation is highly structured, directive and tends to be teacher controlled, collaboration promotes students' initiative and active role in the establishment of governance and in their own learning. Consequently, it could be stated that while collaboration seems closer to the postpositivist perspective on education, cooperation leans more towards the positivist view, albeit to a lesser extent than transmissionist pedagogy, which best epitomises the positivist paradigm. Table 5.6 contains an overview of the major differences between cooperative and collaborative learning regarding activities, governance, procedure, teacher and student roles, outcomes, knowledge developed and assessment.

There are different perspectives on how the two kinds of learning outlined in Table 5.6 should be approached. Bruffee (1995) suggests that

Table 5.6 Cooperative vs. collaborative learning

	Cooperative learning	*Collaborative learning*
Activities	Structured and specified for each individual	Organised by students through negotiation
Governance	In the hands of the teacher, centralised	Assumed by students, shared and negotiated
Procedure	Preestablished	Established by the students, negotiated
Teacher's role	Teacher monitors, observes, intervenes when necessary	Remains on the side, may help if need be
Students' role	Students follow the task rubric and submit final product for assessment	Students come up with ideas, contribute useful resources, procedures and solutions
Outcomes	End product	Increased student involvement in learning
Knowledge developed	Foundational, pre-set, socially accepted, canonical, complicated at best, complicated but reducible	Non-foundational, derived from questioning of canonical knowledge and the learning process, complex and unpredictable
Assessment	The final verdict is issued by the teacher	Students self-assess and jointly assess the outcomes of teamwork

cooperative learning would best lend itself to equipping primary school learners with basic knowledge on which they would found their further education, whereas collaborative education would be more adequate for academic education, where students are tasked with enquiring into the surrounding reality or reestablishing themselves as members of a common culture through questioning, critical thinking and reasoning. However, Panitz (1999) disagrees with what he calls the linear perception of cooperative and collaborative learning and recommends that they be viewed as two ends of a continuum which encompasses instructional setups characterised by varying degrees of teacher and student centredness.

When one adds to that Kiraly's (2000, 2014) belief that constructivist teaching, which involves the development of foundational knowledge and reflects – at least partly – the mechanical and reductionist perspective on education, is as valid an instructional choice in translator education as the transmissionist and emergentist models, it may be posited that teachers do not need to treat cooperative and collaborative learning as competing learning types but rather as mutually complimentary variations which can coexist even within the same telecollaboration project.

The extent to which it is possible to integrate various types of learning within a single telecollaborative project will be demonstrated on the basis of an adaptation of a collaborative translation project discussed by González Davies (2004). What follows is an outline of the adaptation, with the caveat that the framework of the original has been retained (cf. González Davies, 2004), while modifications have been introduced to project details (e.g. translation languages, sub-tasks and the mode of project delivery), which has been changed to telecollaboration exclusively. In the sample project, students from two institutions, one from Italy and the other from Spain, are set to deliver the indirect translation of the Erasmus section of a university website from Italian (source text) into Spanish (target text) via an intermediate translation of the source text into English. The project spans 15 weeks in total, including six weeks of IT-EN translation, six weeks of EN-ES translation and three weeks for project finalisation and feedback; the project work is facilitated by means of a cloud-based CAT tool and a business communication platform (BCP).

The project procedure involves eight stages. At Stage 1, the Italian students translate the entire source text into English in compliance with project specifications delivered by the international office of their university and via a cloud-based CAT tool. They work as a single team and maintain communication via the CAT tool's comments system, which permits them to append segments with notes at both the translation and revision stages, and the BCP, which offers instant messaging (IM). At Stage 2, in exactly

the same mode, the Italian students perform revision of the IT-EN translation which they have completed.

At Stage 3, the text in English is relayed to the Spanish students, who
split it into fragments, distribute the fragments among several teams and
telework to perform EN-ES translation. In some teams, all students work
to the same beat and in collaboration, while in others, individuals or sub-
teams translate their text fragments and then pool their products to compile the Spanish version.

Stage 4 consists in Spanish students jointly revising their translation
against the English text using via the CAT tool and the BCP. At Stage 5,
the Spanish students send the revised Spanish version to their Italian colleagues for verification against the source text, and their Italian partners
jointly perform IT-ES revision via the CAT tool and the BCP. At Stage 6, a
joint videoconference is held where the Italian students provide feedback
on the target text to their Spanish colleagues.

At Stage 7, the Spanish students perform final text editing following
feedback from their Italian partners and deliver the final product to the client, while at Stage 8, a representative of the client, an international officer
from the Italian university, feeds all the students back on the quality of the
translation in a joint online videoconference, where all students also reflect
on translation challenges and applied solutions.

Table 5.7 illustrates what types of learning are likely to occur within each
project stage, as delineated by the procedures and tools used. Particular
student groups are not indicated, as to determine the type of learning promoted at each stage it suffices to analyse the actions performed.

As it can be seen, a single telecollaboration project is likely to involve
both cooperative and telecollaborative learning, depending on the extent
of student-student interaction. In a large team, students are likely to interact, negotiate actions and make individual contributions to the final product on a regular basis, which fosters collaborative learning. At the same
time, if students only delegate work to individuals and subsequently collect
all the outputs to assemble the end product, opportunities for interaction
or negotiation are limited, which implies that they cooperate, rather than
collaborate, to achieve the ultimate goal.

A case in point is Stage 3, where some students collaborate, while others both collaborate and cooperate, depending on the interaction patterns within and between teams. When students work in a whole team or
sub-teams, the joint engagement in task completion fosters collaborative
learning, whereas the limited interaction between the sub-teams and some
individuals, which is limited to job sharing, is more likely to qualify as
cooperation.

All in all, it is possible to arrange for telecollaboration where both cooperative and collaborative learning will occur, in the same way in which – as

Table 5.7 Cooperative vs. collaborative learning

	Procedure	Tools used	Type of learning
Stage 1	Students translate as a single team and communicate online	CAT tool (edit pane, comments), BCP (IM)	Collaborative learning
Stage 2	Students revise as a single team and communicate online	CAT tool (edit pane in revision mode, comments), BCP (IM)	Collaborative learning
Stage 3	Students team-translate text chunks online in three modes: (i) Joint translation (all team members) (ii) Joint translation in sub-teams (iii) Individual translation of text fragments	CAT tool, BCP CAT tool, BCP CAT tool alone	(i) Collaborative learning, (ii) collaborative learning within each sub-team and (iii) cooperative learning between sub-teams
Stage 4	Students revise own translation as a single team and communicate online	CAT tool (edit pane in revision mode, comments), BCP (IM)	Collaborative learning
Stage 5	Students perform joint IT-ES revision of partners' translation	CAT tool (edit pane in revision mode, comments), BCP (IM)	Collaborative learning
Stage 6	Students provide feedback to foreign partners as a single team	Videoconferencing software	Collaborative learning
Stage 7	Students perform final text editing	CAT tool (edit pane in revision mode, comments), BCP (IM)	Collaborative learning
Stage 8	Client provides feedback to all students in a videoconference	Videoconferencing software	Collaborative learning

it has been demonstrated before – it is possible to integrate elements of knowledge transmission into telecollaboration projects (e.g. to outline the project framework). However, it is important that at the planning stage, the right balance is struck between opportunities for learning based on transmission, cooperation and collaboration to facilitate the attainment of intended goals.

Choices relating to online vs. offline work are another important issue that needs considering while planning for telecollaboration. At first sight, the dichotomy might seem to constitute a false choice in telecollaboration, the prefix *tele-* clearly indicates the necessity of collaboration in an online environment. However, as Nissen (2016) remarks, at least certain forms of telecollaboration (e.g. OIEs) tend to be administered in a blended mode, in which they involve both online and offline work. What is more, it is relatively easy to think of reasons for the introduction of an offline component to other kinds of telecollaborative assignments, including telecollaborative translation, simulation of translator-client communication, crowdsourced translation or the running of STBs.

Nissen (2016) has reviewed several blended courses, involving various combinations of f2f and online work, with regard to four major parameters of the two work modes in question: status, sequencing, pedagogical functions and timing. Nissen's (2016) observations refer to the combination of f2f and online work modes in FL learning settings, but if generalised, they are transferrable to other contexts, including that of translator education, hence, their relevance.

The *status of f2f/online work modes* indicates the emphasis that is placed on them, although not necessarily the order in which they are implemented. Thus, one of them may occupy the central position in a course, or it may only be supplementary to the other. In the former case, the core of the work is performed in the mode of choice. For instance, if the online mode takes precedence, students will primarily telecollaborate, while in offline mode, they will perform subsidiary actions. Nissen's (2016) research suggests that it is indeed the online component that teachers often select as the lead because they believe that it best fosters the attainment of set educational goals; in this case, f2f activities may only involve preparation for online work. However, the reverse is also possible, with the offline component taking the lead and online work being reduced to a supplementary role. Interestingly, some forms of online work (e.g. collecting information, creating input for discussion or reflecting on experience) may occasionally supplement other forms of it (e.g. a telecollaboration project or an OIE).

Sequencing. Another choice to be made while implementing telecollaboration concerns the sequencing of online and offline work modes. Three optional arrangements can be distinguished: the linear model, the flipped classroom model and the flex model. Within the first model, students proceed from online to offline activities in a linear fashion, which means that if offline work constitutes preparation for online work, students will proceed from the former to the latter, as FL teachers do through the stages of the canonical presentation-practice-production (PPP) lesson structure (Cook, 2008; Tomlinson, 2011).

The flipped classroom model entails a twofold modification to the linear model. On the one hand, the term *flipped classroom*, which Nissen (2016) uses following the writing of Staker and Horn (2012), reflects the reversal of the order in which offline and online work is implemented (i.e. online learning here will precede offline learning). On the other hand, it also denotes change to the nature of work performed in both modes. "Inverting the classroom means that events that have traditionally taken place inside the classroom now take place outside the classroom and vice versa" (Lage, Platt, & Treglia, 2000, p. 32), which indicates that – contrary to the linear model – content here will be presented or learnt/acquired online, while follow-up work (e.g. practice) will be done in the classroom. Clearly, the flipped classroom model empowers students to explore and learn on their own, taking advantage of the abundance of content accessible online.

The flex model is a possible third way between the two aforementioned solutions where students can flexibly navigate between f2f and online learning, depending on their individual needs, which means that the ratio of online-offline work is not pre-set and will differ depending on students' choices. At times, both learning modes may be relatively balanced, while on other occasions, one of the modes will prevail (Nissen, 2016).

Pedagogical functions. Equally important to the status and sequencing of online and offline learning in telecollaboration is the pedagogical function which each of the learning modes is set to perform. Nissen (2016) distinguishes two major functions: preparative and reflective, which means that if offline work precedes online work, the former is usually devoted to preparation for online interaction, whereas if offline work follows online work, the latter is utilised as a means of reflection on experience.

The exact content of both preparation and reflection will largely depend on the nature of the telecollaboration within which they are performed. For instance, in a telecollaborative translation project, offline preparation could involve the consolidation of knowledge regarding possible translation problems and relevant solutions, professional LSP standards or project management, a review of major translation technologies or CMC tools and their functionalities, as well as introduction to the translation project. In an OIE, the offline preparative stage could be dedicated to the promotion of telecollaboration as a means of intercultural learning but also to raising students' awareness of the prerequisites of intercultural learning or teaching techniques in genuine cultural exploration and intercultural mediation, including those which involve skills of discovery and interpreting and skills of intercultural interaction and reflection.

The teaching modes that could be used to facilitate offline preparative learning need not be limited to knowledge transmission, and they may also involve on-site cooperation and collaboration, enhanced with relevant classroom techniques such as mind-mapping, brainstorming, comparing and contrasting.

The reflective function of offline learning embraces students' attempts to summate the telecollaboration that they have completed, which – as Nissen (2016) reports – may consist in students sharing with others their personal impressions of the telecollaborative experience or comments on the cultural or metacognitive aspects of their learning. The thematic scope of offline reflection will depend on the educational content to which it relates. Hence, while Nissen's (2016) examples of intercultural reflection in FL education contexts will also be pertinent to OIEs implemented in translator education, for other types of telecollaboration, they will require adaptation to match the circumstances at hand. For instance, in a telecollaborative translation project, students could possibly reflect on the impact of online communication tools on the quality of their in-project interaction, the issues in translation, terminology or information searching which they faced in the course of the project or the telework-related challenges which they think could have been avoided had the project been administered in f2f mode. On a metacognitive note, students could also share how they and their colleagues supported one another to mutually augment the learning process or what they had learnt in their project roles.

What merits note is that the offline-online-offline sequence discussed earlier (introduction-telecollaboration-reflection) could be reversed to produce the online-offline-online setup, where the functions ascribed of f2f and online learning would change accordingly; thus, online preparative learning would precede offline collaboration, while online reflective learning would conclude the sequence. Consequently, the content, teaching modes and learning techniques discussed earlier would need to undergo modifications to adjust to the new (online) modality of the preparative and reflective work, as it is exemplified later.

As far as the content goes, in a telecollaborative translation project – to take it as an example – online preparative work could involve introduction to, or consolidation of, knowledge about translation in various modes, translation problems and solutions, professional practices or a review of relevant reference sources. In an OIE, the online preparative stage could be dedicated to the rationale for, and merits of, intercultural education or a review of the constituents of intercultural competence and techniques augmenting their development.

Online preparative work may involve Web-based knowledge transmission, perpetuated by VLEs such as Moodle, or online cooperation/telecollaboration, enhanced by relevant VLE functionalities, CMC tools and the social media, while the relevant techniques (e.g. mind-mapping, brainstorming or comparing and contrasting) may be enriched with multimedia and enhanced with dedicated tools, such as online mind-mappers or brainstorming applications.

Online reflection would aim to help students recapitulate the offline learning experience by sharing anecdotes, comments on project outcomes or learning gains via online channels mediating synchronous or asynchronous interaction (e.g. chat, IM, videoconferencing tools and online forums, e-diaries, e-logs, blogs or vlogs respectively).

The content of online reflection would again depend on the assignment in question. In a telecollaborative translation project, students could hold an online discussion on how the translation decisions they took affected the quality of the target text, or they could analyse examples of particularly problematic language or terminology which they had encountered. Metacognitive reflection could take the form of videoconferencing, whereby students would be expected to jointly rank reported instances of learning failure by the degree of seriousness and suggest future amendments to the learning process. By the same token, they could work on a list of the top five instances of learning success and, on that basis, infer the prerequisites of successful learning, which could be converted into advice for all students to share. The previously cited examples of online reflection are telecollaborative in nature, but it would also be possible to redesign them for less student-student interaction. For example, if each student contributed a wiki entry with an example of learning failure and its potential causes, a reflection-based list would be built in a cooperative rather than collaborative fashion.

In sum, although the suggestions discussed earlier are far from exhaustive, they shed some light on the possible nature of online/offline work, depending on whether the work modes are allocated preparative or reflective functions in particular projects.

Timing relates the proportions of time in a project which are dedicated to online and offline work. It is difficult to set the proportions prescriptively, as they will depend on various factors, including the teaching/learning goals, and thus the focus of a project or infrastructural and technological constraints of on-site and out-of-class learning settings. However, as the research by Nissen (2016) reveals, three major timing patterns are discernible in telecollaboration projects, each with the following rough estimation of the proportions f2f to online work: (i) a 2:1 ratio, (ii) a 1:2 ratio and (iii) a 1:1 ratio. Out of the six projects she analysed, in three, nearly twice as much time was dedicated to f2f work as to online work (21h:9h, 10h:6h and 16h:8h); in another two, the proportion was reversed (1h/week:2h weeks and 15h:36h); and in one, the time dedicated to f2f and online work was roughly balanced (4h/week:5h/week). In other words, in three projects, the f2f mode was subsidiary to online mode; in another two, online work was subsidiary to f2f work; while in one project, neither of the modes was dominant. What additionally stems from Nissen's (2016) findings is that timing must not be equated with workload, which each of the work modes involves. Apparently, it is the nature of learning in each mode that determines learner effort, not the sheer time framework within which the learning occurs.

Authentic vs. simulated work. The last issue to be considered is the extent to which the telecollaborative work with which students engage qualifies as authentic or simulated. Authenticity can be considered with regard to two dimensions of telecollaboration: materials and practices. A discussion of the former can be augmented by the findings of extensive research into the authenticity of FL learning materials and tasks which was conducted in the late 1980s through the 1990s and into the 21st century. Materials in telecollaborative work are either the resources that it involves or the output that it generates. Hence, it seems reasonable to consider what characteristics materials need to have to be dubbed authentic.

Widdowson (1990) believed that authentic FL learning materials are those which have been designed for native speakers of English and are being used in the language classroom in precisely the same way which they were intended for. The concept of native speakers is clearly irrelevant to translator education, but it can be replaced with that of translation or LSP professionals. Analogically, it could be proposed that authentic materials in translator education would be those generated by LSP professionals (e.g. TMs, glossaries, terminology databases and parallel corpora), which students are likely to use in telecollaboration projects. It is important to note that Widdowson's (1990) definition highlights not only provenance but also usage as the distinctive markers of authenticity, with the caveat that both are considered jointly. That is why to him, language FL learning materials which have been originally authored by native speakers but are being used differently than intended (e.g. to develop language skills) are not authentic but genuine. In the light of that, the previously cited materials which could potentially be used in telecollaborative translation projects, ranging from TMs to parallel corpora, will qualify as authentic on condition that they are used for the purposes for which they are originally intended in the professional LSP context.

At the same time, it must be stated that other scholars only partly agreed with Widdowson's (1990) conceptualisation of authenticity. For instance, Little, Devitt, and Singleton (1988) did not dwell on provenance at all but underlined that authentic materials should be utilised in order "to fulfil some social purpose in the language community" (Little et al., 1988, p. 25), which seems to dovetail with Widdowson's (1990) focus on usage. What it implies is that even translations produced by students in telecollaborative translation projects could be regarded as authentic if only the translated content fulfils a purpose in the broader community outside the learning context, which is likely to be the case if students deliver translations to genuine clients (e.g. charitable organisations or institutions oriented towards toll-free service provision or self-help).

As far as task authenticity is concerned, Kiraly (2000) believes that it resides in the extent to which what students do is "representative of the nature and complexity of activities performed by professional translators in the course of their work" (Kiraly, 2000, p. 58). He also adds that in authentic projects, students need to "complete projects for real clients" (Kiraly, 2005, p. 1102) – an argument reiterated in Kiraly (2012) and also apparently supported by Schopp (2006), who maintains that authentic projects need to involve "all stages of the translation process, starting from a price estimate in response to a client's or commissioner's request, to the final proofreading by the client and permission to print" (Schopp, 2006, pp. 175–176).

Fachbereich Translations-, Sprach- und Kulturwissenschaft (FTSK) of Johannes Gutenberg Universität in Mainz, which is an acclaimed translator education institution located in Germersheim, Germany – where both Don Kiraly and Susanne Hagemann are based – defines authentic translation projects highlighting the fact that the projects entail students translating for real-world clients, working with texts which are aimed to facilitate communication with target language readers and stimulating students' sense of involvement through the prospect of remuneration or public acknowledgment (FTSK, 2016).

All in all, the features underpinning authentic telecollaborative project work could be listed as follows:

- completeness (undertaking of complete projects);
- holism (perception of the experience as a whole);
- complexity (challenging and open-ended nature of the experience);
- collaboration with a real-world client; and
- prospect of public acknowledgement or remuneration.

At the opposite end, there is simulation, which by contrast could be defined as telecollaborative translation work characterised by the following:

- incompleteness (undertaking of selected project tasks);
- atomism (focus on selected elements);
- complicatedness (potentially difficult but close-ended nature of the experience);
- collaboration with a simulated client; and
- prospect of instructional feedback.

Authentic and simulated project work should be seen as two ends of a continuum, rather than strict polarities, in that the further away from the model of authentic work a telecollaborative translation project diverts in its design, the closer it will be to the simulation. In fact, it might be posited that to reach the ultimate level of authenticity in any educational setting is an elusive goal, as educational contexts – due to their instruction-oriented nature – are by default different from professional ones. What is more, the relevance of replicating the professional conditions in translator education settings with one-to-one accuracy may be questioned on these grounds:

> Learners may work in a future in which professional conditions have already changed. It is impossible for foretell precisely what the profession will like be in the future, and therefore to prepare the students for any defined set of future conditions.
>
> (Aguilar, 2016, p. 26)

The very same problem is pinpointed by Orlando (2016), who on the one hand advocates for the implementation of "authentic tasks mirroring and taking into account the demands and norms of the industry" (Orlando, 2016, p. 28) but on the other observes that "the rapid changes [to the translation profession] observed seriously challenge the primacy of universities" (Orlando, 2016, p. 28).

Thus, the difficulty in making accurate decisions about students' professional needs indicates that the details of translation projects implemented in educational settings need not be stringently demarcated by the realities of the profession; instead, as Aguilar (2016) suggests, they could be informed by "judgements about what is educationally desirable in relation to a particular constellation of educational purposes" (Aguilar, 2016, p. 26). That creates space for a more open-ended nature of telecollaborative translation projects, which while integrating some elements of professional reality would also allow for unpredictable outcomes, not necessarily driven by the professional needs of the moment. Purposefully or not, Szymczak (2013) implies it in his definition of authentic translation tasks, which he credits with the power to make students "realize the insufficiency of their mental models of reality" (Szymczak, 2013, p. 61). This statement would be best left as it is, without incorporating into it the need for students to gear their mental models towards the professional reality of today. It will suffice if translation projects enable students to reflect on the competences they already have and those they will need to develop to fit into the translation market of the future.

The implementation of simulated projects may also be motivated by other factors (e.g. the need to provide education in an environment which safeguards students against severe consequences of failure in translation tasks), which has been highlighted by Hagemann (2016). In agreement with that, Newmann and Wehlage (1993) append their standards of authentic instruction, including the involvement of higher-order thinking skills, the development of less voluminous but more in-depth knowledge, connectedness to the world and substantive interaction and communication, with social support for student achievement. The latter element refers to the extent to which all students' contributions are valued and how mutually supportive students are in their learning efforts, thus underlining the need for learning to occur in a secure context.

Another argument for simulated work is that, inevitably, students need education which will promote all the desired learning outcomes, but not all of those outcomes will lend themselves to development through authentic project work. For instance, Kelly (2005) observes that especially "large-group project work . . . is not, in all probability, the best way to go about the early acquisition of many of the non-specifically translational competences which are prerequisites for the translational" (Kelly, 2005, p. 116) while also adding the argument originally proposed by Gros Salvat (1995) that the development of expertise – which is one of the goals of contemporary translator education – is not necessarily achievable by merely reproducing experts' actions and knowledge in educational settings. Hence, the need to allow for other types of learning.

The degree of authenticity and simulation in a telecollaboration assignment will ultimately depend on the course instructor, but – in the light of the previous example – (s)he will most realistically need to choose between simulation or a design promoting "closely simulated real-life professional situations" (Kelly, 2005, p. 161) as the most optimal solution, given his or her educational circumstances and set goals.

References

Aguilar, R. P. (2016). The question of authenticity in translator education from the perspective of educational philosophy. In D. C. Kiraly (Ed.), *V&R academic. Towards authentic experiential learning in translator education* (pp. 13–32). Göttingen: V & R Unipress; Mainz University Press.

ALTA. (2015). *Emerging translator mentorship program.* Retrieved from https://literarytranslators.org/mentorships

Amabile, T. M. (1993). Motivational synergy: Toward new conceptualizations of intrinsic and extrinsic motivation in the workplace. *Human Resource Management Review, 3*(3), 185–201. https://doi.org/10.1016/1053-4822(93)90012-S

Belz, J. A. (2003). From the special issue editor. *Language Learning & Technology, 7*(2), 2–5.

Bold, C., & Hutton, P. (2007). Supporting students' critical reflection-on-practice. In A. Campbell & L. Norton (Eds.), *Learning, teaching and assessing in higher education: Developing reflective practice/edited by Anne Campbell, Lin Norton* (pp. 21–30). Exeter: Learning Matters.

Bondarenko, K., Bondarenko, O., Andrienko, T., Potapenko, S., & Slavova, L. (2021). Nurturing collaboration between translation business and academia in Ukraine. *SHS Web of Conferences, 105*(4), 1–15. https://doi.org/10.1051/shsconf/202110505002

Brna, P. (1998). Models of collaboration. *Proceedings of the workshop on informatics in education, XVIII Congresso Nacional da Sociedade Brasileira de Computação,* Belo Horizonte, Brazil.

Bruffee, K. (1995). Sharing our toys – Cooperative learning versus collaborative learning. *Change, 27*(1), 12–18.

Byram, M. (1997). *Teaching and assessing intercultural communicative competence.* Clevedon: Multilingual Matters.

Byram, M. (2000). Assessing intercultural competence in language teaching. *Sprogforum, 18*(6), 8–13.

Byram, M. (2008). *From foreign language education to education for intercultural citizenship.* Clevedon, Buffalo, & Toronto: Multilingual Matters.

Byram, M. (2014). *Intercultural communication.* London: Multilingual Matters.

Byram, M., & Zarate, G. (1998). *The sociocultural and intercultural dimension of language learning and teaching.* Strasbourg: Council of Europe.

Child, S. F. J., & Shaw, S. (2018). Towards an operational framework for establishing and assessing collaborative interactions. *Research Papers in Education, 34*(3), 276–297. https://doi.org/10.1080/02671522.2018.1424928

Chodkiewicz, M. (2014). Student perceptions of the usefulness and effectiveness of a basic course in translation simulating working with a client: The results of a survey. In K. Uzule (Ed.), *Multidimensional translation: From science to art* (pp. 220–230). Riga: Baltic International Academy.

Chodkiewicz, M. (2016). Simulating communication with the client in an undergraduate translation course – Student performance and perceptions. *Linguistica Silesiana, 37*, 379–394.

CoE. (2018). *Reference framework of competences for democratic culture.* Strasbourg: Council of Europe.

Cohen, L., Manion, L., & Morrison, K. (2011). *Research methods in education* (7th ed.). London & New York: Routledge.

Cohen, L., Manion, L., & Morrison, K. (2017). *Research methods in education* (8th ed.). London: Routledge.

Cook, V. (2008). *Second language learning and teaching* (4th ed.). London: Hodder Education.

Cram, B. (1995). Self-assessment: From theory to practice. In G. Brindley (Ed.), *Language assessment in action* (pp. 282–292). Sydney: National Centre for English Language Teaching and Research.

CUP. (2001). *Common European framework of reference for languages: Learning, teaching, assessment.* Cambridge: Cambridge University Press.

Deeley, S. J. (2014). Summative co-assessment: A deep learning approach to enhancing employability skills and attributes. *Active Learning in Higher Education, 15*(1), 39–51. https://doi.org/10.1177/1469787413514649

Dooly, M. (2008). *Telecollaborative language learning: A guidebook to moderating intercultural collaboration online.* Bern: Peter Lang Publishing Group.

Elia Exchange. (2014). *Elia exchange programme internship programme internship: Memorandum of understanding.* Retrieved from www.elia-association.org/fileadmin/files/EliaExch/EE%20Internship%20MoU.pdf

Ellis, R. (2003). *Task-based language teaching and learning.* Oxford: Oxford University Press.

EMT. (2009). *European master's in translation – Competences for professional translators.* Retrieved from https://ec.europa.eu/info/sites/info/files/emt_competences_translators_en.pdf

EMT. (2017). *European master's in translation competence framework 2017.* Retrieved from https://ec.europa.eu/info/sites/info/files/emt_competence_fwk_2017_en_web.pdf

EMT. (2022a). *European master's in translation competence framework 2022.* Retrieved from https://commission.europa.eu/system/files/2022-11/emt_competence_fwk_2022_en.pdf

EMT. (2022b). *List of EMT members 2019–2024.* Retrieved from https://commission.europa.eu/resources-partners/european-masters-translation-emt/list-emt-members-2019-2024_en

Eskelinen, J., & Pakkala-Weckström, M. (2016). Assessing translation students' acquisition of professional competences. *Translation Spaces, 5*(2), 314–331.

Fox, O. (2000). The use of translation diaries in a process-oriented translation teaching methodology. In C. Schäffner & B. J. Adab (Eds.), *Benjamins translation library: Vol. 38. Developing translation competence* (pp. 115–130). Amsterdam & Philadelphia: J. Benjamins Pub. Co.

FTSK. (2016). *Authentic projects at the FTSK.* Retrieved from www.blogs.uni-mainz.de/fb06innovationftsk/authentic-projects-at-ftsk/

González, J., & Wagenaar, R. (2008). *Universities' contribution to the bologna process* (2nd ed.). Bilbao: Publicaciones de la Universidad de Deusto.

González Davies, M. (2004). *Multiple voices in the translation classroom: Activities, tasks, and projects. Benjamins translation library: Vol. 54.* Amsterdam & Philadelphia: J. Benjamins Pub.

González de Sande, J., & Godino-Llorente, J. I. (2014). Peer assessment and self-assessment: Effective learning tools in Higher Education. *International Journal of Engineering Education, 30*(3), 711–721.

Göpferich, S. (2009). Towards a model of translation competence and its acquisition: The longitudinal study of TransComp. In S. Göpferich, A. L. Jakobsen, & I. M. Mees (Eds.), *Copenhagen studies in language: Vol. 37. Behind the mind: Methods, models and results in translation process research* (pp. 11–37). Frederiksberg: Samfundslitteratur.

Görög, A. (2017). *The 8 most used standards and metrics for translation quality evaluation.* Retrieved from https://blog.taus.net/the-8-most-used-standards-and-metrics-for-translation-quality-evaluation

Gros Salvat, B. (1995). *Teorías cognitivas de enseñanza y aprendizaje.* Barcelona: EUB.

Guth, S., & Helm, F. (2010). Introduction. In S. Guth & F. Helm (Eds.), *Telecollaboration 2.0: Language, literacies and intercultural learning in the 21st century* (pp. 13–23). Bern, Berlin, Bruxelles, Frankfurt am Main, New York, Oxford, & Wien: Peter Lang.

Hagemann, S. (2016). (Non-)professional, authentic projects? Why terminology matters. In D. C. Kiraly (Ed.), *V&R academic. Towards authentic experiential learning in translator education* (pp. 33–52). Göttingen: V & R Unipress; Mainz University Press.

Harris, J. (1999). First steps in telecollaboration. *International Society for Technology in Education, 27*(3), 54–57. Retrieved from https://virtual-architecture.wm.edu/Foundation/Articles/First-Steps.pdf

Hodge, S. R. (2010). Adapted physical activity for students with special needs. In P. L. Peterson, E. L. Baker, & B. McGaw (Eds.), *International encyclopedia of education* (3rd ed., pp. 519–529). Kidlington & Oxford: Academic Press.

Hurtado Albir, A. (1995). La didáctica de la traducción. Evolución y estado actual. In P. Fernández & J. M. Bravo (Eds.), *Perspectivas de la traducción* (pp. 9–74). Valladolid: Universidad de Valladoli.

Iglesias Pérez, M. C., Vidal-Puga, J., & Pino Juste, M. R. (2020). The role of self and peer assessment in Higher Education. *Studies in Higher Education, 13*(3), 1–10. https://doi.org/10.1080/03075079.2020.1783526

Jandt, F. (2001). *Intercultural communication.* Thousand Oaks, London, & Delhi: Sage Publications.

Jiménez-Crespo, M. A. (2017). *Crowdsourcing and online collaborative translations: Expanding the limits of translation studies/Miguel A. Jiménez-Crespo, Rutgers University. Benjamins translation library, 0929–7316: Vol. 131.* Amsterdam & Philadelphia: John Benjamins Publishing Company.

Jordan, A., Carlile, O., & Stack, A. (2018). *Approaches to learning: A guide for teachers/Anne Jordan, Orison Carlile, Annetta Stack.* Maidenhead: Open University Press.

Kearns, J. (2006). *Curriculum renewal in translator training: Vocational challenges in academic environments with reference to needs and situation analysis and skills transferability from the contemporary experience of Polish translator training culture* (Unpublished PhD dissertation). Dublin City University: School of Applied Language and Intercultural Studies.

Kelly, D. (2005). *A handbook for translator trainers: A guide to reflective practice.* Manchester: St. Jerome.

Kiraly, D. C. (1995). *Pathways to translation: Pedagogy and process.* Kent, OH & London: Kent State University Press.

Kiraly, D. C. (2000). *A social constructivist approach to translator education: Empowerment from theory to practice.* Manchester: St. Jerome.

Kiraly, D. C. (2005). Project-based learning: A case for situated translation. *Meta, 50*(4), 1098–1111. https://doi.org/10.7202/012063ar

Kiraly, D. C. (2006). Beyond social constructivism: Complexity theory and translator education. *Translation and Interpreting Studies, 6*(1), 68–86.

Kiraly, D. C. (2012). Growing a project-based translation pedagogy: A fractal perspective. *Meta, 57*(1), 82–95.

Kiraly, D. C. (2014). From assumptions about knowing and learning to praxis in translation education. *Intralinea* (Special Issue: Challenges in Translation Pedagogy). Retrieved from www.intralinea.org/specials/article/2100

Kiraly, D. C., & Hofmann, S. (2016). Towards a postpositivist curriculum development model for translator education. In D. C. Kiraly (Ed.), *V&R academic. Towards authentic experiential learning in translator education* (pp. 67–88). Göttingen: V & R Unipress; Mainz University Press.

Kiraly, D. C., Rüth, L., Signer, S., & Stederoth, K. (2019). Enhancing translation course design and didactic interventions with e-learning: Moodle© and beyond. In G. Massey & D. C. Kiraly (Eds.), *Towards authentic experiential learning in translator education* (2nd ed., pp. 101–127). Newcastle upon Tyne: Cambridge Scholars Publishing.

Kohonen, V., Jaantinen, R., Kaikkonen, P., & Lehtovaara, J. (2001). *Experiential learning in foreign language education.* Harlow: Longman.

Kramsch, C., & Whiteside, A. (2015). *What is symbolic competence and what can we do with it?* Retrieved from http://blc.berkeley.edu/wp-content/uploads/2015/08/kramschSC.pdf

Lage, M. J., Platt, G. J., & Treglia, M. (2000). Inverting the classroom: A gateway to creating an inclusive learning environment. *The Journal of Economic Education, 31*(1), 30–43.

Lamy, M. N., & Goodfellow, R. (2010). Telecollaboration and learning 2.0. In S. Guth & F. Helm (Eds.), *Telecollaboration 2.0: Language, literacies and intercultural learning in the 21st century* (pp. 107–138). Bern, Berlin, Bruxelles, Frankfurt am Main, New York, Oxford, & Wien: Peter Lang.

Larsen-Freeman, D., & Anderson, M. (2018). *Techniques & principles in language teaching* (3rd ed.). Oxford [i pozostałe]: Oxford University Press.

Little, D., Devitt, S., & Singleton, D. (1988). *Authentic texts in foreign language teaching: Theory and practice*. Dublin: Authentik.

Liu, M. (2019). The nexus of language and culture: A review of literature on intercultural communicative competence in foreign language education. *Cambridge Open-Review Educational Research e-Journal, 6*, 50–65. Retrieved from https://cerj.educ.cam.ac.uk/archive/v62019/CORERJ-Journal-Volume6-03-TheNexusOfLanguageAndCulture.pdf

Massey, G. (2023, March 16). *The hard thing about soft skills: Educating for today's language industry: TER Symposium on translator and translator trainer education*. Kraków: Jagiellonian University.

Massey, G., & Ehrensberger-Dow, M. (2014). Looking beyond text. The usefulness of translation process data. In D. Knorr, C. Heine, & J. Engberg (Eds.), *Methods in writing process research* (pp. 81–98). Frankfurt am Main: Peter Lang.

Maylath, B., Vandepitte, S., Minacori, P., Isohella, S., Mousten, B., & Humbley, J. (2013). Managing complexity: A technical communication translation case study in multilateral international collaboration. *Technical Communication Quarterly, 22*(1), 67–84. https://doi.org/10.1080/10572252.2013.730967

McAlester, G. (2000). The evaluation of translation into a foreign language. In C. Schäffner & B. J. Adab (Eds.), *Benjamins translation library: Vol. 38. Developing translation competence* (pp. 229–242). Amsterdam & Philadelphia: J. Benjamins Pub. Co.

Merriam-Webster. (n.d.). *Tele. In Merriam-Webster.com dictionary*. Retrieved from www.merriam-webster.com/dictionary/tele

Moodle. (2021). *Workshop activity*. Retrieved from https://docs.moodle.org/311/en/Workshop_activity

Morera-Mesa, A. (2014). *Crowdsourced translation practices from the process flow perspective* (PhD dissertation). University of Limerick, Ireland.

Narayan, A. (2013). ICT: Change of ICT: Change of paradigm, limitations and possible courses for action for future. In D. D'Souza, U. Singh, D. Sharma, & R. Prabhas (Eds.), *Educational technology in teaching and learning: Prospects and challenges* (pp. 9–14). Patna, Bihar: Patna's Women's College Publications.

National Education Association. (2016). *Preparing 21st century students for a global society.: An educator's guide to four Cs*. Retrieved from www.nea.org/assets/docs/A-Guide-to-Four-Cs.pdf

Ness, D., & Lin, C.-L. (2013). *International education: An encyclopedia of contemporary issues and systems*. Armonk, NY: M.E. Sharpe.

Newmann, F., & Wehlage, G. (1993). Five standards of authentic instruction. *Educational Leadership*, *50*(7), 8–12.

Nissen, E. (2016). Combining classroom-based learning and online intercultural exchange in blended learning courses. In T. Lewis & R. O'Dowd (Eds.), *Routledge studies in language and intercultural communication: Vol. 4. Online intercultural exchange: Policy, pedagogy, practice* (pp. 173–191). New York: Routledge.

Nunan, D. (2004). *Task-based language teaching. Cambridge language teaching library*. Cambridge: Cambridge University Press.

O'Brien, S. (2012). Towards a dynamic quality evaluation model for translation. *JoSTrans*, *17*, 55–77.

O'Dowd, R. (2011). Online foreign language interaction: Moving from the periphery to the core of foreign language education? *Language Teaching*, *44*, 368–380. https://doi.org/10.1017/S0261444810000194

O'Dowd, R., & Ware, P. (2009). Critical issues in telecollaborative task design. *Computer Assisted Language Learning*, *22*(2), 173–188. https://doi.org/10.1080/09588220902778369

Orlando, M. (2016). *Training 21st-century translators and interpreters: At the crossroads of practice, research and pedagogy. Transkulturalität – Translation – Transfer*. Berlin: Frank & Timme.

Orozco, M. (2000). Building a measuring instrument for the acquisition of translation competence in trainee translators. In C. Schäffner & B. J. Adab (Eds.), *Benjamins translation library: Vol. 38. Developing translation competence* (pp. 199–214). Amsterdam & Philadelphia: J. Benjamins Pub. Co.

P21. (2016). *Framework for 21st century learning*. Retrieved from http://static. battelleforkids.org/documents/p21/P21_framework_0816_2pgs.pdf

PACTE. (2003). Building a translation competence model. In F. Alves (Ed.), *Triangulating translation: Perspectives in process-oriented research* (pp. 43–66). Amsterdam & Philadelphia: John Benjamins Publishing Company.

PACTE. (2008). First results of a translation competence experiment: 'Knowledge of translation' and 'efficacy of the translation process'. In J. Kearns (Ed.), *Translator and interpreter training: Issues, methods and debates* (pp. 104–126). London & New York: Continuum International Publishing Group.

Panadero, E., & Alqassab, M. (2019). An empirical review of anonymity effects in peer assessment, peer feedback, peer review, peer evaluation and peer grading. *Assessment & Evaluation in Higher Education*, *44*(8), 1253–1278. https://doi.org/10.1080/02602938.2019.1600186

Panitz, T. (1999). *Collaborative versus cooperative learning: A comparison of the two concepts which will help us understand the underlying nature of interactive learning*. Retrieved from https://files.eric.ed.gov/fulltext/ED448443.pdf

Paradowska, U. (2021). Benefits and challenges of an intra-university authentic collaborative translation project. *New Voices in Translation Studies*, *24*, 23–45.

Piaget, J. (1959). *The language and thought of the child. International library of psychology, philosophy and scientific method* (3rd ed.). New York: Humanities Press.

Piotrowska, M. (2007). *Proces decyzyjny tłumacza: Podstawy metodologii nauczania przekładu pisemnego.* Kraków: Wydawnictwo Naukowe Akademii Pedagogicznej.

Piotrowska, M. (2022). *Translation: Inspirations we live by.* Kraków: Księgarnia Akademicka Publishing.

Prabhu, N. (1987). *Second language pedagogy: A perspective.* Oxford: Oxford University Press.

Prieto-Velasco, J. A., & Fuentes-Luque, A. (2016). A collaborative multimodal working environment for the development of instrumental and professional competences of student translators: An innovative teaching experience. *The Interpreter and Translator Trainer, 10*(1), 76–91. https://doi.org/10.1080/1750 399X.2016.1154344

Reiss, K., Vermeer, H. J., Nord, C., & Dudenhöfer, M. (2015). *Towards a general theory of translational action: Skopos theory explained.* London: Routledge Taylor & Francis Group.

Richards, J. C., & Rodgers, T. S. (2014). *Approaches and methods in language teaching* (3rd ed.). New York: Cambridge University Press. Retrieved from www. loc.gov/catdir/enhancements/fy1403/2013041790-d.html

Rico, C. (2017). The ePortfolio: Constructing learning in translation technology. *The Interpreter and Translator Trainer, 11*(1), 79–95. https://doi.org/10.1080/1 750399X.2017.1306995

Risager, K. (Ed.). (2007a). *Language and culture pedagogy.* Clevedon, Buffalo, & Toronto: Multilingual Matters.

Risager, K. (2007b). *Language and culture pedagogy.* Bristol: Blue Ridge Summit: Multilingual Matters.

Saldanha, A. S. (2019). Mentoring in translation: A future reality? In *Proceedings of the conference: Towards the science of mentoring*, University. Retrieved from www.researchgate.net/profile/Ana_Saldanha2/publication/337422982_TITLE_ Mentoring_in_Translation_A_Future_Reality/links/5dd6882e299bf10c5a269344/ TITLE-Mentoring-in-Translation-A-Future-Reality.pdf

Schäffner, C. (2019). Translators' roles and responsibilities. In E. Angelone, M. Ehrensberger-Dow, & G. Massey (Eds.), *Bloomsbury companions. The Bloomsbury companion to language industry studies* (pp. 63–90). London: Bloomsbury Academic.

Schopp, J. F. (2006). How good is an authentic commission for teaching translation? *New Vistas in Translator and Interpreter Training. Special issue of Translation Ireland, 17*(1), 171–180.

Sirena, D. (2004). *Mission impossible: Improve quality, time and speed at the same time.* Retrieved from www.translationdirectory.com/article387.htm

Stahl, G., Koschmann, T., & Suthers, D. (2006). Computer-supported collaborative learning: An historical perspective. In R. K. Sawyer (Ed.), *Cambridge handbook of the learning sciences* (1st ed., pp. 409–426). Cambridge: Cambridge University Press.

Stahl, G., Koschmann, T., & Suthers, D. (2014). Computer-supported collaborative learning. In R. K. Sawyer (Ed.), *Cambridge handbooks in psychology. The Cambridge handbook of the learning sciences* (2nd ed., pp. 479–500). New York: Cambridge University Press.

Staker, H., & Horn, M. B. (2012). *Classifying K-12 blended learning.* Retrieved from www.blendedlearning.org/wp-content/uploads/2014/11/Classifying-K-12-blended-learning.pdf

Szymczak, P. (2013). Translating Wikipedia articles: A preliminary report on authentic translation projects in formal translator training. *Acta Philologica, 44,* 61–70.

Tomalin, B., & Stempleski, S. (1993). *Cultural awareness.* Oxford: Oxford University Press.

Tomlinson, B. (2011). Glossary. In B. Tomlinson (Ed.), *Materials development in language teaching* (pp. ix–xviii). Cambridge: Cambridge University Press.

Tsai, Y. (2020). Collaborative translation in the digital age. *Research in Language, 18*(2), 119–135. https://doi.org/10.18778/1731-7533.18.2.01

UNICEF. (2019). *Global framework on transferable skills.* Retrieved from https://www.unicef.org/media/64751/file/Global-framework-on-transferable-skills-2019.pdf

Van Egdom, G.-W., Konttinen, K., Vandepitte, S., Fernández-Parra, M., Loock, R., & Bindels, J. (2020). Empowering translators through entrepreneurship in simulated translation bureaus. *Hermes, 60.*

Vygotsky, L. S. (1978). *Mind in society.: The development of higher psychological processes.* Cambridge, MA: Harvard University Press.

Wanner, T., & Palmer, E. (2018). Formative self-and peer assessment for improved student learning: The crucial factors of design, teacher participation and feedback. *Assessment & Evaluation in Higher Education, 43*(7), 1032–1047. https://doi.org/10.1080/02602938.2018.1427698

Weigt, Z. (2012). Tekst specjalistyczny w dydaktyce uniwersyteckiej. *Lingwistyka Stosowana, 5,* 135–144.

Widdowson, H. (1990). *Aspects of language teaching.* Oxford: Oxford University Press.

Wood, D. J., Bruner, J. S., & Ross, G. (1976). The role of tutoring in problem solving. *Journal of Child Psychology and Psychiatry, 17*(2), 89–100.

6 Implementing telecollaboration in translator education courses at university level

Research-based insight

What follows is an account of projects involving varying degrees of telecollaboration which have been administered in different courses offered on two-year MA programmes in Translation Studies at the Jagiellonian University in Kraków (UJ) and the Pedagogical University of Kraków (UP), Poland, and the research which was conducted to investigate selected aspects of telecollaborative learning. Interestingly, in 2019, both programmes received the prestigious accreditation of the European Master's in Translation (EMT) network for the years 2019–2024. On the one hand, the report provides information about concrete implementations of different modes of telecollaboration in translator education and as such is a practical illustration of the relevant theories discussed in the previous chapters (see Chapter 4 and Chapter 5). On the other hand, the research results shed some light on the intricacies of telecollaborative learning, including its affordances, learning modes and outcomes, as well as students' perspectives on it.

On a more implicit basis, this chapter – at least partially – may also serve as a set of guidelines on how to implement telecollaboration for particular educational purposes in TS courses and how to research specific aspects of this learning mode. That said, it needs to be underlined that the projects discussed here are by no means to be treated as exemplars. Rather than that, they are to be viewed as possible interpretations of what telecollaborative learning is and how it may possibly be arranged for, with the caveat that numerous alterations or other design options are conceivable, depending on a particular educational context, teaching and learning objectives, expected outcomes, infrastructural setup and context-related constraints. By the same token, the research which is reported on here is selective, if only due to the sheer number of areas of telecollaboration which could possibly be examined; thus, it must not be perceived as exhaustive. Yet it aims to demonstrate what problems could potentially be explored, what research methods could be used to that end and what implications the

DOI: 10.4324/9781003424932-7

research findings might have for the implementation of telecollaboration in translator education.

The examples of telecollaborative learning and the related research will be discussed with regard to the three major design types which are delineated in Chapter 5 (i.e. OIEs, team translation projects and miscellaneous projects, including hybrid implementations with elements of online and f2f interaction).

6.1 Online Intercultural Exchanges

6.1.1 *The Global Understanding project (GPE X)*

Project overview and research context

The two examples of OIEs discussed in the present chapter were administered as part of an elective course in Intercultural Communication in the New Media, offered on a two-year MA programme in Translation Studies at UJ. Both can be viewed as networked, or packaged, projects in that they were externally designed and supervised. They were organised within the framework of the international telecollaboration project Global Understanding, coordinated by the Global Partners in Education (GPE, 2022) – a global virtual exchange network based at East Carolina University in Greenville, NC, USA, which groups 49 higher education institutions from 31 countries and five continents, including North and South America Africa, Europe, Asia and Australia. GPE's major mission is – *inter alia* – to equip students for living in an interconnected world, offer them global experiences, promote intercultural understanding, foster the development of intercultural communication and collaboration skills and promote lifelong global education.

Global Understanding is GPE's flagship programme which every academic year involves students from international partner institutions in videoconferencing and online discussions on various issues, with each of the institutions collaborating with up to three partners per semester, one partner at a time and roughly five online meetings per partner. The project participants work both in and out of class. When in class on most link days – in an alternate fashion from one link day to another – students from each institution are locally split into two groups, one of which works in all-to-all videoconferencing mode while the other in one-to-one online tandems with assigned foreign partners. Both groups discuss the topic of the day, as listed in the GPE Core (GPE, 2014) document available to the institutions involved.

In the 10th iteration of the project, held in the year 2017, the discussion topics comprised: (i) College Life, (ii) Family and Cultural Traditions,

(iii) Meaning of Life and Religion, (iv) Stereotypes and Prejudices and (v) Free Topic, where the last option created room for the exploration of student-initiated topics, with the proviso that their choice would win teacher approval. Overall, in the GPE Global Understanding project (GPE GU) group discussions aimed to highlight diversity in possible understandings of the topics at hand, while tandem interactions were intended to create opportunities for the mutual exploration of personal perspectives. Two project days diverted from the setup explained earlier. The first link day class was normally taught as an all-class videoconference and was usually dedicated to individual introductions and the presentation of partner cultures and institutions, while the last link day often consisted in students delivering multimedia presentations which rounded up the collaborative projects described later.

In 2017, out-of-class work spanned the duration of each partnership and involved students from partner institutions in mini collaborative projects, where individuals worked in pairs – or slightly larger groupings, if need be – to discuss via online communicators of their choice (e.g. Skype or Zoom) a selected topic from a GPE-proposed list to answer a related problem question or prepare a negotiated product, such as a poem, song or cartoon. Two sample topics and the related questions and products are cited next:

7) Collect some examples of jokes, cartoons, and comic pages. What are the common themes?

(GQ/NP): Design a cartoon or joke together that students from both cultures can understand.

8) Discuss two or three people from each culture (past or present) who you think have had the most influence on your culture. Describe their contributions and why you think they are important.

(GQ/NP): Write a description of a fictional character who could have a significant and positive impact on the world.

(GPE, 2014, p. 17; numbering as per original)

The collaborative projects were to help student partners investigate selected aspects of each other's cultures and discern mutual perspectives. All in all, it could be stated that the Global Understanding course involved both telecollaboration proper and e-tandem work, complemented with in-class student-student interaction, which occurred during the videoconferencing sessions and teacher-student interaction in the pre- and post-link stages of each link day class, where the topic of the day was first discussed locally, and the day's events were rounded up through post-link activities (e.g. a short reflection-on-experience session).

The aforementioned Intercultural Communication in the New Media course, which constituted the backdrop of the 10th iteration of the GPE GU project at UJ, was offered to first-year MA translation students as an elective supplement to a core course in Intercultural Pragmatics, which the Polish students had already completed in the spring semester of the 2016/2017 academic year. The course aimed to foster the students' generic intercultural competence, including intercultural communication and mediation skills, and it was completed between 21 March and 6 April 2017, comprising six link days in total.

The project work involved the students from Poland (UJ) in telecollaboration with colleagues from East Carolina University, NC, USA (ECU). The first link day was dedicated entirely to introductions, which on both sides related to the students themselves, their native culture, university and its location. Apart from the six link days, an introductory f2f class was taught to introduce the UJ students to the project and its work modes, as well as delegate individual tasks for completion prior to the first link day. The final link day class was an all-to-all videoconference involving the delivery of students' multimedia presentations designed jointly as part of the out-of-class collaborative project.

Each of the link day classes lasted roughly 60–70 minutes and involved 50–60 minutes' online work, as well as 10–20 minutes of pre-link introduction and post-link reflection led by the course teacher. For an overview of the 10th iteration of the GPE GU project, please consult Table 6.1.

Research aims

The goal of the research based on data obtained during the GPE GU X project was twofold. On the one hand, it aimed to investigate the Polish students' retrospective reflections on the intercultural learning experience occasioned by online interaction with their project partners. On the other hand, it was to explore the implications of the findings regarding the students' learning gains and future learning needs. To that end, three research questions were posed:

RQ1. What areas of culture drew the Polish participants' particular attention in their online interactions?

RQ2. What areas of (inter)cultural learning did the students' online interactions apparently involve?

RQ3. What do the findings imply about the students' potential learning gains and future learning needs with regard to intercultural competence?

Table 6.1 GPE GU X: Project overview

Aspect of the project	Details
Duration	17 days (21 March–6 April 2017)
Related TS course	Intercultural Communication in the New Media (elective)
Goals	To supplement a core course in Intercultural Pragmatics To develop intercultural competence (intercultural communication and mediation skills)
Institutional partners	Jagiellonian University in Kraków, Poland; East Carolina University, USA
Participants	23 participants: 8 UJ students of translation and 15 ECU students of communication and health studies
Procedure	1 introductory f2f class 6 links days: 5 link days proper (in-class videoconferencing and online chat discussions) and 1 round-up link class (in-class videoconferencing with PPT presentations) Online collaborative project (for the duration of the project)

Forms of telecollaboration involved	• Online topic discussions
	  o All-to-all videoconferencing (synchronous)
	  o Team chat (synchronous)
	• Collaborative project (e-tandem videoconferencing; synchronous)

Technologies used	Polycom videoconferencing system (in class) IceChat desktop application (in class) Web communicators, for example, Skype, Zoom, Messenger (out of class)

Research design: Procedures, methods and sampling

The research data were collected in the spring semester of the 2016/2017 academic year, from 21 March to 6 April 2017 at UJ, but they were processed and analysed between January 2019 and July 2021.

To answer RQ1 and RQ2, an ethnographic method was used, whereby structured retrospective reflections were collected from the project participants immediately after each link day via an online forum designed on the university-provided Moodle-based virtual learning platform. To facilitate recall, the forum contained three separate threads within which the students posted reflections on three issues, as recommended in the GPE Core document:

- Highlights of discussion of the day
- Surprising comments or attitudes of classmates & partners at both universities
- Thoughts on the day's discussions.

(GPE, 2014, p. 5)

The students' posts were further exported into .DOCX and .ODT format files, analysed qualitatively and coded by two independent coders in an MS Excel spreadsheet for reflections on discernible areas of culture and (inter) cultural learning. The choice of the tool was determined by the fact that inductive coding was performed (cf. Saldaña, 2013), which means that the coding categories emerged as the analysis progressed. Afterwards, the original categories, developed independently by each coder, were merged into more general categories to reduce data granularity and facilitate the interpretation of the results. Both coders originally identified a total of 71 coding categories which related to areas of culture and components of intercultural competence discernible in UJ students' retrospective reflections. 31 categories were identified in the students' posts on the highlights of the day, 24 categories (in the posts on surprising comments and attitudes of classmates and partners from both institutions) and 16 categories (in the posts containing the students' thoughts on the day's discussions).

The original 71 categories were reviewed to eliminate repetition, which reduced their number to a total of 39. However, due to a high degree of inter-category overlap and to ease data analysis, the 39 were ultimately conflated into six categories, each representing either an area of culture or intercultural learning: (i) affective elements, (ii) (meta)awareness, (iii) shift in perspective, (iv) lifestyle, (v) cultural realities and (vi) values, thought patterns and beliefs. Within each of the categories, the coders independently marked off each relevant instance of the students' retrospective reflections, which produced frequency counts for each of the areas under examination.

To validate the coding procedure, Cohen's Kappa coefficient (κ) (Cohen, 1960; Fleiss, Levin, & Paik, 2003) was computed, which at the value of $\kappa = 0.784$ revealed a substantial level of interrater reliability (cf. Altman, 1999; Landis & Koch, 1977), thus confirming that the coding decisions could be approached with relative trust. The frequency counts for each identified element of intercultural learning were further transferred into a separate MS Excel sheet to generate graphs with which to illustrate the results obtained. At the last stage of the research procedure, the data were also scoured for examples of intercultural learning within the areas identified through the coding.

Sampling

The research subjects were recruited through convenience sampling – the procedure which, as Saldanha and O'Brien (2014) report, is not only very common in humanities and social science research but has also been used in translation research (e.g. to recruit translators). The subjects were ECU and UJ students participating in the GPE GU X project. UJ participants

Table 6.2 Overview of the research design (GPE GU X)

Aspect of research design	Details
Research aims	To investigate areas of culture which drew UJ students' attention in discussions
	To examine what areas of (inter)cultural learning the students' online interactions involved
	To establish what the findings imply about the students' potential learning gains and future learning needs with regard to intercultural competence
Research method	Descriptive research (focused description)
	Structured retrospective reflections collected via an online forum (qualitative and quantitative analysis)
Research instrument	MS Excel spreadsheet (data coding and graph generation)
Sampling	Convenience sampling; 23 GPE GU X project participants from UJ and ECU (N = 23); 8 UJ students (N = 8) and 15 ECU students (N = 15)
	Sub-sample: 8 UJ students (N = 8)
Timing	March–April 2017: data collection
	January 2019–July 2021: data processing and analysis
Data analysis	Qualitative and quantitative

were a group of eight MA-level translation students (N = 8), all in their mid-twenties, seven females (N = 7) and one male (N = 1), whereas their ECU partners were a group of 15 (N=15), 13 females (N = 13) and two males (N = 2), in their early- to mid-twenties and majoring in either communication or health education.

The analysis of the students' retrospective reflections on the intercultural learning experience was conducted on data collected from a sub-sample consisting of UJ students only. An overview of the research design is presented in Table 6.2.

Results and discussion

In total, 210 instances were identified of the students' retrospective reflections regarding the areas of culture and aspects of (inter)cultural learning under examination. Out of them, 74 were found in the forum thread relating to the highlights of the day, 89 in the posts on the surprising comments and attitudes of classmates and international partners and 47 in the posts about thoughts on the day's discussions. The breakdown of the frequency counts for the students' reflections within the five areas, with an indication of the proportions found within each forum thread (highlights, comments and thoughts), is illustrated in Figure 6.1.

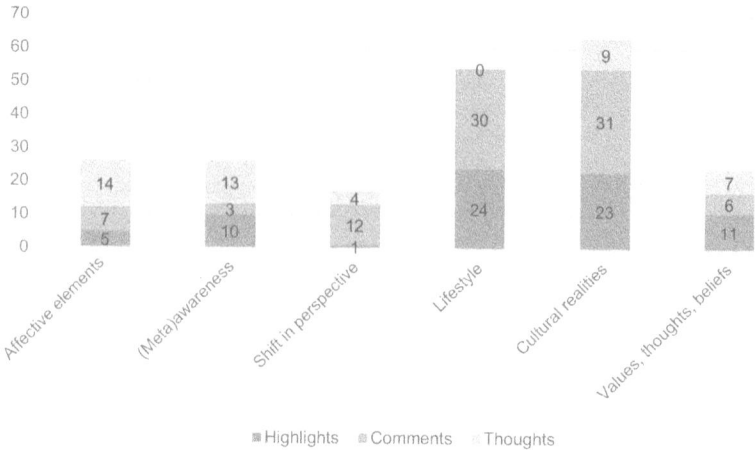

Figure 6.1 Areas of intercultural learning in students' retrospective reflections on highlights, comments and thoughts.

As it has been stated, three areas of intercultural learning were identified in UJ students' retrospective reflections, which were categorised as (i) affective elements (26 reflections), (ii) intercultural and metacognitive awareness – for the purpose of simplicity labelled as (meta)awareness (26) – and (iii) shift in perspective (17), as well as three areas of culture, including lifestyle (54), cultural realities (63) and values, thought patterns and beliefs (24).

The data also demonstrate that the majority of UJ students' reflections on the surprising comments or attitudes of their classmates or international partners related to factual cultural knowledge (cultural realities), lifestyle and the shift of perspective on their native culture or that of their partners. The first two areas are hardly astonishing, as students' comments in an OIE are most likely to regard observable elements of culture, such as practices (lifestyle) and cultural facts (realities). The third is very meaningful, as it implies that at least some of the project participants made inferences about the less explicit – and often subconscious – elements of the culture in question, which is a challenging intercultural learning task.

The students' reflections on the highlights of the day, in turn, mostly pertained to values, thoughts and beliefs, which suggests that either they were elucidated in the students' discussions or that the exchange stimulated reflection on the less obvious. Interestingly, UJ students' final thoughts on the events of the day were clearly dominated by reflections on their initial expectations towards the project, emotions stirred by the project tasks or their partners' apparent attitudes (e.g. relaxed manners, interest or curiosity). Only reflections on (meta)awareness escaped clear categorisation, as most of them were provided either as highlights of the day or final thoughts. The former may imply that some of the realisations about the nature and challenges of intercultural learning occurred to the students more instantly – perhaps, as striking – whereas the latter seems to indicate that at times such realisations required more distance and contemplation.

As far as areas of intercultural learning go, *affective elements* related to the emotions aroused by project partners' degree of involvement in – or apparent attitudes to – the project work and responsibilities, project partners' reactions to the questions asked or issues raised, the atmosphere of the discussion (e.g. emotions stirred by controversial topics) or the perceived ease or difficulty of the discussion task at hand. *(Meta) awareness* embraced two kinds of awareness, hence, the name of this area. On the one hand, it referred to the students' realisations about the challenges and mechanisms of intercultural exploration (intercultural awareness) (e.g. cultural attribution in interpreting intercultural observations). On the other hand, it related to the metacognitive awareness of the students, that is, their insights into the impact of the tool and communication mode being used (e.g. chat vs. videoconferencing), as well as the learning decisions taken (e.g. to go beyond the obvious and the superficial) on the learning process and its outcomes. *Shift of perspective* denoted the ability to perceive reality, including own culture, from the perspective of the other (i.e. the foreign project partner) or to detach from own culture and see it from a new vantage point in response to the intercultural experience.

As the students' reflections on the three areas of intercultural learning defined earlier displayed far less granularity than those on the areas of culture, it was decided that a qualitative analysis of the most revealing, anonymised examples would be conducted, which revealed that the students' reflections on the affective aspects of intercultural learning (26 in total, see Figure 6.1) concerned emotions aroused by the project discussions, their topics, nature and the resulting atmosphere (12) or emotions stirred by the foreign partners' task involvement and apparent attitudes to the issues under discussion (14).

The emotions which the students experienced while participating in the discussions can be illustrated by the two quotations from posts on the highlights of the day. In connection with the discussion on the topic *meaning of life*, Student 1 wrote:

> When it comes to "the meaning of life", we had a lot of laughter and we finally concluded that everyone has to "work it out for himself".

On the one hand, the previously cited reflection reveals the atmosphere in which the students reportedly worked. On the other – very importantly – it implies that the discussion may have been somewhat superficial and the students failed to jointly arrive at conclusions, leaving that part of learning to individuals.

The other quotation comes from a post regarding the highlights of the first linking day on which the students from both institutions introduced to one another their countries, cities and universities via multimedia presentations and video clips while videoconferencing. As the Polish students displayed a video depicting mostly the wars and battles which Poland has endured, Student 2 observed:

> *History is a difficult topic, but with humour we tried to avoid an atmosphere that would have been too serious.*

This time, it seems that the creation of a joyful atmosphere was meant to downplay the seriousness of the topic presented in the video, and while avoiding too serious an atmosphere during the exchange may have been the right strategy, the idea of approaching a nation's traumatic experiences with humour may have trivialised the presentation, thus possibly misrepresenting the students' stance on the events depicted in the video.

The last quotation relating to the affective dimension of intercultural learning comes from a comment on emotions aroused by the project partners' attitude towards the issues being discussed. Student 3 wrote:

> *I was a bit surprised by what I should have expected, namely the openness with which the girls talked about sometimes difficult matters, even encouraging me to carry on the discussion. Surely in America people are more open, but in the "head-on collision" with this fact I felt a little embarrassed.*

Regardless of the difficult matters that this particular reflection concerns, it indicates that at least some of the project partners felt comfortable enough to discuss even problematic topics, which is likely to have increased the depth of the exchange and the resulting intercultural learning. At the same time, it reveals how an open discussion on difficult matters may be intimidating for the more reserved students.

Reflections related to (meta)awareness (26 in total, see Figure 6.1) tackled both the students' cultural awareness (9) and awareness of the nature of intercultural learning (17), including the challenges beyond it, the choice of learning techniques or the perceived opportunities for extended intercultural learning outside the project's mainstream activities (meta-awareness).

The next comment illustrates the cultural awareness of a student who tries to explore the possible motivations behind the project partners' behaviour.

I was surprised by the reaction when I explained to my partners what Śmigus-dyngus was all about. One of them saw sexual connotations in response. This was probably due to the translation [the Polish equivalent] of the phrase "pussy willow" into English. I checked that willows are only found in the North of the United States, so this kind of tree may be less known in this part [the South] of the US; hence, the name may have caused such reactions.

The previously cited comment reveals the student's readiness to suspend judgment in a potentially conflicting intercultural communicative situation. To seek an explanation other than negative – which usually springs to mind first – the student conducted cultural research to attribute the US partners' observed behaviour to the place of residence and limited experience with a particular kind of tree, rather than their personal characteristics.

Another two reflections imply Student 4's awareness of the nature of cultural knowledge and intercultural learning:

How we perceive other cultures is affected by the perception of our own culture.

Sometimes we lack knowledge about our own homeland, let alone other countries.

In the first line, the student underlines that it is hard to objectivise cultural observations, as one's perception of other cultures is to some extent filtered through the prism of one's self-perception of native culture. In the second line, the student apparently realises both the intricacy and incompleteness of people's knowledge of native culture and the essence of intercultural learning, which involves the exploration of both one's own culture and that of the other.

The next three reflections relate to the students' metacognitive awareness, whereby they arrive at certain realisations about ways in which to facilitate their intercultural learning. Student 5 reveals increased awareness of the need to go beyond the obvious in intercultural learning and explore not only visible behaviour (stereotyping in this case) but also the reasons for it and its possible impact on those who can be affected by it when s/he writes:

Rather than listing different stereotypes, we mainly talked about the influences of stereotypes and how people actually use stereotypes.

> *Stereotypes can be "positive", that is, beneficial to people in certain situations. The stereotype is like a knife with two sides – we need it to live comfortably, but we also become its victim.*

Student 6 reflects on the impact of the mode of communication on the quality of intercultural learning, observing the following:

> *Chat is slower than video calls, but it gives you the opportunity to slow down a bit and think about your words before sending your post.*

The quotation earlier implies that the student is also aware of the importance of withdrawing from immediate responses in intercultural communication, which may help the parties involved make more informed decisions about the content they communicate (e.g. in order to avoid potentially conflicting situations).

Student 7 also ponders on the quality of intercultural learning, emphasising the need to discuss even controversial issues in a more open and thus in-depth way.

> *These were perhaps the most "flammable" topics so far, so each of us tried to weigh our words and be careful, especially when we might accidentally have offended someone. I do not know if it is good or bad, certainly good as a sign of our social awareness, but I think that it would have been more interesting for observers if a discussion on one or another "touchy subject" had indeed taken place.*

The third group of reflections referred to the students' apparent shift of perspective (17 in total, see Figure 6.1) which permitted them to see their project partners' perspective on particular issues (6), discern alternative perspectives on their own culture (10) or speculate about the partners' possible intentions in the project interactions (1).

The reflection which follows, regarding the video about traumatic events in the history of Poland, is an example of how the student who produced the post cited later distances themselves from their own culture and takes on a stranger's perspective on it. Their actual interpretation of that perspective is not verbalised, but the closing sentence implies readiness to consider alternative viewpoints.

> *It's a bit as if we like to feel like victims all the time. The film is very interesting, but it seems too serious for the first meeting. I am also curious what the Americans were thinking when we laughed.*

In the reflection later, Student 8 reports on the strategy of the use of conflict avoidance in one of the discussions:

> *I wonder if "avoiding conflict" is their [Americans'] national feature, related to the fact that they do not want to leave a certain zone of security and comfort. Perhaps in private conversations with each other they also avoid controversy? Don't they want to enter into a conversation on difficult topics with Poles because there is something they have not told us, e.g. that they consider us a quarrelsome nation and are afraid of our reaction?*

What transpires from the post earlier is the student's attempt to attribute the partners' observable behaviour either to national culture or to the strategy of conflict avoidance in intercultural communication, which the partners are likely to have adopted. The reflection is interesting, as it indicates the student's ability to shift perspective not only to speculate about the partners' stance on security and comfort in conversations but also to predict their US colleagues' intentions in the communicative situation at hand.

The remainder of UJ students' retrospective reflections related to various elements of culture, but as they displayed a considerable degree of granularity, they will be analysed qualitatively. Figure 6.2 illustrates all the areas of culture which were identified during the coding.

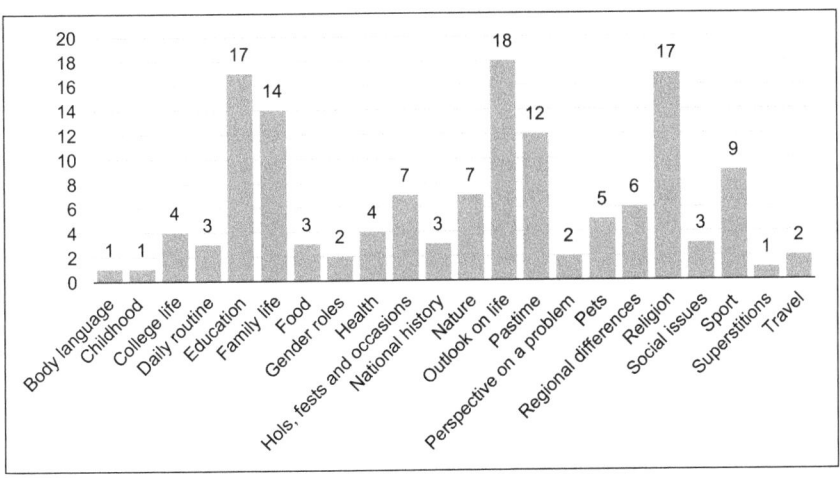

Figure 6.2 Areas of culture identified in UJ students' reflections.

On closer inspection, these areas of culture turned out to fall into three major blocks, which were labelled as lifestyle (54 reflections), cultural realities (63) and values, thought patterns and beliefs (24). *Lifestyle* entailed different cultural practices relating to 11 walks of life, including childhood, college life, daily routine, family life, food, holidays, festivities and special occasions (e.g. weddings), pastime activities, pet keeping, social issues (e.g. gun possession, crime and addictions) and travel. As the frequency counts for the particular elements in this category indicate, the two areas which were most salient, and apparently stuck in UJ students' memory after their online interactions with ECU partners, were aspects of family life (14) and ways of spending free time (pastime), including the pursuing of hobbies and personal interests (12). Much less of the students' attention was caught by cultural practices related to childhood memories (1), food (2), travel (2) or social issues (3).

The reasons for that might have been different. A plausible explanation is that family life and pastime activities are rather obvious topics which are often used as social icebreakers in conversations with strangers whom people have only just met and intend to get to know better. At the same time, social issues may seem too serious a theme for OIEs because the grave problems which the theme entails may be too distant or too depressing for students. That interpretation seems to have been countered by the fact that other relatively light topics, such as travel, daily routine or childhood, did not attract much of the students' attention. However, as the videoconferencing and chat interactions were time limited and the discussion topics were imposed on the students by the GPE Core (GPE, 2014), family life and pastime activities may have seemed the obvious choices for discussion, as they matched the topics of both Link Day 1, which – *inter alia* – was dedicated to personal introductions, and Link Day 2, which focused on family and traditions, with the latter additionally increasing the salience of holidays, festivities and special occasions (7) in UJ students' reflections.

Another area of culture on which the students reflected could be collectively named *cultural realities* – which in the German tradition of cultural studies has been referred to as *Landeskunde* (Risager, 2007) – embracing basic factual knowledge about the project partners' culture. As it is shown in Figure 6.3, the students' reflections revolved around the core cultural studies topics, including education (17), sport (9), national history (3), religion (17), natural life (nature, 7), healthcare (4) and regional differences (6).

Only two of the topics, education and religion, directly related to the topics of discussion tackled on the link days (college life and religion respectively), but – quite tellingly – it is exactly these topics that the students most frequently reflected on. What is more, the third topic most

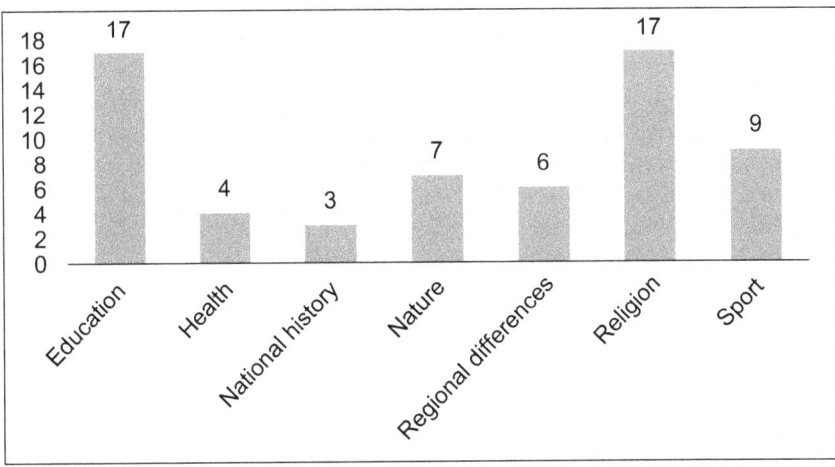

Figure 6.3 Areas of factual cultural knowledge identified in UJ students' reflections.

commonly reflected on was sport, which was not the focus of any link day but nevertheless surfaced vividly in the students' discussions about college life, as the US students recurrently underlined the importance of sport and sporting achievement in American higher education.

Overall, these findings indicate that the students generally adhered to the official project topics in online interactions and reflections, but occasionally, they digressed, focusing on other important threads. A case in point was sport, which extended the topic of education in the American context while additionally illustrating the freedom that the students enjoyed in managing their discussions.

The third area of culture found in UJ students' reflections related to the invisible layer of culture, which in the metaphor of culture as an iceberg (Hall, 1976) is placed underneath the water level to symbolise its implicitness. It is exactly in relation to the iceberg metaphor that this area was named values, thought patterns and beliefs. The frequency counts computed for particular components of this area of culture which were found in UJ students' reflections revealed that by far, the largest proportion of UJ students' reflections related to ECU students' outlook on life (18) (e.g. the role of sporting achievement) and the most important life values, such as family, success, happiness or attitudes to natural life, about which UJ students learnt – both explicitly and implicitly – from their ECU partners. The other components comprised gender roles (2), perspectives on specific problems, such as ways of ensuring success in life or gender roles (2), superstitions (1) and body language (1).

Summary of the findings and conclusions

In the light of the findings discussed earlier, it may be stated that the areas of culture which drew the Polish participants' particular attention were declarative, factual knowledge about life and institutions (i.e. areas of human activity and the related institutions) (cultural realities) and common practices (lifestyle). The third – albeit much less represented – element of culture encompassed the underpinnings of people's observable behaviour, such as values, thought patterns and beliefs.

Given the limited scope of the exchange, it is only natural that the students focused primarily on the most obvious, such as cultural realities. Although this kind of knowledge can be accessed through publications, the merit of the project lies in that the students could learn the facts straight from representatives of the other culture. What is more, they had opportunities – albeit limited due to time constraints – to ask for clarification or further explanation, which might have helped them explore the culture of the other beyond the bookish picture available in materials for cultural learning.

At the same time, the students used the project to additionally delve into one another's cultural practices, which tend to be less accessible to outsiders. Most importantly, though, the research results demonstrate that the project interactions permitted the students to tackle the elements of culture which are most difficult to explore and thus impossible to access through conventional learning methods such as reading. A case in point were the values, thought patterns and beliefs of the other but also their own, which most often remain subconscious. Perhaps it was the latter that helped some of the students to reportedly shift their cultural perspectives and objectivise their own culture by looking at it from a different standpoint, as well as take the vantage point of the other to see an alternative outlook on life. This, complemented with awareness of the nature of intercultural discovery and learning ([meta-]awareness), is likely not only to augment the students' further development of intercultural competence as an indispensable element of translation competence but also to facilitate their transferrable self- and lifelong learning skills, which build translator competence.

The results additionally indicate the students' immediate intercultural learning needs. Firstly, the students apparently need to work more on the less explicit elements of culture (i.e. values, thought patterns and beliefs underlying culture-bound behaviour). It is essential that the students balance these elements with the more explicit ones not only to learn about culture-bound behaviours and practices and understand the factors underlying what is observable but also, first and foremost, because this kind of knowledge is necessary for effective translation. The realisation of what determines the communicative choices of the text authors facilitates source text comprehension, which helps translators produce culturally adequate renditions of the source content in the target language.

Towards that end, the students need to advance their metacognitive awareness and consciously explore the affective/emotive aspects of their learning. For instance, increased metacognitive awareness can augment their efforts to consciously shift perspective, which surfaced in a limited number of reflections and seems to be a challenge. Moreover, by increasingly reflecting on emotions involved in intercultural interactions, the students are likely to realise that negative emotions are often a natural response to otherness and learn to rationalise those emotions through objectivising; they may also predict and avoid potentially conflicting situations in intercultural communication, of which translation is a form.

All in all, the project had a two-pronged pedagogical merit. From the students' perspective, it was a chance to test own intercultural competence in action and make experience-based intercultural observations. From the teacher's perspective, it was an opportunity to research the nature of intercultural learning and its outcomes thanks to the networked character of the project, which took the onus of design off his shoulders. Although the research results most certainly depicted only a limited picture of the intercultural learning under examination – be it due to the sampling method, whereby reflections were collected from UJ students only or the limited reliability of students' reflections – the collected responses, as planned, highlighted the most salient aspects of intercultural learning occasioned by GPE X.

6.1.2 *The Global Understanding project (GPE XII)*

Project overview and research context

The OIE that will be discussed here was also held as part of the 12th edition of the GPE GU (GPE XII) project; thus, the generic details of the project, including the link day discussion topics and the procedures of the video-conferencing, chat mode and the collaborative projects remained the same as those described in Chapter 6.1.1.

The GPE GU XII at UJ was again integrated into the Intercultural Communication in the New Media elective course for first-year MA translation students, who telecollaborated with colleagues from ECU. This time, the project was administered in the fall semester, lasted from 6 to 27 November 2018 and spanned six link days in total, on top of which an additional two classes were also taught. On 25 October 2018, in an introductory f2f class, UJ students were introduced to the details of the project and negotiated the sharing of tasks and responsibilities ahead of the first

Table 6.3 GPE GU XII: Project overview

Aspect of the project	Details
Duration	22 days (6–27 November 2018)
Related TS course	Intercultural Communication in the New Media (elective)
Goals	To supplement a core course in Intercultural Pragmatics
	To develop intercultural competence (intercultural communication and mediation skills)
Institutional partners	Jagiellonian University in Kraków, Poland; East Carolina University, USA
Participants	26 participants: 12 UJ students of translation, 14 ECU students of psychology
Procedure	1 introductory f2f class
	5 link days proper (in-class videoconferencing and online chat discussions)
	Online collaborative projects (for the duration of the project)
	1 round-up link class (in-class videoconferencing with PPT presentations)
Forms of telecollaboration involved	• Online topic discussions
	o All-to-all videoconferencing (synchronous)
	o Team chat (synchronous)
	• Collaborative project (e-tandem videoconferencing; synchronous)
Technologies used	Polycom videoconferencing system (in class)
	IceChat desktop application (in class)
	Web communicators, for example, Skype, Zoom, Messenger (out of class)

link day. On 27 November 2018, the last link day involved all-to-all video-conferencing with the students delivering multimedia presentations which they had prepared with their ECU partners within the out-of-class collaborative project. The duration of the project classes remained unchanged; thus, each link day class was roughly 60–70 minutes long and involved 50–60 minutes' telecollaboration, complemented with 10–20 minutes of teacher-led pre-link introduction and post-link reflection. An overview of the GPE GU XII project is presented in Table 6.3.

Research aims

The primary goal of the research relating to the GPE GU XII project was to go beyond students' reflections or comments on experience and delve into their involvement in online chat interactions by examining their use of specific interactional features. The secondary research goal was to explore the possible implications of the findings in relation the students' learning and areas of possible improvement. To that end, three research questions were posed:

RQ1. What markers of involvement did the students use in online chat interactions?
RQ2. What can be inferred from the findings about the nature of chat communication?
RQ3. What do the findings imply about the students' intercultural learning in the project and areas of improvement to better foster the development of intercultural competence?

Research design: Procedures, methods and sampling

The data collection was performed in the fall semester of the 2018/2019 academic year, between 6 and 27 November 2018, in the 12th edition of the GPE GU project, as it was implemented at UJ. Data processing and analysis was completed in the period spanning January 2019 and March 2021.

The research involved the use of *virtual ethnography* (Carel, 2001; Corbett, 2003), which is an ethnographic method used to examine interactions in online environments, where communication is mediated through the digital media. Although the research method originated in anthropological studies, Domínguez et al. (2007) rightly point out that it has now been adopted in numerous other areas, including sociology, pedagogy, philosophy, psychology or economics, hence, the choice. Only data from the students' online chat communication were analysed, as records of their text-based interactions were automatically saved in .TXT file format by IceChat – the desktop chat application which the students used when working in e-tandems in class. 24 recorded chat discussions were selected for analysis, two discussions by each of the 12 chat teams, of which ten were pairs and two were groups of three. In each team, the first and last discussion was selected to build a picture of interaction at the beginning and at the end of the project.

The coding performed in this research was deductive (cf. Saldaña, 2013) (i.e. based on the preconceived coding categories listed later). Thus, the records of students' chat interactions were imported into R (www.r--project.org/) – the software for statistical computing and graphics – and coded in the program's package for qualitative data analysis (RQDA) (https://rqda.r-forge.r-project.org/) for eight interactional features, as defined by Ware (2013): the use of (i) emotive words and phrases, (ii) personal forms of address, (iii) topic development, (iv) question posing,

(v) personal information, (vi) display of alignment, (vii) emoticons and tone tags and (viii) unconventional capitalisation.

The features listed earlier were collectively named *markers of effective collaboration* due to the fact that they are likely indicators of student involvement, alignment seeking and interest in interactions with project partners. The markers were operationalised in congruence with Ware's (2013) proposition and could be described as follows. The emotive elements, as the name indicates, were emotionally charged words and phrases such as *great, lovely* or *love*. Personal forms of address involved the use of the project partners' first names, the second-person pronoun (*you*) or the related possessive adjective (*your*). Topic development denoted the sentences or phrases that the students used to elaborate on what had already been written by the project partner or to contribute more to-the-point details. Question posing referred to the questions which the students asked their partners to elicit information or redirect the conversation. Personal information signified all cases where the students shared information relating to their private life, including personal experiences and memories, as well as those of their relatives and friends. Therefore, most of the sentences or phrases in this category began with the person personal pronoun singular (*I*, to denote self) or plural (*we*, to talk about family or friends). Display of alignment comprised sentences or phrases through which the students apparently sought to underline the things that they and their chat partners had in common (e.g. likes, interests or viewpoints). Thus, they were (e.g. statements or short phrases such as "*Oh, I like it too!*" or "*Same here*" respectively). Emoticons and tone tags were those elements which, as *The Oxford Handbook of Internet Psychology* (Joinson, McKenna, Postmes, & Reips, 2009) reports, are used in online communication to provide textual or graphical replacements for the kinds of nonverbal devices (e.g. body movements or facial expressions) which people normally use in f2f interactions in order to strengthen the emotional dimension of a message or the paraverbal devices through which the tone of what is being said can be indicated. In the students' chat conversations, emoticons were, for example, smileys produced through punctuation marks (:) or ;)), while tone tags were, for example, written representations of onomatopoeia (*hahaha*). Finally, unconventional capitalisation referred to instances where students emphasised the content of their messages by capitalising words, phrases, longer fragments of their written messages or even entire sentences (e.g. "*YOU DON'T SAY!*"). More examples of the actual realisations of the markers of involvement operationalised earlier will be provided when the results of the research are discussed.

In total, records of students' interactions in 12 teams were examined and coded for the markers defined earlier. Two records per team were selected for analysis, one from the chat conversation on the second link day and the other from the chat discussion held on the penultimate link day. The decision to examine chat interactions on these particular days stemmed from the fact that these classes involved chat-based communication at all and that the students' discussions at the time concerned the first and last topic listed in the GPE GU Core (GPE, 2014). In GPE GU XII, the first and last link days involved whole-class videoconferencing exclusively.

Again, as the coding was performed independently by two coders, Cohen's Kappa coefficient (κ) was computed to verify interrater reliability, and the result of the computation (κ=0.757) revealed a substantial level of interrater agreement as interpreted by Landis and Koch (1977). Finally, the linguistic markers of involvement identified in the textual data were summated to obtain frequency counts for each marker. This quantification of the findings, together with the generation of graphs illustrating the numerical data, was supposed to facilitate the interpretation of the results by possibly revealing certain trends in the students' communication patterns.

Sampling

Convenience sampling (Saldanha & O'Brien, 2014) was used to recruit the research subjects, who were participants of the GPE GU XII project from ECU and UJ. All the students were in their mid-twenties. The 12 UJ (N = 12) participants were MA-level translation students, eight females (N = 8) and four males (N = 4), while the 14-strong group of ECU students (N = 14) consisted of 12 females (N = 12) and two males (N = 2), who majored in psychology. Table 6.4 provides a summary of the search design.

Results and discussion

Overall, 2,919 instances were found in the students' online chat interactions under examination, and the breakdown of the frequency counts for each marker category is presented in Figure 6.4.

As the graph earlier illustrates, by far, the largest proportions of the markers identified in the students' chat interactions involved sentences, whereby the students developed the topic initiated or tackled by their colleagues (topic development – 831) and question posing (573). Lower counts were found for personal forms of address (394), personal information (359) and emoticons and tone tags (336). The students used considerably less emotive words and phrases (242), sentences or phrases denoting display of alignment (169) and – very sporadically – unconventional capitalisation (15).

Table 6.4 Overview of the research design (GPE GU XII)

Aspect of research design	Details
Research aims	To examine UJ and ECU students' use of linguistic markers of effective telecollaboration (Ware's, 2013, features of online interactions)
	To explore implications of the findings about the nature of the students' intercultural communication in the project and areas for further development of intercultural competence
Research method	Descriptive research (focused description)
	Records of students' chat interactions coded for the markers cited earlier (quantitative analysis). 24 records were analysed from 12 teams (two records per team)
Research instrument	R software for statistical computing (coding)
	MS Excel spreadsheet (graph generation)
Sampling	Convenience sampling; 26 GPE GU XII project participants from UJ and ECU (N = 26); 12 UJ students (N = 12) and 14 ECU students (N = 14)
	Sub-sample: 8 UJ students (N = 8)
Timing	March–April 2017: data collection
	January 2020–July 2022: data processing and analysis
Data analysis	Qualitative and quantitative

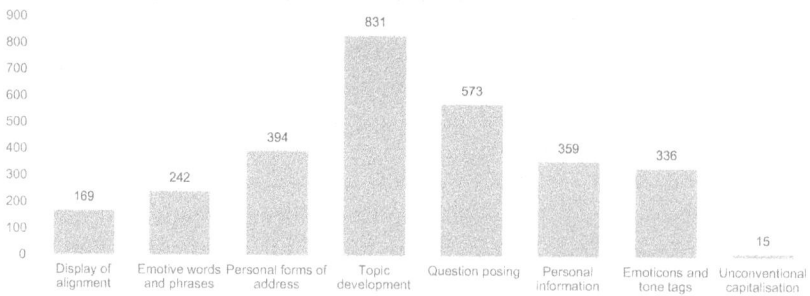

Figure 6.4 Linguistic markers of effective telecollaboration in GPE GU XII students' chat interactions.

The data suggest that the students apparently focused on the completion of the project task, which involved the discussion of the day's topic. Thus, their communication was dominated by the two actions which were most indispensable for that purpose (i.e. eliciting and providing information by asking questions and developing on what had already been said respectively). It needs to be underlined that the students' conversations seem to have reached beyond the mere question-and-answer pattern, which is inferable from the much larger number of the observed instances of topic development *vis-à-vis* the number of questions asked. If one is cognisant of the fact that topic development by definition did not comprise mere answers to questions but cases where the students elaborated on the issues being discussed, it indicates that the messages produced by the students in response to questions embraced more than simple fact giving, which facilitates intercultural learning. The latter finds corroboration in the number of instances in which the students personalised the information they provided and the extent to which they used markers of emotional involvement. Although not quite clear judging by the sheer number of emotive words and phrases used in the chat conversations, it becomes evident when one realises that emotional involvement was additionally marked by the use of emoticons and tone tags. Having said that, it must be noted that the aggregated number of both means of expressing emotions (242 and 336 respectively) amounts to as many as 578, which implies a substantial emotional load carried by the messages exchanged, and may in turn be indicative of a high level of student interest and involvement in the project activities.

More can be inferred from the juxtaposition of the counts for particular markers of effective telecollaboration identified in chat discussions on link day two and link day five, which is illustrated in Figure 6.5.

As the data reveal, the number of four of the eight marker types under examination increased from the second to the fifth link day. Such increases were observed for emoticons and tone tags (from 120 to 216), topic development (from 377 to 454), personal form of address (from 175 to 219)

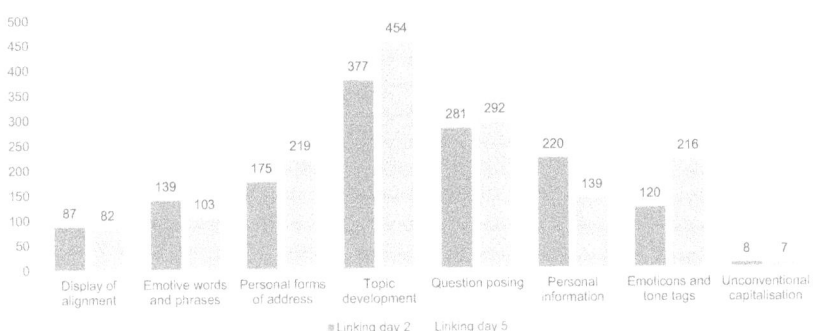

Figure 6.5 Linguistic markers of effective telecollaboration in students' chat interactions (Link Day 2 vs. Link Day 5).

and question posing (from 281 to 292). In yet another two categories, there was either a marginal or very small decrease for unconventional capitalisation (from eight down to seven) and for display of alignment (from 87 to 82), respectively. Only in two areas was the decrease in the number of markers of involvement greater. For personal information, the number decreased from 220 to 139, and for emotive words and phrases, it decreased from 139 to 103. The changes may be indicative of several issues regarding the students' interaction.

Firstly, given that as projects unfold, students' motivation and involvement are likely to decrease (e.g. due to the wearing off of the relative novelty of the tasks at hand), it seems very positive that five markers of involvement either increased or only slightly decreased, thus revealing that the aforementioned drop in motivation levels did not occur. Interestingly, Kurek's (2015) observation that the feeling of belonging and common purpose helps to maintain students' motivation levels in telecollaboration projects implies that the use of the interactional features under examination may not only indicate student involvement but also catalyse it, thus increasing motivation and involvement over time.

Secondly, the decrease in the number of instances where the project participants provided personal information in the chat conversations might have been caused by the topic of the conversation on the fifth link day, which was *Stereotypes and prejudices*. On the one hand, the topic was very general; thus, the students may have naturally decided to discuss it without referring to particular individuals. On the other hand – and more pertinently, perhaps – it is very likely that, due to the sensitive nature of the issue being discussed (e.g. the negative stereotypes and prejudices), at least some of the students decided to distance themselves from it, either to avoid potential misunderstandings or conflicts with their foreign partners or to save face and project a positive image of themselves to the rest of the team.

For at least two reasons, it seems rather ungrounded to attribute the decrease in the provision of personal information in chat conversations on the fifth link day to the students' decreased involvement or motivation. One of them is that, as it has been demonstrated, the levels of other markers of involvement in the students' exchanges remained relatively high. The other reason relates to the apparently high level of the students' emotional engagement. Given that the number of emotive words and phrases actually had decreased from the 139 to 103 from the second to the fifth link day, the latter might be viewed as a surprising proposition. However, it must be noted that simultaneously, the number of other markers of emotional involvement (emoticons and tone tags) had nearly doubled, increasing from 120 on the second link day to 219 on the fifth. A possible explanation of the growth in the students' use of emoticons and tone tags could be that with time, they might have felt more relaxed and thus less compelled to use formal markers of emotional involvement, replacing the latter with graphic symbols. Moreover, as the intensity of the discussion had seemingly increased, which is signified by increases in the number of questions asked and topic development messages posted, the choice of emoticons and tone tags over emotive words and phrases might denote the students' prioritisation of brevity. Lastly, as Maíz-Arévalo (2015) maintains that emoticons are frequently used to save one's own or one's interlocutors' face, the students might have utilised them as a mitigating strategy, particularly when dealing with the topic of stereotypes and prejudices.

To gain more insight into the nature of the students' chat interactions, an example of interaction within one team will be analysed in greater detail. The record of the team's conversation was randomly extracted from the batch of all of the chat conversations recorded in the GPE GU XII project, and it happens to be a discussion about *Family life* which a team of three students (one UJ and two ECU students) held on the third link day (see Figure 6.6).

As it can be seen, Student 1's (S1, UJ) conversation was dominated largely by topic development (67) and the use of emoticons and tone tags (27). The student asked 12 questions (e.g. to elicit information) and mostly elaborated on their partners' messages, thus contributing intensively to the discussion. The student seems to have been emotionally involved in the conversation, which – apart from emoticons and tone tags – they additionally manifested through the use of emotive words and phrases (8). At the same time, the student contributed relatively little personal information to the discussion (8).

Student 2's (S2, ECU) interaction displayed a similar pattern in that it was also dominated by topic development (50) and the use of emoticons

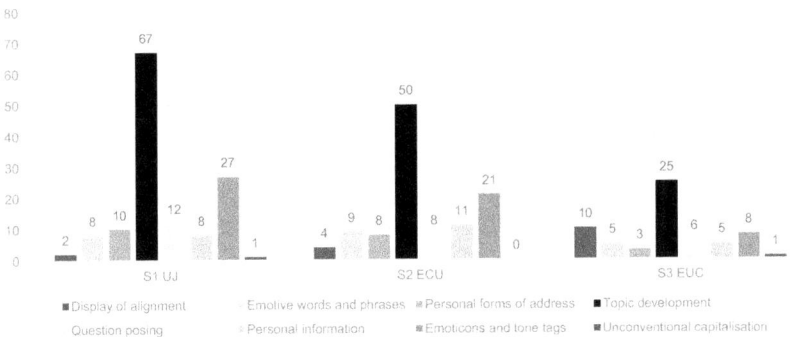

Figure 6.6 Linguistic markers of effective telecollaboration in chat interactions within a team of three students.

and tone tags (21). S2 asked slightly less questions (8), which were supposed to stimulate the discussion, but contributed more personal information (11). Alike S1, this student also asked questions to stir the discussion and elaborated on the topic tackled by their chat partners while displaying a relatively high level of emotional involvement.

Student 3 (S3, ECU) visibly differed in their performance from the other two colleagues, not so much in the pattern of interaction but in the level of its intensity. S3 also mostly developed on the conversation topics (25), asked some questions (6) and displayed emotional involvement through used emoticons and tone tags but, as Figure 6.6 illustrates, scored considerably lower than their partners in all the three departments. Since the student's pattern of performance does diverge from that of their partners, it might be suggested that although the student was indeed involved in the conversation, apparently, (s)he gave way to the other two colleagues. Consequently, S1 and S2 led the discussion, while S3 contributed whenever they deemed it necessary. Notably, though, S3 used sentences and phrases displaying alignment much more frequently than the other two partners (10 instances vs. 2 and 4 for S1 and S2 respectively). In light of that, the implications of S3's limited interaction do not need to be negative, as S3's low-key profile may have stemmed from the fact that (s)he simply did not want to infringe on the other two colleagues' conversation. What is more, their increased alignment building may have been a way in which the student attempted to compensate for their limited contributions to the discussion.

Quite notably, only two instances of unconventional capitalisation were found in the students' chat interactions. However, as this kind of device is usually used to strengthen the message, it is quite possible that instead, the students chose to use emoticons and tone tags, which all of them did extensively, perhaps due the commonality of this communicative feature in online communication (cf. Maíz-Arévalo, 2015).

It is also interesting to compare the aggregated scores on the markers of effective collaboration under examination for the UJ student (S1) vs. their two ECU colleagues (S2 and S3) in this conversation. The scores are graphically presented in Figure 6.7.

The data produce an interesting picture of the chat interaction within the team. Firstly, as it can be seen in the graph earlier, in most of the departments, the UJ student (S1) used so many markers of effective collaboration in their performance that their scores matched the aggregated corresponding scores of the ECU partners (S2 + S3). For instance, although the number of occasions on which S1 used personal forms to address their chat partners may appear to be low (10), it must be observed that the number is nearly as high as the aggregated number of personal forms of address used in the conversation by the two ECU students.

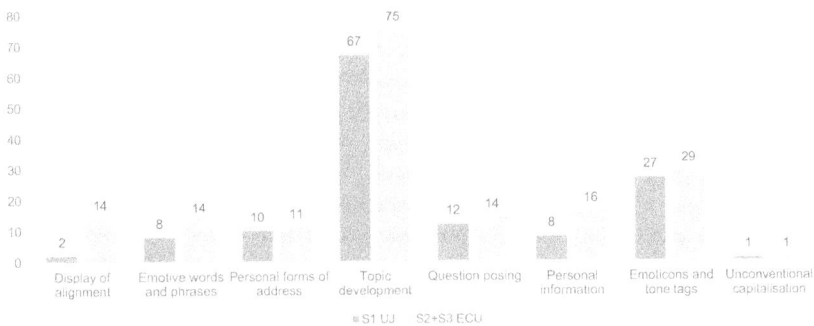

Figure 6.7 Linguistic markers of effective telecollaboration in chat interactions (S1 vs. S2 + S3).

The three areas with a reversed score pattern comprised the use of emotive words and phrases and the contribution of personal information, where the ECU students used nearly twice as many markers as the UJ student, as well as the display of alignment, in which case, the ECU students completely dominated the scene. Having said that, it must be underlined that S1 performed remarkably well, as through their active involvement in the conversation they compensated for the one-to-two ratio of conversational partners in this exchange. Thanks to it, it is likely that both cultures were aptly presented in the discussion. What is more, the relative balance between UJ and ECU students' interaction may also be attributed to the low-key profile adopted by S3. Perhaps one more reason for which S3 partly withdrew from the conversation was to make room for more contributions from S1 so that the UJ representative would not feel intimidated by the conversational dominance of the ECU partners.

To complement the analysis, several examples will be cited of the linguistic markers of effective collaboration used by the team members. To display alignment with the project partners, the students on the team used *I hear ya!!, Agreed, From what we have already talked about I assume it is the same? Oh yeah, I love Disney cartoons too, I saw it I saw it* [about a film a partner has seen], or *It seems that the "ton-of-food" thing is something we share, cool* and *interesting.* The words and phrases through which the students expressed emotions were, for example, *Too funny! Loved talking with you guys as always!* and *Yes love Disney stories!* Personal forms of address involved the use of first names, for example, *[First name], what about you?* or second-person pronouns and possessive adjectives (*You* and *Your*, respectively). Topic development was realised through messages which elaborated on what had been said by a project partner (e.g. *I see.*

Here in Poland I think they don't go on vacations together that often).
Examples of personal information provided by the team members: *I do*
plan to have children, I have some friends who are married, with kids,
and divorced, Then my dad will read from the Bible about the birth of
Jesus, Ok [sic!], *I will type what my own experience is like,* or *Oh yeah!*
Xmas is my favorite holiday of the year. Emoticons and tone tags were
typically: :)))), :D :D, and :(, while YEAH and RIGHT were the only two
instances of unconventional capitalisation, which was apparently used
for emphasis.

Summary of the findings and conclusions

The findings presented earlier reveal that the students' chat interactions
were dominated by question posing and topic development, which suggests a focus on the task at hand, which was to discuss the topic of the day.
Apparently, in their chat exchanges, the students made efforts to offer more
than straightforward responses to the questions asked by their colleagues,
frequently elaborating on the colleagues' responses and thus potentially
increasing the depth of the discussion. To a slightly lesser extent, they
personalised the messages they produced, thus transcending beyond generalities, which otherwise might have been learnt through (inter)cultural
learning materials. It seems sound to also conclude that the chat discussions under investigation stirred the students' emotions, to which the students gave vent either by using emotive words and phrases or emoticons
and tone tags. What draws attention is the lower frequency of alignment
displays, which might have affected the overall level of rapport.

The results signal an important problem, namely, how the choice of the
topic in a task may affect the nature of student-student interaction. Exactly
that may have happened when the students were required to talk about
stereotypes and prejudices in their cultures, and they provided 40% less
personalised information (a drop from 220 on the second link day to 139
on the fifth link day), possibly sharing fewer topic-related personal anecdotes. By the same token, the decreasing sense of relative initial novelty
involved in the project work may with time have an impact on the nature
of students' interaction, lowering motivation and engagement levels. Last
but not least, student grouping alone may be a factor affecting the quantity
of students' contributions to online interaction. As it was observed in a
team of three, a conversation may be essentially dominated by two of the
students, for which there may be multiple reasons. For instance, one of
the students may feel intimidated by the other two's conversational dominance. The *third* student may also intentionally give the floor to other two
for fear of interference. Alternatively, if two cultures are being represented
by three students in a team (one student vs. two student partners), it is

likely that a student in the two-strong team will reduce their contributions in good faith, so as to restore the balance between the conversational turns taken by the representatives of the two cultures involved.

A number of inferences can be made based on the research results. As it has been demonstrated, although the project participants used all the linguistic markers of effective telecollaboration in chat interactions, the extent to which they did so differed for particular markers. It would be unjustifiable to expect that all the markers would be used with the same intensity. Nevertheless, it needs to be ensured that the differences in the frequency of use observable from one marker to another are an outcome of informed decisions made by the students in concrete communicative situations. Therefore, prior to an OIE of the kind exemplified by the GPE GU XII, it seems desirable to introduce students to the repertoire of linguistic markers of effective telecollaboration which they can potentially use while interacting with the project partners and increase their awareness of the functions of particular markers, as well as the impact those markers can have on the nature and outcomes of online interaction.

Moreover, it seems reasonable to recommend that individual students test the use of particular markers in practice during the project and reflect on the achieved, or unachieved, outcomes. In this way, the salience of the means by which students can improve the effectiveness of telecollaboration will increase, thus fostering their development in this area. At the same time, students will be able to plan and monitor the development of their telecollaboration skills and – indirectly – intercultural competence, as the former may be both a learning goal in and an instrument with which to develop the latter.

Yet students need to be sensitised towards the extent to which they maximise opportunities for intercultural learning in an OIE (e.g. by raising their awareness of the role of active participation in online interactions). It is also important to draw students' attention to the manner in which the topic of discussion or the number of team members may affect their participation levels and thus the learning process. As a result, even when discussing potentially problematic topics, students will be able to avoid conflicts, or save face, without necessarily withdrawing from the use of particular markers of effective telecollaboration. In a similar vein, students working in teams with an uneven number of partners will be able to consciously alternate between lowering and raising their conversational profile to foster the other partners' development and secure room for their own learning.

All in all, the project can be deemed a success, as it promoted the development of linguistic, intercultural and metacognitive competence. It gave students insight into possible linguistic markers of collaboration, the extent to which their communicative turns are collaborative and how their dominance in a communicative exchange can affect their own and partners' learning.

Again, the packaged nature of the project freed the teacher's resources to let him investigate the nature of student-student interaction and the impact of task design on actual in-project communication and learning outcomes.

What merits note is that both OIEs discussed earlier were not originally designed specifically for TS students and with emergentist learning in mind. That is why they were neatly structured, involved a degree of scaffolding, if only through the set structure, and created little room for the degree of complexity conducive to emergentist learning. However, they permitted the students to hone their intercultural competence, which is targeted in translator education, while also giving them a chance to experience telecollaboration.

6.2   Team translation projects

As it has been explained in Chapter 5, another format of telecollaboration, which directly relates to translator education, is that of team translation projects. Three examples of such projects will be discussed here, albeit administered in two different modes. One project was implemented in hybrid mode (i.e. involving both f2f and online collaboration), while the other two were completed entirely online. The first project was part of a specialisation course in Telecollaborative Translation, while the other two were held in two subsequent iterations of a course in CAT Tools. Both courses were offered to students on a two-year EMT programme at the Jagiellonian University in Kraków, Poland, following the accreditation of the European Master's in Translation (EMT) network which the programme had been awarded for the years 2019–2024.

Each of the team translation projects constituted the backdrop of research on the implementation of telecollaborative translation on TS programmes with regard to issues such as the learning context, project roles, online interaction patterns and students' views on the efficacy of the use of telecollaboration projects in translator education. Accounts of the project details will be followed by reports on the results of the ensuing research. To findings will additionally be complemented the results of a survey conducted in the years 2017–2022 on the participants of several team translation projects with a view to examining students' learning preferences vs. actual learning experience in translation courses at large.

6.2.1   Therapeutic Gardens Project (TG)

Project overview and research context

The first of the projects was implemented in the academic year 2017/2018 in the Chair for Translation Studies at the Jagiellonian University in

Kraków in a specialisation course in telecollaborative translation. The project started in October 2017 and continued until February 2018, with a holiday break spanning December 2017 to January 2018.

The project was conducted in association with an external client, which was a locally based charitable foundation called Ogrody Terapeutyczne (Therapeutic Gardens) in Kraków, who commissioned the project participants to translate three chapters from a book on horticultural therapy, also known as garden therapy, from English into Polish. The source text was expository and informative, and the target text users were the employees and volunteers of the aforementioned charity, who needed to familiarise themselves with the content in question to obtain guidelines for the design of therapeutic gardens. Therefore, the project had both educational and social value, as on the one hand, it gave the students the opportunity to learn team translation while, on the other, to potentially contribute to the well-being of the members of the local community.

The project was performed by a team of 13 students who needed to complete three major stages of the project, including the pre-production, production and post-production, as delineated by the 11669:2012 (ISO 11669, 2012) standard for translation services. The pre-production phase comprised initial negotiations with the client, agreement on project specifications, which were written down as a translation brief, source text analysis, terminology work, role assignment, the writing of a style guide and the preparation of technical resources (i.e. a business communication platform and a computer-assisted translation tool). The production phase largely involved translation *per se*, self-revision, revision by another translator, final verification performed by the project manager and product delivery, while the post-production phase involved the provision of client feedback and the issuance of certificates confirming the students' timely completion of the project.

The rendering of the source text in the target language involved dealing with content such as image captions and descriptions, descriptions of garden plans, a calendar, footnotes, as well as in and out-of-text citations. The two major digital tools used in the project were Slack (slack.com), a cloud-based business messaging platform which was utilised to facilitate in-project communication, coordinate team actions but also exchange project resources, and Smartcat (smartcat.com), a cloud platform for computer assisted and automatic translation with features supporting collaborative workflows. The other tools which were also used in the project included memoQ – a desktop CAT tool whose terminology – related functionalities the students used to extract terminology from relevant reference texts and the university's MS OneDrive, which the students used to store project documentation (e.g. the translation brief or style guide).

Most of the project work was performed online, with the students working from home, and involved email communication with the client, resource sharing, project coordination and communication on Slack, as well as team translation proper and workflow management on Smartcat. However, simultaneously, regular f2f classes were taught throughout the semester in which the students were first introduced to the general concept of the project and its details which were already available at that stage, largely based on an analogous project which had been completed by their colleagues the year before. At that time, the students also decided on the actual line-up of smaller sub-teams in which they would be working and the roles (translators, revisers, terminologists, project managers) which they wanted to adopt. The remainder of the class meetings were dedicated to other course content, which all related – albeit to varying degrees – to the project work (e.g. the concept of specialised translation, terminology and its various dimensions), the importance of terminology (work) in, and out of, translation contexts, guidelines for terminology work or terminology management tools. It occasionally happened that some of the f2f class time was used as an opportunity for the students to brief the teacher on progress in the project work or to discuss some problematic issues (e.g. terminological choices which needed to be made while translating). It is this two-pronged nature of the students' work that makes the team translation project a hybrid rather than pure telecollaboration, although it needs to be underlined that the translation workflow was telecollaborative.

Although the students performed the translation as one large team, to facilitate collaboration and increase opportunities for more individuals to work in roles other than that of a translator, three smaller sub-teams were formed, each consisting of four students. By default, each project participant was tasked with translation, which was the core activity. However, in addition, two students in each team were assigned additional role each; one was a reviser and the other worked as a team terminologist. The project work was overseen by the remaining student, who acted as the project manager (PM). One of the three team terminologists simultaneously acted as project terminologist (PT) and one of the revisers was project reviser (PR). Both the PT and PR supervised the work of team terminologists and revisers respectively and, along with all the other project participants, reported to the PM. For an overview of the project, consult Table 6.5.

The research-based TG project was conducted in two modules, which in total aimed to provide insight into the details of telecollaboration stimulated by the performance of team translation. Module I aimed to survey the students on the perceived learning gains, forms for peer learning

Table 6.5 TG: Project overview

Aspect of the project	Details
Duration	17 October 2017–23 February 2018 (on and off, due to Christmas break)
Related TS course	Specialisation course in telecollaborative translation
Goals	To develop competences relevant to team translation through informed, reflection-based practice
	To develop technological competence (use of CAT tools and terminology management tools)
	To introduce students to terminology work in translation
	To occasion self- and peer learning
External client	Ogrody Terapeutyczne (Therapeutic Gardens) in Kraków (horticultural charity)
Source text (domain)	Social horticultural therapy (MED)
Participants	13 UJ students of translation
Project roles	Project manager, project reviser, project terminologist, team terminologists, team revisers, translators (all students)
Team structure	1 project manager, 1 project terminologist, 1 project reviser
	3 sub-teams of 4 (each with 4 translators, 1 team terminologist and 1 team reviser*)
	*1 team terminologist and 1 team reviser acted as project terminologist and project reviser respectively
Procedure	Hybrid (f2f and online collaboration)
	1 f2f introductory pre-project class
	Online team translation (students working from home)
	Simultaneous f2f course classes throughout the semester (involving project briefings and discussion of pressing issues)
	1 round-up class (in-class reflections on the project work)
Forms of telecollaboration involved	• Online communication, resource sharing and project workflow coordination
	• Online team translation
Technologies used	Slack (platform for communication, resource sharing and work coordination)
	Smartcat (CAT tool for team translation and use of shared resources, for example, TMs and TBs)
	MemoQ (CAT tool for pre-project terminology work, for example, term extraction)
	OneDrive (cloud storage for documentation)
	Trello (project management tool added by the students)

occasioned by the project (with the students acting mutually as both learners and teachers), learning difficulties and challenges, as well as the choice of the communication platform. For better recall, the data were collected as the project was still in progress, with the intended auxiliary effect of raising the students' awareness of opportunities for peer learning in the remainder of the project.

Four major research questions were posed, one complemented with two sub-questions:

RQ1. What are the perceived learning gains in the team translation project?
RQ2. What forms of peer learning occurred in the project?

- What did the students learn from their colleagues?
- What did the students teach to their peers?

RQ3. What learning difficulties and challenges did the project participants face?
RQ4. What are the students' views on the choice of the project communication tool?

Module II involved the administration of a post-project survey in which the students were asked to share their viewpoints on the possible purposes of telecollaboration projects in translator education, major learning gains, the nature of post-experience reflections and forms of elicitation, as well as teacher presence, including its effects possible teacher roles. This part of research was motivated by four major research questions and a set of sub-questions, two for RQ3 and three for RQ4:

RQ1. For what purposes could telecollaboration projects be used in translator education?
RQ2. Overall, what are the perceived major learning gains in the telecollaborative team translation project?
RQ3. What is the nature of post-experience reflections in team translation projects?

- Do they occur naturally or need to be elicited?
- What forms of elicitation would be most effective, if needed at all?

RQ4. Is teacher presence needed in telecollaborative team translation projects?

- To what extent does the teacher need to be present?
- What effects are the possible of various degrees of teacher presence?
- What roles does the teacher need to adopt in telecollaborative team translation projects?

Research design: Procedures, methods and sampling

In this research, data were collected at two points: in December 2017 (i.e. as the TG project was still in progress) and in March 2018, after the project had been completed. Data processing and analysis were conducted afterwards from March 2018 to February 2019.

In Module I, the research was conducted through a self-reflection form with a total of six open-ended questions; the first two of them were supplemented with sub-questions, which aimed to elicit detailed responses. The questions fell into four categories: questions 1 and 2 related to RQ1 and RQ2, questions 3 and 4 to RQ3, while questions 5 and 6 to RQ4. The questions are listed in the next section:

1. Think of the little, or more elaborate, things (consider skills, knowledge, awareness, tools) which you have already learnt while participating in the project. List them here and be ready to report on the following:

   • How did you learn them?
   • From whom?
   • How useful have they been in your work so far?

2. Think of the little, or more elaborate, things (consider skills, knowledge, awareness) which you have already taught your colleague(s) while participating in the project. List them here and be ready to report on the following:

   • How did you teach them?
   • To whom?
   • What did your colleague(s) need them for?

3. What have you found to be the greatest, and yet surmountable, problem/difficulty while performing the project tasks?
4. What has been the greatest deterrent to your involvement in the project work?
5. What are your impressions of Slack so far?
6. Can you see any room or need for another communication channel to be used for project work?

The self-reflection form was distributed in .DOCX format, with the students asked to respond to the questions in writing and submit the file via Moodle. It is important to underline that the survey was administered when the project was on-going and the students' memories of the experience were supposedly very fresh. Thus, although the results obtained provide a cross-sectional image of the issues under examination, it is believed that their validity is increased through better recall than in the case of retrospective research.

In Module II, the post-project survey was designed and conducted in February 2018 online with the use of LimeSurvey (limesurvey.org), which is a free, open-source platform for survey development and administration, as well as the generation of basic statistics and data export. A hyperlink to the survey was published on the university Moodle site, which the project participants used for regular coursework. The survey contained ten questions, including five close-ended questions (three multiple-choice questions and two array questions). There was also one filter question which, depending on the answer given to it, redirected the respondents to the next relevant question. However, as all the respondents selected the same response option and, consequently, followed exactly the same path through the survey. Question 4 – as irrelevant – was not answered at all.

The survey questions came in four categories relating to the aforementioned RQs: question 1 related to RQ1, questions 2 and 3 and 4 (filter question) to RQ2, questions 5 and 6 to RQ3 and questions 7–10 to RQ4. The return rate for the survey was also 100%. Yet several missing responses were noted in the following questions (each marked as QN): Q3 (one missing response), Q8 (1) and Q9 (3). An overview of the research is presented in Table 6.6.

Sampling

The research participants were recruited through convenience sampling (Saldanha & O'Brien, 2014) in that they were all UJ participants of the TG project. The 13 (N = 13) participants, all in their mid-twenties, were MA-level translation students, 11 females (N = 11) and two males (N = 2). Table 6.6 provides a summary of the search design.

Results and discussion

Module I. Before the results are presented, it must be explained that, as the mid-project self-reflection questions were open-ended, with an unlimited number of response options provided by each research participant, the figures cited later indicate how many responses of a given type were obtained but cannot be paralleled to the number of respondents who provided particular answers. The figures only demonstrate how many responses of a given type were provided in total.

In the self-reflection form, the students reported learning gains in a total of 12 areas, which could be conflated into the following categories: (i) procedural knowledge and skills relating to (translation) technologies (29 responses), (ii) knowledge at the interface of declarative and procedural (7), (iii) soft skills (6) and (iv) declarative knowledge about CAT tools and project resources (5), as Figure 6.8 depicts.

Table 6.6 Overview of the research design (TG)

Aspect of research design	Details
Research aims	Module I. To examine perceived learning gains, forms for peer learning occasioned by the project, learning difficulties and challenges, the choice of the communication platform, as reported by students at the mid-project stage
	Module II. To investigate possible purposes of telecollaboration projects in translator education, major learning gains, the nature of post-experience reflections and forms of elicitation, teacher presence and teacher roles
Research method	Descriptive research (focused description)
	Module I. Self-reflection form (with six open-ended questions).
	Module II. Post-project survey (with 10 close- and open-ended questions)
Research instrument	MS Excel spreadsheet (computations of frequency counts and graph generation)
Sampling	Convenience sampling; 12 UJ MA-level students of translation (N = 13); 11 females (N = 11) and 2 males (N = 2)
Timing	December 2017–March 2018: data collection
	March 2018–February 2019: data processing and analysis
Data analysis	Qualitative and quantitative

Figure 6.8 General areas of student-reported learning gains in the TG project.

Knowledge in the first of those categories pertained, first and foremost, to the functionalities of the CAT tool (Smartcat) (10 responses), communication and scheduling tools (Slack and Trello) (11 responses), other generic IT tools often used to enhance the translation process, such as unnamed optical character recognition (OCR) software (4) and the office suite MS Office 365 (4), as well as knowledge about the management of translation project resources (4), such as TMs and glossaries or reference documents (style sheets).

Declarative knowledge about project resources and CAT tools (5) comprised basic theoretical knowledge about translation technologies and the resources which can be used in translation projects to facilitate both the workflow and translation *per se* (e.g. term banks). The knowledge at the interface of declarative and procedural knowledge covered domain knowledge (terminology) (3), generic translation skills (1), the logistics of translation projects (1) and the practical application of declarative knowledge learnt in the classroom (2), while the soft skills that the students reportedly learnt through the team translation project comprised time management (4) and telecollaboration skills (2), including communication with the client. A detailed breakdown of the responses reported earlier is presented in Figure 6.9.

What draws attention is that in the students' views, the project occasioned learning which mostly comprised procedural knowledge and skills, the practical application of the knowledge which they had internalised

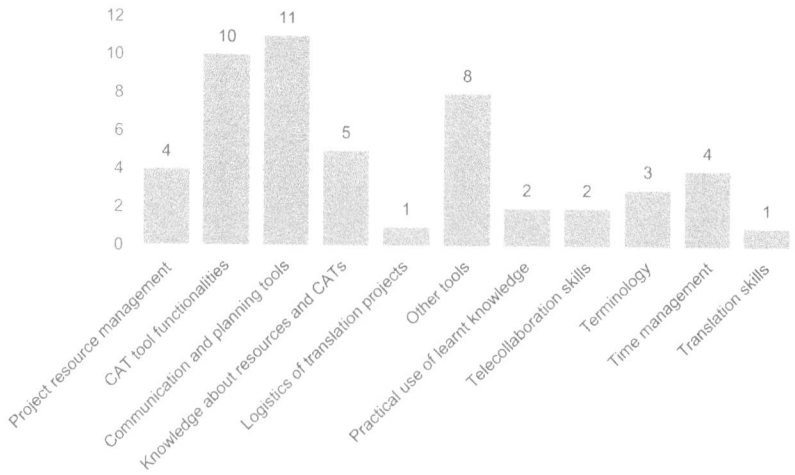

Figure 6.9 Student-reported learning gains in the TG team translation project.

through classwork and soft skills. Purely declarative knowledge as a learning gain was reported in five responses only, which indicates the salience of the largely practical nature of the learning involved in the TG team translation project.

Interesting is the students' attribution of the learning reported earlier to particular stakeholders in the project. In most of the responses (20), the students claimed they had been learning from peers (i.e. the other team members), in a slightly lower proportion of responses they maintained they had been self-learning (16), either through trial and error or via online resources, and only marginally had the students reported learning from the course teacher (4). Given that the aim of the team translation project in question was indeed to promote self- and peer learning, it seems that the project work did occasion both. The little learning directly from the teacher was most certainly a consequence of the low profile which the teacher had intentionally adopted to give the floor to the students and thus instigate student-centred learning. What may be striking, though, is lack of learning from the client, which had originally been planned for. It was so because the f2f feedback session, which had been arranged for, was unexpectedly cancelled by the client due to an emergency, and only very general feedback in writing was provided by email, mostly expressing gratitude to the students for the timely completion of the project work and the submission of a high-quality translation with adequate field-related terminology.

As in peer learning, students are not only at the receiving end but also act as teachers, it is interesting to analyse what the project participants had taught to their colleagues midway through the project. The students' responses to the relevant question fell into two major categories: (i) procedural knowledge and skills relating to (translation) technologies, including the use of various functionalities of CAT tools (3), project resources (2) – this time the term bank only – OCR (1), cloud file storage (1), communication management on Slack (1) and file management (1) but also (ii) declarative/procedural knowledge, mostly relating to terminology issues (3) and text editing (2). Interestingly, three responses (this time, each came from the same student) revealed no peer teaching had been performed yet, which may mean that they had not been done or realised yet. In the former case, the student in question still had opportunities to do peer teaching in the remainder of the project. What merits note is that the overall number to students' responses confirming involvement in peer learning (53) considerably outnumbers the responses related to reported peer teaching (17), which may indicate that either peer learning was more salient to the students, for example, because they had instantly benefited from it in the project or that they peer taught only to a limited extent (e.g. due to lack of relevant competence, confidence or motivation). In either case, the implications are rather negative, as the students' contributions to team-work had apparently been limited.

With regard to the initial, yet surmountable, difficulties which the project participants faced, the respondents' answers were quite granular, with most of them appearing in single responses only; thus, no hierarchy can be built. However, the responses can be considered as an insight into potential hardships involved in telecollaborative team translation. The difficulties will be discussed in four emerging groups, with the number of responses provided only for items with a count above 1.

The first group was attitudinal in nature and comprised poor rapport or, on a more personal level, initial anxiety about the project and the students' inclinations for procrastination. The cited technical difficulties related to the proliferation of tools (2) and the workings of the communication platform. Translation-related challenges referred to the coordination of (stylistic) consistency in the target text or students' lack of domain knowledge (3). Finally, the soft skills which were problematic at first included communication and project management, as well as time management (2).

In a similar vein, deterrents to participation in a telecollaborative translation project fell into similar categories. Attitudinal deterrents entailed anxiety, initial fear of the (CAT) tools to be used in the project (3) and lack of motivation. The only technical deterrent mentioned by the respondents was that of the proliferation of tools, and the only translation-related deterrent was lack of domain knowledge and field-relevant terminology. The most often cited deterrent was excessive workload related to the students' other responsibilities in and outside university (5). Interestingly, one student stated that they perceived no deterrents at all, as they enjoyed facing novelty and were happy to embark on the project.

It is also interesting to see the students' views of the major project communication tool, Slack, as the software is normally used in business contexts and may have been a novelty to the students, as before the project, they had most certainly relied on personal communication tools. As it turns out, the students appreciated the program's good quality and user-friendliness (2). They maintained that Slack is an effective business solution, facilitates communication (9) and teamwork (2), as well as fosters rapport thanks to the inclusion of emoticons. At the same time, the students observed that the program may be overwhelming due to the relatively large number of messages posted in various communication channels (3) and indicated – as if suggesting a solution to the problem – that it requires proper communication management (3). One respondent even suggested that a communication manager should have been appointed to that end.

By and large, the adequacy of the choice of the project tools was corroborated by the fact that as many as nine students (75% of the entire team) stated that they would not have selected any other tools for the project work. One student advocated the use of Trello – a visual project and workflow management program with task tracking functionalities, which the students had eventually added to the pool of project tools of their own accord. Only two students suggested that Facebook, which in itself might indicate the lingering sentiment for the social networking tool due to the students' use of it for private purposes. At the same time, the small proportion of students who saw its applicability to the project might imply that the majority of the team realised Facebook had not been developed with project management in mind.

Module II. In survey Q1, which tackled the purposes for which online projects can be used, the students' responses could be conflated into three main categories. The majority of the responses were all congruent with the purposes of the TG project, in which the respondents had participated and comprised: the development of soft skills (5 responses), the provision of professional experience to translation students (4) and the fostering of teamwork (2) and telecollaboration (2) skills, as well as translation competence (1). Other purposes were suggested in single responses only, and they mostly concerned forms of student activity potentially related to the learning of – but not directly involving – translation: the preparation of large term banks, collaboration with foreign partners, the completion of research projects and information mining. A third group of responses were general-educational in nature and comprised the close monitoring of students' performance and increasing students' motivation, while the last purpose cited was very pragmatic (to save time), although the respondent who provided it failed to specify in what circumstances and how time was supposed to be saved and who in particular would benefit from it.

In Q2 (close-ended), all respondents maintained that their participation in the telecollaborative translation project had brought them learning gains. As they further specified in Q3, the most significant learning gains which they discerned were those corresponding to soft skills (22 responses), translation practice (4), the workings of telecollaboration (3), metacognitive awareness (2) and rapport (2), as Figure 6.10 illustrates.

The data demonstrate that once they had completed the project work, the students apparently attached the most significance to learning gains within the area of soft skills, with the others remaining clearly in the background. Given that telecollaboration is often credited with the potential to develop transferrable skills (see Chapter 4), it means not only that the team translation project had potentially succeeded in this area but it had also drawn the students' attention to the importance of universal competences. It is interesting to relate these findings to the areas of student-reported learning gains in the TG project reported in the mid-project self-reflection

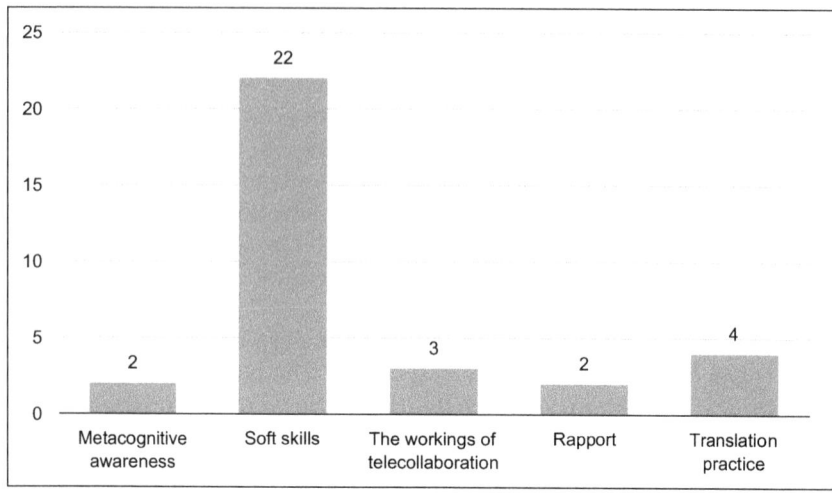

Figure 6.10 Student-reported most significant learning gains in the TG project.

form (see Figure 6.10). When juxtaposing the data from both sources, it may be observed that while the project was still in progress, the greatest salience had been gained by learning benefits in the area of procedural knowledge and translation-related skills; after the project, the students mostly appreciated the development of soft skills. Firstly, there is no conflict between the data, as the mid-project form elicited all potential areas of student-perceived learning gains, while the post-project survey examined the most significant of those gains. Secondly, and most importantly, the apparent elevation of the status of transferable skills in the team translation project may stem from the fact that while translation competence was extensively prioritised in numerous other courses offered as part of the MA programme which the students were on, soft skills may not have been focused on so much. As a result, the students may have appreciated that the team translation project had offered them a chance to redress the balance between the two.

Responses to Q5 (close-ended) revealed that a light majority of the students believed that reflections in telecollaboration projects both occurred naturally and needed to be additionally elicited through tasks (6 responses). Others were of the opinion that reflections are largely natural (5), while only one response suggested that reflections are not natural and they need to be induced. As for the students' preferred forms of elicitation provided in Q6 (close-ended), the respondents made the following choices: class discussion (9), group discussion with peers (8), a questionnaire (8), individual teacher-student discussions (7), purpose-designed elicitation class tasks (6) and student journals (4) (see Figure 6.11).

It seems that the students' preferences were inclined towards discussion at large (with the aggregated frequency count of 24) in three formats: whole class, group peer-to-peer and teacher-student discussion. Questionnaires and class elicitation tasks scored comparably to each of the three types of discussion. However, the least preference was visibly displayed for student journals, which require considerably more effort than the other elicitation formats.

Q7 (close-ended) revealed that seven students would rather the teacher remained in the background, while five would prefer the teacher to provide systematic feedback throughout the project. Therefore, it is difficult to draw a definitive conclusion as to which is the preferred mode of teacher presence in telecollaboration projects within the sample. Either way, in Q8 (open-ended), the students shared their views on what effects teacher presence is likely to have in telecollaboration projects, and although the responses were granular, they could be arranged into three major categories: (i) project procedures (14 responses in total), (ii) learner involvement (7) and (iii) project prestige (1).

Most of the responses pointed to the impact of teacher presence on project procedures, including the provision of systematic feedback (3), the clarity of project goals (2), increased supervision (2) and support (2), stimulation of self-reflection (1), provision of a behaviour model (1) and round-up (1), presentation of an external perspective on the project work (1) and assurance of higher quality (1). 50% of the responses less highlighted increased

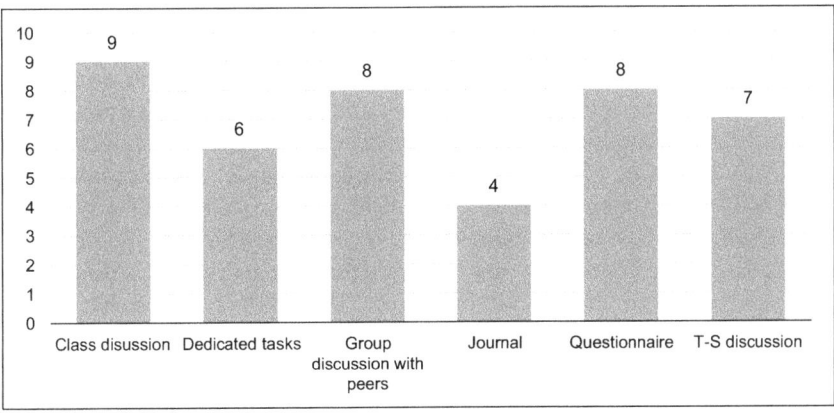

Figure 6.11 Preferred forms of elicitation for reflections.

learner motivation (4) and involvement (3), while one response underlined the effect of teacher presence on a rise in project status (1).

Q9 and Q10 related to the students' perceptions of teacher roles in telecollaboration projects. Q9 examined the preferred teacher roles, which were as follows: monitor (4 responses), mentor (4), support (3), guide (2), demonstrator (2), manager (2), stimulator of students' reflection (1), participant (1) and mediator (1). As it can be seen, the first four roles, which happen to have the highest frequency count (13), sideline the teacher, placing them away from the students' mainstream project activity. This perspective was somewhat metaphorically summarised in the answer to Q9 cited next, where a student described the teacher:

GANDALF *from* THE LORD OF THE RINGS, *however silly it might sound. The guide and mentor at the* start, *dies (metaphorically of course) when real work begins, but is still present in the "hearts" of the team, like a beacon for the rest of the journey. He comes back, dressed all in white, to settle students' consciences.*

The other five roles which featured in the students' responses, with a total frequency count of seven, indicate more direct teacher involvement in the project work, for example, to provide models or instruct (demonstrate), manage the project, elicit reflection, join the students and act as a team member or mediate in case of problems. In other words, although the students largely demonstrated the understanding that in telecollaboration projects, the teacher plays a subsidiary role only, they nevertheless seemed, at least to some extent, to adhere to a sentiment for more active teacher involvement.

In Q10 (close-ended), the students were asked to indicate at which of the three stages, course planning, task introduction and monitoring, the students would deem teacher presence most essential. Course planning was operationalised as the planning of an entire course so as to weave the telecollaboration project into its texture and make students aware of the goals of telecollaboration. Task introduction and support were described as clearly defining project tasks, verifying students' understanding of them, providing on-going feedback and supporting students at work (e.g. by providing advice or guidance on the technologies used in the project). Monitoring was defined as observing students at work and aiding with problem resolution throughout the project. The results revealed that all the three response options were equally endorsed by the students, with each selected exactly ten times, which implies that, quite naturally, students need to be first clearly introduced to the goals of telecollaborative translation projects, the tasks involved and their responsibilities. Throughout the project, they would like to have their work monitored, be provided with guidance if need be and receive systematic feedback. However, they would also expect a relatively high degree of teacher involvement in problem resolution. Last but not least – and interestingly – it seems that students would like to see telecollaborative translation projects seamlessly integrated into translator education courses so that team translation projects are not *ad hoc* events and are performed with the students' full realisation of the goals of telecollaborative work modes.

Summary of the findings and conclusions

Several important observations arise from the research findings in both modules, which have been reported earlier. Firstly, students examined in the TG project demonstrated increased realisation that the learning outcome of telecollaborative team translation projects is primarily the development of procedural knowledge and skills, transferrable skills and, only to some extent, declarative knowledge. What is more, the students also seemed to recognise telecollaboration projects as the opportunity to use in practice the theoretical knowledge which they had acquired in the course of their translator education.

When the students learnt in the project, they did so mostly from colleagues (peer learning) and by themselves (self-learning), with very little direct contribution to that process from the teacher. That kind of setup lies at the core to transformative/transgressionist learning, which telecollaboration is likely to stimulate. What draws attention is definitely the need for feedback from the client, which in the TG project was minimal due to unforeseen circumstances. Yet it needs to be underlined that feedback provided by a third party (e.g. a market representative) is not only likely to have a motivational effect on the project participants. It may also be a way in which to professionalise translator education and thus narrow the gap between academia and the LSP industry.

The aforementioned gains seem to stem from all the kinds of learning involved in telecollaboration, including peer-to-peer learning, which found corroboration in the fact that the TG project participants taught other colleagues mostly procedural knowledge, or knowledge with declarative and procedural elements (e.g. when the students explored concepts behind field-relevant terminology and researched definitions while simultaneously investigating usage and seeking the most optimal translation options). At the same time, the research results highlight the need for increasing the salience of peer teaching in telecollaboration, as some students claimed they had not done it yet, while others seemed to lack awareness of their contributions to the project partners' knowledge. In the former case, it must be borne in mind that if team members concentrate on peer learning and its benefits to themselves without making contributions to the work of the others, and thus to the entire product of the team translation effort, their participation is largely cooperative, which does not lie at the core of telecollaboration.

As far as potential difficulties and challenges in telecollaborative translation projects are concerned, they originate from the students' personal dispositions, for example, attitude (anxiety, procrastination) or limited transferable skills (in-project communication management, project management, time management), but they may also derive from the nature of the task at hand and be technical (e.g. caused by the proliferation of tools to be used) or translation-related (the need to maintain consistency in team-produced translations). Some of these problems may be so serious that they will act as potential deterrents to participation in telecollaborative translation projects. The respondents clearly indicated that anxiety, the number of tools or lack of domain knowledge and terminology may be the discouraging factors. In addition, it turns out that at times, very pragmatic motives, such as excessive workload, may play a role in discouraging student involvement, which implies that if telecollaboration projects are to be successful, they must not involve students in work beyond capacity, however difficult it may be to appraise.

As one respondent pointed out, it is possible that students with increased levels of self-confidence, who could be categorised as adventurous learners, will happily embark on projects even despite the apparent hardships, but all learner profiles need to be catered for lest more careful learners should be inhibited. Thus, the aforementioned deterrents must not be downplayed. Instead, it seems desirable to explain to prospective project participants that although challenges are inherent to project work, they create learning opportunities, mostly through team effort and mutual support (e.g. peer-to-peer teaching).

The students' opinions about the project communication tool may be an illustration of how a novel, and potentially challenging, element of the project can be mastered successfully through practice. It is demonstrable when one realises that although the TG project participants were not initially familiar with Slack, they had eventually mastered the tool, claiming that overall, it was an effective business platform which facilitated in-project communication. At the same time, some of the respondents signalled the need for the appointment of a communication manager, who would streamline communication on Slack and thus reduce the number of messages posted there. The latter suggestion indicates raised awareness of possible solutions through which to improve project management, which may be indispensable in professional life.

In Module II, when asked about the usefulness of online projects, the students pointed to their role in the development of transferable skills, the provision of professional experience and the fostering of teamwork/

telecollaboration skills, with transferrable skills perceived as the major learning gain from participation in the TG project. It does not necessarily mean that the students downgrade the other competences as less important but may be indicative of the fact that either the project occasioned the development of multiple transferrable skills or that other work modes did not foster the development of those skills to such a great extent, hence, their salience. In the latter case, the implementation of telecollaboration in translator education would by all means be desirable as a work mode complementary to the other forms of coursework being used.

The research results also demonstrate that for the majority of the students surveyed, reflections in telecollaboration projects occur naturally, and the students only disagreed on whether or not reflections needed to be additionally elicited. From the perspective of a translation teacher, it is important to infer from these findings that although reflections can indeed be a natural element of project-based learning, there might be a need to help students focus on what is most pertinent to the learning to be induced in a particular course. The students seemed open to all forms of reflection elicitation (e.g. questionnaires or purpose-designed tasks), with the majority displaying preference for different modes of discussion. However, they least commonly appreciated elicitation through a student journal, perhaps due to the large amount of workload which it potentially involves. Consequently, if teachers are cognisant of students' workload in other courses, coupled with that involved in telecollaboration, it seems reasonable that in team translation projects, they use this and other work-costly elicitation formats (e.g. portfolios) with caution.

Finally, when asked to voice their preferences towards teacher presence in telecollaboration projects, the students seemed unable to provide a definitive answer. Yet when they listed preferred teacher roles, they apparently leaned towards the teacher staying in the background. Thus, it could be concluded that while the students would be relatively comfortable with the teacher playing a supportive role in their learning, at the same time, they would expect a degree of intervention, at least if need be. Overall, the students expressed the belief that teacher presence has an impact mostly on project completion (e.g. through support and feedback), learner involvement (motivation) and the prestige of the project.

All in all, despite its open nature and the freedom of decision making it offered to the students – when compared to OIEs – it led to the successful completion of the translation commission around which it was woven. Additionally, the research results provided insight into otherwise implicit aspects of project work, including perceived learning gains, involved forms of peer learning and students' preferences about elicitation and reflection modes, as well as teacher roles and presence. Given the range of data collected, it seems likely that continuous research of this kind will help teachers demystify the intricacies of telecollaboration projects and gain greater confidence in this learning mode.

6.2.2   *Cochrane Project 2021 (CP 2021)*

Project overview and research context

The second project to be discussed was implemented in the academic year 2020/2021 in the Chair for Translation Studies at the Jagiellonian University in Kraków in a CAT Tools course. The project started in mid-April and had been completed by 12 May 2021.

As in the case of the TG project, the project in question was also performed for an external client, which this time was Cochrane (cochrane. org), a London-based, internationally acclaimed charitable organisation for disseminating high-quality information necessary to make health decisions. The organisation is a network of member entities based in 190 countries which serves clinicians, patients, carers, researchers and policy makers by enhancing their healthcare knowledge and decision making by organising and disseminating reviews of health evidence. In 2021, Cochrane commissioned the project participants to translate from English into Polish 48 specialised texts from the domain of medicine which were short summaries of publications mainly – but not exclusively – on medical research results and medical advice relating to various conditions (e.g. treatment of COVID-19 patients). The client required that the translations were of publishable quality, as they would ultimately be uploaded to the Cochrane Library (www.cochranelibrary.com), whereby they would be disseminated among the end users. By dint of the subject matter, the project was educationally and socially significant, providing an opportunity for students to involve in team translation while also potentially benefiting the international and local (Polish) healthcare community.

The participants were a team of 24 students in total, who needed to complete the project work, at the pre-production, production and post-production stages, in compliance with the 11699:2012 (ISO 11669, 2012) standard for translation projects.

The source texts were 400–700 words long each, contained basic medical terminology and were expository and formal in style. They were delivered in .XML format, with no text embedded in graphics, via the project's translation tool, the cloud TMS called Memsource Cloud (memsource. com). Courtesy of Memsource Cloud (Phrase), a proper licensing plan had been arranged for, which permitted the management of a team translation project, with access to project resources, including TMs, glossaries and professional MT provided by DeepL. All the stages of the translation workflow were completed on Memsource Cloud, including the delivery of the target text to the client. The final review was performed by Cochrane's medical editors, and the publication of the translations was at the discretion of the client.

The major communication platform in the project was Slack (slack.com) and, occasionally, university-provided MS SharePoint, which was utilised as cloud for project documentation. What differentiated CP 2021 from TG was that in the former project, all work, including the preparation of project documentation, in-project communication, email communication with the client, resource sharing, project coordination, team translation and workflow management, was performed online, with the students working from home. An introductory class was taught before the project; however, it did not involve any collaboration and introduced the students to quality management in (translation) projects and an overview of the quality management principles (ISO, 2015), as delineated by the International Standards Organisation. Consequently, CP 2021 qualifies as a telecollaborative team translation project.

To facilitate collaboration, the students split into four teams of six. Each project participant acted as a translator, but in each team, three students were additionally assigned the role of revisers, and one acted as team project manager. One of the translators was the project manager (PM), to whom the students in all the roles reported, who also managed the entire workflow, coordinating it with team project managers. The decision to appoint four team project managers was motivated by the need to create learning opportunities for more than one student to gain experience in project management and to facilitate workflow management at team level. The adoption of particular project roles by individuals was either voluntary or it was the outcome of student-student negotiations, with the final decision taken by the students in a position of power (e.g. the project manager or team project managers). For reference purposes, an overview of the project is provided in Table 6.7.

Research aims

The implementation of the CP 2021 project was used as an opportunity to zero in on the problem of quality management and the measures which were taken to observe quality management principles throughout the project, as reported by the project managers. In this way, it was examined to what extent elements of professional translation service provision and project delivery were integrated into the project work.

The research was motivated by two major research questions, the first of which was supplemented with four detailed questions which were supposed

Table 6.7 Cochrane 2021: Project overview

Aspect of the project	Details
Duration	mid-April–mid-May 2021
Related TS course	CAT Tools
Goals	To develop competences relevant to team translation through informed, reflection-based practice
	To develop technological competence (use of CAT tools and terminology management tools)
	To introduce students to terminology work in translation
External client	Cochrane (international non-profit organisations for disseminating high-quality information to make health decisions)
Source text (domain)	Summaries of medical evidence (MED); 60 texts in total
Participants	24 UJ students of translation
Project roles	Project manager, team project managers (team leaders), translators (all students), revisers
Team structure	1 project manager* (*a team translator at the same time)
	4 sub-teams of 6 (each with 6 translators, 3 team revisers and 1 team project manager*)
	*team revisers and project team managers were translators at the same time
Procedure	1 introductory f2f class devoted to project quality management
	Online team translation (students working from home)
	Workflow: ST delivery, translation (by student translators), revision (by student revisers), final review at provider level (by PM), TT delivery, final review at client level (by Cochrane medical editors), publication on Cochrane website
Forms of telecollaboration involved	• Online communication, resource sharing and project workflow coordination
	• Online team translation
Technologies used	Slack (platform for communication, resource sharing and work coordination)
	Memsource Cloud/Phrase (CAT tool for team translation, use of shared resources, for example, TMs and TBs and workflow management)
	MS SharePoint (cloud storage for documentation)

to focus the resulting description on the most essential dimensions of quality management. The research questions were worded as follows:

RQ1. Did the students take measures to observe quality management principles in the CP 2021 project? If so:

- What actions were taken?
- By whom?
- What communication channels were used for that purpose (where relevant)?
- What resources were used for that purpose (where relevant)?

RQ2. To what extent were the principles of professional translation service provision integrated into project with regard to selected elements of quality management?

Research design: Procedures, methods and sampling

To investigate the issue at hand, an online written interview (Saldanha & O'Brien, 2014) was conducted. The choice of the research instrument was determined by several factors. As Saldanha and O'Brien (2014) report, both synchronous and asynchronous interviews are being increasingly held online. However, those administered in asynchronous mode – such as the written interview in question – not only permit time-effective administration and automatic data logging but also potentially promote increased reflection and the provision of more accurate answers on the part of the interviewees. Although written interviews are often distributed via email, to further increase the time-effectiveness of the research, a decision was taken to create and disseminate the interview as an online forum, which was created and distributed via LimeSurvey (limesurvey.org). As a result, while all the advantages of email interviews cited earlier were potentially assured, the distribution of the interview questions and the collection of responses were fully automated.

The interview (Saldanha & O'Brien, 2014) comprised a total of 46 open-ended questions about selected aspects of quality management principles (QMPs), as delineated by ISO (2015), to which the students had been introduced prior to the project.

The principles covered seven areas (i) customer focus, (ii) leadership, (iii) engagement of people, (iv) process approach, (v) improvement, (vi) evidence-based decision making and (vii) relationship management but only selected dimensions of each area were operationalised through loosely adapted descriptors which had been developed specifically with the CP 2021 team translation project in mind. All in all, the students were introduced to 23 descriptors, which are listed in the next section:

1. Customer focus

   - on-time delivery of services according to project specifications;
   - clear and prompt communication with the customer; and
   - following the customer's recommendations.

2. Leadership

    - meeting the deadlines;
    - delivering a high-quality translation revised and reviewed prior to delivery;
    - tracking and coordinating the tasks assigned to team members; and
    - writing announcements about deadlines and forthcoming work-flow stages.

3. Engagement of people

    - stimulating involvement of the entire team with reminders posted on Slack;
    - monitoring progress;
    - ensuring team members' swift responses to MP's calls;
    - praising the team;
    - answering questions asked by team members; and
    - supporting each other's activities.

4. Process approach

    - providing clear task descriptions;
    - using Slack to inform about tasks; and
    - ensuring team members understand, and can do, tasks.

5. Improvement

    - developing translation, revision and other relevant skills; and
    - self-revising the text for compliance with specifications and errors at all stages.

6. Evidence-based decision making

    - revising the text for compliance with specifications and errors;
    - introducing necessary text modifications;
    - modifying text status on Memsource Cloud; and
    - researching field terminology to create a term bank to inform the translation.

7. Relationship management

    - maintaining contact between all parties involved in the project.

Each of the interview questions contained a definition of a particular QMP and required the respondents to provide the details of how its selected dimensions were catered for in the project, especially with regard to the actions which were taken and the actors involved. Additionally, some questions also elicited information about the resources that were used to implement a given QMP, as was the case with *improvement: developing translation, revision and other relevant skills*, and the communication channel which facilitated the implementation (e.g. in the case of *engagement of people: answering questions asked by team members*).

As, by definition, interviews are usually conducted with a limited number of respondents, who nevertheless are expected to provide a more in-depth description of the issue(s) under examination, the quantification of data is either impossible or tends to be deprioritised. The same vantage point was adopted within the research under discussion; the more that individual responses to the interview questions were not perceived as disparate voices to be compared with one another but rather mutually complementary accounts of the project reality with which to build a more comprehensive picture of quality management in CP 2021. Consequently, it was decided that the analysis of the data provided by the five interviewees (MPs involved in the CP 2021 project) would be qualitative in nature.

Sampling

Recruitment for this research happened in two stages. At first, the 24 participants of the CP 2021 project (N = 24) were recruited through convenience sampling (i.e. following the students' course enrolment decisions). However, as the research targeted project managers exclusively, a purposive (Saldanha & O'Brien, 2014) sub-sample was identified based on the critical parameter of student role in the project. As a result, five respondents ultimately constituted the research sample, including the CP 2021 project manager and four team project managers (team leaders). All the five (N = 5) participants were MA-level female students of translation in their mid-twenties. The research design is summarised in Table 6.8.

Results and discussion

The results of the qualitative analysis of the interview responses not only reveal interesting details about quality management in the CP 2021 project but also provide insight into the opportunities which the project apparently created for the students to learn how to implement QMPs in a concrete context. Therefore, at first, measures will be discussed which the students reportedly took to observe the QMPs that had been set to guide the project work, while subsequently, a summary will be provided of QM-related learning affordances which the project work seems to have created.

Customer focus. As the interviewees reported, to ensure the *timely delivery of the final product*, that is, summaries of medical evidence translated into Polish for Cochrane, the project manager general (PMGen)

Table 6.8 Overview of the research design (CP 2021)

Aspect of research design	Details
Research aims	To examine ways in which quality management principles were observed in the project, as reported by the project managers
	To examine the extent to which elements of professional translation service provision and project delivery (quality management) were integrated into the project work
Research method	Descriptive research (focused description)
Research instrument	Post-project written, asynchronous interview (with 46 open-ended questions)
Sampling	I. Convenience sampling: 24 UJ MA-level students of translation (N = 24);
	II. Purposive sampling: sub-sample of 5 PMs (N = 5), all females in mid-twenties
Timing	December 2017–March 2018: data collection
	March 2018–February 2019: data processing and analysis
Data analysis	Quantitative

introduced the time frame for the project work and systematically notified all the participants about the completion of particular workflow stages via a dedicated Slack channel. Team project managers (TPMs) relayed necessary information from PMGen to their team members via Slack updating colleagues on approaching deadlines. PMGen also designed an Excel grid with a list of the translation jobs (source texts to be translated) and a column for comments and information on the job status. The project participants could update the status of their tasks in the grid according to an agreed colour-coding scheme. As the interviewees maintained, the assignment of specific project roles to individual team members also reportedly helped them meet deadlines as, consequently, they focused only on the tasks which were relevant to their roles.

The interview data revealed that the monitoring of deadline observation throughout the project was the responsibility of PMGen and TPMs, but all team members reported on the status of their jobs by marking them as completed in the aforementioned Excel grid. As far as the transmission of information in the project is concerned, messages were mostly distributed in the top-bottom mode (i.e. PMGen communicated with TPMs, who relayed relevant messages to their teams).

The interviewees stated that *communication with the client* was handled single-handedly by PMGen, who ensured clarity by writing emails to the client in formal language and consulting the content with TMPs. When reporting back to the team, PMGen shared emails from the client with TPMs on Slack, thus allowing all team members to ask for clarification if need be. Promptness of the communication was ensured in two ways. The project inbox was regularly monitored, lest correspondence from Cochrane be overlooked, while the client was contacted only on urgent matters to ensure that emails from PMGen would be fast-tracked.

To follow the client's recommendations at the pre-production stage, PMGen and a client representative from Cochrane Poland negotiated the style guide and translation brief, which had been drafted by the team. If need be, PMGen emailed additional queries to the Cochrane contact person.

Leadership. The interviewees stated that *to meet deadlines*, PMGen set additional intermediate deadlines and informed team members about the completion of each workflow stage. TPMs also regularly reminded team-mates about the obligations and tasks at hand. *To cater for the high quality of the final product*, the translators and revisers were initially instructed that they each needed to run automated quality assurance (QA) in Memsource Cloud and correct errors identified in the process. Adherence to this requirement was reportedly monitored through Memsource, which displayed the QA status for particular translator. Target text quality regarding terminological accuracy and consistency was additionally ensured through the use of a shared project term base, whose content was verified for consistency against other Polish translations already published on the Cochrane website. Last but not least, the aforementioned Excel document was also helpful in tracking the performance of QA checks by particular team members.

The interviewees revealed that *coordination of the project tasks* lay primarily with PMGen and TMPs, who systematically wrote announcements and reminder messages about forthcoming deadlines and workflow stages in the general channel and in team channels on Slack respectively. However, all team members could additionally *track task completion* in Memsource Cloud, where the current status of each job was displayed, and in the aforementioned Excel grid.

Engagement of people. *Involvement* of the entire team was stimulated through PMGen's and TPMs' reminders about deadlines, which they posted in advance on Slack. All project members were constantly updated on overall progress and in case of problems, and individuals could consult other team members for help to ensure the timely completion of tasks. Moreover, particular tasks were clearly described on Slack and checked for comprehension not to leave anyone behind and to ensure task doability. Tracking and monitoring progress in Memsource Cloud and the Excel grid were also used towards that end. Moreover, to enhance the team spirit, problems, such as those reported by individuals who believed they might miss a deadline, were publicly consulted and team resolved on Slack.

The interviewees maintained that the *monitoring of progress* was chiefly the responsibility of PMGen and TPMs. For instance, PMGen *monitored* the revisers' work for status on Memsource Cloud and through the Excel grid, while TPMs verified translations for language quality and compliance with project specifications.

To ensure that team *members swiftly responded to MP's calls*, the project participants were reportedly advised to download the Slack app to their smartphones and the desktop Slack client to their computers so that everyone could receive instant notifications about incoming messages. Interestingly, the team members' readiness to respond was also built through *praise*, as TPMs constantly emphasised that the whole team was working towards a shared goal and time discipline was required. Translators and revisers were also continuously being motivated by PMGen and TPMs, who worded their Slack messages in a positive manner and also stressed their readiness to provide additional explanation to those in need. What is more, it was made clear that team members could also contact PMGen directly, bypassing their TPMs if need be. Overall, as a TPM observed, *keeping positive spirit amongst everyone was crucial during the whole project.*

Engagement was additionally enhanced through TPMs, who would *respond to queries* and help team members with immediate problems. Only when problems escalated would PMGen be notified and possibly involved in finding an adequate solution. Simultaneously, all team members could provide *mutual support*. For instance, some would take the floor and offer advice to colleagues on the meaning of field-relevant terms or final terminological decisions based on prior internet research. Efforts were also made to help the team strike a healthy work-life balance, which a TMP illustrated reporting that the long May weekend, which fell within the time bracket of the project, was officially declared a time off to ensure the team members would feel rested and ready to sustain high levels of engagement afterwards.

Process approach. To help the team members focus on the process a number of measures were used. One of them was to provide clear task descriptions, to which end Slack posts were written in plain language, with PMGen and TMPs encouraging team members to ask for further explanation or comment on expected challenges. Slack messages were also streamlined in the general channel or team channels, depending on their relevance to all or specific teams respectively. Process-related communication was reportedly held on Slack exclusively.

Improvement. The interviewees stated that the team members had opportunities to develop translation, revision and other relevant skills, although what transpired was that – in congruence with findings of the research into the TG project – the vast majority of the learning opportunities related to the development of soft skills, such as the ability to work under the pressure of time, collaboration or cooperation skills, problem-solving skills, time management, organisational skills, teamwork skills and self-motivation.

Translation and revision skills, whose development was also purportedly occasioned by the project work, pertained to three areas: (i) linguistic knowledge (e.g. the use of field-relevant terminology), (ii) communication skills, including computer-mediated communication within the team and the client – albeit in the latter case, only one person (PMGen) had a chance to practise – and (iii) computer-assisted translation skills, mostly regarding the use of Memsource Cloud for the delivery of the project, translation and revision.

Evidence-based decision making. From the interviewees' perspective, several steps were taken to ensure that each team member would revise their translations for errors and compliance with specifications. Firstly, at the inception of the project, it was underlined that the goal was to produce high-quality translations and that each translator was required to self-revise (i.e. critically revise their own work to identify possible errors). At the same time, all the team members were familiarised with the client expectations, as stipulated in the translation brief, which was available throughout the project on Slack (through a link to MS SharePoint) and in Memsource Cloud (as a reference text). After self-revision, it was important that individuals introduced necessary modifications to their translations before the texts were transferred to revisers.

An important part of evidence-based decision making in the project was the use in the translations of *field-relevant terminology which had been researched*, verified and accepted as the team jointly built a term bank that would subsequently inform the translators' terminological choices. As the interviewees maintained, the team members were sensitised to the need for the verification of terminology to be used in the project through online research based on reliable sources, such as medical websites or the client-provided term base. The project participants were also granted access to the term base designed by their colleagues in the very first iteration of the Cochrane Project at UJ in the year 2020, which ultimately was used for reference as yet another project resource.

Relationship management. The interviewees reported that contact between all the parties involved in the project was maintained through Slack. Therefore, all team members were required to regularly monitor Slack posts. PMGen, TPMs and revisers used the platform to consult one another, as well as the other colleagues. PMGen additionally handled email communication with the client.

Slack was used for various purposes but mostly to introduce and assign tasks, resolve problems, share resources and inform about current workflow stages. In addition, communication on task completion was augmented by the editable Excel grid, which permitted individuals to report progress or share comments. Finally, Memsource Cloud was used for in-project communication, permitting the translators to append translation units (corresponding source and target segments) with comments addressed to the revisers.

Summary of the findings and conclusions

As the interview findings reveal, to follow the set QMPs, project managers used several solutions for handling various project areas, including communication management (e.g. information flow), workflow management (e.g. task coordination and progress tracking), individual engagement and quality assurance.

Two major steps were taken to manage the project communication. One of them involved the adoption of specific communication channels through which to augment internal correspondence (Slack) and correspondence with the client (email), with latter being handled by PMGen alone. This step also comprised the streamlining of communication on Slack through several Slack channels, which were set up to deal with issues relevant to the whole team (general channel) or members of particular sub-teams (dedicated team channels).

The other measure was the establishment of the default information flow pattern for the project, which could be summarised as PMGen-TPMs-other team members (translators and revisers). As a result, information primarily flew from the top to the bottom of the power hierarchy in the team (i.e. from the management to the rank and file). The reverse was also possible, but even then – with some exceptions only – information would flow hierarchically, that is, translators and revisers would first contact their immediate supervisors (TMPs), who would in turn report to PMGen if need be. Provisions were also made for those at the bottom of the hierarchy to contact PMGen, as if bypassing the mediation of TPMs, but that option was reserved only for critical problem-solving.

There was also considerable information flow cutting across this hierarchy within two major tiers: the management, where PMGen was in communication with and TPMs, and the teams, where translators and revisers exchanged messages communicating on the tasks at hand. The intermediaries, so to speak, between the two tiers were TPMs, who on the one hand acted as subsidiary managers to PMGen while simultaneously performing translation along the other team members. Therefore, TPMs seem to have provided an important link between the two aforementioned tiers in the project, as they had insight into both managerial matters and the work being performed in particular teams. The information flow pattern for the CP 2021 project has been visualised in Figure 6.12, which demonstrates who communicated with whom in the project, which was the primary (solid arrows) and secondary (dashed arrows) direction of information

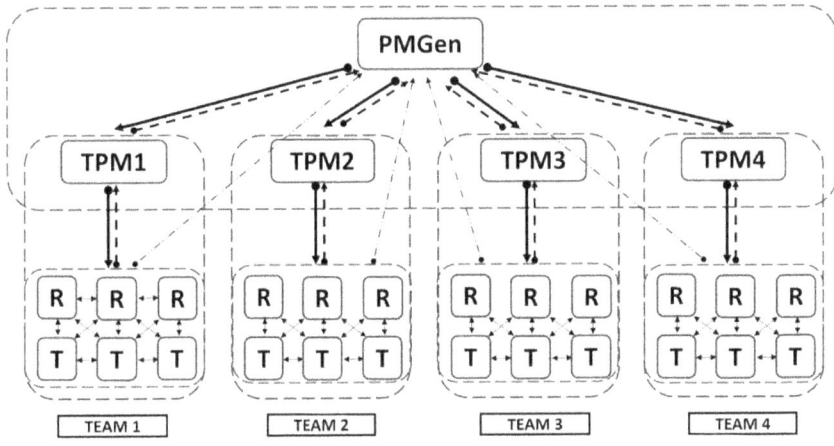

Figure 6.12 Information flow pattern in the CP 2021 project.

flow, and which instances of information of flow occurred only sporadically (thin dashed arrows).

To ensure that the project would be completed in agreement with the client's recommendations and on time, precise specifications of the product were initially delineated in the translation brief, style guide and style recommendations, which had all been negotiated with the client, and information was provided outlining the project time frame, workflow, work modes and tools. Subsequently, the ensuing work was coordinated by means of task-related notifications and reminders sent mostly by TPMs on Slack, modifications of the status of the current workflow stage, which PMGen handled on Memsource Cloud, but the sharing of relevant PMGen-client communication with other team members. What needs to be underlined is the particularly interesting solution which involved the creation of a dedicated MS Excel grid where the students updated one another on work progress and task status through comments or, visually, through a colour-coding scheme.

The measures which the students implemented to ensure the high quality of the final product entailed the maintenance of terminological accuracy and consistency across the translations through the joint preparation and subsequent use of a shared term base, which prompted individual translators to use specific TL translations of field-relevant terminology. The term base was being systematically updated through team consultations on Slack and online research. Moreover, automated QA checks were run in Memsource Cloud by translators and revisers to generate a list of language (e.g. grammar, punctuation and spelling errors) and technical (spacing, text tags) issues which the CAT tool detected. Eliminating those issues helped the team to ensure the linguistic accuracy, correct text formatting and proper layout of the translated documents.

To facilitate teamwork, effort was also made to maintain a high level of engagement on the part of team members. It was done by clearly laying out tasks and monitoring progress but also by ensuring a positive attitude of particular individuals to the project through praise, the underlining of team spirit and the importance of individual contributions towards the shared goal or by showing respect for the team members' right to rest.

As far as the learning affordances the CP 2021 project go, the testimony provided by the interviewees indicates that the project-induced learning potentially fostered the development of soft skills (the ability to cope with the pressure of time, problem-solving skills, time management and self-motivation skills), organisational skills, people skills, teamwork and collaboration skills.

At the same time, the project reportedly occasioned the learning of translation and revision skills within the realms of language, including linguistic accuracy (error correction in target texts), domain knowledge (the exploration and use of field-relevant terminology), generic communication management (the establishment of information flow patterns) and CMC management (the use of Slack as a communication platform); translation *per se*, including translation skills and CAT skills (the use of the TMS); as well as LSP skills, including the management and delivery of telecollaborative team translation projects, which entailed translation workflow management (e.g. the use of shared resources) and different dimensions of quality assurance (e.g. self-revision and automated QA).

Overall, the project seems to have been a successful implementation of emergentist learning on several plains. On the one hand, it turned out that when left to their own devices, students can indeed take independent decisions to cater for an aspect of project work (quality management) on which they are primed. On the other hand, the research results revealed that, as envisaged by the proponents of emergentist learning, projects can foster the simultaneous harnessing and potential development of both hard (linguistic, field knowledge, computer-assisted translation) and transferrable skills (teamwork, interpersonal and management skills).

6.2.3 *Cochrane Project 2022 (CP 2022)*

Project overview and research context

The third project was administered in the academic year 2021/2022 in the Chair for Translation Studies at the Jagiellonian University in Kraków in a CAT Tools course and lasted from mid-April to mid-May 2022.

By and large, CP 2022 was a mirror reflection of the earlier iteration of the same project (CP 2021), and it was performed for the same external client (Cochrane). As the project shared its general characteristics, including educational and social significance, with the preceding edition, only the slight differences will be discussed later regarding the profile of the involved student population.

This time, the project was performed by 28 students, who were tasked with the translation of short summaries of medical texts, varying in length between 200 to 800 words each. The client delivered a total of 60 source texts in .XML format via Memsource Cloud, whose configuration was analogous to that of CP 2021, including access to shared project resources such as TMs, glossaries and professional MT.

The project communication was managed on Slack (slack.com) again, and project documentation was shared on MS SharePoint, with the caveat that the most important files, including the translation brief, style sheet or a file with dictionary links, were also attached to the project files on Memsource Cloud as reference texts. CP 2022 was also a telecollaborative team translation project, as it was completed entirely online.

As far the structure of the translation team is concerned, the 28 students worked in four teams of seven, with each student performing translation. In each team, three students were assigned the role of a reviser. One of the translators was appointed as the project manager (PM), who coordinated the project work via four TPMs, who were both translators and team leaders supervising the translation workflow at team level and reporting to the PM. The adoption of project roles was voluntary, but occasionally, roles were peer appointed by the students with more jurisdiction (e.g. the PM or TPMs). An overview of the project is presented in Table 6.9.

Research aims

The CP 2022 project was used as an opportunity to conduct cross-sectional, survey-based research rounding up the project participants' experience in four major areas: (i) attitudes to telecollaborative project work, (ii) motivating and demotivating factors in project work, (iii) areas of translator competence, as defined in the EMT framework (EMT, 2017), developed in projects, and (iv) students' recommendations for changes to project design. The research aimed to answer the following questions:

RQ1. With what expectations do students embark on telecollaborative translation projects?

RQ2. What are students' attitudes towards project work?

- What are their attitudes towards projects and teamwork at large?
- Are their attitudes likely to change during the project?

Table 6.9 Cochrane 2022: Project overview

Aspect of the project	Details
Duration	mid-April–mid-May 2022
Related TS course	CAT Tools
Goals	To develop competences relevant to team translation through informed, reflection-based practice
	To develop technological competence (use of CAT tools and terminology management tools)
	To introduce students to terminology work in translation
External client	Cochrane (international non-profit organisations for disseminating high-quality information to make health decisions)
Source text (domain)	Summaries of medical evidence (MED)
Participants	28 UJ students of translation
Project roles	Project manager, team project managers (team leaders), translators (all students), revisers
Team structure	1 project manager* (*a team translator at the same time)
	4 smaller teams of seven (each with 7 translators, 3 team revisers and 1 team project manager*)
	*team revisers and team project managers were translators at the same time
Procedure	Online team translation (students working from home)
	Workflow: ST delivery, translation (by student translators), revision (by student revisers), final review at provider level (by PM), TT delivery, final review at client level (by Cochrane medical editors), publication on Cochrane website
Forms of telecollaboration involved	• Online communication, resource sharing and project workflow coordination
	• Online team translation
Technologies used	Slack (platform for communication, resource sharing and work coordination)
	Memsource Cloud (CAT tool for team translation, use of shared resources, for example, TMs and TBs, and workflow management)
	MS SharePoint (cloud storage for documentation)

RQ3. What factors can affect students' motivation in projects?

RQ4. In student's views, what translator competences are developed in team projects?

RQ5. What modifications to project design, if any, do students deem desirable?

Research design: Procedures, methods and sampling

The research helped to produce a focused description of the issues cited earlier based on data elicited from the participants of the CP 2022 through an online survey, which was designed in May 2022 and administered via the open-source LimeSurvey (limesurvey.org) platform within a period spanning 6–12 June 2022.

The survey contained a total of 20 questions: 14 close-ended questions, including three radio list questions which permitted a single response and 11 multiple choice questions, as well as six open-ended questions, four requiring short write-in responses and two permitting the provision of more elaborate answers. The survey questions fell into nine categories which related to the following areas: student profile, competences developed, initial expectations, attitudes to the project before and after it, motivating factors, demotivating factors, attitudes to project work and teamwork, perceptions of project work and teamwork and students' suggested amendments and recommendations for project design. Despite the online administration of the survey, the response rate (Cohen, Manion, & Morrison, 2017) was very high and amounted to 96.5%, which means that 27 students in all filled in the survey form and only one failed to so.

The data obtained in the research were largely quantitative; thus, they were exported from LimeSurvey to IBM's Statistical Package for the Social Sciences (SPSS, v.28) to compute descriptive statistics, mostly frequency distributions. The data collected through open-ended short text questions with three write-in responses were reviewed for repetitions and emerging categories, which were subsequently also quantified; data collected through the other open-ended questions were analysed qualitatively. The results will be reported in percentage points to reveal the proportions of students who opted for specific answers. However, it must be noted that for questions which permitted multiple responses, the cumulative percentage scores will exceed 100%.

Sampling

The research subjects were recruited through convenience sampling (Saldanha & O'Brien, 2014); they were students who had enrolled in the CAT Tools course in the 2021/2022 academic year and participated in the CP 2022 project as part of their coursework. The sample consisted of 28 subjects (N = 28), 25 females (N = 25), two males (N = 2) and a person who labelled themselves as gender nonconforming. The majority of the subjects fell into the 22–24 age bracket (N = 22), while the others were below the age of 22 (N = 3) and above the age of 24 (N = 2). An overview of the research design is presented in Table 6.10.

Table 6.10 Overview of the research design (CP 2022)

Aspect of research design	Details
Research aims	To examine attitudes to telecollaborative project work, motivating and demotivating factors in project work, areas of translator competence, as delineated in the EMT framework (EMT, 2017), developed in projects and students' recommendations for changes to project design.
Research method	Descriptive research (focused description) Post-project survey of 20 questions (14 close-ended and 6 open-ended questions)
Research instrument	SPSS statistical package, v.28 (data processing and statistical analysis) MS Excel spreadsheet (graph generation)
Sampling	Convenience sampling; 28 UJ MA-level students of translation (N = 28), 25 females, 2 males, 1 gender nonconforming person
Timing	6–12 June 2022: data collection June–August 2022: data processing and analysis
Data analysis	Qualitative and quantitative

Results and discussion

Prior translation experience. Nearly 67% (18) of the subjects declared they had no experience in professional translation at all, 26% (7) had less than a year's experience, while 7% (2) had experience ranging between one and two years. Therefore, it may be stated that for the majority of the students the CP 2022 project was the first-ever LSP experience. Furthermore, for 93% of the project participants, CP 2022 was most likely the first-ever team translation project they had completed, as the professional experience of another quarter of the students examined had very limited experience in the LSP industry.

Project roles. Interesting results were obtained when the students were asked what project roles they had adopted. They declared that four of them were team project managers, one was project manager general, 24 were translators, 16 were revisers and one student wrote in their own response stating that they managed customer contact. Although the responses largely reflect the original role distribution, some disparities are observable. Firstly, it seems that eventually, 16 students, rather than the original 12 (three per group), were involved in revision, which implies that the team saw the need to appoint four more revisers to complete the task. Besides, one student was tasked with managing team-client communication, although originally, no person had been assigned to that role.

However, quite remarkably, three students did not indicate that they were translators in the project, thus contradicting evidence from the CAT tool. As the question about project roles permitted multiple answers, it seems plausible that the additional roles which those three students played, most probably acting as additional revisers or customer contact, overshadowed their original roles to such an extent that the students chose not to report on their dual responsibilities.

Competences developed. When it comes to the translator/translation competences, as defined by the then latest version of the EMT competence framework (EMT, 2017), which the students believe to have developed throughout the CP 2022 project, most of the responses pointed towards the following four: technology (23%), translation competence (22%), personal and interpersonal (21%) competence and service provision competence (21%).

The only competence which received a considerably lower proportion of responses was that relating to language and culture (13% of responses vs. 21–23% for each of the remaining competences). It is interesting to discern exactly which aspects of the competences listed earlier the students reported to have developed, as accents fell unevenly within each of them.

As for language and culture competence, most of the respondents reported to have predominantly developed its linguistic dimension, with L2 competence (the students' foreign language) competence and L1 (native language) competence selected by the highest proportions of respondents (78% and 63% respectively). Generic cultural competence was claimed to have been developed by nearly half of the respondents (48%), while considerable smaller proportions of students maintained they had developed specifically their knowledge of culture 2 (23%) and culture 1 (19%).

The salience of linguistic development in the responses might be attributed to the fact that the students' main concern in the project was to produce functionally adequate and linguistically accurate TL translations, which inevitably required a great focus on various aspects of the languages involved. On the one hand, increased attention to the learning of L2 might imply that the students recognised potential challenges behind their attempts to comprehend the source texts (written in L2), which warrants high-quality translation at large. On the other hand, as the students translated into L1, they might have taken their L1 competence for granted and thus – at least to some extent – remained unaware of its potential development. The fact that generic cultural competence was reportedly developed more than cultural competence relating specifically to the L1 and L2 language pair might in turn derive from the fact that while dealing with the specialised texts, the students perhaps had generic cultural realisations (e.g. with regard to the domain) rather than the specific cultures involved in the translation. Last but not least, it is possible that the students ignored the inseparability of language and culture, as indicated through concepts such as *languaculture* (Agar, 2008), whereby the examination of a language element automatically induces the exploration of its cultural underpinnings.

The students also reported the development of all the dimensions of translation competence; however, most of them (82%) maintained to have developed thematic competence, which in the project entailed the medical domain specifically, while the lowest proportion of students (41%) believed they had developed knowledge of translation methods. The remaining dimensions of translation competence, including document analysis skills, meaning transfer between L2 and L1, translation strategies and final quality control procedures, were reported to have been developed in the project by majorities ranging from slightly over two-thirds (for meaning transfer and final quality control) of the respondents to nearly three-quarters (for document analysis skills).

Technology competence in the survey embraced the use of tools facilitating various stages of the LSP process, including document processing (generic solutions, for example, office software), information mining (search engines and corpus-based tools), translation *per se* (CAT tools) or file management, the basics of MT and assessment of MT systems. Figure 6.13, which provides an overview of the results obtained within the area of technology competence, illustrates the breakdown of frequency counts identified for a particular tool and reveals that the largest proportions of students reported development mostly in three dimensions of the competence: using CAT tools (93%), using search engines (70%) and the basics of MT (63%).

Another three areas which were reportedly developed in the project by nearly 40% of respondents each comprised: using relevant IT apps, using corpus-based tools and assessing MT systems. Considerably smaller proportions of respondents reported the development of file management skills (22%) and skills relating to the use of other tools (15%).

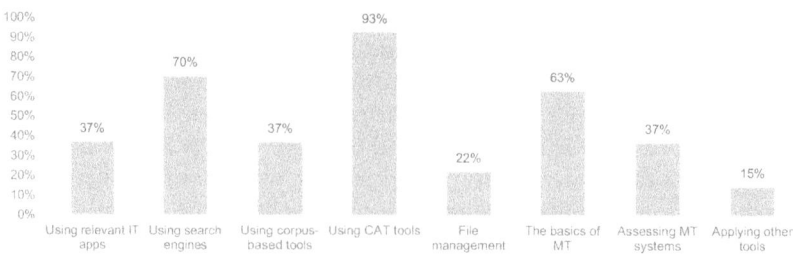

Figure 6.13 Areas of technology competence allegedly developed in the CP 2022 project.

The results seem to reflect the use of technology in the CP 2022 project, as the students mostly used the CAT tool and TMS in one (Memsource Cloud) to translate the source texts, they were backed up with the MT system (DeepL) provided by the client and they used online search engines to research field-relevant terminology in order to compile the project term base or to support the terminological decisions which they needed to take. Evidently, the extensive use of these tools led to increased competence development.

The lowest numbers of students maintained to have developed file management skills and skills in using other apps, which could be attributed to at least two factors. Firstly, prior to the project, the students had already been introduced to the basics of file management; thus, at least some may have believed there was little room for development in that area. Secondly, the need to handle files in the project was quite limited, as the project CAT tool permitted the storing, editing and real-time sharing of all the source and target texts, as well as other resources (term bases, translation memories and reference documents) with all the stakeholders in the translation process, including the client and the entire translation team. That might have reduced learning opportunities in this department, as the students did not need to concern themselves with file formats nor did they need to convert or send any files. Consequently, if file management was involved in the project work, it concerned only those students who performed tasks outside the mainstream project activities.

By the same token, opportunities for the development of skills related to the use of other apps may have been limited, as the default tools (Memsource Cloud and Slack) were evidently sufficient for the students to perform their project tasks, which means that even if other applications were occasionally used, it was the choice of a low number of individuals. Finally, actions promoting advancement in technology competences which had reportedly been developed by roughly 40% of the project team also seem to have been performed sporadically, hence, the lower frequency counts which were computed for them.

The constituents of personal and interpersonal competence which the students had reportedly developed in the CP 2022 project were time management skills, stress management, people management skills, teamwork skills, communication skills, social media skills, adapting, organisation and physical ergonomics of the working environment, as well as self-evaluation skills. However, while the most prominent areas of development comprised four skill sets – time management skills (82%), teamwork skills (78%), communication skills (74%) and self-evaluation skills (67%) – the remaining elements, such as working environment skills (37%), stress management skills (33%) and people management skills (26%), were claimed to have been developed by smaller proportions of respondents, with social media skills selected by only 15% of respondents.

Apparently, most of the project participants reported development in those dimensions of personal and interpersonal competence which corresponded to the most essential aspects of the team translation project and which were emphasised right from the onset. The students were made aware at all times that (i) they needed to complete assigned project tasks and complete the translation on time (time management), (ii) the translation was being performed by a team, whose members were all working towards a shared goal to which they needed to contribute, for example, by translating texts or providing mutual support (teamwork), (iii) they were to be in communication through different channels with their teammates and the client (communication skills) and (iv) they were to critically revise the outcomes of their work, for example, by self-revising their translations (self-evaluation).

The other skills may have been backgrounded to some extent for two possible reasons. While the learning and use of some of those skills were at the discretion of the project participants (e.g. no guidance was provided on how to deal with stress, organise the working environment or responsibly use the social media), the other skills, such as people management – although important – may have been perceived as the responsibility of those in managerial project roles (i.e. PMGen and TPMs).

In the case of service provision competence, all the areas were reported to have been developed in the project, albeit to varying degrees. The three areas of this competence which the largest proportions of respondents claimed to have developed were knowledge about professional standards (78%), analysing and reviewing language services to suggest improvements (69%) and applying quality management and quality assurance procedures to meet pre-defined standards (63%), which all directly related to LSP, which lied at the core of the CP 2022 project.

The two competences whose development was testified by the lowest proportions of respondents were communicating with the client (7%) and dealing and negotiating with the client (4%), which is not striking when it is realised that communication and negotiation with the client were delegated to only two team members, with the customer contact in charge of the former, and PMGen in a position to do both.

Development in the other areas had been noted by varying numbers of respondents ranging from 44% to 22%. The areas covered either elements to which the project participants had not been particularly alerted, such as knowledge about ethical issues in LSP (33%) and complying with ethical codes (26%), or those which lay in the hands of only some team members – clarifying the client's and end users' requirements, objectives and purposes (22%).

The most outstanding is the relatively large proportion of students who believe to have caught up with new industry demands (44%). On the one hand, it could be said that elements of this competence had not been high-lighted to the students involved in the project, but on the other hand, it might be that while working on the project tasks, the participants were under the impression that the actions they were involved in gave them an opportunity to see the new industry demands, including the need to work in teams or use cloud-based TMSs such as that used in the project.

Initial attitudes towards the project. As far as the students' initial expectations towards the project go, the vast majority reported that they looked forward to experiencing the reality of a translation project (85%), with very high proportions of respondents also hoping for the improvement of their CAT tool skills (78%) or the development of translation competence (74%). The students' initial attitudes towards the project varied and fell into the categories illustrated by Figure 6.14.

As it can be seen, slightly more than half the students (52%) experienced anxiety before the project work started, while 30–41% felt excited (44%), motivated (41%), curious (37%) and interested (33%). The other attitudes were reported by much lower proportions. As many as 11% of the students declared that they felt positive, unsure or they anticipated challenge, while 7% stated that they felt enthusiastic, professional, determined, focused and ready, or they anticipated complexity. Only single students (4% in each case) additionally listed attitudes such as responsibility, a sense of importance or anticipation of work heaviness and novelty. Interestingly, out of the 17 attitudes which the students displayed before the project, only one was markedly negative (anxiety); the others were either positive, indicating expectations of concrete learning, interest and readiness to embark on the project, or realistic, marking expectations of challenge, heavy work or complexity.

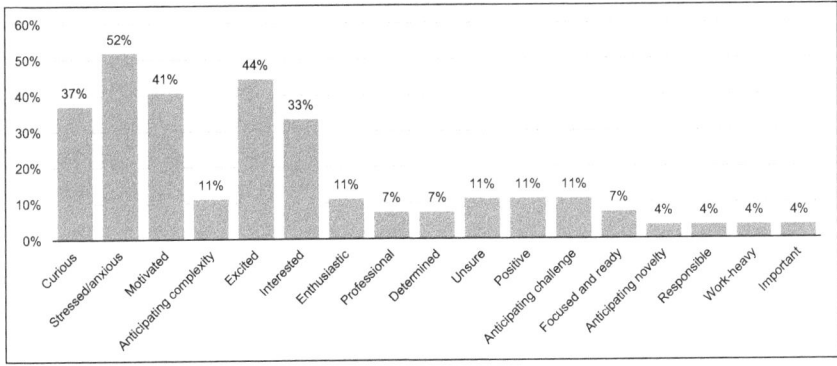

Figure 6.14 Students' initial attitudes towards the CP 2022 project.

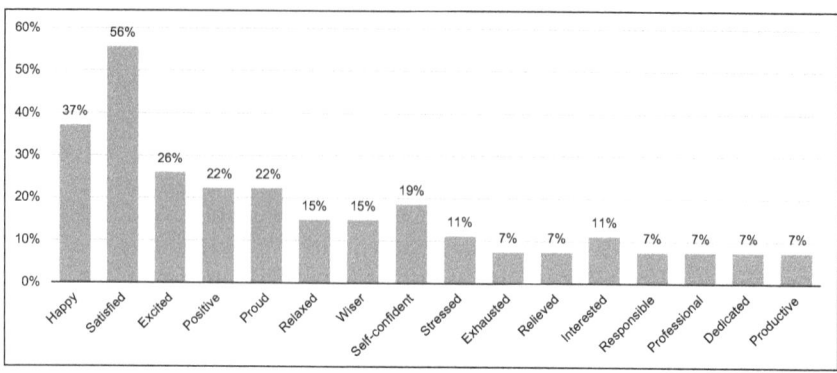

Figure 6.15 Students' attitudes after the CP 2022 project.

Post-experience attitudes towards the project. The students' attitudes reported after the completion of the project are depicted in Figure 6.15.

This time, over half the students (56%) maintained they felt satisfied with the project, 37% of them felt happy and 26% felt excited. As many as 22% stated that they felt positive, without providing further details, or that they were proud to have completed the project. 19% claimed they felt self-confident, 15% reported they felt wiser or relaxed, while 11% declared stress or interest in project-related matters. The smallest proportions of the students (7% in each case) stated that they felt exhausted, relieved, responsible for the job done, professional, dedicated (without specifying to what) and productive. All in all, out of the 16 attitudes which the students reported after the project, only three were negative (stress, exhaustion and relief), denoting the emotional and physical burden which the project work had entailed. Simultaneously, no negative attitudes were recorded towards the concept of the project as a didactic solution in translator education.

For the record, four invalid responses were also provided, which apparently referred to particular characteristics of the project work (challenging, demanding, complex and unpredictable) rather than the students' attitudes to it.

A comparison of the students' attitudes recorded before and after the project reveals that while before the project started the students felt stressed – perhaps due to the anticipation of the unknown – yet excited, motivated, curious and interested, afterwards, their anticipation gave way to satisfaction, content, excitement, pride and positive spirit, which implies that their perceptions of the project experience were very positive.

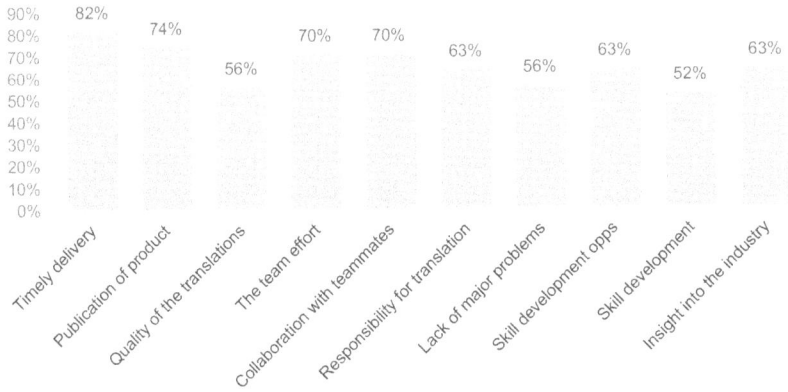

Figure 6.16 Motivating factors in the CP 2022 project.

(De)motivating factors in the project. The survey results revealed that over half of the students found the project-related factors named in Figure 6.16 motivating.

Three-quarters and more of the respondents reportedly derived motivation from the timely delivery of the final product (82%) and the prospect of their translations being published and acknowledgment for authorship, which – as it was suggested in the relevant survey question – might strengthen the students' CVs. As many as 70% of the students were motivated by the team effort, or collaboration with teammates, required to complete the project. Over 60% of the students found it motivating that the project placed responsibility for the translation on them (63%) and offered them an opportunity to develop new skills (63%), as well as gain insight into the workings of the translation industry (63%). The quality of the final product (i.e. the translations which the team had produced and lack of major problems in the project) was the source of motivation for 56% of the students, while the actual development of new skills motivated 52% of them.

What draws attention is that most students derived motivation from four factors: (i) the timely delivery of the final product, that is, the team-produced translations, (ii) the publication of the final product appended with the translators' names, (iii) the team effort involved in the project and (iv) the collaboration with colleagues, which has important implications. The first factor implies that the students took the project very seriously and thus strived to complete it on time. However, when coupled with the third and fourth factor, it may also be viewed as evidence confirming that the collaborative nature of translation projects may be an important student motivator. The second factor seems to highlight another two sources of student motivation. One of them is project authenticity (i.e. the fact that the project was performed for a real client and the team-produced translations were meant to serve a community of specific end users), while the other is the students' increased sense of achievement, which was fostered by the publication of translations on the client website and the acknowledgement of authorship.

As far are the demotivating factors in the project are concerned, the frequency counts for the students' responses are depicted in Figure 6.17.

The results reveal that all the students (100%) unanimously agreed that they found the delayed publication of their translations by the client demotivating, which only corroborates the aforementioned importance that the project participants apparently attached to product publication. The other demotivating factors were reported by much lower proportions of respondents. Time pressure and the burden of students' responsibility for the quality of the final translations were demotivating for 41% of the students each. The complexity of the project task at large was a demotivator for roughly one-third of the students (33%); the provision of limited and indirect feedback by the client was an issue for slightly more than a quarter of the students (26%). The remaining demotivators included the students' perceived lack of adequate competences (15%), the need to perform teamwork (11%) and the occurrence of major problems (4%). It must also be underlined that as many as 22% did not perceive any of the factors listed in the survey as demotivating at all.

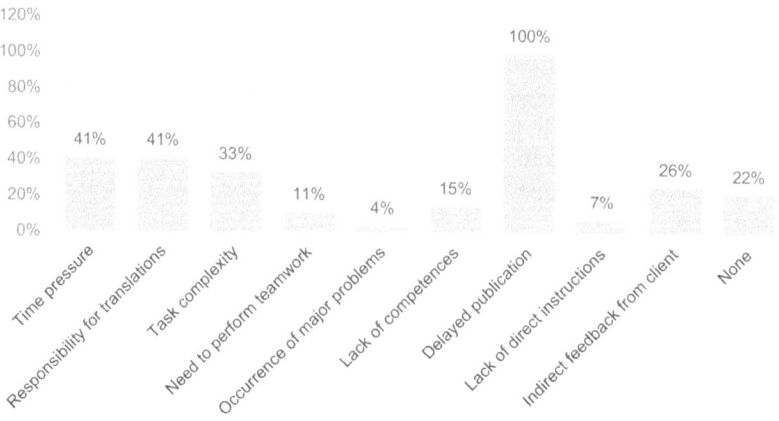

Figure 6.17 Demotivating factors in the CP 2022 project.

It is interesting to see the results cited earlier as checks, so to speak, of the validity of the students' responses to the question on motivators in the project. When responses regarding motivating and demotivating factors are juxtaposed, it is clear they do not contradict, which affirms the consistency of the students' responses.

The data additionally indicate that, although the vast majority of the CP 2022 participants found teamwork motivating, not all students are likely to share the sentiment. As individual perceptions of difficulty levels in the project differed, some students saw major problems where others could not. Some were demotivated by the inherent characteristics of translation projects (e.g. stress, responsibility or task complexity) while others by their own weaknesses such as lack of adequate skills – regardless of how grounded their self-perception was. Some felt they would rather obtain clear instructions on how to proceed; yet others simply preferred individual work by default.

Attitudes towards teamwork. It is interesting to see what the CP 2022 project participants' general attitudes were towards teamwork-based learning. As the survey data revealed, nearly two-thirds of the students maintained that they unreservedly enjoyed teamwork (63%), while roughly one-third (33%) stated that would be willing to do teamwork, albeit with some caveats (e.g. the right team), as they were introverted. While 11% found teamwork exhausting, only 4% (one student) stated that they did not enjoy working with others at all. The results are illustrated in Figure 6.18.

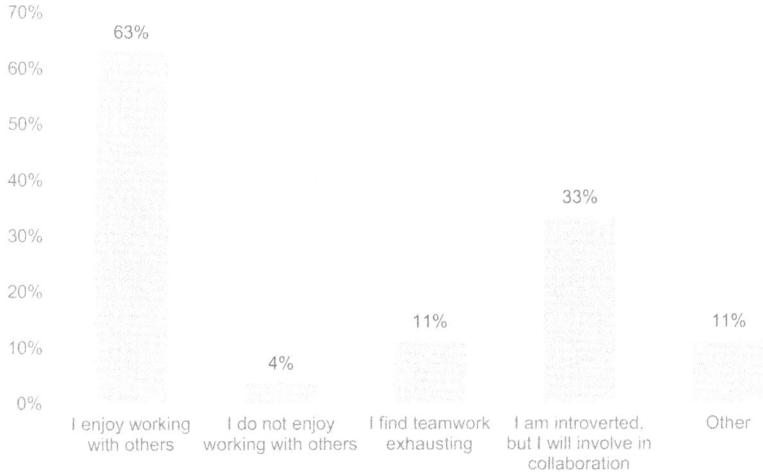

Figure 6.18 General attitudes to teamwork in the CP 2022 project.

In addition, 11% of the students also contributed their own responses. One claimed that they equally enjoyed teamwork and individual work, another stated that they enjoyed teamwork but found individual work comfortable, while one more stated that they would normally involve in teamwork although they preferred individual work and got frustrated if individuals on the team were not cooperative enough. Overall, the results cited earlier indicate that while some students may happily embark on teamwork, for others, the level of involvement will depend on the quality of the teamwork (e.g. the partners' commitment).

Perceptions of translation projects at large. The students were also surveyed on how they perceive team translation projects as a form of learning vs. other conventional methods used in translator education. Figure 6.19 contains a visualisation of the responses.

As the graph in Figure 6.19 illustrates, the largest proportions of students, two-thirds and considerably more, indicated that team translation projects involve an increased sense of responsibility (85%), real-life practices and reflect market requirements (82%), help students develop teamwork skills (74%) and provide an opportunity for contact with a real client. Roughly half the students (48%) agreed that team translation projects help to develop a range of translation and other, generic skills, as well as communication skills. A slightly lesser proportion (44%) believed that such projects diversify the learning experience by placing students in different roles and involve the use of various tools. As many as 41% noted that in team translation projects, students develop planning skills, and 30%

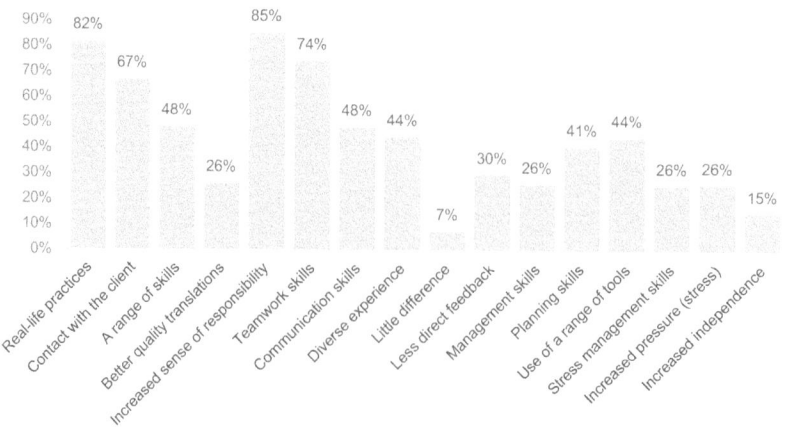

Figure 6.19 Students' perceptions of team translation projects at large.

observed that such projects involve less direct feedback than other forms of learning.

Slightly over a quarter of the students (26%) expressed the view that the projects in question facilitate the production of higher-quality translations, help to develop management skills and stress management skills, but also involve increased pressure levels. Only 15% of the students believed that in team translation projects individuals have more independence, while as little as 7% saw little difference between this and other learning methods.

All in all, it seems that most of the students appreciated the use of team translation projects in translator education mostly as an opportunity to develop teamwork skills and gain some insight into professional practices, including contact with the client or a sense of responsibility related to genuine professional LSP. They also valued projects for other reasons (e.g. as a chance to develop various skills), but individuals displayed different preferences in this respect, hence, the lower frequency counts computed for these responses.

Advantages and disadvantages of the CP 2022 project. In an open-ended question with three write-in responses, the students were asked to list the advantages of the team translation project in which they participated which they thought may have particularly facilitated their learning. When all the 81 responses – three per respondent, with no missing responses – were reviewed, it turned out that they fell into nine emerging categories of advantages related to the following areas: (i) teamwork, (ii) the use of CAT tools, (iii) the translation process, (iv) time management, (v) peer support, (vi) communication, (vii) insight into the realities of a professional team translation project, (viii) management and (ix) attitudinal factors. What follows is a qualitative analysis of the responses within each of the aforementioned areas.

As far as teamwork is concerned, the students maintained they found it particularly helpful in learning, as it enabled them to work on the same problem together, brainstorm – and thus produce better ideas than through individual work – hold discussions and consult others to take the most optimal terminological decisions, jointly resolve translation problems and job-share by delegating tasks in a team to individuals. They also underlined the outcomes of teamwork, which they mainly saw as the development of stronger bonds with colleagues, a sense of sharing the experience, higher motivation, the proliferation of ideas through collaboration and increased productivity.

Within the area embracing the use of CAT tools, the students appreciated access to an unrestricted version of the cloud-based professional TMS (Memsource Cloud), the user-friendliness of the CAT tool, the ability to learning how to work with a CAT tool in team mode and to use CAT tool resources such as TMs or MT.

When it comes to the translation process, the greatest learning advantages listed by the students were the quest for optimal translation solutions and the learning of new solutions, which stemmed from the former, the opportunity to learn how to find relevant terminology and research problematic terms, to translate domain-specific (medical) texts and to develop new skills (e.g. revision). In addition, the students also stated that the unproblematic provision of the source texts enhanced their learning, and although they did not explain why, most probably, they meant that the provision of the source texts in editable format and via the CAT tool helped them focus on the very translation, without the need to exchange file packages, convert file formats or OCR texts.

As for time management, the students relished the fact that punctuality was required and time pressure was exerted, as it helped individuals learn to respect their own and other team members' time. Time management helped to maintain discipline, which was necessary to meet the project deadlines. One of the students also stressed that what helped them to learn better was the high intensity of the project actions, perhaps due to the realisation that in professional LSP, time is always a key factor.

Other advantages related to peer support and comprised the ability to obtain direct advice from colleagues and team members' readiness to assist others. The forms of help that the students reported involved collaboration on optimal translation solutions, joint search for supporting materials or assistance with technical issues. Simultaneously, the students observed that peer support was a source of mutual motivation and a factor decreasing the amount of stress that they experienced while working on the project.

The elements of communication which facilitated learning in the project comprised the need for maintaining permanent contact with other team members, possibility of communicating with others for help and the implementation of a dedicated communication tool (Slack). Interestingly, while some students perceived Slack as the hub for communication and resource sharing, others appreciated the fact that it was a new tool, which in itself increased learning opportunities in the project. A student also reported that the intensive in-project communication helped them develop stronger communication skills.

What some students also appreciated was that the project gave them insight into the realities of professional team translation. They particularly valued the fact that they could work for, and collaborate with, a real client, which made them sense the resulting responsibility throughout the project. They also valued the clarity of information on the client's expectations, which helped them focus on what was most essential throughout the project. In addition, the students reported that what facilitated their learning was the organisation of the workflow, including flexible working hours and resource sharing.

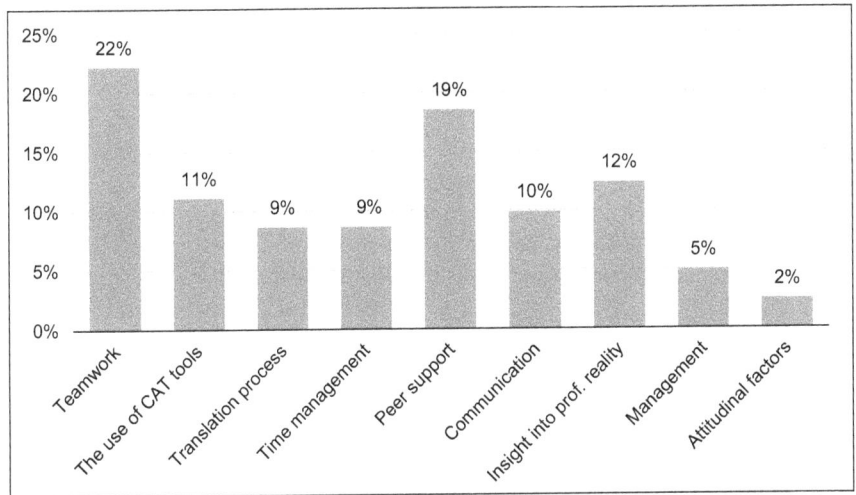

Figure 6.20 Learning-enhancing advantages of the CP 2022 project.

As far as management-related advantages go, the students mostly underlined the handling of the project by managers, including PMGen's readiness to help others and effective work management within teams through role assignment.

Finally, the students emphasised that their learning was facilitated by attitudinal factors such as their own and colleagues' positive attitude and motivation to work, which stemmed from the nature of the project work.

The computation of counts within each response category revealed which areas prevailed in the students' comments, as depicted in Figure 6.20.

As it can be seen in Figure 6.20, most of the students saw advantages regarding elements of teamwork (22%) and peer support (19%), while the lowest proportions appreciated aspects of project and team management (5%), as well as attitudinal factors (2%). The results seem to strongly support the concept of teamwork and collaboration as a valid learning solution, especially in translator education, as the highest percentage scores for the remaining advantages which the students listed related directly to translator education: insight into professional reality (12%) and the use of CAT tools (11%).

A parallel question of the same design as cited earlier was also asked about the disadvantages of the CP 2022 project which the students viewed as detrimental to their learning. This time, as many as 27 responses (33% of the maximum possible) indicate that no detriments to the learning process were observed, which means that for one-third of the students, no factors apparently interfered with their learning. When the remaining responses were reviewed, it occurred that they fell into eight major areas: (i) organisational challenges, (ii) lack of experience, (iii) team management and issues, (iv) challenges in translation, (v) time pressure, (vi) stress, (vii) materials and (viii) lack of feedback. Again, the students' responses within these areas will be qualitatively analysed later.

The disadvantages related to organisational challenges comprised the variety of work modes used within the project, limited control of individuals over time management, the number and range of project tasks, the multiple roles assigned to individuals, which bred confusion, the need to align individual work with that of other team members (e.g. revisers could not do their tasks until the translations had been completed), the need to consult the Slack platform for project updates, team size, which apparently was too large for some, the lack of time discipline on the part of some team members and the unauthorised text modifications.

Another group of disadvantages regarded the students' lack of experience in professional (team) translation and lack of adequate skills, which resulted in problems such the correction of translated texts by less competent colleagues, the fear of sub-standard performance or even incapacity.

Detriments pertaining to team management included problems with in-team communication, misunderstandings and conflicts of opinion (e.g. on terminological choices or project schedule, negligence on the part of particular team members and greater susceptibility of the team effort to failure due to diluted accountability).

The challenges which related directly to translation involved the necessity to deal with complicated texts and an unfamiliar domain (medicine), errors in translation which caused confusion at the revision stage and uncertainty about the choice of translation solutions due to conflicting ideas offered by individual team members.

When it comes to learning disadvantages which contributed to time pressure, the students cited short project duration, high-paced work and the necessity to meet deadlines, which resulted in little time for task completion and verification.

As far as stress goes, the students stated that it was caused by the unpredictability of the work, the sense of responsibility for the entire team and the shared goal, the huge workload and the realisation that the final product (translations) would be published.

The reported disadvantages connected with the materials used in the project comprised the lack of prototypical or past examples of the final product, which counters reality, as the students could access the entire Cochrane Library for examples of other English-Polish translations. The other disadvantages within this area reportedly included lack of materials of unspecified nature and the sub-standard quality of the term base which the students had been provided with at the onset.

Yet another disadvantage which reportedly affected the students' learning was the lack of direct and immediate feedback from the client, which some students had originally expected. Ultimately, the feedback was delivered as soon as the translations had been client reviewed, with the students receiving bilingual files for each of their translations with tracked corrections introduced by the client's medical editors. Nevertheless, it appears that the students would have rather obtained feedback sooner.

To summarise the findings discussed earlier and reveal identifiable tendencies within them, the students' responses were quantified, as illustrated in Figure 6.21.

However detrimental to the students' learning the previously cited factors were, they must be seen as opportunities for learning; that is why they had not eliminated from the project setup. After all, it is these factors that introduce students to the less pleasant aspects of professional LSP so that they can learn how to deal with issues such as intense pressure, increased responsibility and the high-stakes context of the translation of publishable content or the necessity to meet short deadlines due to increased demand. In addition, the findings reveal that while certain features of project work (e.g. the fast pace of work) are a learning advantage for some students, for others, they are likely to be the cause of stress. One more element

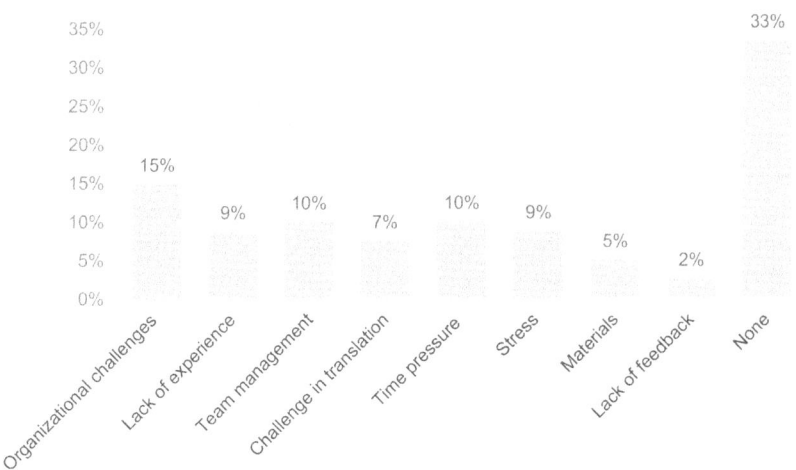

Figure 6.21 Detriments to learning in the CP 2022 project.

which needs to be commented on is the low proportion of those students who were unhappy about the lack of client feedback. Their colleagues did not find it problematic, but it is most probably because they remembered that delayed client feedback would be provided in due course, as it had announced right at the onset.

In the final part of the survey, the students were asked to suggest amendments to the design of the team translation project with a view to increasing its effectiveness in stimulating the learning process. A total of 13 students provided responses, which might be an additional indicator of the students' involvement in the project and the ensuing sense of responsibility. The 13 students shared 14 actual recommendations for amendments, with one invalid response which contained words of praise on the good organisation of the project. Interestingly, some of the recommendations regarded those aspects of the project over which the students had in fact had control. Those amendments comprised reducing team size, delegating responsibilities more fairly to make the learning more enjoyable for all, improving the quality of the project term base prior to translation and encouraging team members to find materials of unspecified nature that could facilitate work.

The remaining responses contained suggestions about modifications to the project design, such as extending project deadlines to give students more time for producing better-quality translations, increasing contact with the client throughout and after the project for more tips and feedback respectively, increasing the availability of specialised terminology, holding discussions to give those who are shy admit that they needed help, introducing students to field-related terminology prior to the project, giving students more freedom in establishing the rules for communication and assigning a single role to each project participant.

The closing question of the survey elicited any final comments which the students wished to share. Two of those comments called for further amendments, one for breaking down project tasks into smaller steps to improve self-agency and the other for the implementation of more field-relevant term bases in the project. At the same time, in congruence with the words of praise which had already featured in some of the responses to the penultimate survey question, four students expressed appreciation of the chance to participate in the project or the pleasure which they had derived from it, as evidenced by the following quotes:

S1: *Everything was well prepared. I would suggest that those kinds of projects are organised more often.*

S2: *The texts I translated were interesting and an opportunity to translate them broadened my medical terminology and improved my CAT-tool skills. I am grateful for the opportunity to participate in the project.*

S3: *I think it was really nice to be a part of this project. I really enjoyed the teamwork. I think it made the project more fun, because we could share our experiences within the chat and have the same goal.*

S4: *I really enjoyed the project.*

Summary of the findings and conclusions

In the light of the findings, the questions which motivated the research can now be answered. As far RQ1 goes, it may be concluded that students seem to have focused expectations towards telecollaborative translation projects, which mostly embrace the development of translation technologies (e.g. CAT tool skills), and broadly understood translation competences. Generally, students perceive projects as real-life practice, a chance to delve into professional reality (translation market requirements) and to develop teamwork skills, as well as transferrable skills, which are – very importantly – likely to equip them for professional life, even outside the LSP industry.

As for RQ2, students seem to eagerly embark on project work, and they display very positive attitudes towards it. In the research, a vast majority of the participants unreservedly declared that they enjoyed collaboration and felt involved in project work, even if they were introverted. What is more, the students' positive attitudes did not change after the completion of the project, at which point they reported a sense of satisfaction, happiness, pride and increased self-confidence.

As far RQ3 goes, motivation in team translation projects seems to derive from various sources, including the sense of achievement, which is enhanced by task completion, the sense of responsibility, which projects seem to induce, the ensuing learning opportunities and – very significantly – the team effort and collaboration with colleagues which project work inherently involves. The latter seems to provide a very strong argument for the implementation of telecollaboration in translator education courses.

At the same time, the factors which are most likely to demotivate students are a lower sense of accomplishment, which in projects involving publishable content can be caused by the delayed publication of students' translations, the time pressure exerted by short deadlines, the complexity of the project work or the lack of immediate feedback from the client. What draws attention is the problem of complexity, which on the one hand, the students viewed as a demotivating factor but which, as the advocates of emergentist learning maintain (see Chapter 4), perpetuates learning by occasioning the emergence of knowledge. As this perceived downside may potentially be an advantage, it seems advisable that teachers increase students' awareness in this respect.

The students also mentioned other demotivators, such as anxiety, fear of the unknown and unexpected, prospective challenges and heavy work. The apparent lack of confidence on the students' part seems to call for a degree of counselling, which has been used in FL education courses to support students' learning (Larsen-Freeman & Anderson, 2018). When implemented prior to translation projects, it is likely to increase students' morality and persuade students to believe that the tasks at hand are doable.

RQ4 enquired about the translation competences which can potentially be developed through team translation projects. The research results indicate that a plethora of competences are amenable to development, including hard and soft skills. For instance, the project apparently fostered autonomous decision making, as the students appointed additional roles to team members in response to the amount of work and nature of work which they needed to handle. Three more revisers and a customer contact person were appointed, which implies that the students first strategically estimated the task at hand and made relevant decisions. On the one hand, it might mean that the students took full responsibility for the project and took the necessary steps to complete it on time, while on the other, by acting independently of the teacher, they may have increased their sense of self-reliance.

The project also created opportunities for developing competences other than translation *per se*, which the students evidently found very significant. They testified to it as they reportedly took on project roles other than that of a translator, as if trying to go beyond the role they would normally take for granted in more conventional forms of coursework.

The reported development of the students' cultural competence seems to raise an important issue pertaining to the students' perception of culture. While large proportions of students maintained to have developed general cultural competence, much lower proportions reported on the development of cultures related to the project language pair (i.e. English and Polish). What it seems to indicate is that students possibly tend to overlook the interconnectedness of language and culture without realising that elements of a given language are underpinned by, and carry, the related culture; thus, their exploration often entails the development of language-specific cultural competence. It is perhaps the teacher's role to attract students to that fact and the learning affordances which stem from it.

As far as the development of translation competence in the project is concerned, the research results revealed that development in that area was inclusive and covered not only the learning of translation solutions, such as translation methods and strategies, but also other elements of the translation process, including document analysis skills and quality control.

The data regarding the development of (translation) technology competence highlights another important issue. The students primarily claimed to have developed in areas most indispensable for the project work, such as CAT tool skills, Web-searching skills (use of search engines) or the basics of MT. At the same time, relatively low proportions of students reportedly developed skills pertaining to file management or the use of corpus-based tools, which indicates that the development of specific areas of (technology) competence in team translation projects inevitably hinges upon the choice of project procedures and tools. Consequently, if particular areas of competence are to be targeted for development, projects must be planned with that in mind. For instance, to foster the development of file management skills, the file delivery modes and formats which were originally used in the CP 2022 project would need to be modified so that the client would not deliver files through a TMS and content would be delivered in non-editable formats. That would require students to arrange for the reception, organisation and naming of files, as well as file conversion (e.g. through the use of OCR technologies).

The research results demonstrated that personal and interpersonal competence was largely developed in the areas of time management skills, teamwork skills, communication skills and self-evaluation skills. However, they simultaneously seem to indicate that guidance may be necessary to foster the development of other relevant skills (e.g. stress management or the organisation of work environment), for which development was reported by lower student proportions. It seems that without support, students may find development in these areas impossible (e.g. due to the lack of necessary means of coping with stress). Thus, to advance in this department, students might require an incentive to explore optimal solutions.

All in all, it is impossible to expect that in telecollaboration projects, all skills will be developed simultaneously and to the same degree each, as opportunities for development will inevitably differ (e.g. depending on the project roles which students adopt). A case in point is the development of skills related to negotiations with the client, which was reported by only one project participant who handled team-client communication. Besides, it would be a tall order to target all competences – the more that the less obvious ones, such as compliance with ethical codes, which is part of service provision competence, may require a specific focus.

Finally, the possible modifications of project design which the students suggested (RQ5) also have interesting implications. For instance, changes to team size, the delegation of responsibilities, task structure (smaller steps for better control), the degree of student involvement (encouraging participants to find materials that could facilitate their work) or the nature of pre-project work (preparation of the project resources prior to translation), which some students advocated, were all elements of project management, and as such, they were at the discretion of the students themselves. Such recommendations seem to indicate that, apparently, not all students fully realised the degree of autonomy which they had been granted within the project, possibly due to the nature of their learning experience and the teaching modes which are prevalent in translator education, as the research related to the LP 2018 project (to be discussed in the following section of the present chapter) demonstrates. Consequently, there is a need to elucidate to students the degree of freedom and control they have in a project.

Other student recommendations regarded modifications to project design, such as pre-project introduction to terminology and even the collection of relevant terminological resources, the need to limit the number of project roles to one per person, more freedom in establishing the rules for in-project communication, the introduction of discussion sessions to give shy students the voice and more client involvement throughout the project for tips and feedback.

The list of student-recommended modifications will most probably differ from project to project; thus, the modifications cited earlier need not be treated as universally applicable propositions. However, they offer interesting implications for translation teachers. One of them is the extent to which teachers' intentions converge with students' expectations. For instance, in the project, some students were assigned more than one role with a view to increasing their learning opportunities and perhaps the repertoire of competences to be developed. Evidently, students' perspective on this kind of solution will not necessarily dovetail with that of the teacher. Thus, it seems advisable to increase students' awareness of the justification of role assignment. At the same time, it is not necessarily desirable to meet students' expectations in this respect. If projects are to introduce students to professional reality, students need to realise that in professional contexts, they will be frequently asked to multitask and perform multiple roles. That is why it is an advantage that they are first asked to leave their comfort zone and rehearse this scenario in the learning context.

The students' remarks about the lack of freedom in deciding on the mode of communication in the project highlights another problem, namely, that of pedagogical and professional motivations behind translation project design. To avoid students' disappointment and confusion, it seems reasonable that the motivations, especially those behind any project elements which are imposed on the students, are clearly explained. Had it been done in the CP 2022 project, the students would have learnt that they were required to communicate on Slack for two reasons. On the one hand, it was meant to facilitate the teacher's monitoring of student involvement in the project (pedagogical motivation); on the other hand, it was supposed to reflect the fact that, despite their preferences for private channels of communication, in professional settings, the students would nonetheless be expected to use corporate tools (professional motivation).

Last but not least, although most of the project participants were adamant that teamwork and the opportunity to collaborate with colleagues were advantages of project work, not all individuals subscribed to that point of view. Consequently, as some students may apparently feel readier to interact with the other team members (e.g. to share problems) in the teacher's presence, it may be necessary – in congruence with the findings obtained in research related to the TG project – to ensure that presence and regulate it flexibly.

All in all, it may be stated that the CP 2022 project was completed successfully, as the students delivered the translations to the client on time. Moreover, they appreciated the relative autonomy which they had but also the responsibility which they needed to accept. Particularly motivating were the authenticity of the project, which had been commissioned by a genuine client and the recognition of students' achievement through the publication of their translations on the client's website with the acknowledgement of authorship. In the light of that, translation projects seem to increase students' confidence in their own competences and promote further learning.

The team translation projects discussed earlier involved increased authenticity when compared to the OIEs (see Chapter 6.1) not only in that they were completed for genuine clients but also because they addressed the needs of local (TG) or national (CP 2021, CP 2022) communities. That alone enhanced students' motivation and sense of responsibility while also providing opportunities for students to develop varied components of translator competence. Given the time at which the projects were administered, they also reflected changing trends in language service delivery; while TG involved the use of a SaaS tool mostly to facilitate team translation, in CP 2021 and CP 2022, a client-owned TMS was used to facilitate workflow and resource management.

6.3   Miscellaneous projects

The third category of projects applicable to translator education, as discussed in Chapter 5, is that of *miscellaneous projects*, where a degree of telecollaboration is either complemented with f2f work (hybrid courses) or used to perform actions other than translation *per se*. Two examples of such projects will be presented as possible implementations of telecollaboration: one dedicated to terminology work (Terminology Project) and the other involving the exploration of localisation practices (localisation project).

Each of the projects also served as the context of research into selected aspects of telecollaboration. The student participants of the former project were surveyed on the operational, cultural and critical literacies developed in the project and the characteristics of the telecollaboration tools which they used in their work, while the participants of the latter project constituted a sub-sample of research conducted in the years 2017 and 2022 to examine students' expectations towards translator education vs. their actual learning experience, which was inspired by research of a similar kind originally conducted by Klimkowski and Klimkowska (2013). Descriptions of the two projects will be followed by reports on the accompanying research.

6.3.1 Terminology Project (TP 2016)

Project overview and research context

The project was held in the year 2016 in the Chair for Translator Education at the Pedagogical University in Kraków, Poland (UP), as part of a Terminology course and lasted from November 2015 to January 2016, with a view to developing the participants' knowledge about terminology building and management, helping them to explore CAT-related terminology, offering them hands-on practice in the use of the terminology-related functionalities of a selected CAT tool (Wordfast Plus Tools, tlTerm or memoQ) and giving them a chance to telecollaborate.

The project was completed by 11 students whose major, ultimate goal was to produce an electronic term base comprising terminology (45–60 terms) in computer-assisted translation as a TS research area or a translation mode. To complete the project, the students needed to perform several steps, including online search for reference texts, alignment of parallel texts, term extraction with the use of a CAT tool, research, exploration and definition of extracted terms to collect data necessary to build term entries, import of the collected data into an electronic term base designed with a CAT tool and transfer of the data into the Mail Merge tool of MS Word to generate a printed version of the term base.

The students worked in groups and telecollaborated using Web 2.0 tools selected from the following: social networking sites (e.g. Facebook), online text editors with team-editing functionalities (e.g. TitanPad, PrimaryPad or Google Docs), file sharing services (e.g. Padlet, OneDrive, Dropbox or Google Docs), a purpose-created Moodle forum and online text/audio/video communicators (e.g. chat apps or Skype). Each group autonomously appointed a leader responsible for coordinating group/individual tasks in the project and contacting the course teacher in case of problems. An overview of the project, including the ultimate choice of the tools, is presented in Table 6.11.

Table 6.11 Overview of Terminology Project 2016 (TP 2016)

Aspect of the project	Details
Duration	November 2015–January 2016
Related TS course	Terminology
Goals	To develop students' knowledge about terminology building and management
	To make students explore CAT-related terminology
	To involve students in telecollaborative terminology work consisting in the preparation of an electronic term base with the use of Web 2.0 tools
External client	N/A (not a translation project)
Terminology (domain)	computer-assisted translation (linguistics)
Participants	11 UP students of translation (MA level),
Project roles	Team leader (1 per team), terminologists
Team structure	3 teams, each with a team leader appointed to coordinate the work
Procedure	Search for reference texts, alignment of parallel texts (optional), term extraction, term exploration, collection of (meta)data to build term entries, import of data into an electronic database (e.g. in memoQ), transfer of data into Mail Merge (MS Word) to generate a printed version of the term base
Forms of telecollaboration involved	• Online communication, resource sharing and project work coordination
	• Team text editing (in the cloud)
Technologies used	Web 2.0 tools:
	• Online text editors (TitanPad)
	• Resource sharing services (Padlet)
	• Moodle forum (purpose-created on the course site)
	• Online text/audio/video communicators (e.g. Messenger)

Research aims

Research conducted in connection with the TP 2016 project focused on the two kinds of communication tools which the students used to facilitate telecollaboration: the cloud-based application for team text editing, TitanPad (titanpad.com), and the instant messaging app, Messenger (messenger. com). The research was motivated by the need to investigate the extent to which general-purpose software, such as TitanPad and Messenger, could be used to facilitate work in projects administered to develop selected elements of translator competence, which in this case involved knowledge about terminology (building) and management skills.

The research was guided by the three questions listed in the next section:

RQ1. In students' views, what work modes did the general-purpose communication and telecollaboration tools (Messenger and TitanPad) facilitate?

RQ2. What are the telecollaboration-related strengths and weaknesses of the tools?

RQ3. What is the students' evaluation of the suitability of the tools for telecollaboration?

Research design and procedures

The research was designed to produce a focused description of the TP 2016 project participants' views on the extent to which general-purpose communication and telecollaboration software (Messenger and TitanPad respectively) could lend itself to facilitating telecollaborative tasks aimed to develop selected elements of translator competence, namely, terminology-related knowledge and skills. The research data were elicited through a tool evaluation sheet in MS Word format, which was distributed via the university Moodle system in January 2016, while the responses were analysed in February 2016.

The evaluation sheet contained a table of five columns, with each eliciting responses regarding the purpose of a given tool, work modes facilitated by the tool, major functionalities of the software, strong and weak points, overall evaluation of the tool in terms of functionality (e.g. ease of use or the clarity of the user interface) and the students' evaluation of the suitability of the tool for telecollaboration. The table cell size was adaptable; thus, the volume of the written responses which the students provided was unlimited. The format of the responses was open; thus, the students either entered run-on text or provided responses as bulleted lists. As the research was administered via the official university Moodle platform, the response rate (Cohen et al., 2017) was 100%, which means that all the 11 students returned the survey form.

Due to the small sample size and open nature of the responses elicited through the tool evaluation sheet, the data obtained from individuals were approached as cumulative, and they were analysed qualitatively to profile the students' perceptions of the issues at hand. To augment the analysis, responses relating to the two tools under examination from individual students were transferred to two separate sheets, one for each tool, to review the entire team's views collectively, with the caveat that only the content relevant to the research questions was analysed.

Sampling

The research subjects were recruited through convenience sampling (Saldanha & O'Brien, 2014) (i.e. they were students enrolled in the Terminology course in the 2015/2016 academic year, who participated in the Terminology Project. The research sample comprised all the course participants, that is, 11 subjects (N = 11), nine females (N = 9) and two males (N = 2), whose age was roughly defined as the mid-twenties. Table 6.12 provides an overview of the research design.

Results and discussion

Messenger. The respondents characterised Messenger as a tool which primarily facilitates individual and group communication via online text-based chat or video call functionalities, which may be useful for people involved in remote teamwork. It also enables users to create separate activity- or topic-dedicated groups and permits file and resource sharing,

Table 6.12 Overview of the research design (TP 2016)

Aspect of research design	Details
Research aims	To investigate the extent to which general-purpose software (TitanPad and Messenger) could be used to facilitate work in projects administered to develop selected elements of translator competence (knowledge about terminology and terminology building and management skills).
Research method	Descriptive research (focused description) Collection of students' post-experience evaluations of the tools in question via a purpose-designed MS Word sheet
Research instrument	Post-experience tool evaluation sheet with 5 columns for write-in responses (unlimited in volume) regarding the purpose of the tool, work modes facilitated by the tool, major functionalities, strong and weak points, overall evaluation of the tool for functionality and overall evaluation of the tool for suitability for telecollaboration
Sampling	Convenience sampling; 11 UP MA-level students of translation (N = 11), 9 females, 2 males in their mid-twenties, participants of the Terminology course
Timing	January 2016: data collection February 2016: data processing and analysis
Data analysis	Quantitative

enabling chat participants to upload files in various formats (e.g. .DOCX, .PDF) or share hyperlinks to external resources, such as relevant websites or online videos.

The work modes for which the students reportedly used Messenger to facilitate telecollaboration in the project involved discussing terminological issues, exchanging information about terminology management, functionalities and troubleshooting in memoQ and, occasionally, holding quick question-and-answer sessions to decide on the most pressing matters. In addition, they used Messenger for file sharing, including the exchange of ready-made products, such as terminology entries prepared by particular team members, or screenshots evidencing individuals' work at each project stage. The students also used the application to mediate external file sharing, sending one another notifications about content updates in third-party storage software (e.g. the cloud-based storage service Padlet).

Through Messenger, the students communicated to establish and modify collaboration and job-sharing rules within teams or to delegate term base management tasks. Some team members admitted that they also contacted the other team members via Messenger voice or video phone calls, particularly when they were away from their desktop computer. In two teams, the program was used to vote for the team leader prior to the project, and in one team, to increase security, a closed group was created so that the team members could comfortably exchange project-related text and visual content without concerns about privacy.

As for the strengths which the students identified in the program, the respondents observed that Messenger augments fast and efficient communication and helps users keep up to date with in-project communication thanks to text and audio notifications which alert them to new content. It permits working on an any-time-any-place basis through the mobile phone app. It also gives users flexibility in handling communication, allowing them to disable chat and notifications or block messages from individuals. The program does not limit the number of characters in chat posts; it helps append conversations with graphics and shared resources and allows video calls. The students additionally underlined that what made Messenger truly convenient to use was its popularity, thanks to which the software was immediately available to the project participants without the need for installation or account setting and individuals could be easily invited to join the project group.

The features of the program which the students found disadvantageous for telecollaboration were the necessity to have a Facebook account to use the program, problems with antivirus software blocking file downloads, lack the possibility to modify the user interface, the need for good connectivity, lags in the delivery of messages, which can break the flow of communication and cause misunderstandings, limited upload size, as well as the small size of the message box and the scroll bar which is used to navigate the content.

The students also displayed awareness of issues related to privacy and copyright, which involved the possibility of sharing content without the necessary consent or access to users' private details unrelated to the project work. One student also remarked that Messenger may not be the optimal choice for professional communication, as its users are likely to be distracted by private messages.

The students noted the suitability of Messenger for telecollaboration due to several capacities, including quick and easy exchange of information, a record of previous conversations, available even if one failed to join them in real time, the handling of varied communication modes, such as longer conversations, shorter exchanges or video calls, the configurability of the chat groups, the sharing of multimedia content, portability and the instantaneousness of feedback due to people's online presence. Simultaneously, a respondent noted that Messenger is most useful for handling communication in small projects, which do not require constant commitment, but they offered no further explanation.

As for *TitanPad*, the students viewed it as a program for the joint editing of text documents which additionally permits real-time communication with co-editors via an online chat box. Although the tool was designed with synchronous work in mind, the students observed that it also enabled them to leave information on the pad so that others could comment on it at their convenience.

The work modes in which the students engaged, and which TitanPad reportedly facilitated, involved uploading documents and sharing them with team members, the team editing of terminological entries or terminology lists in synchronous and asynchronous mode, discussions on project-related ideas and important issues (e.g. the selection of reference texts, the listing of terms for extraction or further management and the provision of updates on progress in the project).

The advantages of TitanPad which, in the students' views, supported telecollaboration included the accessibility and visibility of important content uploaded to the program due to main window size and, most essentially, the facilitation of real-time collaboration through the easy identification of the authorship of particular contributions by means of colour coding. What the students appreciated was the possibility of reviewing and time-tracking the process of text editing, and thus modifications made by particular individuals, through the time slider functionality, which additionally permitted the restoration of the previous versions of edited documents. Other advantages comprised the possibility of using the chat box for real-time communication while team-editing uploaded content, the capacity to invite others to edit the pad documents, auto-save, which prevented data loss, export options for various file formats, including .DOC, .PDF, .HTML and .TXT, easy orientation in documents and identification of specific text fragments thanks to line numbering and the monitoring of the co-editors' online presence through the display of their nicknames in the chat box.

The major disadvantage of the tool for telecollaboration which the students reported was, most importantly, support for only basic forms of text editing and occasional problems with character encoding, which caused Polish diacritics to display incorrectly. Other disadvantages related to the fact that comments entered in the main program window did not bear users' names, as a result of which individuals needed to append their messages with first names in brackets, which slowed down collaboration. Besides, contributions were limited to text only, as the program did not support diagrams, tables or charts, which are useful for illustrative purposes. In addition, new members could be invited to the editing team through an invitation email which needed to be sent by the pad admin, and the content would automatically be deleted after some time if a pad was not created by a registered user. Occasional problems were also reported with inviting other users or setting pad passwords, but they were easy to resolve.

Despite the aforementioned problems, the students generally perceived TitanPad as a tool which could effectively support telecollaboration in real time, as it permitted joint text editing and the tracking of contributions through the colour-coding scheme. The program also auto-saved modifications introduced to the text and permitted the archiving of content through data export. The students acknowledged the usefulness of the time slider, which fostered control over the work progress, and the chat box, which helped users to separate comments and notes from the content being edited. In retrospect, a student remarked that the team editing of content was a little-known form of collaboration at the time of the project, which indicates that the task was a novelty, albeit the same student admitted that (s)he did not particularly enjoy teamwork.

At the same time, some project participants did not overlook telecollaboration-related shortcomings of the program, which included missing user identification for edits introduced to the team-edited content, or the lack of functionalities which would permit the integration of TitanPad with other tools.

Summary of the findings and conclusions

The qualitative analysis of the findings revealed that both the tools facilitated particular aspects of students' telecollaboration, albeit each to a different degree and in its own ways. All in all, RQ 1 may be answered by stating that the work modes supported by both tools collectively comprised text-based discussion, information exchange, decision making (vote) and brief Q and A sessions, video calls, file sharing, including the exchange of hyperlinks to external resources, as well as recoding and evidencing progress and individual contributions to the project.

With regard to RQ2, it needs to be observed that the telecollaboration-related strengths of the tools under examination lied in their capacity for facilitating in-project communication through text chat, length limit-free posts, video calls, updates on progress in the project (e.g. through text and audio alerts) and the use of graphics and shared resources with which to append conversations. What is more, while Messenger was instantly usable due to its popularity among the students, TitanPad offered additional advantages such as the capacity for reviewing, time-tracking and content versioning, automated content archiving and export features. The disadvantages of Messenger included unmodifiable user interface, connectivity-induced problems, including lags in the delivery of messages, and blocked downloads due to conflicts with antivirus software, while the downsides of TitanPad related to very basic text-editing functionalities, limited format of contributions, unreliable storage in unregistered accounts and occasional problems with inviting new team members to the platform.

As far as RQ3 is concerned, the students perceived both tools as suitable for telecollaboration in that they permitted quick and fast exchange of information, facilitated varying communication modes, helped to keep a record of previous communication, tracked individual contributions – albeit with problems (TitanPad) – and archived team-edited content (TitanPad). Simultaneously, the respondents noted that both programs had limitations (e.g. Messenger was best suited for small projects, while TitanPad could not be integrated with other tools).

To sum up, the project was successful not only in terms of task completion but also in that it permitted the students to evaluate the tools that they used. Although the use of Messenger or TitanPad for telecollaboration might seem obsolete today, when multiple other tools have been developed, the TP 2016 research corroborated the validity of the project demonstrating how even an experience with less obvious telecollaboration tools, supplemented with post-project reflection, could be a valid pedagogical choice persuading students to look critically at the resources they use and drawing their attention to the need for tool evaluation on a fit-for-purpose basis and with regard to potential technology-related problems that can be encountered in telecollaborative settings. The project seems to have fostered the critical dimension of any kind of literacy, which Lankshear and Knobel aptly define as "awareness that all social practices, and thus all literacies, are socially constructed and 'selective': they include some representations and classifications – values, purposes, rules, standards, and perspectives – and exclude others" (Lankshear & Knobel, 2011, p. 18). It is by making project participants reflect critically on their telecollaboration practices (e.g. the tools that they use to complete project work) that teachers can potentially transform learning into a liberating experience, whereby students will learn to approach each new translation task with a fresh pair of eyes to make informed choices of the tools and work modes most adequate for the new context rather than relying on presumptions or routine.

6.3.2   Localisation project (LP 2018)

Project overview and research context

The last project to be discussed was administered in the 2017/2018 academic year in the Chair for Translation Studies and Intercultural Communication in Kraków at the Jagiellonian University in Kraków, Poland (UP), as part of a course in Specialised Translation. It could be characterised as a f2f collaboration project with telecollaborative modalities, depending on the students' choice of tasks and project tools. Consequently, for some of the participants, the project ultimately involved a hybrid of f2f teamwork and telecollaboration, which was the case in the team which decided to complete Scenario 2 (see next section) and use the cloud CAT tool Smartcat to perform online team translation.

The project, which started in May and ended in June 2018, aimed to introduce students to localisation practices and tools through hands-on experience and (tele)collaboration. The 12 project participants worked in three teams of four, and within each team, they were asked to complete three localisation tasks, which they selected on a pick-and-mix basis from the list of five scenarios with which they were provided in advance.

Scenario 1 involved the localisation of the user interface of a computer game in MS Excel or alternative software (e.g. Open Office Calc or Libré Office Calc), with the source text provided in .XLSX format. To visualise the source content, the students needed to either play the game, find walkthrough instructions for it or rely on screenshots. Scenario 2 pertained to the localisation of the user interface and technical documentation of the office bundle Apache Open Office, which was supposed to be completed in telecollaborative mode via the SaaS community translation platform Pootle, provided by Apache. In this case, the source content was delivered mostly in .PO and .TXT file formats. To visually explore the content being localised, the students used the original Apache software. In Scenario 3, the students were supposed to localise the user interface of a computer application using XML Notepad or the cloud CAT tool Memsource, with the source text strings provided in .XML or .PROPERTIES file formats. For visual support, the students needed to consult the original application or screenshots of the interface. Scenario 4 consisted in translating a mobile phone app, which was delivered as an .APK file and the accompanying .XML files with text strings to be translated. To preview the content to be localised, the students needed to use a mobile phone emulator installed on their computers or rely on screenshots from the app. In Scenario 5, the students' task was to localise fragments of a website directly in a content management system (CMS) via a language plug-in, in the free source code editor Notepad++ or in the Web CAT tool CatsCradle. The source content was delivered in .HTML files containing tagged text and tag attributes to be translated. For previewing the source content, the students used either the CMS, Web browsers or the CatsCradle visualiser tool.

The project procedure required each of the three teams to self-organise (i.e. select the localisation tasks which they wanted to complete), explore and select relevant tools, through trial and error, and decide on the work-flow. Subsequently, the students engaged with the project work. For the duration of the course, the teams met once a week in class and collabo-rated in f2f mode, but they if they decided to take on the task involving community translation (Scenario 2) or to use tools permitting online team translation, they embarked on telecollaboration, either with external local-isers on the Pootle platform in the former case, or with their teammates in the latter case. It must be explained at this stage at the array of tools that the students could use in the project was not limited only to those listed in the descriptions of the five scenarios. To enable the students to test the applicability of other tools to the tasks at hand, it was announced that they could find, learn and explore other software as long as they believed that it would facilitate the localisation process. An overview of the project is provided in Table 6.13.

Research aims

Due to its manifold provenance, the research related to the LP 2018 pro-ject differs in character and scope from all the other project-based research which has been reported on so far.

Firstly, it was motivated by observations which were made about the students' choice of tasks and tools in the LP 2018 project. As it was noted, only one team decided to involve in telecollaboration to complete the project work, which meant that a third of the project participants (four students) took the opportunity to delve into both work modes which the project potentially occasioned, while the others preferred to collaborate on site. That drew the present researcher's attention to the problem of stu-dents' learning preferences and the compatibility of their expectations with what less conventional forms of learning, such as telecollaboration, entail.

Secondly – and very much in connection with the aforementioned obser-vation – the research was inspired by Klimkowski and Klimkowska's

Table 6.13 LP 2018: Project overview

Aspect of the project	Details
Duration	May–June 2018
Related TS course	Specialised Translation
Goals	To introduce students to localisation practices and tools
	To provide hands-on experience in translation
	To foster learning through f2f teamwork and/or telecollaboration (depending on task choice)
External client	N/A
Participants	12 UJ students of translation (MA level)
Project roles	Team leaders (1 per team), localisers (all students)
Team structure	3 teams of four, each with a team leader appointed to coordinate the work
Procedure	Task selection, examination of the source content, hands-on exploration and selection of tools, localisation work, submission of the final products (mostly in-class f2f work, supplemented with individual out-of-class work)
Work modes (with potential telecollaboration involved)	Hybrid mode: f2f in-class collaboration with voluntary telecollaborative modalities (community translation via a SaaS platform or online team translation)
Technologies used	Localisation tools (subject to choice):
	• Spreadsheets (MS Excel/Open Office Calc/Libré Office Calc)
	• SaaS community translation platform (Pootle)
	• CAT tool (Memsource)
	• Open-source XML editor (XML Notepad)
	• Web CAT tool (CatsCradle)
	• Content Management System (WordPress)
	• Source code editor (Notepad++)
	• .PO file editor (PoEditor)*
	• SaaS CAT tool (Smartcat)*
	*students' own choice

(2013) study of students' opinions on the modes of classroom management which they actually experienced in academic translation courses *vis-à-vis* their expectations. The aforementioned researchers reported that students' expectations were somewhat inconsistent in that on the one hand, they leaned towards the anthropocentric, collaborative approach to education, while on the other hand, they tended to display preferences towards transmissionist teaching. Interestingly, the latter was also what the students under examination reported as the dominant mode of instruction in the translation courses they had attended.

With that in mind, the present author administered research into students' preferences towards the learning experience on university-level programmes in translation and their actual experience of instructional practices used in that context. In sum, the research aimed to answer the following questions:

RQ1. What are students' general preferences towards the learning experience on university-level programmes in translation?

RQ2. What is students' actual experience of instructional practices on university-level programmes in translation?

RQ3. How do translation students' preferences and actual instructional practices compare?

Research design and procedures

As the research aimed to explore translation students' preferences towards learning vs. the instructional practices of translation teachers, the results were to provide a focused description of the aforementioned aspect of translator education. The research data were collected through an online survey, which was developed and administered via the LimeSurvey platform, with the link to it distributed via the university Moodle platform. The research was originally conceptualised and launched in the year 2018, but due relatively small group sizes on the translation programme in question, it was conducted in four consecutive academic years (2017/2018, 2018/2019, 2019/2020 and 2020/2021) so as to increase its scope.

The survey contained two major questions. Question 1 related to the respondents' learning preferences and was worded as follows:

Define your preferences as a student in relation to the teaching solutions listed below. Do it by marking the appropriate position on the scale. Note that by selecting a specific answer you lean more towards one or the other didactic solution (answers –2, –1, 1, 2), or you place yourself exactly between them.

Question 2 was analogous to question 1, only it referred to the respondents' actual classroom experience; thus, only the first part of it is cited next:

Based on your experience at university, define below what the didactic solutions used by teachers look like in reality.

Both questions shared the same nine response options involving a semantic differential scale, which, as Cohen, Manion, and Morrison (2011) explain, is a means of eliciting degrees or intensity of response rather than definitive responses that would normally be collected through dichotomous questions. In a conventional differential scale, two opposite adjectives (e.g. *satisfactory* and *unsatisfactory*) are placed at each end of the scale, with an array of numbers (e.g. 1, 2, 3, 4, 5 or –2, –1, 0, 1, 2) in between, which respondents mark to indicate their stance on the issue under investigation. In the survey designed for the purpose of the present research, short sentences, rather than adjectives, were provided which described contrasting instructional modes reflective of transmissionist, teacher-led class management vs. more open, student-centred class management, which could be associated with telecollaboration. A five-point scale was placed between those statements with equidistant points on it numbered –2, –1, 0, 1 and 2, where –2 and –1 marked allegiance to transmissionist instruction, 0 marked the middle ground featuring elements of both extremes, while 1 and 2 marked adherence to open, student-centred instruction.

Due to the distribution of the survey link via the official university Moodle learning management platform, the response rate (Cohen et al., 2017) was high and amounted to 81% of the target population, which means that a total of 84 students responded to the survey.

The survey data were exported into SPSS for preview, and they were further transferred to MS Excel, where the response options were recoded into a scale of 1, 2, 3, 4 and 5 to facilitate the computation of mean scores for each of the nine differential scales. As the LP 2018 project participants' educational choices inspired the research, the students were treated as a purposive sub-sample, and their response data were additionally extracted from the entire batch to compute the mean scores for the sub-sample alone. The means for the complete sample and the sub-sample were then marked on two separate purpose-prepared graphs, which were designed in MS PowerPoint and exported to two graphic files illustrating the degree of congruence between the respondents' learning expectations and instructional experience. The response options for both survey questions will be revealed when the results of the research are discussed; thus, they will not be presented here.

Sampling

The research subjects were recruited through convenience sampling, and they were the students enrolled on the MA programme in translation at the Jagiellonian University in Kraków. The research sample comprised a total of 84 subjects (N = 84), all roughly in their mid-twenties. No information was collected about the gender of the research participants.

In addition, a purposive sub-sample was singled out from the entire sample to analyse and report the findings specifically for the participants of the LP 2018 project. The sub-sample comprised 12 students (N = 12),

Table 6.14 Overview of the research design (LP 2018 + 2018–2021 samples)

Aspect of research design	Details
Research aims	To examine students' preferences towards the learning experience on university-level programmes in translation and their actual experience of instructional practices
Research method	Descriptive research (focused description) Online survey, 2 array questions with 9 response options, each based on a 5-point differential scale
Research instrument	SPSS statistical package, v.28 (data reviewing) MS Excel spreadsheet (data recoding and computations) MS PowerPoint (graph design)
Sampling	Convenience sampling; 11 UP MA-level students of translation (N = 11), 9 females, 2 males in their mid-twenties, participants of the Terminology course
Timing	June 2018–June 2021: data collection August 2022: data processing and analysis
Data analysis	Quantitative

ten females (N = 10) and two males (N = 2). An overview of the research design is presented in Table 6.14.

Results and discussion

The mean scores computed for each of the nine differential scales accompanying both survey questions were mapped onto a purpose-prepared graph, which produced a visualisation of the students' learning preferences and actual experiences. The graph depicting how all the 84 members of the sample responded to the survey questions in the years 2018–2021 can be seen in Figure 6.30. On either side, it features nine descriptors of the following aspects of instruction: (i) learning goals, (ii) class organisation and management, (iii) task completion mode, (iv) nature of instruction (and knowledge), (v) error correction mode, (vi) task assessment mode, (vii) course assessment mode, (viii) the role of assessment and (ix) the subject of assessment. The descriptors on the left-hand side are worded so that they reflect the transmissionist paradigm, while those of the right-hand side represent the principles which will be adhered to in student-centred, transformative/transgressionist teaching, which is likely to be involved in telecollaboration.

As Figure 6.22 demonstrates, for the top five descriptors, the students' learning preferences locate exactly in the middle of the spectrum between

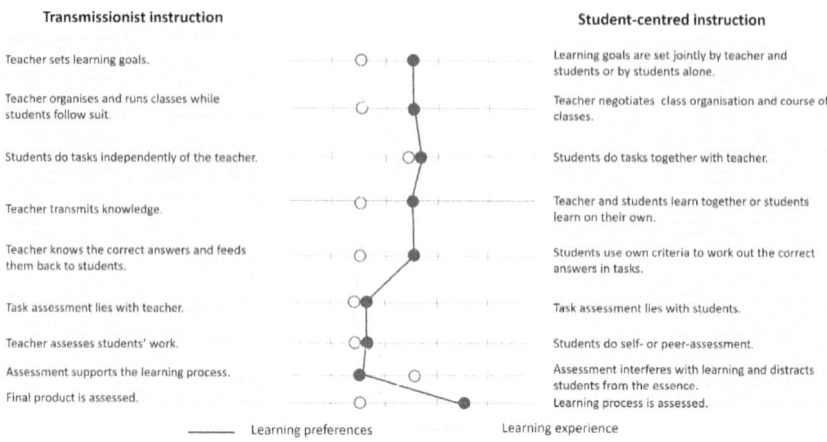

Figure 6.22 Students' learning preferences vs. actual learning experience.

transmissionist and student-centred instruction, which each scale represents. For another three descriptors, they are skewed towards knowledge transmission, while only for the last descriptor do the students' preferences lean towards more liberating student-centred instruction. What this implies in practical terms is that when it comes to who sets the learning goals, organises and manages classwork, is responsible for course task completion, relays knowledge and corrects errors, the students either hesitated between the two alternative instructional modes in question or perhaps they believed that the most optimal educational solutions would entail elements of both transmissionist and transformative/transgressionist instruction.

At the same time, the students displayed preferences towards instruction where the teacher rather than they themselves assesses tasks, without them having any say in this department, where general course assessment also lies in the hands of the teacher, with no room for self- or peer assessment and where assessment is indiscriminately viewed as supportive to learning. Only as far as the subject of assessment goes did the students indicate that they would rather the learning process – not the final product – was assessed.

It is interesting to see that the students' actual learning experience was predominantly transmissionist (i.e. strongly teacher controlled) in nature. The only two exceptions to this rule pertained to (i) task completion, which according to the subjects was typically the responsibility of the students alone or an outcome of joint student-teacher effort, and (ii) assessment, which the students viewed as a factor potentially supporting the learning process or interfering with it, depending on the circumstances.

The findings discussed earlier demonstrate that in at least some translation courses, teachers evidently tend to hold a firm grip on classroom control, which builds a rather archaic image of the learning process. Apparently, teachers impose the learning goals on their students without allowing negotiation or autonomy in that area. Teachers also seem to authoritatively manage the classwork without letting students have some say about the organisation and course of the classes. They transmit knowledge rather than take on the role of co-learners who would explore problems and seek answers together with the students. They provide the correct answers and do not allow students to work out the answers on their own. They also assess tasks and entire coursework without permitting students to do so (e.g. through self- or peer assessment), and when assessing, they focus on the final product, most likely the translated text, rather than the learning process.

As Figure 6.23 illustrates, the picture is not much different when the research results are analysed with regard to only the participants of the LP 2018 project.

The data for the LP 2018 sub-sample reveal that the students' learning preferences and actual experience were nearly identical to those reported by their colleagues in the years 2019–2021. What strikes is that while in 2018, the respondents reported that they were given some say in class

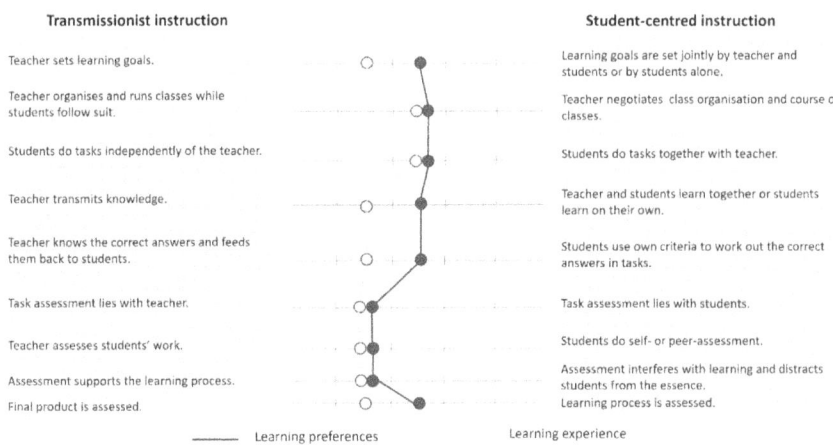

Figure 6.23 Students' learning preferences vs. actual learning experience in LP 2018.

organisation and the course of classes, in the years to come, such practices were not reported, which implies that teachers are rather reluctant to change their ways; and if at times instructional modes shift slightly towards the transformative end of the spectrum, it appears to be rather exceptional and perhaps dependent on the individual choices of the minority of teachers. Simultaneously, it seems that more recently, students' preferences have slightly evolved towards the transformative/transgressionist view of what needs to be assessed in the sense that in the years 2019–2021, the respondents believed that assessment needs to focus on the learning process rather than the product. Interesting as it may be, it is hard to state whether the little shift is an exception to the rule caused by specific circumstances or whether it is indicative of a more permanent change in students' learning preferences.

Summary of the findings and conclusions

The research findings cited earlier depict that translation students' expectations towards learning and their past learning experiences may only to some degree predispose them for telecollaboration-based learning. When it comes to their perceptions of learning goals, class organisation and management, task completion mode, nature of instruction and knowledge, as well as error correction procedures, the students examined did not display clearly discernible preferences either towards the transmissionist or transformative/transgressionist instructional paradigm. Whether it was an indication of the students' hesitation as to which option to choose or evidence of balanced expectations towards the learning experience, overall, it does not exclude telecollaboration as a valid learning solution. If the former is true, involvement in telecollaboration projects might help the students decide on where they stand on the two instructional paradigms in question. In the latter case, telecollaboration will not plainly contradict their learning expectations. At the same time, the students' expectations regarding task and course assessment mode, as well as the role of assessment, leaned towards transmissionist teaching, which means that if telecollaboration were to be used with them, it would require design modifications which would allow for instances of such instruction.

On the basis of their learning experience to date, the students reported the prevalence of transmissionist instructional modes in translation courses, which in the students' view may render telecollaboration a rather unconventional practice. Noticeably, it is not to say that the respondents had never participated in transformative/transgressionist learning (e.g. a project or teamwork), which would be too implausible a generalisation to make. However, what it demonstrates is that occasions on which this work mode was implemented may have been so scarce, when compared to transmission-based instruction, that they had not registered well in students' memories.

All in all, the localisation project could be deemed successful in that the student teams completed the tasks of their choice. Interestingly, although the students were free to choose the mode of collaboration and tools most adequate for their purposes, only in two teams did they decide to experiment with telecollaboration via a community translation platform (Pootle) or online team translation platform (Smartcat). Consequently, it seems reasonable to suggest that due to its voluntary nature, the LP 2018 project design might be used to prime students for full-scale telecollaboration, enabling them to experiment with the format and compare f2f to online work.

The project-related research findings have important implications for those translation teachers who are intent on implementing telecollaboration in their courses, as apparently, some students might not be expecting it. Teachers must be cognisant that despite the advocacy of the implementation of telecollaborative and project-based work modes in translator education and the affordances which team projects potentially create, telecollaboration may be an experience which in its nature diverges – at least with regard to some of its dimensions – from students' expectations and learning experience. It is by no means an argument against the use of telecollaboration in translator education courses. In an era where distant learning and telework have gained so much ground in and outside translation and where telecollaboration has already established itself as a mainstream solution in other areas of education, for example, FL learning or intercultural learning (see Chapter 1), it would be a heresy to make such a proposition. Rather than that, the findings seem to signal the need to slightly adjust the design of telecollaboration projects so that they do not strongly contradict students' learning initial expectations while also trying to help students advance in their mentality beyond the archetypal teacher-centred learning mode and thus open their minds to alternative solutions – the more that, as all the research reported on in this chapter demonstrates, telecollaboration may be a useful means of fostering the development of various components of translator and translation competence.

References

Agar, M. (2008). *Language shock: Understanding the culture of conversation*. New York: Perennial.

Altman, D. (1999). *Practical statistics for medical research*. Chapman: Hall/CRC Press.

Carel, S. (2001). Students as virtual ethnographers: Exploring the language culture connections. In M. Byram, A. Nichols, & D. Stevens (Eds.), *Developing intercultural competence in practice* (pp. 146–161). Clevedon: Multilingual Matters.

Cohen, J. (1960). A coefficient of agreement for nominal scales. *Educational and Psychological Measurement*, 20(1), 37–46. https://doi.org/10.1177/00131644 6002000104

Cohen, L., Manion, L., & Morrison, K. (2011). *Research methods in education* (7th ed.). London & New York: Routledge.

Cohen, L., Manion, L., & Morrison, K. (2017). *Research methods in education* (8th ed.). London: Routledge.

Corbett, J. (2003). *An intercultural approach to English language teaching. Languages for intercultural communication and education* (1st ed). Bristol: Multilingual Matters.

Domínguez, D., Beaulieu, A., Estalella, A., Gómez, E., Schnettler, B., & Read, R. (2007). Virtual ethnography. *Forum Qualitative Sozialforschung/Forum: Qualitative Social*, 8(3).

EMT. (2017). *European master's in translation competence framework 2017.* Retrieved from https://ec.europa.eu/info/sites/info/files/emt_competence_fwk_2017_en_web.pdf

Fleiss, J. L., Levin, B. A., & Paik, M. C. (2003). *Statistical methods for rates and proportions* (3rd ed., Joseph L. Fleiss, Bruce Levin, Myunghee Cho Paik, Eds.). Wiley series in probability and statistics. Hoboken, NJ & Chichester: Wiley-Interscience. Retrieved from www.loc.gov/catdir/bios/wiley042/2002191005.html

GPE. (2014). *Global understanding core 2015. East Carolina University, Greenville, NC, USA.* PDF: GPE.

GPE. (2022). *About GPE.* Retrieved from www.thegpe.org/about-gpe/

Hall, E. T. (1976). *Beyond culture.* New York, London, Toronto, Sydney, & Auckland: Doubleday.

ISO. (2015). *Quality management principles.* Geneva: ISO.

ISO 11669. (2012). *Translation projects – General guidance* (ISO, 11669:2012). Switzerland: ISO.

Joinson, A. N., McKenna, K. Y., Postmes, T., & Reips, U.-D. (2009). *The Oxford handbook of internet psychology* (Reprint). Oxford: University Press.

Klimkowski, K., & Klimkowska, K. (2013). Towards empowerment in translation education: Students' opinions and expectations of the translation training course. In M. Borodo & S. Hubscher-Davidson (Eds.), *Bloomsbury advances in translation. Global trends in translator and interpreter training: Mediation and culture/edited by Séverine Hubscher-Davidson and Michal Borodo* (pp. 180–194). London: Bloomsbury Academic.

Kurek, M. (2015). Designing tasks for complex virtual learning environments. *Bellaterra Journal of Teaching & Learning Language & Literature*, 8(2), 13. https://doi.org/10.5565/rev/jtl3.633

Landis, J. R., & Koch, G. G. (1977). The measurement of observer agreement for categorical data. *Biometrics*, 1(33), 159–174.

Lankshear, C., & Knobel, M. (2011). *New literacies* (3rd ed.). Maidenhead: McGraw-Hill Open University Press.

Larsen-Freeman, D., & Anderson, M. (2018). *Techniques & principles in language teaching* (3rd ed.). Oxford [i pozostałe]: Oxford University Press.

Maíz-Arévalo, C. (2015). Typographic alteration in formal computer-mediated communication. *Procedia – Social and Behavioral Sciences*, *212*, 140–145.

Risager, K. (2007). *Language and culture pedagogy*. Bristol: Blue Ridge Summit: Multilingual Matters.

Saldaña, J. (2013). *The coding manual for qualitative researchers* (2nd ed.). Los Angeles, CA & London: SAGE.

Saldanha, G., & O'Brien, S. (2014). *Research methodologies in translation studies*. London: Routledge.

Ware, P. (2013). Teaching comments: Intercultural communication skills in the digital age. *Intercultural Education*, *24*(4), 315–326. https://doi.org/10.1080/1 4675986.2013.809249

7 Conclusions

To illustrate how the theories behind telecollaboration-based instruction may translate into actual instructional practices, seven implementations of telecollaboration were accounted, including two OIEs, three online team translation projects and two miscellaneous projects, each held to develop an array of translator and translation competences in various translator education courses. Moreover, to shed light on the intricacies of telecollaborative learning, including students' perspectives on it, the affordances which it carries, the learning modes which it involves and the possible learning outcomes, the description of each project was also supplemented with a report on research based on the project data.

The telecollaboration projects are summarised later through a top-level analysis of how they incorporated the three discussed pedagogical approaches (transmissionist, transformative and situated, praxis oriented) and what design modifications they involved, complemented with general conclusions regarding their pedagogical efficacy and related implications.

The *OIEs* (GPE X an GPE XII) exemplified externally organised and coordinated projects with a pre-set framework, which left little room for alterations. They were implemented to supplement other courses on an EMT programme to develop students' intercultural competence. The OIEs involved elements of transmissionist, transformative and situated, praxis-oriented pedagogy. Knowledge transmission prevailed in the f2f introductory classes. Transformative learning was promoted in the in-class videoconferencing and online chat sessions, which gave the floor to the students but permitted online communication within the imposed project structure and thematic scope, without genuine teacher-independent decision-making or product-oriented collaboration. Situated learning was part of the out-of-class collaborative project, whereby the students worked jointly towards a negotiated end product, which was, however, limited to a specific format namely that of a multimedia presentation.

The projects resulted in the students exploring both explicit and implicit elements of culture, although the latter seemed to require more conscious

DOI: 10.4324/9781003424932-8

attention and increased metacognitive awareness for more effective control of emotions and greater objectivisation of experience in contact with otherness. It also that turned out that the efficacy of student-student intercultural interaction could be improved by expounding to students' concrete elements of communication (e.g. interaction markers) prior to the project to help them make informed communicative choices.

It must be underlined that although the projects did not involve translation, they facilitated the development of intercultural competence as an integral part of translation competence. Moreover, it would have been possible to incorporate translation per se – if only through a pivot language – into the project texture (e.g. the out-of-class collaborative project) had the students from both partner institutions majored in translation.

The *team translation projects* (TG, CP 2021, CP 2022) illustrated how telecollaboration may be geared not to merely involve translation but keep it at the core of student activity while simultaneously targeting the development of multiple components of translation/translator competence. Overall, their design was by far less predetermined than that of the aforementioned OIEs, as the student groupings and project stages were tailored to match the negotiated workflow of the translation jobs which the students needed to complete for an external client. In that respect, the projects were at least to some extent modelled on professional LSP practices.

The TG project primarily aimed to develop competences relevant to team translation and technological competence through self- and peer learning, and it was administered in hybrid mode, featuring f2f and online work, which made room for transmissionist, transformative and situated learning. The f2f classes largely involved knowledge transmission, through which the project was introduced and the theoretical course content was taught, but also transformative learning (cooperation and knowledge co-construction), which occurred during the student-student or student-teacher discussion of pressing issues and project briefings. Last but not least, situated, praxis-oriented learning was promoted by online team translation, which the students performed from home, with the decision taking and telecollaboration procedures lying at their discretion.

The project largely fostered the development of procedural skills and helped the students use their theoretical knowledge in practice. Moreover, as originally planned, it involved the students in self- and peer learning. However, it also highlighted several issues, including the need to highlight individual students' proactive role in peer learning and encourage them to peer teach more or the students' expectations of client feedback, which despite the instructor's efforts was not provided due to an emergency. Additionally, it turned out necessary to explain to students that complexity and the ensuing challenges, which may be inherent to project work, need to be approached as learning opportunities rather than obstacles.

The other two translation projects (CP 2021 and CP 2022) differed from TG in that they involved very little transmissionist teaching, which occurred only in the introductory f2f class. Instead, both projects occasioned a mixture of situated, praxis-oriented learning – predominantly in the form of telecollaborative team translation – and a degree of transformative learning, where students cooperated (e.g. by delegating tasks to individuals).

The CP 2021 increased the professionalisation of learning, as it reportedly helped the students develop a wide range of competences related to LSP and various soft skills. Very importantly, the participants self-organised and worked out measures which aimed to implement some of the QMPs to which they had been formally introduced prior to the project to ensure quality in the teamwork which they performed. The project also honed the students' other LSP-related competences, including translation, revision or CAT skills, and an array of soft skills, such as CMC management skills and generic communication skills.

In the CP 2022 project, the students worked on their personal and interpersonal competences, albeit with different success. While some skills (e.g. time management skills, teamwork skills, communication skills and self-evaluation skills) were reportedly developed without the teacher's intervention, others (e.g. stress management or the organisation of work environment) turned out to be problematic. In the latter case, an apparent need emerged for guidance that would have optimised the students' development in that area or incentives that would have helped the students explore relevant learning opportunities on their own.

The project facilitated the development of competences most indispensable for the project work at hand. Yet other areas (e.g. generic computer skills) remained seemingly underdeveloped and apparently required instructional stimulation, if only through elements of project design, such as the choice of project procedures or tools. Most importantly, the project induced the students to act independently of the teacher, which potentially increased their confidence and self-reliance.

The *miscellaneous projects* (TP 2016, LP 2018) involved only a limited amount of telecollaboration, but they nonetheless turned out successful in fostering competence development in the targeted areas. In the TP 2016 project, the students were explicitly introduced to terminology building and management (knowledge transmission), but they also (team-)explored CAT-related terminology and telecollaborated to perform terminology work and build an electronic term base, which produced opportunities for both transformative and situated learning. The former consisted in the students delegating tasks, sharing jobs and exchanging resources, while the latter involved online communication, joint coordination of project work, self-organisation within teams and team text editing in the cloud. What the project lacked was a greater degree of situatedness, which would have embedded it in a concrete professional context; it was mostly a learning assignment with pedagogical rather than a professional purpose.

The LP 2018 project introduced students to localisation practices and tools through hands-on experience and predominantly fostered f2f teamwork, with a degree of voluntary telecollaboration (community translation via a SaaS platform or online team translation). The learning involved a combination of transformative and situated learning, permitting a degree of cooperation and, for volunteers, online team (community) translation via a SaaS platform respectively, with no elements of knowledge transmission.

What draws attention is the voluntary nature of telecollaboration in the project, which on the one hand allowed the less adventurous learners to avoid telecollaboration – or involve in it to a limited extent – while on the other hand limited the scope of the learning experience. Consequently, only some students worked in hybrid mode. This kind of design might be advisable to use at the transition stage from f2f collaboration to telecollaboration or from transformative to situated learning. However, ultimately, all students would need to work in all these modes to ensure that they receive education compatible with requirements of the contemporary LSP industry.

Later, an overview of the project-related research is provided with a set of conclusions drawn on the basis of the findings and recommendations for teachers planning to use telecollaboration in translation courses.

Online Intercultural Exchanges. Research based on the GPE X project examined areas of culture developed in OIEs. As its results revealed, OIEs can be useful in developing translation students' cultural competence, particularly with regard to declarative, factual knowledge about public life and institutions and the common practices related to individual lifestyles. Albeit in the GPE X project it was observed to a lesser extent, OIEs may also help students develop metacognitive awareness, which augments not only intercultural learning but also 21st-century skills (Orlando, 2016), such as self- and lifelong learning, which are often listed in contemporary translator competence models. At the same time, it occurred that although in OIEs students have opportunities to elicit cultural information straight from representatives of other cultures, whom they can ask for clarification or further explanation, their learning may largely focus on the most obvious (i.e. most observable or easily transmittable cultural elements).

Consequently, the learning needs which were identified on the basis of the research data comprised implicit cultural knowledge, metacognitive awareness and the emotive dimension of intercultural learning. Firstly, it seems desirable to involve students more in work on the implicit elements of culture, such as values, beliefs and thought patterns, which seem to have been neglected in GPE X. This kind of knowledge is necessary not only for a deeper understanding of other cultures but also for effective translation, as it augments text comprehension and helps translators to take appropriate translation decisions. That in turn increases the high quality of translations and permits the avoidance of potential conflicts in intercultural communication, which translation mediates. In addition, as only limited evidence was gathered of perspective shifting and cultural distancing, which helps students perceive reality through the eyes of the cultural other, the need to foster students' metacognitive awareness was identified. Last but not least, the fact that emotions observably ran high in GPE X highlighted the need to increase students' understanding of affective factors in intercultural learning, which could them predict potential conflicts in intercultural communicative situations or rationalise their negative reactions to otherness.

The GPE XII research examined interaction patterns in OIE students' online chat communication, as revealed by the linguistic markers of effective telecollaboration which the project participants used. As the results revealed, the students' use of these markers differed in intensity between tasks and individuals. The markers identified in the students' communication also showed that while students posed numerous questions, developed on the topics introduced by their project partners and personalised the information which they provided, they displayed relatively little alignment. It was also observed that the choice of task topics, the duration of project involvement and the composition of chat teams apparently affected the nature and intensity of student-student interaction.

Thus, it was posited that students needed to be explicitly introduced to the linguistic markers of effective telecollaboration before an OIE to raise their awareness of the marker functions so that they make informed communicative choices while interacting with project partners, thereby testing the ensuing outcomes. It was also recommended that students' metacognitive awareness be increased to maximise learning opportunities in less favourable conditions (i.e. even when the discussion topic is challenging and potentially involves face loss or when the team composition is culturally biased).

Online team translation projects. The TG research revealed the students' expectations that telecollaborative team translation projects at large would predominantly help them develop procedural knowledge and skills, transferrable skills and only some declarative knowledge, which in fact was the case in TG. They also saw online projects as a chance to gain professional experience and foster teamwork/telecollaboration skills.

In the project, the students largely learnt by themselves (self-learning) or from colleagues (peer learning) while only marginally relying on the teacher in this respect. Individuals also taught project partners whatever was necessary, mostly procedural knowledge and skills necessary for completing specific tasks.

Challenges and difficulties in the project mostly derived from the students' personal dispositions (e.g. anxiety or procrastination), limited soft skills or the nature of the task at hand (e.g. the need to use multiple tools). Simultaneously, the research results revealed that while adventurous learners might feel ready to embark on team translation projects despite the anticipated difficulties, others might need a degree of counselling to raise their awareness of that fact challenge might be conducive to learning. It found corroboration in the research data, which demonstrated that although the project participants initially viewed the use of the communication platform Slack as challenging, they mastered it through practice.

The project participants emphasised the need for client feedback, whose prospect apparently had a motivational effect on them; they may have viewed it as a means of professionalising translator education and narrowing the gap between academia and the LSP industry. The students believed that reflections in online team translation projects were natural but might also be additionally elicited as long as elicitation formats did not involve excessive workload. In fact, occasionally, the elicitation of post-experience reflection might be necessary focus on students' attention on a specific aspect of their project work.

Finally, the research exposed ambivalence in the students' stance on teacher presence in translation projects. On the one hand, they would rather the teacher remained in the background, while on the other, they would expect direct intervention (e.g. to stimulate student performance, raise motivation levels and simply increase the project prestige), which implies the need to flexibly negotiate the teacher presence/absence continuum within or between projects, depending on educational objectives.

The CP 2021 research focused on the measures which the participants took to observe quality management principles (QMPs) while completing the project tasks. The results showed that giving students room for initiative might involve them in extensive decision making, which in the CP 2021 project manifested itself in the plethora of solutions the participants had developed to adhere to the aforementioned QMPs.

As it turned out, the students established the rules of communication management, workflow and information flow (e.g. regarding the choice of adequate communication channels). They also took measures to perform the commissioned translation in agreement with the client's recommendations, for example, the delineation of precise product specifications in the project documentation (translation brief, style guide and style recommendations), and the coordination and tracking of progress.

To deliver a high-quality product, the students monitored the translated texts and project resources (e.g. the term base) for the terminological accuracy and consistency and ran automated quality assurance checks in the project CAT tool. To facilitate teamwork, they took steps to enhance the team spirit and thus sustain high levels of individuals' engagement by systematically monitoring the project work, ensuring positive attitudes through praise and emphasis on the importance of individual contributions, as well as respect for the project participants' time off work.

The learning affordances created by the project which the research revealed comprised opportunities to foster the development of soft skills, teamwork and collaboration skills, language competence, CMC skills, translation and revision skills and LSP skills.

The research occasioned by the CP 2022 project, which – *inter alia* – investigated students' expectations towards telecollaborative translation projects, revealed that those expectations focused mostly on the learning of translation technologies and the development of translation competences. In congruence with the findings of the TG research, for the CP 2022 project participants, telecollaborative translation projects were also an opportunity to delve into professional reality, explore market requirements and enhance teamwork and transferrable skills.

The research results also showed that in general, students tend to eagerly embark on project work and have positive attitudes towards collaboration with colleagues, which – coupled with the sense of achievement and responsibility which projects potentially carry – is the source of motivation for them. At the same time, what demotivates students is lower sense of accomplishment (e.g. if the final product not published immediately), the complexity of project work, lack of immediate feedback, personal dispositions (e.g. anxiety or fear of the unknown and the unexpected), anticipated challenges and hard work. The demotivating factors indicate that seemingly, students join projects with relatively low levels of self-confidence, which highlights an apparent need for counselling and pre-project support from the teacher to enhance students' self-esteem and rationalise their fears.

The research demonstrated that all areas of translator and translation competence delineated in the new EMT (2017) model (i.e. language and culture, translation, technology, personal and interpersonal competence and service provision) are amenable to development through online translation projects, albeit individual students declare the development of particular sub-competences to varying degrees. Both hard and soft skills are possible to develop, while project work involves extensive decision making, which was also corroborated by the CP 2021 research.

What needs to be reiterated at this point is that in translation projects, balanced development of particular competences – if only due to their intricate nature – is hard to expect and so is the simultaneous development of all competences. If one adopts the emergentist view of learning, one needs to realise that what actually develops will be occasioned by the nature of the project tasks and individual learning experiences. In contrast, if the development of particular competences is to be specifically targeted, appropriate guidance may be necessary. For instance, to foster the development of stress management skills or workplace organisation skills, students might need to be introduced to relevant techniques, either through explicit instruction or student-research.

The research also examined students' recommendations for possible amendments to the design of translation projects, and although such recommendations would certainly differ from one context to another, the students' responses highlighted several important issues.

Firstly, teachers' intentions will not always meet students' expectations. While teachers might assign multiple roles to individual students so as to increase learning opportunities, students might view it as confusing and counterproductive. Therefore, it seems desirable to explicate to students the rationale behind role assignment in a project so that they realise – as the findings by other researchers (cf. Mastela, 2022) also indicate – that the roles which they adopt will affect the range and quality of their learning experience.

Secondly, professional reality, which projects often aim to reflect, may diverge from educational reality. For example, while from the professional perspective deadlines need to be tight, educational reality might require a slower pace to reduce students' workload.

Thirdly, although students may generally approach teamwork with enthusiasm, it does not mean that they will indiscriminately favour it. Simultaneously, as in professional settings translation tends to be done in an virtual environment and through teamwork (Pietrzak, 2020; Pietrzak & Kornacki, 2021), it is necessary for students to gain experience involving this work mode, regardless of their personal preferences.

Fourthly, while by default the teacher's role in translation projects is limited, students may nevertheless see the need for teacher intervention (e.g. to help them resolve pressing problems or to support individuals' learning effort). When coupled with the findings of other researchers, for example, that by Mastela (2022), who reported that in team translation projects students appreciate opportunities for discussion and reflection with both teammates and the teacher, the observation implies that prior to the project, teacher presence needs to be carefully considered and, again, consulted with the students.

Miscellaneous projects. The TP 2016 research, which involved terminology work, zeroed in on the choice of project tools and their advantages and disadvantages for telecollaboration. As the results indicated, the choice of tools inevitably affects student-student interaction and collaboration in the project (e.g. while Messenger mostly – although not exclusively – facilitates text-based discussion, TitanPad augments team editing). Moreover, tools vary in suitability not only for telecollaboration but also for post-experience reflection; thus, their choice is critical.

It is crucial to underline that the research in question focused on the analysis of tools used in the concrete Terminology Project; thus, it did not aim to determine what tools would be most appropriate for the performance of miscellaneous projects, the more that projects within this category will vary greatly in design. Instead, it demonstrated that even the choice of less obvious project tools, such as a social media communicator and a team text editor, creates opportunities for tool evaluation, which is a vital professional skill. Through reflection on the project tools, teachers may draw students' attention to the fact that, considering the multitude of software which can potentially facilitate different forms of LSP today, to ensure maximum efficiency, tools need to be selected through decisions taken on a fit-for-purpose basis, rather than as a matter of routine.

The research inspired by the hybrid localisation project (LP 2018) in fact constitutes a bracket for all the other research reported on in this publication, as it delved into translation students' learning expectations and actual learning experiences regarding transmissionist and transformative instruction, as examined in the years 2018–2021.

As the results demonstrate, while no clear preferences for either of the two paradigms under examination were identified in the collected responses, the students' learning experience was reportedly dominated by transmissionist instruction, which implies that telecollaboration, as representative of transformative or situated pedagogy, is likely to diverge from translation students' learning experience, and before it is implemented, it needs to be properly introduced to the prospective participants to ensure the clarity of its purpose and work modes. The latter may need to be negotiated with students and, perhaps slightly modified, to help students advance in their mentality and learning practices beyond the archetypal teacher-centred learning and make them embrace the less conventional without completely contradicting their learning expectations.

All in all, the findings obtained through the research discussed in Chapter 6 make it possible to propose the following recommendations for instructors with an interest in implementing telecollaboration in translation courses:

- if you lack confidence, begin with networked, pre-designed projects, which are clearly structured and thus more manageable;
- prime students for telecollaboration through hybrid projects involving a mixture of online/offline work;
- introduce students to emergentist learning so that they perceive complexity as a learning opportunity;

- vary telecollaboration projects and encourage students to take on various project roles to diversify the ensuing learning experience;
- review project design and bring team translation projects up to date with current LSP practices;
- increase students' motivation by maximising project (near-)authenticity; for instance, involve genuine stakeholders (clients, market representatives) or organise projects responding to concrete social needs;
- develop students' meta-awareness regarding goal setting, auto-feedback and learning needs analysis and stimulate self-reflection to foster self-learning;
- use focused reflection to gear learning outcomes towards specific goals;
- ensure the provision of auto-, peer, teacher or client feedback to increase project takeaways;
- research the project work(ings); fragmentary as it may be, the research builds expertise and informs future design;
- do focused research, as projects are too inclusive for thorough examination;
- accept that some of the in-project learning will remain opaque;
- involve students in project research, as it extends their learning experience; and
- share research results with students to sensitise them to telecollaboration-related issues.

References

EMT. (2017). *European master's in translation competence framework 2017.* Retrieved from https://ec.europa.eu/info/sites/info/files/emt_competence_fwk_2017_en_web.pdf

Mastela, O. (2022). Zaangażowana dydaktyka akademicka i jej wpływ na jakość kształcenia tłumaczy. In J. Bugaj & M. Budzanowska-Drzewiecka (Eds.), *Jakość kształcenia akademickiego* (pp. 182–198). Kraków: Wydawnictwo Uniwersytetu Jagiellońskiego.

Orlando, M. (2016). *Training 21st-century translators and interpreters: At the crossroads of practice, research and pedagogy. Transkulturalität – Translation – Transfer.* Berlin: Frank & Timme.

Pietrzak, P. (2020). Inside and outside the translation classroom. *Research in Language, 18*(2), 109–117. https://doi.org/10.18778/1731-7533.18.2.07

Pietrzak, P., & Kornacki, M. (2021). *Using CAT tools in freelance translation: Insights from a case study.* London: Routledge.

Index

Note: Page numbers in **bold** indicate a table on the corresponding page.

For Product Safety Concerns and Information please contact our EU
representative GPSR@taylorandfrancis.com
Taylor & Francis Verlag GmbH, Kaufingerstraße 24, 80331 München, Germany

www.ingramcontent.com/pod-product-compliance
Ingram Content Group UK Ltd.
Pitfield, Milton Keynes, MK11 3LW, UK
UKHW020032260325
456732UK00014B/151